THE **Bruce R. McConkie Story**
Reflections of a Son

Bruce R. McConkie

THE Bruce R. McConkie Story
Reflections of a Son

Joseph Fielding McConkie

DESERET BOOK

SALT LAKE CITY, UTAH

© 2003 Joseph Fielding McConkie

All rights reserved. No part of this book may be reproduced in any form or by any means without permission in writing from the publisher, Deseret Book Company, P. O. Box 30178, Salt Lake City, Utah 84130. This work is not an official publication of The Church of Jesus Christ of Latter-day Saints. The views expressed herein are the responsibility of the author and do not necessarily represent the position of the Church or of Deseret Book Company.

DESERET BOOK is a registered trademark of Deseret Book Company.

Visit us at deseretbook.com

Library of Congress Cataloging-in-Publication Data

McConkie, Joseph F.
  The Bruce R. McConkie story : reflections of a son / Joseph Fielding McConkie.
    p.   cm.
  Includes bibliographical references and index.
  ISBN 1-59038-205-6 (alk. paper)
  1. McConkie, Bruce R.   2. Mormons—United States—Biography.   3. Mormon Church—Apostles—Biography.   I. Title.
BX8695.M258M33 2003
289.3'092—dc22   2003018211

Printed in the United States of America   18961-7153
R. R. Donnelley and Sons, Crawfordsville, IN

10   9   8   7   6   5   4   3   2   1

A life well lived contains lessons well worth remembering. Kindred spirits, though separated by time, are nonetheless still bound by purpose, for no great cause is accomplished in a generation. The hope, vision, and faith of our noble forebears must become ours. As we stand upon their shoulders, so in some future day others may be blessed to stand on ours.

Contents

Acknowledgments ix

Introduction 1

1. "Let This Then Be Our Covenant" 7
2. The Hearts of the Fathers 13
3. The House of Faith 30
4. Boyhood in Monticello, 1915 to 1926 56
5. Youthful Years, 1926 to 1934 73
6. Service as a Missionary, 1934 to 1936 87
7. Marriage to Amelia and the Death
   of Bruce Jr., 1937 to 1941 108
8. The War Years, 1942 to 1946 127
9. Called as a Seventy, 1946 and 1947 143
10. Things Great and Small, 1948 to 1961 162

Contents

11. The *Mormon Doctrine* Saga, 1958 and 1966 . . 182
12. The Australia Years, 1961 to 1964 194
13. Family Traditions 231
14. "What Was It Like?" 245
15. The Nature of the Man 264
16. As He Saw It 290
17. A Time to Laugh 307
18. Call to the Apostleship 322
19. Among the Nations, 1968 to 1982 333
20. The Nature of His Ministry, 1946 to 1985 . . . 354
21. Great Events 373
22. Special Contributions 386
23. His Final Testimony 399
24. Reflections of a Son 419

    Notes 433

    Index 439

Acknowledgments

Although I have sought and received much good counsel in the course of writing this work, I alone am responsible for it. Because for the most part it draws on personal recollections and family letters, to which most readers will not have access, these materials have generally not been formally referenced.

Thanks are extended particularly to my uncles Briton and Oscar McConkie and to my aunt Margaret Pope, the siblings closest in age to my father. Each was a delightful companion in reminiscence. Mother, of course, was a primary source, as were my brothers and sisters. Glen and Marva Rudd represented wonderfully the Lambourne neighborhood group that Mom and Dad enjoyed so much. Velma Harvey, Dad's trusted secretary for more than thirty years, shared helpful insights, as did Robert J. Matthews, who labored with Dad for over a decade on the Scriptures Publication Committee. Virtually everyone I have ever met who knew my father has a story to tell. People loved him and warmed to the subject.

Acknowledgments

As to the tedious matter of reading and rereading, which was attended by many helpful suggestions, special thanks are extended to my uncle Oscar and to my wife, Brenda. Thanks are also extended to Robert L. Millet, my colleague at Brigham Young University, and to Cory Maxwell and John Bytheway of Deseret Book. The painstaking labor of editing was ably done by Suzanne Brady. And this work would not be what it is were it not for my research assistant, Matthew B. Christensen.

Introduction

Among the many names that hold a place of honor as great theologians of this dispensation, Joseph Smith stands preeminent. He is the Prophet of the Restoration. He penned more scripture than any twelve Bible prophets combined. As a preacher his discourses are unequaled for clarity, power, and truth. He truly represented the voice of heaven, and his life matched his teachings.

In the providence of God, Joseph Smith was surrounded by men of remarkable ability to expound the truths he restored. They are men whose sermons we continue to read with profit and whose eloquence we can only hope to attain. The day simply will not come when we as a people cease to quote from the sermons of Brigham Young, John Taylor, and Wilford Woodruff. As long as there is so much as a flicker of light left in our souls, we will revel in the sermons and writings of Parley P. Pratt, Orson Pratt, and Heber C. Kimball. Who would not have been willing to endure the hardships of Zion's Camp—the fifteen-hundred-mile march from Kirtland to

Introduction

Missouri under the most difficult of circumstances—to have walked beside such men and heard their conversations one with another? Each of these men has a written history, and each is a treasure of faith and courage.

In our own day, the Lord has not left us without men of like spirit and wisdom with whom we can rub shoulders. From them we can gain knowledge and understanding held by the noble and great of all gospel dispensations. Bruce Redd McConkie, the subject of this work, was such a man. Like those of his counterparts in earlier days, his, too, is a story of great faith.

To the rising generation he may be only a name they hear appended to a quotation in a talk or lesson. But to many of their parents, he is a man held in particular love and esteem. They remember the plainness with which he spoke and the power in the principles he expounded. Thousands of them remember the spirit that attended his final testimony of Christ given in the Tabernacle on Temple Square only two weeks before his death. If they met him, they probably have a story to tell of the occasion, just as did their parents or grandparents before them who noted in personal histories their associations with Joseph or Hyrum, with Brigham or Heber, with John Taylor or Wilford Woodruff or others because of their faith and the fire in their sermons.

EXPOUNDING SCRIPTURE

Like those so honored from generations past, Bruce R. McConkie was a disciple of Jesus Christ, and he echoed with eloquence the message of the Restoration taught by Joseph Smith, the great revelator of Christ for our dispensation. One cannot come to know Elder McConkie and his teachings without coming to know Christ. Bruce McConkie saw the revelations of the Restoration as the "key of knowledge" (Luke 11:52). With them he unlocked the past, and with them he unsealed the heavens. Their spirit became his spirit,

Introduction

and as one revelation unfolded another, he found himself writing volumes of scriptural commentary and doctrinal explanation. His first venture into print was the three-volume work entitled *Doctrines of Salvation*, in which he edited material from letters and other writings of Joseph Fielding Smith. When correspondence did not adequately cover a particular subject, he would elicit it from President Smith, put it into writing, and have him sign it. President Smith never found it necessary to change so much as a word of what Elder McConkie had written. Gospel insights from one of the great theologians of the Church were thus preserved.

These volumes were followed by the publication of *Mormon Doctrine*, an encyclopedic work covering hundreds of gospel topics from "Aaron" to "Zoramites" and whose publication constitutes a story in itself (see chapter 11). Perhaps no other book has had a greater influence on synthesizing and codifying Latter-day Saint doctrine. That influence is reflected in the Bible Dictionary, which is now a part of the Latter-day Saint edition of the King James Bible.

Then came Elder McConkie's three-volume *Doctrinal New Testament Commentary*, the only Bible commentary ever written by a general authority. Perhaps its most significant contribution was to introduce the Church to the Inspired Version (now called the Joseph Smith Translation) during a period in which it was viewed with considerable suspicion. Today the Joseph Smith Translation is recognized as a significant key that unlocks a great host of gospel truths to our understanding. The *Doctrinal New Testament Commentary* is a classic illustration of the light which the revelations of the Restoration shine on ancient scripture. It shows how all scripture under the tutelage of the Spirit becomes one and how, for instance, we cannot properly understand the writings of the apostle Paul without first having read what Alma and other Book of Mormon writers have to say about salvation by grace.

Elder McConkie's work on the New Testament was followed by

Introduction

a six-volume series on the Messiah. The first volume deals with the promise of a Messiah, as that promise is unfolded in scripture recorded before the birth of the Savior. The next four volumes detail the life and ministry of the Savior, particularly as the story is found in the Gospels. Again with the use of the Joseph Smith Translation and the revelations of the Restoration, Elder McConkie gave the Latter-day Saints a clearer view of the Messiah than they had previously enjoyed. His work weans us from secular scholarship and attunes our understanding with modern revelation. The concluding volume of this work, *The Millennial Messiah,* is a most refreshing and original approach to the subject of the return of Christ and his millennial reign. Rather than rehashing what others had said, Elder McConkie went back to the scriptural sources and began anew. In so doing, he shattered a host of Mormon myths dealing with the gathering of Israel, the return of the ten tribes, and the second coming of Christ.

The last of Elder McConkie's published works was *A New Witness for the Articles of Faith.* In his treatment of the Articles of Faith, Elder James E. Talmage had related them to the Bible. Elder McConkie approached them from the perspective of the revelations of the Restoration, the perspective from which Joseph Smith had written them. By showing that they are summary statements of great principles revealed to the great Prophet of this dispensation, Elder McConkie illustrated the power and spirit associated with them. His work thus becomes a new, or modern, witness that Joseph Smith is a prophet and the principles restored through him are true.

Having written ten volumes of scriptural commentary (not including *Mormon Doctrine*) that together number almost six thousand pages, Elder McConkie has become a principal source for virtually every search for scriptural understanding made by Church members. In addition to these works, he wrote under the direction of the Brethren a number of landmark articles on such subjects as

Introduction

the gathering of Israel, the salvation of little children, the Creation, the Fall, and the Atonement. He loved to teach doctrine and was especially at home teaching the doctrine of the divine Sonship of Christ, the importance of eternal marriage, and the hope of salvation possessed by all faithful Latter-day Saints.

His sermons—and he delivered thousands in the nearly forty years he served as a general authority—were always doctrinally oriented. He was an avid and disciplined student of scripture. Scripture and the Spirit from whence it came were the primary source for all that he taught and wrote. Thus he both spoke and wrote as one having authority. Because of this, he is one of the general authorities most often quoted on doctrinal matters. As a true messenger, he conveyed the message in the same uncompromising manner in which he received it. In doing so he gave offense to some, nor could it be otherwise. To stand for one thing is to stand against another.

FAITH AND KNOWLEDGE

In his final general conference address, Elder McConkie observed that "if we are to have faith like that of Enoch and Elijah"—which was the kind of faith he sought and which he urged all Latter-day Saints to have—"we must believe what they believed, know what they knew, and live as they lived."[1] That is to say, we cannot be a people of faith without at the same time being a people of sound gospel understanding. The one cannot be had without the other. In like manner, we must be a people given to righteousness if we are to be a people endowed with the power of faith. But again, there can be no righteousness in indolence or in ignorance. Each of these principles brings us to the same point: We cannot, individually or as a people, suppose that our profession of faith can excuse our responsibility to obtain a sound understanding of gospel principles.

The story told in the following pages is that of a man who

Introduction

sought above all else to raise the level of gospel understanding in the Church, so that we in turn might raise the level of our faith. He would not have presumed for a moment that this meant anyone should know anything about his life, only that they know something about the principles by which and for which he lived. This volume finds justification in the thought that to know something about the life of an Enoch, an Elijah, or one of their modern-day counterparts might be of help to some in obtaining the faith common to such great witnesses of Christ. A life well lived is a story worth telling.

1

"Let This Then Be Our Covenant"

Let this then be our covenant, that we will keep the commandments of God and be living witnesses of the truth and divinity of this glorious work, which is destined to sweep the earth as with a flood.
—Bruce R. McConkie

On Sunday evening, July 2, 1972, my grandfather Joseph Fielding Smith, then the tenth president of the Church, passed away quietly at the home of my parents, Bruce and Amelia McConkie. At the time of his passing he was seated in the living room in his favorite chair, a reddish leather recliner, and had been visiting with my mother. She was writing letters and had excused herself for a moment to get some stamps for the envelopes. When she returned, she found that her father had slipped away. She said, "I think his father and perhaps others had come to take him and were just waiting for me to turn my back so they could snatch him." She added, "I was born in his home, and he died in mine." President Smith was just seventeen days short of his ninety-sixth birthday.

At the death of a president of the Church, his counselors are released, they having been set apart as counselors to the man, not to the Church. Thus the Quorum of the First Presidency is dissolved, leaving the Quorum of the Twelve Apostles as the governing quorum in the Church. The president of that quorum is thus the only man on earth who can call the quorum into a meeting or receive revelation for that body. Thus he automatically presides over the Church because he is presiding over its leading quorum. As my father once explained, "at the last heartbeat of the president of the Church, the mantle of leadership passes to the president of the Quorum of the Twelve Apostles, whose next heartbeat is that of the presiding authority of God on earth." In this instance, that man was Harold B. Lee.

Within minutes after being notified of President Smith's death, President Lee arrived at our home. By this time Granddaddy had been laid on the couch. President Lee, without saying a word, went to him, knelt, took his hand, and spoke quietly. When he stood, there were tears in his eyes. It was obvious, Mother said, that "the mantle had fallen on him."

Five days later, on July 7, 1972, the new First Presidency was announced. Elder N. Eldon Tanner, who had been serving as second counselor to President Smith, was called to be first counselor to President Lee. Elder Marion G. Romney, then a member of the Quorum of the Twelve, was called as second counselor. Spencer W. Kimball, who had been the acting president of the Quorum of the Twelve while President Lee served in the First Presidency, was set apart as the president of that Quorum.

At the October 1972 general conference, the Church as a whole had the opportunity to sustain this action, and the first session of that conference was a solemn assembly held for that purpose. The vacancy occasioned by Elder Romney's call to serve in the First Presidency was filled by Elder Bruce R. McConkie.

After the sustaining, President Lee spoke with great feeling and power, referring to those on the other side of the veil who had joined the Saints in the meeting. He then called upon Elder McConkie to make his first address as an apostle.

"Let This Then Be Our Covenant"

Elder McConkie, with the spiritual confidence that typified his life and ministry, first expressed gratitude for the blessings that had been showered upon him, his family, and the Saints. He reminded his listeners that special spiritual gifts had been given to the members of the Church and noted that the first of the gifts mentioned in scripture is the gift of testimony or revelation. That gift centers in knowing of the truth and divinity of the work in which we are engaged, Elder McConkie explained. "This," he said, "is my gift."

He testified: "I have a perfect knowledge that Jesus Christ is the Son of the living God and that he was crucified for the sins of the world. I know that Joseph Smith is a prophet of God through whose instrumentality the fullness of the everlasting gospel has been restored again in our day. And I know that this Church of Jesus Christ of Latter-day Saints is the kingdom of God on earth, and that as now constituted, with President Harold B. Lee at its head, it has the approval and approbation of the Lord, is in the line of its duty, and is preparing a people for the second coming of the Son of Man."

Elder McConkie testified further that he knew the Lord poured out his Spirit on the Latter-day Saints as he did upon the Saints in ancient days. To evidence the point he said, "I know there is revelation in the Church because I have received revelation. I know God speaks in this day because he has spoken to me." He bore witness of the Lord's system—which, he said, remained the same in all gospel dispensations—to reveal His mind and will to apostles, prophets, and other righteous men. These in turn were to declare those truths and to seal their declaration with their testimony of the verity of that which they had taught. "I rejoice," he said, "in the privilege of standing as a witness of the truth in this day."

He expressed gratitude for the privilege of raising his arm to the square in covenant to sustain, uphold, and take counsel from the newly sustained First Presidency of the Church. He spoke of President Lee as a man filled with the spirit of revelation and wisdom, one who was on intimate terms with the Lord; of President Tanner as the embodiment of integrity and Christian virtue, one who loved the Lord and kept his commandments; and of President Romney as a spiritual giant and preacher of righteousness who knew the Lord and his doctrines.[1]

Elder McConkie then made two statements, both of which were enclosed in quotation marks in the report of the October 1972 general conference, although only one of them is given a scriptural citation. First, he quoted the voice of the Lord as saying: "These are they whom I have chosen as the First Presidency of my Church. Follow them." Next, he quoted from the Doctrine and Covenants a revelation given in 1837 to Thomas B. Marsh, then president of the Quorum of the Twelve, relative to the First Presidency: "On them have I laid the burden of all the churches [the various branches, or congregations, extant at that time]. . . . and whosoever receiveth me, receiveth those, the First Presidency, whom I have sent" (D&C 112:18–20).[2]

The first of these quotations was a revelation given to Elder McConkie personally more than twenty years earlier on the occasion of the solemn assembly at which David O. McKay, Stephen L Richards, and J. Reuben Clark Jr. were sustained as the First Presidency of the Church. Elder McConkie cited it as evidence that he had heard the voice of the Lord and that he had firsthand knowledge of the principles of which he spoke. At the 1951 October general conference he had said:

"I have never told this to any person before, except my wife. Six months ago in the Solemn Assembly, when the First Presidency of the Church were sustained, as I sat down here behind one of these lower pulpits, the voice of the Lord came into my mind as certainly, I am sure, as the voice of the Lord came into the mind of Enos, and the very words were formed, and it said: *'These are they whom I have chosen as the First Presidency of my Church. Follow them'*—those few words." To his recounting of that experience, he added: "I have had a testimony of the divinity of this work from my youth. I was reared in a family where love was the motive force, where my parents taught me righteousness, and I have grown up with a testimony. But that witness [received in the 1951 general conference] was an added assurance. It meant to me, if I hadn't known before, which I did know before, that this is the Lord's Church; that his hand is over it; that he organized it; that these men who preside are called of him: that they are his anointed; that if we will follow them as they follow Christ, we will have eternal life, which is my prayer for myself and for all Israel."[3]

Elder McConkie commented in his 1972 conference address that he and President Marion G. Romney came from the same family. (Later, after Elder McConkie received his call to the apostleship, President Romney said to him privately, "I think Granddad Redd [Lemuel Hardison Redd] will be glad to receive us." Elder McConkie said, "I am going to live so I will be worthy to go where he is." President Romney replied, "So am I.")

Speaking not for himself alone but rather as a spokesman for faithful progenitors, Elder McConkie continued: "Let this then be our covenant—whatever the past has been—let this then be our covenant that we will walk in all the ordinances of the Lord blameless. Let this be our covenant, that we will keep the commandments of God and be living witnesses of the truth and divinity of this glorious work, which is destined to sweep the earth as with a flood and which shall cover the earth as the waters cover the sea.

"O God, grant that I and my family and all the faithful members of the house of Israel may walk in truth and light, and having enjoyed the fellowship and kinship and association that is found nowhere else on earth outside the Church, let us enjoy that same spirit, that same fellowship in its eternal fulness in the mansions and realms which are ahead."[4]

While Elder McConkie spoke, his wife, Amelia, seated a short distance away with the wives of other general authorities, did not hear her husband speak these words; rather, she heard the voice of his father, Oscar W. McConkie, who had died in 1966.

As Elder McConkie stood at the pulpit in the Tabernacle, he knew that his voice was but an echo of the testimony of his father and his mother and indeed his progenitors from the dawn of the Restoration. It was from them that the seeds of his faith had come. The last time he had stood at that same pulpit was to speak at the funeral of President Joseph Fielding Smith. The veil had been lifted, and he had seen President Joseph F. Smith and others from the world of the spirits who had come, as he expressed it, "to manifest their interest in the family." He knew well the nature of our covenants, that salvation is a family affair, and that in the gospel plan none of us stands alone.

2

THE HEARTS OF THE FATHERS

And he shall turn the heart of the fathers to the children, and the heart of the children to their fathers, lest I come and smite the earth with a curse.

—Malachi 4:6

It is a hope natural to many of us that in the search for our ancestors we find ourselves descended from royal blood. Of much greater moment, however, is to find that we are descended from men and women of proven faith, courage, and character—people whose deeds bespeak true nobility. If such a legacy is accounted of worth, then Bruce Redd McConkie was born a child of wealth.

His mother was a woman of very determined nature. She never admitted a day of sickness in her life. At the age of ninety-five and in apparent good health, she decided that she had seen enough of this world and announced that it was time for her to die. She went to bed and seemingly willed herself to death, dying three days later. Bruce's father was a man whose faith was like unto Enoch's, and he preached the gospel with power. When he spoke in church, it was said, you did not need to attend, for you could hear all that he had to say perfectly well while sitting on your front doorstep.

The union of Oscar Walter McConkie and Margaret Vivian

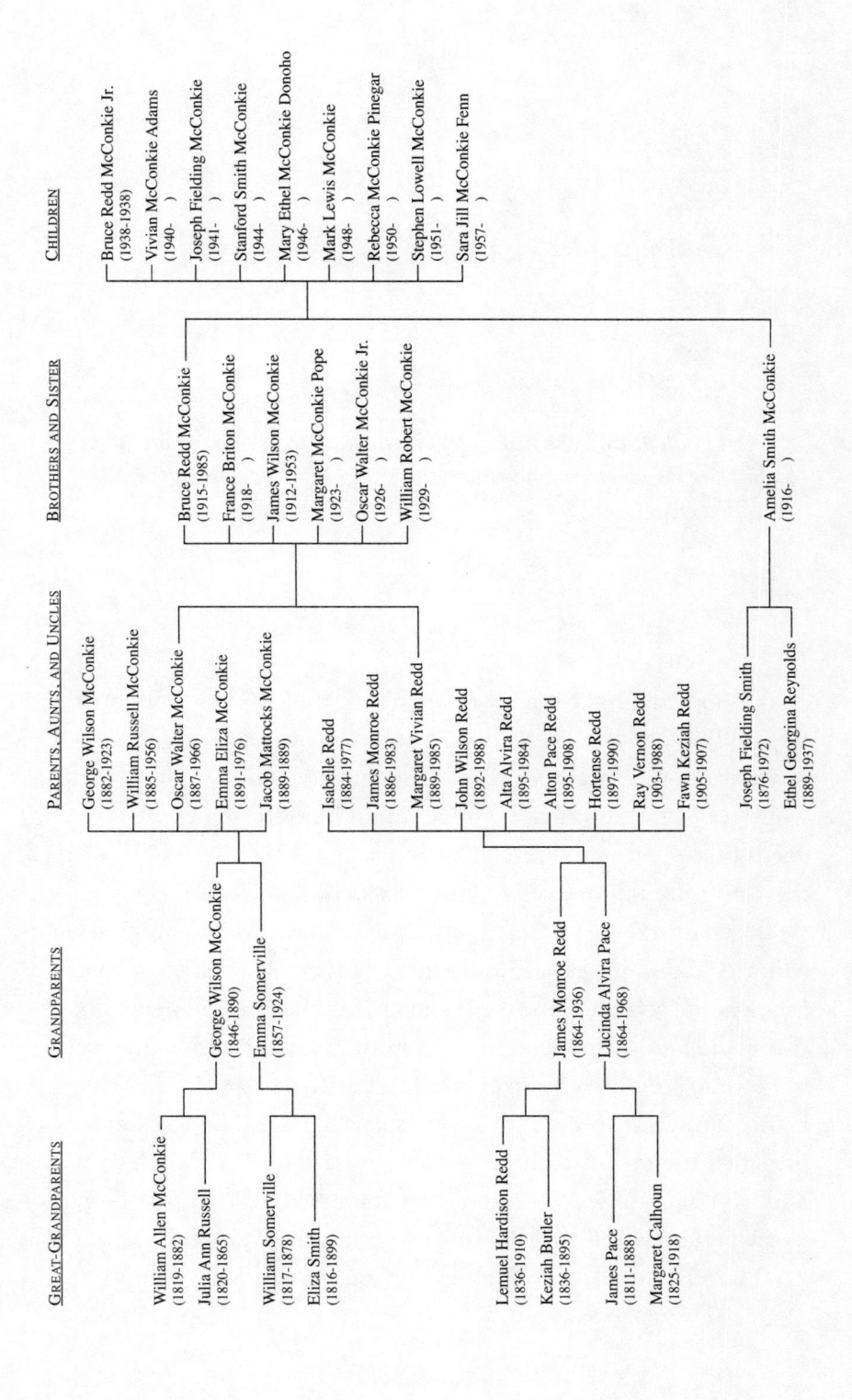

GREAT-GRANDPARENTS

William Allen McConkie
(1819-1882)

Julia Ann Russell
(1820-1865)

William Somerville
(1817-1924)

Eliza Smith
(1816-1899)

Lemuel Hardison Redd
(1836-1910)

Keziah Butler
(1836-1895)

James Pace
(1811-1888)

Margaret Calhoun
(1825-1918)

GRANDPARENTS

George Wilson McConkie
(1846-1890)

Emma Somerville
(1857-1924)

James Monroe Redd
(1864-1936)

Lucinda Alvira Pace
(1864-1968)

PARENTS, AUNTS, AND UNCLES

George Wilson McConkie
(1882-1923)

William Russell McConkie
(1885-1956)

Oscar Walter McConkie
(1887-1966)

Emma Eliza McConkie
(1891-1976)

Jacob Mattocks McConkie
(1889-1889)

Isabelle Redd
(1884-1977)

James Monroe Redd
(1886-1983)

Margaret Vivian Redd
(1889-1985)

John Wilson Redd
(1892-1988)

Alta Alvira Redd
(1895-1984)

Alton Pace Redd
(1895-1908)

Hortense Redd
(1897-1990)

Ray Vernon Redd
(1903-1988)

Fawn Keziah Redd
(1905-1907)

Joseph Fielding Smith
(1876-1972)

Ethel Georgina Reynolds
(1889-1937)

BROTHERS AND SISTER

Bruce Redd McConkie
(1915-1985)

France Briton McConkie
(1918-)

James Wilson McConkie
(1912-1953)

Margaret McConkie Pope
(1923-)

Oscar Walter McConkie Jr.
(1926-)

William Robert McConkie
(1929-)

Amelia Smith McConkie
(1916-)

CHILDREN

Bruce Redd McConkie Jr.
(1938-1938)

Vivian McConkie Adams
(1940-)

Joseph Fielding McConkie
(1941-)

Stanford Smith McConkie
(1944-)

Mary Ethel McConkie Donoho
(1946-)

Mark Lewis McConkie
(1948-)

Rebecca McConkie Pinegar
(1950-)

Stephen Lowell McConkie
(1951-)

Sara Jill McConkie Fenn
(1957-)

Redd, though humble as mortals measure such things, united two families of proven faith and courage. Both were from families who had shouldered their lot virtually from the dawn of the Restoration. These were people who had borne the heat of the day and never thought themselves due any special accolades for having done so. Theirs is the story of family trees that found a place in the sun, rooted themselves deeply, weathered harsh seasons, and reached to the heavens.

Kindred Spirits Drawn to the Gospel

All four of Bruce's maternal great-grandparents—Lemuel H. and Keziah Butler Redd, and James and Margaret Calhoun Pace, a plural wife he married after he moved west—came out of Nauvoo. Six of Bruce's eight maternal great-great-grandparents had also joined with the Saints in Nauvoo. They each carried their own memories of the Prophet Joseph Smith. By the hand of providence, the lives of these people were bound together like the strands of a rope.

Their paths in turn crisscrossed those of Bruce's paternal ancestors, for they too were rooted in Nauvoo and the pioneer era. William Somerville, a paternal great-grandfather to Bruce, fired the final shot in defense of Nauvoo as the last of the Saints left in September 1846. A Scot, he had been baptized by Orson Pratt in Edinburgh in 1840. His daughter Emma would mold the character of her son Oscar W. McConkie, who in turn would mold the character of Bruce.

As to the McConkie family, the missionaries had not yet found them. Instead, like the merchant seeking goodly pearls, the McConkies traveled west in 1874, learned about the Church, and, like Bruce's other progenitors, having heard the message, put their hand to the plow and never looked back. Although none of these people held prominent positions in the Church, they were always found where faith and courage were needed. All of them appear to have been drawn to the gospel.

Nauvoo

Nauvoo was home to most of Bruce's progenitors during the early years of the Restoration. It was, he believed, a place of reunion, a place where they renewed kinships formed long before they were born.

On his maternal side, among the first to arrive were James and Lucinda Strickland Pace. They had courted in Murfreesboro, Rutherford County, Tennessee. After their marriage, they homesteaded in Shelby County, Illinois, less than a hundred miles from Nauvoo. It would have been only with some difficulty that they could have avoided hearing the Mormon elders preach. In April 1839, Dominicus Carter came their way. He preached, and they listened. When he said amen, they asked to be baptized. Elder Carter baptized them and confirmed them at the water's edge. Before another seedtime arrived, they had packed their wagons and were on their way to join the Saints. In Nauvoo, James labored on the temple and served as a bodyguard for Joseph Smith; after the Prophet's death, James became a bodyguard for Brigham Young.

James and Lucinda took pen in hand to share with their families back in Tennessee what they had found. Their testimony found place in the heart of James's older brother William. He in turn befriended some new settlers from North Carolina, the family of a sea captain and merchant-turned-plantation-owner named John Hardison Redd. It was John Redd who wrote Joseph Smith, asking him to send them a Mormon preacher. The Prophet responded by sending a powerful preacher by the name of John D. Lee.

It was explained to Elder Lee that he would not be able to preach publicly without endangering his life as many of the citizens were very hostile to the Mormons. In fact, they had driven the Mormons out of that part of the country. Lee responded that he would come only if an announcement of his visit was made publicly, stating where and when he was going to preach.

General notice was given of the meeting. John D. Lee did not get within twenty miles of the place before he was met by a guard of ten men, headed by Captain Redd, who had come to protect him. John D. preached, and the Redds went forward to apply for baptism. As expected, this was more than a good southern community could bear. Word arrived that a group of citizens was on its way to tar and feather the Mormon preacher. When the mob arrived, the women in the congregation surrounded John D. Lee so that the mobbers would have to fight their way through them to get at him. After some fuss, they withdrew to reconsider their strategy, not caring to fight the women. At this point Captain Redd announced that the meeting would be continued at his home under his protection. When the meeting reconvened, John Hardison Redd sat next to John D. Lee with two large pistols, which he called his peacemakers. Apparently, respect for Captain Redd's ability to use the pistols was sufficient to allow the meeting to continue without interruption, except for one drunk he booted out.

After his baptism, John Hardison Redd decided it was inconsistent with the covenant he and his wife had made to continue to be slaveholders. They sold their plantation and freed their slaves. By an act of the court and at considerable personal loss, they made financial provisions for each of these people.

John Lowe Butler and his wife, Caroline Skeen Butler, whose daughter Keziah would eventually marry John Hardison's son Lemuel, joined the Church in Kentucky. They were among those who moved to Nauvoo. The spotlight of history fell on John Butler on August 6, 1838, in Gallatin, Missouri. It was election day, and the Missourians had sworn that Mormons would not be allowed to vote; the Mormons, in turn, were determined to exercise the right for which their kin had fought the Revolutionary War. Hatred of the Mormons and a keg of whiskey solidified the Missourians' resolve, and a brawl ensued. The Mormons, eleven in number, attempted to establish their voting rights against odds reckoned at about eight to one. At this moment, John Lowe Butler introduced himself to the Missourians. A rugged, muscular man standing slightly less than six feet, three inches in height, he made that introduction with a four-foot piece of oak timber he wielded with a deftness reminiscent of Samson when he slew a thousand Philistines with the jawbone of an ass.

It was reported that the club of John Butler removed nineteen Missourians from the fray that day. The blows he administered had the effect of sharpening their memories, for none of them ever forgot him. The years that followed witnessed hatred on the part of the Missourians for John Lowe Butler, a feeling matched in intensity by the affection in which he was held by the Prophet Joseph Smith. He became a trusted friend, a bodyguard, and a messenger for the Prophet.

In 1831 John Butler had married the beautiful, dark-haired Caroline Skeen. Caroline had been raised in a slaveholding family whose position was somewhere between the gentry and that of the yeomen class from which her husband came. At their wedding, her parents presented them with two slaves, one of whom was the woman who served Caroline all her life. The newlyweds gave the slaves their freedom that very day. This action undoubtedly commenced a strain with her family, which erupted a few years later when Caroline and John embraced Mormonism.

Caroline's faith matched her husband's strength. In Nauvoo, when Mary Fielding Smith asked the sisters to contribute to the building of the temple, Caroline was penniless and her husband off on an assignment for the Prophet. She made it a matter of prayer and then took her little children for a walk. They found two dead buffalo, from which they pulled the hair. She washed the hair, carded it, spun it into thread, and then wove the thread into gloves to be worn by the men working on the Temple.

On the paternal side of Bruce McConkie's family, William Somerville arrived in Nauvoo in March 1841. A year later he was ordained a seventy and called on a mission to Canada. Having served for a year, he returned to Nauvoo, where he helped guard the city as a member of the First Company of the Nauvoo Legion. He became a close friend of the Prophet and his brother Hyrum. He frequently stood guard over the Prophet's home at night. In defending the Prophet, he was shot in the knee and carried the bullet with him to his grave. When the Saints were expelled from Nauvoo, William Somerville's company of the Nauvoo Legion assisted Brigham Young and others to cross the Mississippi. He helped start the settlements of Garden Grove and Mount Pisgah as the Saints crossed Iowa.

William returned to Nauvoo sick with ague. He was immediately raised from his bed of affliction by the power of the priesthood and placed in command of ten men to aid in defending the city. The mob militia, armed with five pieces of artillery, had commenced their march toward Nauvoo. There was no artillery in Nauvoo to counter them. Two steamboat shafts were found on the banks of the Mississippi, and it was decided to make them into cannons. The shafts were cut to a proper length with a piece of iron bolted at one end. There was some danger that when these crude cannons were fired, they might blow up and kill those who manned them. William declared, "If that happens, I will still take a lot of them [the mob] with me."

For four days he and his men withstood the mob, until a cease-fire was agreed upon. On September 30, 1846, the mob, in violation of that treaty, fired on the position guarded by William Somerville and his men. William was hit in the forehead by a rock chipped from a stone by a bullet from one of the mob. He responded with a bit of Scottish wrath, ordering his men to return fire. They did so and scattered those who had fired upon their position. This secured to them the honor of firing the last shots in defense of Nauvoo.

Leaving Nauvoo

James Pace was among those called as missionaries to declare the candidacy of Joseph Smith for president of the United States. He labored in Arkansas from the middle of May until the end of July. Thus, he was not in Nauvoo when Joseph and Hyrum were killed or when their bodies were returned. Lucinda, however, was among those who went out to meet the brethren who brought the bodies of Joseph and Hyrum back to the city, and she was in the meeting on August 8, 1844, when Brigham Young was transfigured so that he looked and sounded like Joseph Smith to many who were present.

On January 10, 1845, with mobs threatening the city and the Saints preparing to leave, James and Lucinda were sealed in the Nauvoo Temple. They left Nauvoo in the dark of night on the 8th of February to cross the Mississippi, taking with them only what two horse-drawn wagons could carry. Lucinda and the children were taken to the home of her brother-in-law, William Pace, about five miles from the river. James returned to Nauvoo to stand guard at Brigham Young's home.

The Trek West

At Council Bluffs, William Somerville met a young woman by the name of Eliza Smith. Love blossomed, and they were married there on February 3, 1847. They traveled west in 1852, settling first in Palmyra, Utah County, and later moving to Spanish Fork. There the last of their six children, Emma Somerville, was born May 21,

1857. There too they became close friends with the Paces, the Redds, and the Butlers.

On July 6, 1846, Brigham Young had called James Pace to serve in the Mormon Battalion. He was formally enlisted and was then elected—that being the way officers were chosen in that day—first lieutenant. As an officer, he was entitled to a servant, who would be paid fifteen dollars a month. He chose his son William to fill that position as he was too young to enlist. Lieutenant Pace left a journal account of the Battalion march. He was discharged in Los Angeles one year to the day after his enlistment. From there James and William journeyed back to Mount Pisgah, where they were reunited with their family on December 17, 1847. "I can well remember," recalled his daughter Margaret, "the day of their return home, how overjoyed we all were, my mother shed many tears of joy."

The Paces crossed the plains in the summer of 1850, with James a captain of fifty. One of the families in their company was that of John Hardison Redd, who kept a daily journal of the trek, which, except for the first and last pages, has been preserved. It reads very much like a seaman's log, without reference to either himself or his family, notwithstanding that both he and his son Lemuel contracted cholera during the trek and almost died.

Spanish Fork and Payson

Upon the Paces' arrival in the Salt Lake Valley, Brigham Young assigned James to settle on a small creek named Peteetneet about eighty miles south of Salt Lake City. One of James's daughters recalled: "We went there with five or six other families, but soon enough more came and we built a fort which we lived in on account of the Indians. While we were on the road, we camped at Battle Creek, there we found my Uncle William Pace and family, and a happy meeting it was. They had come in the year before and were getting scarce of groceries, and my mother gave them a good supply, for which they were very thankful. We had not been on the little creek long, when President Young and quite a number of the twelve Apostles came, and organized a branch for us, and put my father in to preside over the branch." President Young named the community Payson in honor of James Pace and his son William.

Shortly after the establishment of Payson, the Paces, the Redds, and the Butlers were assigned to settle Spanish Fork. For protection against the Indians, these early settlers built their houses in such a manner as to form a fort. That marital ties would bind them even closer was almost inevitable. The first of their number to marry were Lemuel Hardison Redd, eldest son of John and Elizabeth Redd, and Keziah Jane Butler, third child of John and Caroline Butler. They were pronounced husband and wife by Bishop William Pace on January 2, 1856.

In the summer of 1855, John Butler took two of his older daughters to Fort Bridger to see what money could be earned. Caroline remained in Spanish Fork to tend the younger children, care for their newborn child, and run the farm. The grasshoppers were so bad that summer that the Butlers, like the rest of the Saints, had a struggle harvesting any crop at all.

Amid these difficulties, a man and his son sought food and shelter from Caroline. She had cornmeal, which she cooked and divided between the two visitors. She also gave each of them a bowl of milk. They felt the sweet spirit of the home, and as they were preparing to leave, the elder of the two men said, "Sister Butler, I am prompted to give you a blessing." The two men placed their hands upon her head and, among other things, promised her in the name of the Lord that she and her children would never go hungry.

In later years Caroline testified to the truth of this promise. She said she sometimes scraped the bottom of the meal barrel for the last bit of flour, mixed it, and baked it. Then, when she could not find

*James Monroe Redd
and Lucinda Pace Redd*

food anywhere else, she would go back to the same barrel and scrape up enough meal for another batch of bread. The promise seemed one and the same with that of the widow whose barrel of meal had been blessed by Elijah (1 Kings 17:13–16).

NEW HARMONY

In the early 1860s the call came for help in settling southern Utah. The Butlers, having anticipated the call, had already moved to Panguitch. The Paces and the Redds also responded. In October 1861, James Pace made the move south. After two weeks' travel, his family arrived at New Harmony, Washington County, where on the advice of Erastus Snow they remained. They spent the winter cooking in a dugout and sleeping in a wagon box.

The Redds joined them there the following spring. On August 24, 1863, Keziah Redd presented her husband, Lemuel, with a son they named James Monroe Redd. On September 21 of the following year, another new citizen of New Harmony graced the home of James Pace and his second wife, Margaret Calhoun. She was named Lucinda, as an expression of her parents' love for James's first wife. We may suppose that as the new mothers talked, it was mentioned that it would be nice if the two babies grew up to marry each other. Nineteen years were required to bring such talk to reality. Monroe and Lucinda entered the new and everlasting covenant of marriage on April 2, 1884.

In the 1860s William Somerville responded to a call from Brigham Young to help settle Mona in Juab County. William and part of his family joined the united order in Mona in 1875, putting his cattle and sheep in the company herd. When the order failed, he lost all his livestock, making his sons bitter. He commented, "If I lose my sons because of their lack of faith, then I am a poor man indeed." Because of their love and respect for their father, they returned to the Church. They eventually became the holders of the largest herd of cattle in the United States permitted to graze on government land. William died on April 25, 1878, and was buried in Mona. So was his wife Eliza, who died April 17, 1899. She had been Mona's first Relief Society president and was known as a woman of "faultless soul."

THE HOLE IN THE ROCK

In the fall of 1879, yet another call went out for families to aid in colonizing the Great Basin. Saints living in Iron, Garfield, and Washington counties were asked to colonize the valley of the San Juan River in southeastern Utah, the most isolated area left in the United States. This effort was called the Peace Mission because the settlers were to locate between two warring tribes of Indians—Navajos and Piutes—who for countless generations had survived by their cunning and thievery. This venture proved to be the toughest bit of pioneering in the annals of the western United States. Lemuel Hardison Redd and two of his sons, James Monroe and Lemuel Jr., together with Lemuel Jr.'s wife Eliza Ann Westover and their little daughter, Lula, made the epic trek.

Lemuel Sr. was one of four men chosen as a scouting party. They were four consecutive days without food. To survive the lack of water, he found it necessary to keep a little flat stone in his mouth for days to prevent his tongue from swelling. Then, in a dream, it was revealed to him where water could be found. His companions thought him to be delusional and refused to accompany him to the place. Nonetheless, he went directly to the spring, found its lifesaving waters, and then led his companions to it.

A short time later, the scouts were lost for three days in snow and fog with neither sun nor stars to guide them. Lemuel was again favored with a dream. In the morning he told his companions to walk with him to the top of a knoll, where he would show them the San Juan River. As they stood on the spot where he had stood in his dream, they were able, with the aid of field glasses, to see the river.

These pioneers had undertaken this journey thinking it would take three weeks. It took six months. The terrain was so difficult that these veteran pioneers averaged little more than a mile a day. Their journey from southwestern to southeastern Utah took twice the time it had taken them to cross the plains and wend their way through the Rocky Mountains to the Salt Lake Valley. Their first settlement in the valley of the San Juan River was called Bluff.

The Mexican Colonies

Because it was so isolated, Bluff became a place of refuge for polygamists who otherwise had to be in constant hiding as a result of the Edmunds-Tucker Act. It would not be long, however, before the United States marshals made their appearance. This left Mexico as the final resort for these families. Once again many Saints found themselves packing their wagons, Lemuel Hardison Redd among them. He felt that if he took one family to Mexico, the other family could live in Utah in peace. The trip was long and hard. There were no roads, and there is some question whether they even had maps. They just knew they must travel south. It took three weeks to get to Nutrioso, Arizona, were they bathed, washed their clothes, and regrouped. Then they took to the road again. Nine weeks later, in January 1892, they arrived in Colonia Dublán. Lemuel bought a fruit farm, and the family began to rebuild. Thereafter he divided the year between his family in New Harmony and the one in Dublán. In Mexico he served as a counselor to stake president Alexander F. McDonald, then in the same capacity to Miles P. Romney, and yet again to Albert D. Thurber. He was ordained a patriarch in March 1908. Lemuel Hardison Redd died June 9, 1910, in Colonia Juárez, where he is buried.

THE LATECOMERS

The McConkie clan did not find its way into the Church until 1874. George Wilson McConkie, born October 26, 1846, in Mansfield, Ohio, was passing through Salt Lake City with his wife, Susan Smith of Alabama, on their way to California. They felt impressed to stay, ask questions, and learn. The restored gospel struck a responsive chord with them. They were baptized in City Creek and eventually found their way to Mona, Utah, where George taught school. Susan felt it proper for her husband to take a second wife. Together they chose Emma Somerville, whom Susan had repeatedly invited to dinner so that they could all become acquainted. Emma became the second wife of George Wilson McConkie on April 7, 1881, in the Endowment House in Salt Lake City. Later, George married a third wife, a sixteen-year-old young woman named Elizabeth (Lizzie) Slade. Susan bore him eight children; Emma, five, one of whom was stillborn; and Lizzie, two.

In the 1880s, George McConkie moved all three of his families to Moab, Utah, where they shared two small cabins. His efforts centered primarily on eluding United States marshals, who were hunting for polygamists. It was not long until they decided to flee to Mexico. The journey was most difficult, as it was necessary for them to stop and work along the way to sustain themselves. Two years after they

Emma Somerville McConkie and George Wilson McConkie

left Moab, they arrived in Pacheco, Chihuahua, where they once again put down roots. George Wilson McConkie died there on December 9, 1890; all three of his wives survived him. After his death, Emma and her family returned to Mona, Utah, where the Somervilles resided.

In family lore Emma is remembered for a dream she once had. While she was serving as Relief Society president in Moab, one of the sisters under her care required special help as a result of childbirth. This woman had married a Gentile, and because of the hard feelings between many of the Saints and the Gentiles, none of the other sisters in the ward would go into her home to help. The burden of caring for her rested entirely on Emma.

Each morning she rose early and walked a considerable distance to the woman's house. There she saw to it that the other children were fed and also cared for the mother and baby. Then she gathered the laundry to carry it home to launder and take back the next day when she returned. One morning, sick herself, she lay in bed thinking she was just too weak to go, but as she thought on it, she realized that if she did not go, the woman and her children would not be cared for. Despite her own condition, she went.

When she returned that day, she immediately sat down and, as she did so, fell asleep. She dreamed that she was bathing the Christ child and marveling at what a privilege it would have been to have done so. A feeling of warmth encompassed her, which she said felt as if it would melt the very marrow of her bones. She then heard a very distinct voice, which said, "Inasmuch as ye have done it unto one of the least of these . . . , ye have done it unto me" (Matthew 25:40).

The Promises Made to the Fathers

Bruce Redd McConkie had no claim to royalty as men count such things. His kin were common folk whose names did not find their way into history books, nor have they been recorded among the noble leaders of the Church. They were people who did not wait for the gospel to find them; rather, they sought it out. Having found it, they embraced it; and having embraced it, they never looked back. It was the nature of these people to treat all men with dignity in a day when such treatment was not expected and, in fact, often strongly discouraged. They never hesitated to share what they had, and when volunteers were needed, they were among the first to step forward. They could fight with the strength of Samson and exercise faith like that of the widow who gave the last of her meal to Elijah. They served as bodyguards for the Prophet, fought in defense of Nauvoo, marched with the Mormon Battalion, crossed the plains, and aided in colonizing one city after another. When the toughest pioneering was needed to go through the Hole in the Rock, they were there. They became builders and colonizers because that was what needed to be done. They were, as the Good Book says, "a brand plucked out of the fire" (Zechariah 3:2), and through it all they elicited special promises from the Lord relative to what they held to be of higher worth than all the treasures of the earth.

Indeed, the greatest blessing that can be given a faithful man or woman, beyond the promise of his or her own salvation, is that of a righteous posterity. Such a promise was common to the patriarchal blessings given to all of them. Though the language differed from one blessing to another, the essence of the promises was that theirs would be a legacy of righteous men and righteous women and that prophets would come of their loins. The women were blessed with the blessings of Sarah and Rachel and told that the Lord would reveal to them in visions and dreams those things necessary for the welfare of their children. Another thread common to their blessings was the promise that their tables would be "crowned with blessings of the earth," that they might be as ministering angels to the oppressed, feeding those who hungered and comforting the fatherless. Common to the blessings of their companions was the promise that the power of the priesthood would rest upon their sons to the latest generation.

Perhaps their spirit is best caught in events attending the death of John Butler. Realizing that he was dying, he called his family together and bore wonderful testimony of the truthfulness of the restored gospel. He told his children that the great desire of his heart was that they and their children after them remain faithful to that message. He "paced the floor and his face turned blue with anxiety over his children."

Such were the hearts of the fathers from whom Bruce Redd McConkie was descended, and such were the promises made to them.

3

THE HOUSE OF FAITH

I never indulged the deceitful hope that I could win God's favor while I, at the same time, opposed him in any particular.

—Oscar W. McConkie

In answer to my question, "Who other than Joseph Smith would you rank as the greatest spiritual giants of our dispensation?" without a moment's thought Dad responded, "Wilford Woodruff and my father." Such was his measure of the spiritual stature of his father, Oscar W. McConkie. None who knew him would rank him less. Of his mother, Margaret Vivian Redd, Bruce McConkie would say, "They were equally yoked."

LIKE FATHER, LIKE SON

To understand the father is in large measure to understand the son. I have heard people say that had they been blindfolded and heard one of them preach, they could not have told which of the two had done the preaching. On politics their views differed sharply—one a Democrat and the other a Republican. On matters of gospel principle or doctrine, they were of one mind. Oscar

The House of Faith

McConkie possessed the gift of healing and the ability to dream dreams and see visions as few men have. Bruce McConkie possessed the gift of knowledge and prophecy in like measure. They held the gift of faith equally; either man could have moved mountains or raised the dead.

Both were born to believe, and both had a hard time being patient with or understanding those who knew no faith. Elder McConkie learned some degree of patience in this matter after spending what seemed to him countless hours in the councils of the Church. He said his father would have been frustrated with the ambivalence of some in those councils. Neither of these men understood uncertainty.

As to their gospel understanding, both were self-taught, though the father was a marvelous mentor for his children. Neither man had access to a gospel library in his youth; each had the scriptures, the Spirit, and little else. They learned to drink from the fountainhead. Neither man ever lacked confidence in the things of the Spirit. Oscar told his children that they knew more about God than anyone they would ever meet in the world.

If it can rightly be said that making money is a talent, then that is one talent neither Oscar nor Bruce possessed or sought to develop. Given the opportunity to make a few dollars or preach a sermon, they would preach the sermon any day of the week. In running his law practice, Oscar McConkie could not bring himself to bill a widow or a woman in distress. Styles and fashions were of no interest to either the father or the son, nor were either of them particularly interested in sports—though they each had sons who excelled in athletics. On the other hand, Oscar would not miss watching the Kentucky Derby on television and exacted a promise from me that I too would watch it.

Like his father, Bruce took employment with a newspaper after completing law school. He was also following in the footsteps of his father when he took up his pen to teach the doctrines of the gospel. Oscar was the author of two Church books. *A Dialogue at Golgotha*, published in 1945, is a scholarly discussion showing the oneness of the teachings of the ancient prophets about Christ. It analyzes the people's rights, obligations, government, and judicial system in those ancient days and concludes with a discussion of the Hebrew and Roman trials of the Savior, his crucifixion, and his resurrection. Oscar's second book, *The Holy Ghost*, published in 1952, masterfully describes the personage, power, purposes, and functions of the Holy Ghost.

In dedicating his first book, *Mormon Doctrine*, Bruce wrote: "To Oscar W. McConkie, my father, a pillar of spiritual strength, a scripturian and theologian, who has brought up his children in light and truth and instilled in the heart of each of them a desire for excellence in Gospel scholarship."

Oscar Walter McConkie

Oscar McConkie was raised on a diet of faith. During his growing-up years, that is the only thing his family had plenty of. His father, George Wilson McConkie, who lived during that era in which the plurality of wives was sanctioned by the Lord, had three wives. At the time of Oscar's birth, the three families shared two small cabins at Buena Vista, near Moab, an area commonly known as Poverty Flats. His mother, Emma Somerville, and his two older brothers, George Jr. (then age four) and Russell (age two), shared a cabin with Elizabeth Slade, his father's third wife. Elizabeth had given birth to her first child, Mary Elizabeth, a month and two days before Oscar's arrival on May 9, 1887. Susan Smith, George's first wife, and her seven children occupied the other cabin.

Were we to step inside one of those cabins, we would find a wood stove, a few mattresses stuffed with straw or cornhusks, a homemade bedstead, candles or perhaps a small lamp, and cribs for

Oscar (sitting), surrounded by his siblings Emma, George, and Russell

the babies. As for food, little more than flour and molasses could be found. It is said that venison was plentiful, but then, so were United States marshals hunting for polygamists. Neither Oscar's father nor venison was to be found at their dinner table very often.

Before Oscar was old enough to remember, the family took refuge in the Mormon colonies in Mexico. There his father died in December 1890 and was buried in Pacheco, Galeana, Chihuahua. After George's death, Emma became the chief architect of Oscar's character. She and her children moved back to Mona, Utah, where her husband had taught school years before and where she had family. The log home in which they lived still stands as a point of community pride.

Oscar's youthful memories begin in Mona. "I carried milk from Uncle Orson's for our evening meal. Tiring of the task, I became careless and spilled the milk now and then. Mother's patience was exhausted. She gave me a good spanking one day, which I considered very inappropriate in view of the fact that I thought I did not purposely do it, but this one fact remained: I did not spill any more milk—not once more."

From age seven to ten, Oscar herded rams, dug potatoes, and did like tasks for twenty-five cents a day. Years later he took his family back to Mona. Pulling off the road in what seemed a particularly barren spot, he gave directions to get the picnic basket out of the trunk. When asked why he had chosen such a barren spot, he replied, "As a boy I herded goats out here and promised myself that some day I would return and eat all that I wanted to." In his journal he recorded the story thus: "One day I was at Garfield's when they were eating, and they had a piece of cheese on the table that I never forgot. It was probably three or four pounds, it could have been five. I had never seen so much cheese outside the store and resolved that someday I would buy a piece of cheese like that. When I was on the Bench of the District Court I went to a grocery store in Salt Lake, had a piece of cheese cut to fit my precise memory, took it, a lunch, and the family and went to Mona, spread out a table cloth and we had a meal with cheese as near as I could tell like Garfield's had that day, upwards of forty years before."

He recalled of his boyhood years: "Mother told me once, that I had asked for something to read when I was bedfast in Mona. She reached up and took down a Book of Mormon, and she said that there came over her, when she handed it to me, a glorious feeling that she never forgot, such as to give her a testimony that she had acted wisely and that the book was from the Lord. The Holy Ghost seemed to burn her whole soul as with fire, a fire that soothed and sweetened her mind and body. The Lord warmed her soul."

The House of Faith

When Oscar was ten, the family moved back to Moab so that his mother could help care for her brother Will's children (Annie and Ray), as their mother had passed away. Responsible by nature, Oscar was called as president of the deacons quorum shortly after his ordination to that office. "I passed the sacrament in overalls, oft times bare footed," he recalled.

Because temporal matters rest with the Aaronic Priesthood, it was the duty of the deacons to cut and haul wood for the widows, the wives of missionaries, and the building in which church meetings were held. It became a contest among the young men to see who could find the best wood, get the biggest wagon load, and cut the biggest pile. Oscar began to put muscle on the Nephi-like stature that would be his: "My long arms and physical strength came in well in all these contests. It required two days to get a good load of wood, so we camped out at night when we were in earnest about it." Another mark of manhood in that day was the ability to pitch hay. Two men would work a wagon, one pitching on each side. Each would try to outdo the other and then walk ahead of the wagon to wait for their slower companion, as if to say, "I am the best." It was with considerable pride that Oscar McConkie said, "No one was ever able to do that to me." He always drew top wages of two dollars a day for pitching hay.

As a youth, Oscar idolized his older brother George Wilson, who served as a missionary in the Southern States. While there, George contracted malaria and became quite ill. Those nursing him wanted him to drink coffee, which he refused. Finally, one day he sipped a few swallows. His companion told the mission president George was not observing the Word of Wisdom. George wrote home that as soon as he got well, he was going to whip that companion good. Upon receiving the letter, Oscar said, "I visualized him coming home in disgrace [for fighting], and fasted three days and nights, and daily went up into the belfry of the Central School

Brothers George, Oscar, and Russell

at Moab, where I was janitor, and prayed about it. At the end of three days the Spirit of the Lord told me not to fast any longer, that my prayer was answered." In the course of time, a letter came from George saying that he had read an article by President Joseph F. Smith in the *Improvement Era* that had changed his mind, so he wasn't going to fight the other missionary. In his letter George gave the very hour in which he had made this decision. It was the same time that the Spirit had told Oscar to eat.

Oscar was promised in his patriarchal blessing that he would dream dreams and see visions. This privilege was accorded him even from the days of his youth. In this manner he was frequently warned of the deaths of friends and relatives. When his uncle Andrew Somerville was sick, he dreamed that he went to see him, and as he stood in the room looking at him, a man came into the room. He did not come through the door nor leave by it but passed through the wall. "I observed him closely," Oscar recalled, "both his appearance, features, and manners," though he had never seen him before. The man walked straight to his uncle's bedside and studied him, shook his head, and with a very grave look on his face turned and left the room with no acknowledgment of Oscar's presence.

It was Oscar's habit to share such experiences with his mother. From his description, Emma recognized that the man he had seen was her father. She asked her son the meaning of the dream and was told that her brother was going to die. She got up, put on her shawl, and went immediately to Andrew's bedside. When she returned, she said he seemed much better and that the doctor had said he would be fine. Two days later he passed away.

From such experiences Oscar learned much about the workings of the Spirit. For instance, he said that in the dream when the father saw that his son would die, his face became very grave and the lines on it deepened, not because he was going to die but because his work was not finished and because he had not been as faithful as he should have been. This alone, he was able to determine, was the source of his sorrow.

Oscar recalled that his mother, who had the spirit of discernment, believed the spirit of the Gadianton robbers infested the area around Moab, where he grew to manhood. He said, "I saw drunken men on the streets and staggering in the gutter, heard their oaths, saw them fight, saw the flash of knives and heard the crack of pistol fire, and saw hell boiling over upon many." Of those who employed him in those days, he recalled that the non-Mormons were kinder to him and paid him better wages than did members of the Church.

When he became old enough to vote, Oscar walked ten miles to cast his first ballot. He voted for Will Knight, who was running for governor. Will was the son of Jesse Knight and a Democrat, which Oscar felt was recommendation enough for any man. He then sat up all night waiting for the election returns.

Politics were part of his religion. He recorded: "I ran for a number of offices in San Juan, and in each instance the Lord told me the outcome."

He was active and interested in political and governmental affairs all his life. He served two terms as a state senator from the Twelfth District, was the Salt Lake City commissioner of finance for three years, and sought to be a candidate for governor on the Democratic ticket in 1940. As in all things, he felt his political convictions strongly. In the following letter, he expressed his feelings about the Constitution of the United States and illustrated the manner in which he regarded his responsibility to his country.

> To My Posterity,
>
> I am pleased beyond expression that I live in a land of liberty, where I can act in a voluntary manner, with no obstacle in the way of my doing so. The will to be free may be feeble in some, their air of liberty may be impure, but I bear my civil responsibilities faithfully and possess genuine love for the Constitution. World-wide trends leave me wanting in ease. I feel the sting of asps as they strike at the Constitution, as fully as though their poisonous fangs were buried in my flesh. I hate the destructive clamor that would annihilate Constitutional liberty.
>
> This Christmas finds me thankful to Almighty God for vital liberty, and that the grotesque state of political disorder that has settled upon so much of the world, like a giant cloud of darkness that leaves mankind in a state of anesthesia, has not captivated my reason nor lulled me into hope of false security.
>
> The Constitution is beneficial to my soul. Those who shoot at it fill me with arrows. I accept the Constitution of the United States as God ordained, God inspired, God established, and believe the agency it guarantees to be as essential to the peace of mankind as any other principle of the Restored Gospel. Its principles are a part of the cable that ties man to

The House of Faith

Oscar and Vivian with their children and grandchildren, 1951

God. I cherish the Constitution like I cherish life. I love it like I love liberty.

Men who can see the light must lead those who cannot. We must teach men to cherish virtue, but there can be no virtue without agency, and there can be no agency without vindication of the principles of the Constitution. Falsehood brews in every port. Let my family double strength its wisdom, its patriotism, its devotion to God and to the Constitution of the United States. Let my family stand amongst those who befriend it. Let them pledge their worldly goods, their sacred honor and their lives to the end that it may be preserved. God will not forsake it. We must not do so. God brought it forth to be preserved. He will defend it. While he has a true prophet upon the earth, he will speak for the Constitution of the United States and against those who are against it. As to myself, I am commanded by the mandate of God. I live and I shall die by these principles.

When Oscar was twenty-one years old, he dreamed that he had

a terrible tussle with a great snake that was longer than he was tall. In this dream, he became all but exhausted. Finally, summoning all of his strength and exerting his full powers, he killed the snake. The dream had its fulfillment in a battle he had with a severe case of typhoid. At a stake conference held May 15, 1909, he received a sustaining vote to be ordained to the Melchizedek Priesthood. Four months passed, however, before he was ordained. Typhoid fever intervened and came close to taking his life. For nearly sixty days he lay unconscious with a temperature running to 106 degrees. His weight dropped from two hundred pounds to less than ninety. He became so thin that he could hold his hand to the light and see through it. Serious sores developed on his hips and shoulders.

One night, Oscar recalled, "the boys" came to see him before he died. (There were no hospital regulations about visitors, because the doctor thought he was going to die anyway.) "I heard one of them say that if Oscar had drunk liquor and tea and coffee instead of the water of the Colorado River, he would not be sick." Oscar responded from what appeared to be his deathbed, saying, "If it kills me to keep the commandments of the Lord, I'll die." He added that he had always boiled his drinking water.

"The year I had the typhoid, during a ten-month period, these also had it: Lewis Larson, Elmer Martin, George McConkie, Tom Parrot, Roy Shafer, and a Cisco stage driver whose name I cannot remember. George and I were the only two who observed the Word of Wisdom and we were the only two who survived. All the rest died. All of us were between 22 and 26, I believe, except one who was around 40 years old. We were all strong and able-bodied. The doctor told me that I should have died and all the rest should have lived."

The doctor told him later that if he had had any poison in his system at all, he would not have survived. Asked what he meant, the doctor, who was not a member of the Church, replied, "Tea, coffee, tobacco, or liquor."

A year passed before Oscar regained his strength. Because of the illness, his bishop did not submit his mission papers, and he did not serve as a missionary until years later when he was called to preside over the California Mission.

Vivian Redd

Margaret Vivian Redd was born October 13, 1889, in Bluff, Utah, to James Monroe Redd and Lucinda Pace Redd. She grew to maturity in that community. Oscar and Vivian first met at a basketball game between Monticello and Moab. They were both working at the officials table. He often told his children, "God ordained and appointed your mother and me" and "our union was according to a divine plan." To date her, Oscar rode the sixty miles between his home in Moab and her home in Monticello on horseback. He loved to tell the story of a time when he had made that ride and, being weary, had stopped to rest under a tree. Using his saddle as a pillow he lay down to nap. Vivian, who knew he was coming, rode out to meet him. Finding her handsome prince soundly sleeping beneath a tree, she knelt down to wake him with a kiss. "I woke up," as Oscar would tell the story, "to the most beautiful sight I have ever seen in this life."

Both Oscar and Vivian attended the University of Utah. Vivian did so on a basketball scholarship. "While I was courting your mother," Oscar told his children, "we were both very busy." They were serious students and carried heavy class loads. "We would meet by appointment on the campus," Oscar explained, "and walk amongst the trees and shrubbery, sit on the grass, and enjoy 'love' as it crept up upon us. I would arrange to meet her and we would walk home together now and then from school, but not often as our classes did not allow it. On Sunday I would walk over to her house

Above: *Lucinda Pace Redd surrounded by seven of her children. Back, John and James Monroe Jr.; middle, Belle, Hortense, Lucinda, and Vivian; front, twins Alta and Alton*
Left: *Vivian (second from bottom) with University of Utah basketball teammates, 1909*

in the evening. She, Alta, and Hortense [her sisters] were batching." She was wearing, he recalled, a dress that she had made. "She was very popular and I watched closely to make sure no one got her away from me. From the very first, it seemed to me that I knew we were for each other, or at least, that she was for me. I never gave any thought as to whether I was for her. I just knew she was for me. On Sunday, we attended the same Sunday School, where Dr. Widtsoe was the teacher. It was a class for college students. Always we walked home together."

When something special was held in the Tabernacle, they would walk together to attend the event. "Our courtship was walking and visiting." The two of them found little reason to seek out other forms of entertainment. "My happiness seemed complete if I

Oscar and Vivian about the time of their marriage

could get Miss Redd to be with me." Again, he added, "We knew each other before we were born and we knew what we would do about it after we were born, and that is why we fit in the same picture so well. It was as if we had always known each other. She never seemed strange to me. My heart was knit to her from the beginning. All our ambitions have integrated into one great desire, and that desire includes you," he said in reference to his posterity.

LIFE TOGETHER

Oscar Walter McConkie and Margaret Vivian Redd were married September 10, 1913, in the Salt Lake Temple. The day after their marriage they left for Ann Arbor, Michigan, where Oscar was to study law. One of the first things Vivian did there was to make her new husband a shirt. An excellent seamstress, she made him shirts for many years. It was in Ann Arbor that their first son, Bruce Redd McConkie, was born.

After his second year of law school, Oscar experienced difficulties with his eyes that made it necessary for him to withdraw from school. He, Vivian, and their baby returned to Monticello, where a job as the editor of the *San Juan Record* awaited him, as did the

Oscar and Vivian in Ann Arbor, Michigan

opportunity to practice law. They lived with Vivian's parents while a house was built for them.

Writing to his children in November 1948, Oscar said, "Your mother is like unto beautiful Rebecca. She has lived up to the full measure of her foreordination, thus far. She knew you all before you were born, and she rejoiced as she looked forward to the day when she should mother you in the flesh, for the arrangement was made there. Our family is not by chance, nor did it begin here. . . . God chose her to bring forth prophets. . . . Out of her womb have come those who if they are true, will shape the opinions of many, even nations, and who will stand with the greatest of the great, and will be numbered with them. . . . Her seed shall stand in the front ranks in defense of Jesus Christ, and in mortality, they will walk and talk with God. . . . *One day I shall stand before him in judgment, but I shall not know better then than I know now that he lives. My knowledge that he lives is now perfect.*

"She was sent forth from God for the special purpose of mothering special spirits, which were born for a special purpose, and the special purpose is to establish the will of God." Of those who would come of her lineage, he said, "These spirits which God has given her are foreordained to special assignments in the plan of salvation, and great shall be their power and their glory if they endure in all things in righteousness. But if they do not, the scythe of the Lord will cut them down as quickly as it would have severed me from amongst the children of men."

Vivian in her middle years

The promises given to her husband relative to his posterity had also been given to his wife by a patriarch in her youth. "From thy children shall come prophets and prophetesses," she was told, "and they shall be called to fill very responsible positions of trust in the Church and Kingdom of God." She was promised that she would have great influence for good, live to a rich old age, die in peace, hear the plaudit, "Well done, thou good and faithful servant," and be crowned as a queen. She was to be as Sarah of old.

Both Oscar and Vivian believed that the strength of their union rested on their willingness to keep the commandments of the Lord. They claimed never to have had any disagreement on anything of importance. Oscar observed, "To say that we never disagreed would be to confess a dominating force on the one hand or a weakness of intellect upon the other, or would be a confession that I am as big a liar as the others I have heard say it." After many years of marriage Oscar would write of his wife: "I have learned to love her more deeply as the years passed. Today, she is as much a part of me as the food and drink that sustain my life—as the air that I breathe. My eyes are ever filled with the beauty of her charm. I always look and wonder as to how greatly God has blessed me. My ears have never heard enough of her voice and counsel. When she is away my heart aches for her presence. She is in me and we are one. Our children have been her special assignment. Anxiety for them, plus the war, plus the spoken threat of Lucifer, then concern for them on missions, with all the anxiety and sorrows of the years, all these and more have left the mark of time upon her, but out of it all she emerges as glorious, faithful, true, a helpmate like Sarah, Rebecca and Rachel."

Bruce believed that faith could be inherited, that his father had inherited the faith of his mother, Emma Somerville, and that he, in like manner, had inherited the faith of his mother, Margaret Vivian Redd. He quoted Paul's statement to Timothy to evidence that belief: "I call to remembrance the unfeigned faith that is in thee, which dwelt first in thy grandmother Lois, and thy mother Eunice; and I am persuaded that in thee also" (2 Timothy 1:5).

Oscar told his children that he and his wife had made a covenant with the Lord to teach them principles of righteousness and truth. With such principles, he held, "there is no half way." There was to be no picking and choosing among the commandments, nor was there to be any compromise with principles of truth. Each of his children, he asserted, had been foreordained in the councils of heaven to be mighty in the testimony of Christ.

As a Mission President

On April 1, 1946, the First Presidency announced the appointment of Oscar W. McConkie to serve as president of the California Mission. His experiences as a mission president are legendary. After touring President McConkie's mission, Elder Harold B. Lee said that more great spiritual experiences were taking place there than anywhere else in the Church.

One day, one of Oscar's young missionaries came into his office and told the president it was necessary for him to leave the mission

The House of Faith

Missionary Farewell

in honor of
OSCAR W. McCONKIE AND WIFE VIVIAN

Called to preside over the California Mission

SUNDAY EVENING, APRIL 28, 1946
7:00 p.m.
SOUTH 20th WARD CHAPEL
Cor. 2nd Ave. and G St.

field and return home. He was a farm boy from Idaho and had just received word from his mother that his father had run off and left her. She was unable to care for the farm and had written asking him to come home, as she could not get along without his help. To complicate matters, the young elder was going blind.

President McConkie told him that if it were necessary for him to return home, he would release him, but he asked him to visit an eye specialist first. The elder had his eyes examined by one of the finest eye doctors in the country, who told him that the disease in them was too far along to be helped and it would be a matter of only a few weeks before he was completely blind.

Having received this report, President McConkie told the young man that he would like to give him a blessing before he was released, to which the elder agreed. In the blessing, this young man was told that the Lord wanted him to remain in the mission field so that He could give him two blessings. Those blessings were, first, that he might have perfect eyesight restored to him, and second, that his father might return to his mother.

After the blessing, President McConkie directed the elder to go back to the eye specialist and be examined again. He did so. The second examination showed that the young man's eyes were healing and that he would soon have perfect sight. He went back to his field of labor and continued his missionary activities.

About two weeks later, President McConkie received a copy of a letter written to the elder by his father. In the letter, his father explained that after he had left his wife, he received a report that his missionary son had conducted a funeral service. As he thought about it, he became so proud to think that his son could conduct a funeral service that he was inspired to straighten out his own life. This he did, and he returned to his wife, asking for her forgiveness.

On another occasion, President McConkie called the missionaries serving in Hemet, where there were about twenty-five

The House of Faith

members of the Church, to tell them he would be there in two weeks to speak.

The missionaries were laboring at the time with a man by the name of Ed Dover, a farmer living about thirty miles south of town. Staying at his home while tracting without purse or scrip, they learned that Ed Dover had been born in the Church. After his parents had left Cedar City to move to California twenty years earlier, the family gradually fell into inactivity. When his mother died, Ed took up the use of both alcohol and tobacco. It was this addiction that kept him from returning to the Church.

Ed refused to give up his bad habits; the missionaries refused to give up on him. Concerned that President McConkie might be too forceful in speaking about the Word of Wisdom and thus drive Ed and his family away, the missionaries took it upon themselves to fast and pray that he would be directed to speak on some other subject.

The day of the meeting came, as did President McConkie. He spoke for an hour and fifteen minutes in his great booming voice, railing the whole time against the use of alcohol and tobacco. He told his listeners that unless they lived the Word of Wisdom they would never find happiness in this world or the next. He made the subject the very hinge upon which the door of their salvation would swing.

The entire time President McConkie was speaking, the missionaries were thinking that Ed would just get up and walk out of the building, never to be heard of again. At the meeting's end, Ed walked up to the missionaries, reached into his pocket, took out a pack of cigarettes, and handed it to them, saying he would never smoke again. He never did.

Ed became the rock upon which the Church in that area was built. He died a happy and prosperous man with all of his family firmly in the faith. Some fifty years have come and gone since that sermon was given, and today eighty-five members of his family are active in the Church. One hundred ten people can be identified whom Ed alone introduced to the waters of baptism, including nine men who have served in bishoprics and seventeen who have served full-time missions.

At this time, the California Mission included Arizona. During his travels in that state, President McConkie made the acquaintance of an Indian named Mark Johnson Vest. Their acquaintance soon grew into a great love for each other. Mark Johnson Vest stood six feet, five inches tall and weighed more than three hundred pounds. President McConkie described him as "a rugged outdoors man, and yet a man of refinement. A man's man, big physically, and equally big spiritually." It would have been Mark's right by birth, had his people been following the tradition of their fathers, to be the chief of his tribe, the Cochapas.

Mark Johnson Vest accepted the gospel and was baptized. Shortly thereafter he was called to be the branch president over the handful of his people who had also accepted the gospel. He labored among his people and in a short time increased the size of the branch to about seventy-five members. Then he became very ill and in the course of the illness lost more than a hundred pounds. President McConkie administered to him, but it did not seem to help. When Elder Harold B. Lee toured the mission, President McConkie asked him to administer to Brother Vest. Elder Lee did so and gave him a beautiful blessing. Mark seemed to improve for a while but then got worse. Despite the illness, he continued his work among his people. He did not live on the reservation but traveled out on the bus each weekend and borrowed an old milk truck to make his visits. One day while he was in the bus station, his legs ached so badly that he asked a stranger to rub them. Then, as he went to sit down on a bench, he died.

When President McConkie received word that Brother Vest had died, he and Sister McConkie immediately got on a train for

Arizona to attend the funeral. All night long as they traveled, President McConkie prayed, seeking to understand why Brother Vest had been taken. He had been doing such a fine work and was so greatly needed among his people that President McConkie could not understand why the Lord had not allowed him to be healed. As he prayed, a vision was opened to him of the spirit world. He saw Mark Johnson Vest standing in front of a large group of Lamanites, which he estimated to be about ten thousand. Mark was preaching the gospel to them. As he did so, a Lamanite in the middle of the group stood up and said, "Do not listen to this man. He is not a Lamanite. He is a Nephite!" Mark Johnson Vest rose to the full stature of his height and said, "I am not a Nephite! I am a Lamanite, and when I died I was cremated according to the custom of my people." The vision then closed up.

When President and Sister McConkie arrived at the train station, they were met by the district president, who took them immediately to the chapel where the service was to be held. On the way, he told them that a serious problem had developed. Mark's tribe, the Cochapas, wanted him cremated, according to their ancient customs. His wife's tribe would not stand for such a thing and wanted him buried properly. The Cochapas had said that if his body were buried, they would dig it up and cremate it. By the time the district president had finished relating the problem, they had arrived at the chapel. As they walked in, President McConkie noted that programs had been printed announcing he was to speak.

In his talk, he related the vision that he had had during the night. This settled the problem of cremation to the satisfaction of both tribes, and no more fighting took place over the matter. After the funeral service, President and Sister McConkie witnessed the cremation of Mark Johnson Vest.

At this time, President George Albert Smith was convalescing at a private home in California. He was extremely ill, and Oscar McConkie was called to give him a blessing. In administering to the prophet, it was made known to President McConkie that President Smith would be restored to health, and he so promised him. It was further made known to him that the Lord wanted his prophet to leave a last great testimony with the world before he passed away. President McConkie said he did not tell that to President Smith, because it was not his place to instruct the prophet of God. President Smith regained his health, and in the next general conference (October 1950), he bore a powerful testimony to the world. He passed away two days before April conference the next year.

Faith like Enoch's

In the Saturday morning session of general conference in October 1952, President David O. McKay announced that the concluding speaker in that session would be Oscar W. McConkie, who had previously presided over the California Mission. He then invited the choir and congregation to sign a hymn. Both the hymn and the invitation to speak were extemporaneous. What makes the story of particular interest is that Oscar McConkie was not in the meeting. That morning when he and his law partner, Oscar Jr., had met at their office, he said, "Oscar, we need to keep the office open today, but one of us could attend conference. You are the youngest; you go to conference."

When Oscar Jr. heard the announcement that his father was to speak, he sprang to his feet, left the Tabernacle, and dashed to their office on Main Street and South Temple to tell his father. Fortunately, his mother, who was listening to the radio broadcast, also heard the announcement and immediately called her husband.

Oscar Jr. met his father about halfway, running toward the Tabernacle. They completed the race together and stepped into the Tabernacle just as the hymn ended. In his remarks, President

The House of Faith

President Oscar W. McConkie

McConkie told of an occasion while he presided over the California Mission when he prayed for the faith of Enoch and Elijah. When he arose from his knees, the voice of the Spirit spoke to him, saying, "Enoch and Elijah obtained their faith through righteousness." To this expression he added, "We may pray until our voices fade away, but if we do not have righteousness in our daily lives, we will never have enough faith to win salvation." He declared, "I never indulged the deceitful hope that I could win God's favor while I, at the same time, opposed him in any particular."

The following day, his son Bruce was called on to speak, but his allotted time had already been taken by the previous speakers. President McKay told him to take the time given him. Knowing that would take from the time President McKay was to speak and despite the invitation to do otherwise, Bruce spoke for exactly a minute and a half. One of his aunts observed afterwards that this was a matter of breeding. "Either you are born with good sense or you don't have it," she said.

A Warning to His Posterity

By revelation Oscar learned of the special promise that had been given to his posterity and of the special challenges they would face. "It is true that the Lord has given me inspiration by day and visions by day and by night, according to the promise, and many things have been made known to me in that manner. The promise that my sons and daughters, for these wives of my sons are my daughters, will be mighty in Israel is already being fulfilled." It was also made known to him that "Lucifer covenanted with himself that he would destroy not only me," Oscar learned, "but those whom the Lord had ordained should be my children, and not only my immediate children but my posterity also. Lucifer once said to my face: 'I'll destroy you and your family, if I can.' As he laughed, at a time thereafter, in hope of expectation of his triumphant purpose, I saw the jaws of hell. At another time, when I approached the open door of his house, and when my feet were at the threshold of it, I being in search of Lucifer to demand that he molest none of you, my children, and he asked me to enter, I refused, answering his invitation . . . 'No, I will not come in; the house of Lucifer is the house of sin.'"

In vision, Oscar also learned that the Lord had covenanted with his mother, Emma Somerville McConkie, that he would bless her posterity according to their faithfulness in following the same path she had chosen to follow: the path of selfless service, love of the gospel, and profound respect for those who represented the Lord in the offices of the priesthood. Further, he reported (the year was

1952) "that some of her posterity would sit amongst the mighty and great ones of the earth" and that those who were faithful would be called to rule over those who were not. "I knew," he said, "that God would bless my mother's posterity forever, with a special blessing, if they honored her" through emulating the example she set.

4

BOYHOOD IN MONTICELLO
1915 TO 1926

Life was discovered in me and I began to mend and grow, to fulfill a controversial destiny of which my trying birth was symptomatic.
—Bruce R. McConkie

"Whether earth was refusing to receive me or heaven declining to give me up, I do not know," observed Bruce McConkie about his birth, "but be that as it may, a torturing struggle attended my advent into mortality." Bruce was born July 29, 1915, at a private hospital in Ann Arbor, Michigan. His mother was on the operating table for nine hours. Complications, said to have been caused by her involvement in athletics, forced her doctor to send for help. Providentially, the doctor who owned the hospital and who was generally believed to be the finest obstetrician in Ann Arbor, was available.

As Oscar McConkie watched the doctors pull and twist his infant son from his mother's womb, he asked if the child would be born dead. "We abandoned the hope of saving the child long ago," was the response. "Our only hope now is to save the mother." Oscar went immediately to his wife and placed his hands on her head and blessed her by the power of the priesthood. "The Lord did the rest," he said.

Boyhood in Monticello, 1915 to 1926

Oscar and Vivian with their firstborn son

Bruce as a barefooted farm boy

As to the baby, his head, face, and mouth were so twisted that Oscar wondered whether his firstborn son could ever be normal should he live. The baby was set aside and forgotten while full attention centered on saving his mother. Not until her condition stabilized did the doctors turn to the child and discovered, to their surprise, that the little fellow still had life in him.

In years to come, when Bruce would tell the story of his birth, he would point to the marks on the side of his head made by the doctor's forceps as he was pulled from his mother's womb. "Life was discovered in me," he said, "and I began to mend and grow, to fulfill a controversial destiny of which my trying birth was symptomatic."

THE RETURN TO MONTICELLO

Oscar and Vivian returned from Ann Arbor, Michigan, to Monticello before Bruce was a year old. Monticello, which means

Above: *Bruce with his grandmother Emma Somerville McConkie*

Left: *Bruce learning to stand tall*

"little mountain," is a majestic and fertile valley nestled beneath the Blue Mountains in southeastern Utah, some seven thousand feet above sea level. It boasted at the time a population of 343. Its earliest settlers had arrived less than thirty years before. The townspeople were primarily Mormon families who tended little farms, grazing their cattle and sheep on the Blue Mountains in the summer and out on the great dry desert to the east or in lower canyons along the banks of the San Juan River in the winter. The church, built of red brick, stood in the center of the town. Near it was the traditional building for the Relief Society—in this instance, a log cabin—and a block and a half to the south was the tithing yard. The Monticello of 1916 had neither running water nor electricity.

Francis A. Hammond had been called by the First Presidency to preside over the San Juan Stake in 1885. To do so, he moved from Huntsville, near Ogden, to Bluff, Utah. On the journey he camped near Piute Springs (now Monticello) and concluded it would be an excellent place for the Saints to colonize. Good water was available,

Boyhood in Monticello, 1915 to 1926

the mountains not more than six miles distant would supply wood, and the land appeared fertile. "Snow," he said, "will fall here a foot to two feet in February. Here also may be found one of the best places for extensive dry farming I have ever seen, there being thousands of acres of the choicest soil near enough to the base of the mountains to afford rain enough, as I believe, to produce crops without irrigation." Under his direction, settlers moved to Monticello from Bluff. The first to weather a winter there did so in 1888.

The Blue Mountains are, according to Bruce McConkie, "mountains that look like mountains are supposed to look." When natives of Monticello look at them, their eyes are immediately drawn to the features of a horse's head. The configuration, about as big as the peak itself, is of spruce trees on an otherwise sparse slope. The horse's head has a bald face. The snow down the center of the forehead looks like white hair. Although this whole vista is plain to the locals, those whose imagination has been tainted by the outside world often have difficulty identifying these features.

Oscar and Vivian were the children of pioneers. Both were born in log cabins, he at Poverty Flats, near Moab, she in Bluff only nine years after the arrival of those hardy souls who had come down through the Hole in the Rock. In Monticello, which was little more than a wide place in the road, both family and opportunity welcomed them. Oscar quickly became a moving force in the community. He was the editor of the *San Juan Record,* a weekly small-town newspaper, practiced law, and served on every board or committee necessary for the survival of the town. Bruce's grandfather James Monroe Redd owned land beginning at the first crossroads as one entered town from the north. His was the lot northwest of the crossroads; his home was on the southwest corner of that intersection. The home, built by Daniel Dalton in 1897, was purchased by James Monroe and Lucinda Redd in 1905 for one thousand dollars, a handsome sum at the time. It was known as a place from which the hungry or weary would never be turned away. An upper room was reserved for use of the stake president. No one else could use this room, thus assuring him of a place to stay whenever he visited Monticello.

Continuing south from the Redd home was the road to Blanding and from there to Bluff. A left turn at the edge of town would take the traveler east to Colorado. James Monroe ("Roe") Redd Jr. had a home on the northwest corner of the same block as the Redd home. The old Redd corral was west of Roe's home, as were about eighty acres of pasture and farmland owned by the family. It is on this land that the Monticello Utah Temple now stands.

Oscar and Vivian had a small home built on the same lot where James Monroe and Lucinda Redd lived. It had a kitchen, a front room, and one bedroom. As a young boy, Bruce gathered scrap pieces of wood and built a path some fifty feet long from his parents' home to that of his grandparents so he could get cookies from his grandmother's kitchen without walking through the mud.

Rather than have everyone continue to carry water to their homes from the town well, Oscar promoted the idea of having the Blue Mountain Irrigation Company—which held the water rights—to provide both water and light to each home. A meeting of the stockholders was held for that purpose, but only the officers showed up. The consensus was that they leave the matter until there was greater interest. Oscar disagreed, holding that the time for light and water had come. He asked those present to wait. He went to his law office and drew up proxies for voting. He then returned to the meeting, divided them up among the board members, and sent them out to get the necessary signatures. It was good and dark by then, so everyone had gone to bed, but it seemed a small matter to wake them, and the necessary proxies were collected. The board members returned to resume the meeting and voted themselves the necessary authority to bring water and light to the community.

Oscar passed the bar exam in 1917. The press of other responsibilities precluded his spending so much as a single minute preparing for the test. Nevertheless, he felt compelled to take it. "I knew nothing about Common Law pleading," he acknowledged. When he took the exam, those administering it forgot to give that part of the test.

Because there was no hospital in Monticello and because of the difficulty she had had in delivering her first child, Vivian went to the hospital in Moab to give birth to her children. Two weeks before their due date she would go to Moab and stay with Emma Dalton, her husband's sister, where she was always welcome. Briton, James, Margaret, and Oscar Jr. made their entrance into the world in Moab. So it was that the family sank their roots into the soil of San Juan County and tied their hearts to the little community of Monticello. Even after they moved to Salt Lake in 1926, they returned each summer to visit family, work on the farm, and revitalize their souls.

RECOLLECTIONS

"In the winter of 1920," Oscar recalled, "while Vivian was at Moab on Stake M.I.A. business, I was stricken with flu. As I lay in my bed, Bruce, 5 years old, knelt by the side of the bed and asked the Lord to heal me and it was done immediately." His father also recalled an occasion when Bruce suddenly developed stomach pains. Dr. George W. Middleton, a famous physician, said he had appendicitis and must have an operation immediately. The pain increased, so Bruce's mother took him to Salt Lake City. When she got there, she was impressed to have a child specialist examine him. No appendicitis was found and thus the operation avoided.

Another of Bruce's early recollections was of again having a serious pain in his stomach. His father got him up out of bed and had him kneel down by the bed to pray. The last thing he remembered was getting up from his knees and getting into bed. He slept all night. Of that experience his father said, "I administered to him previously, and did not have the faith to stop the pain. I was prompted that he did have, so I told him if he would ask the Lord himself the Lord would do it for him. And the Lord did."

"One of my earliest memories of Monticello as a child," Bruce recalled, "was being awakened in the middle of the night when people from Blanding knocked at our door to get rifles from my father. They were collecting guns to take back to Blanding for the last Indian war fought in America." He would have been seven years of age at the time. "An old Indian named Posey started the small war. I learned later that Posey died by a campfire near some ledge out of Blanding. He had a broken leg that apparently was inflicted in the course of the war."

Bruce remembered that they "had a woodpile out near our back door. Our cooking and heating of the house was by wood stoves. I went barefooted in the summertime and was one day chopping wood barefooted when I sliced into the middle of my big toe on my left foot. Ever since then the toenail has grown in with the healed slash mark in it."

Impressed that they should grow turkeys, Vivian purchased a number of baby turkeys that she nurtured for some weeks in her kitchen behind the wood stove where it was nice and warm. Bruce recalled: "As a boy I herded turkeys in the summer, meaning that we drove the turkeys out in groups where the grasshoppers were and let them eat. There would be about 100 to 150 turkeys in the flock, and we would drive them back in the evening into turkey pens provided for the purpose. My mother was raising turkeys in Monticello to try and help introduce a new industry and also to make a little supplemental income.

"The winters during my childhood were severe. Ofttimes the snow was deep enough with a hard crust on it so that we could walk over the tops of the fences. My mother had a complex about fresh air. She thought there always had to be fresh air in a bedroom, and so we slept with the windows open. The snow would swirl in and sometimes a couple of inches would be on top of the bed in the morning.

"My father got a goat for me and Brit. It pulled a little wagon. We had a collie dog that we called by the name Collie." Oscar believed he had the best dog, the best horse, and the best rifle in the county.

Two blocks from Grandfather Redd's home on the corner of Main and the State Road was a country grocery store called the L. H. Redd Company and also known as the Monticello Co-op. "My father," Bruce said, "had some kind of an interest in it. L. H. Redd, Jr., was the president of the stake in my youth and my father, after he was bishop of the Monticello Ward, served as a counselor to him in the stake presidency. The store was a large two-story red brick building facing east. It had a hitching post in the front, a large porch, and large display windows on each side of the door. Inside it had a wood floor and a high ceiling." A. J. Redd's son recalled, "There used to be shoes all around the walls high up, and a ladder that could be pushed around the walls to get them. An elevator went from the basement, where groceries were stored, to the second floor. It was manually operated with a rope and a brake. Originally, the store had a pot-bellied stove, but I remember the coal furnace with its steam. In front of the store was an upright gas pump with a glass-enclosed top that showed the number of gallons pumped, up to ten. The Monticello post office was once attached to a part of the store. There was an office on the south side, behind the meat counter, and a walk-in safe where Jay Redd kept a loaded .45 revolver to keep himself from getting locked in. There was a large metal file that held charge receipts. In the northeast corner of the store was a large, glass-enclosed display of Stetson hats, yard goods, and clothes. The south front side held groceries, candies, and drugs."

"My Uncle Roe and Aunt Anna and their family lived in Monticello," Bruce remembered. "He was a traveling salesman, once for ZCMI and once for the J. G. McDonald Candy Company. When he traveled for the candy company, he had large cases filled with samples. His children, Venice, Shirley, and Jim, along with Brit and me, found it convenient to search his closet and sample profusely the various kinds of candy provided by J. G. McDonald's."

Each winter in Monticello, to diminish the effect of jackrabbits on the agriculture of the area, the men of the town divided into Red and Blue groups and went out to shoot rabbits. When they shot a rabbit, they cut off its ears so they could be counted. The losing side gave a banquet to the families of the winning side. "I remember my father being on the losing side only once," Bruce said.

It was customary for people to help each other thresh. They did not pay money but rather traded work. When the threshers came to your place, you fed them. Grandmother Redd often fed the threshers, and that meant enormous meals of meat and vegetables to satisfy the appetites of these hard-working men. The food, of course, was all cooked on wood stoves, so Bruce and Brit were assigned to cut the wood and peel potatoes.

In that day, people milked their own cows and made their own butter and cheese. Vivian made butter in a large round crockery jar. The cream was beaten with a wooden paddle that was moved up and down by hand. She made cheese in a large copper vat made for that purpose. It held twelve or fifteen gallons of milk. It was necessary to put the whey in presses and let the cheese ripen for at least six months. Even then it was very mild cheese. Vegetables such as potatoes and carrots were stored in root cellars. Fruit was bottled or dried. It was customary to dry apricots and apples and corn. These were put out on sheets in the sun. A piece of gauze or other cloth was put over the top to keep the flies off. Dried corn is a real delicacy. It has a flavor far superior to that of canned corn.

Hay, meaning alfalfa or grass, was cut and raked. After it dried it was loaded with pitchforks onto slips. Each slip was made of wood with a couple of logs underneath and was pulled by a team of horses. A sling on the slip was fastened to a cable, which was pulled by a horse up over the stack, then the sling was tripped, and the hay fell onto the stack. Bruce used to drive a slip and occasionally ride the horse. He said, "It was more fun to drive a slip because that meant a team of horses, than it was to ride the derrick horse back and forth pulling the various slip loads up for deposit on the stack. One man sat on the stack to engineer the placement of the falling hay from the slips."

Bruce's grandfather Redd had a couple of old saddle horses that the children rode almost daily. One of them, a bay horse called Old Cherry, was considered to be Brit's. Bruce remembered, "There was another one called Old Buck which was a buckskin which I suppose was considered to belong to Uncle Roe's children. There was yet another, Buckskin, that was a little skittish and not so tame for children, that more or less was considered to be mine. We did a great deal of riding."

The children of Vivian and Oscar have fond memories of growing up in Monticello. Margaret remembered that once a week they were allowed to take two eggs over to the Co-op and trade them for a frozen Snickers bar. All remembered the sugar cookies baked on Grandmother Redd's wood stove. Oscar Jr. recalled the preparations that were made for stake conference. The people traveling to the meetings would need to be fed. So Granddad Redd would hitch up the wagon and go out to cut cedar wood to heat the oven. Then Grandmother Redd would bake bread. As loaf after loaf came out of her oven, each would be placed in a large chest. When the chest was full, everyone knew it was time for conference. Brit recalled going to the tithing office, where he would give a nickel or dime to his father, who was then the bishop of the Monticello Ward, and his father getting out the large record book, carefully recording his donation, and then giving him a receipt that was the size of half a normal sheet of paper. Bruce remembered being baptized on his eighth birthday by his father and being confirmed the same day. The baptism took place in a little font constructed in the building called the Bishop's Office, adjacent to the wardhouse. His mother and family were present.

Aaronic Priesthood Outings

Bruce was ordained a deacon five months before his twelfth birthday by his father. Of that he said simply, "They were not so hide bound as to years and ages and rules in that day."

He recalled going on fathers and sons outings in the Blue Mountains. "These were ward affairs. We went by horseback and camped out several nights." At night Oscar would have his sons put their blankets together so they could keep each other warm, and as they lay out under the stars, he would tell the story of Abraham's vision of Kolob and the other wonders of eternity as they are unfolded in the revelations given to Joseph Smith.

Of another occasion Bruce remembered, "The Aaronic Priesthood had an outing to go to Mesa Verde National Park. We traveled in trucks. Our bedrolls and the like were in the back of the trucks and we sat on them. As we returned from Mesa Verde, a priesthood advisor, Jay Redd, gave me instructions to see that everything was quiet and peaceful in the back of the truck in which we were riding. We had not gone very far before I got in a fight with a fellow by the name of Lyle Hyde. We were standing up in the back of the truck slugging it out when this came to the attention of those in the cab and they had to stop the truck and then stop the fight."

When he was a bit younger, Bruce, who was a tall gangly kid, got into a heated tussle at some sort of public gathering with another boy about his own age but smaller. The two of them decided the most equitable way to settle the matter was with their fists. At this point the fathers intervened. Oscar sought to prevent the fight. The other boy's father responded, "Leave them alone, Oscar. My boy can whip your son any day of the week!" To this Oscar responded, "That may be so, but my son is going to grow up to be a good man." Both fathers reaped as they had sown. Oscar's son indeed became a good man, and the other father's son spent a fruitless life fighting a battle he lost with life, responsibility, and alcohol.

SCHOOLING IN MONTICELLO

So it was that pleasant, youthful years were spent in Monticello running barefoot in the summer, herding turkeys in the pastures and alfalfa fields, riding the derrick horse and driving slips in the haying season, milking cows, getting thrown from the backs of bucking calves, and (as he learned much later) surviving polio.

"I started school in Monticello," Bruce recalled. "The first and second grades were in the same room. The PTA bought and installed a slippery slide on the school ground for the children. In that day it seemed like a high and large slide. We would line up and climb the stairs and go down it. My younger brother Briton was once pushed off from near the top. It did not hurt him. I was pushed off from near the bottom and as a result got into a good fist fight with a boy named Bailey."

As evidence that the heavens did not always smile upon him, copies of Bruce's report cards for the first and fourth grades have survived. They consist mostly of C's and B's and only an occasional A. Thus the testimony of teachers Celia Jenson and Elsie Edwards appears to be that Bruce was a remarkably ordinary boy.

Bruce about five years old

Back: *Brit and Bruce McConkie;* front: *William McConkie and Jim Redd*

Family

The McConkie boys remembered James Monroe Redd, their grandfather, as a cowboy who stood about five feet, eight or nine inches tall, and had a slight build. His build was particularly pronounced when he stood beside their own father, who thought it a good day when he could get his six foot, three- or four-inch frame to weigh less than two hundred fifty pounds.

James Monroe Redd had a cowboy mustache and could go nowhere without his horse. "My grandfather had lived so much in the saddle during most of his years," recalled Bruce, "that he had the reputation of walking a block to the corral, catching a horse and saddling him in order to run an errand that was one block away."

Lucinda Redd was a spirited and sprightly lady. She lived to be one hundred four and never turned a soul from her table, be they

Indian, cowboy, or prisoner from the jail down the street. She served as Relief Society president for thirty-eight years during a time when Relief Society presidents not only took in meals to help a new mother but went as a midwife and brought her child into the world as well.

"I remember visiting my grandmother Emma Somerville McConkie a time or two in Moab," Bruce recalled. "She seemed to be a very old lady. She was a very good woman and had been the ward Relief Society president for many years in the Moab Ward. She was one of the plural wives of my grandfather George W. McConkie, who died when my father was a very young boy."

THE HAND OF THE LORD

It was Oscar McConkie's custom to relax with the newspaper each evening in his living room. One evening as he did so, a still small voice whispered in his ear, "Get up and run!" Surprised, he was not sure what to do. The voice repeated, "Get up and run!" Upon hearing the voice the second time, he immediately responded. Throwing the paper aside, he ran through the kitchen and out the back door, past his bewildered wife, who wondered what had overcome him. As he dashed out of the house, the first thing he saw was a large black stallion without a rider racing across the backyard. Without time for thought, he ran alongside the horse and grabbed its reins, pulling it to a halt. It was only after calming the horse down for a few moments that he looked on the other side and discovered his eldest son, Bruce, with his foot caught in the stirrup. He had been riding the horse when he was knocked off by a limb, catching his foot in the stirrup. Had his father failed to heed the promptings of the Spirit, Bruce could well have been dragged to death.

Grandfather Redd had some land east of the community some ten or twelve miles. The area was identified simply as "out east," though it was also called Boulder. To get there, one had to cross a big wash called Montezuma Canyon. Oscar owned some land a couple of miles east of Monticello, which was called the Brunson Farm. He raised hay and some grain on it and also used it as pasture.

Bruce's brother Brit recounted an occasion when he went "out east" with Granddad Redd to get a load of wood. Granddad sent Brit back with the heavily loaded wagon. "As I drove the team along the road toward home I came to a point where the road started downward and at the bottom of the hill was a narrow bridge and on the other side of the bridge the road made a sharp turn. Because of the steepness of the terrain, the wagon seemed to push the team forward, and I was unable to control them; they went faster and faster as they approached the bridge. I could not stop or slow the horses. I realized the peril I was in; the wagon could not negotiate the turn at the speed it was traveling. As I reached a critical point a log became displaced and locked the rear wheel dragging the wagon and team to a stop."

In like manner, Bruce told of "being on a wagon loaded with fence posts. We had just pulled up the east side of the Montezuma Creek Road and were coming out onto level ground. I was very young and my Uncle Ray Redd was with me. He had permitted me to drive the team. Something, I do not know what, spooked the horses and they bolted. The posts on the wagon were not chained down. I remember that he grabbed the reins from me and was standing up yanking and pulling and trying to stop the bolting horses and shouting to me to jump. I didn't know enough to jump and just remember that the logs were swaying from one side of the wagon to the other, and I was seated on them. In due course he got the team calmed down and then demanded of me why I didn't jump off and told me that he thought we were going to tip over and I would be killed at any moment." To this Bruce added, "As far as I know I was not killed at any moment."

Boyhood in Monticello, 1915 to 1926

RETURN TO ANN ARBOR

In 1925 Oscar and his family moved back to Ann Arbor, Michigan, to return to law school. That move meant he had to be released from the stake presidency. The stake president, for whom he had great respect, suggested that it was not worth the effort to return to Ann Arbor. But an influencing factor for Oscar was the promise in his patriarchal blessing that he would be called on "to protect the innocent and pass judgment on the guilty." This proved to be true when he was appointed to serve as a United States district judge.

The McConkie family were the only members of the Church in Ann Arbor at that time. There was a small branch of the Church in Detroit, which they visited a time or two. For the most part, however, they held Sunday School in the home they had rented on 216 Packard Street. Each Sunday Bruce would give a lesson from what was his first reading of the Book of Mormon. On occasion Oscar would take his family to the Presbyterian church. When asked why, he said that he just felt it was important for his children to form the habit of attending church meetings.

"The summer we arrived there Mother wanted Briton to go to summer school on the theory that it would help him make up what he had not learned in Monticello under very poor teachers. She sent me to summer school with him," Bruce said. "Instead of doing what they normally would have done, that is, have me take over again the grade that I had previously had, they put me in the fifth grade. I suppose it was by mistake. I went two hours a day for six weeks and thus passed the whole fifth grade, getting myself out of kilter socially for my age."

After completing his studies in Ann Arbor, Oscar and Vivian decided that they should move to Salt Lake, where the schools would better prepare their children for college and where they could go to the University of Utah while living at home. So it was that

The Bruce R. McConkie Story

Oscar McConkie sold the land they had farmed in Monticello on which oil was discovered a few years later. Had he been asked whether he had second thoughts about that decision, he would have responded that his family was his real wealth and no amount of money would have been worth more than assuring them of a good education to develop the talents God had given them.

5

YOUTHFUL YEARS
1926 TO 1934

It shall be given you to become strong like unto prophets of old, and you shall lead your brethren in the fight for righteousness against the enemies of truth.

—A priesthood blessing to Bruce R. McConkie

The McConkie family made the move to Salt Lake City and took up residence on C Street in the Avenues, a hill in the northeastern part of the city that begins its rise eastward just across State Street from the Church Office Building and extends to the campus of the University of Utah. In the fall of 1926 Bruce was enrolled in seventh grade at Lowell Elementary School because of the extra schooling he had taken during the summer in Ann Arbor. From there he went to Bryant Junior High for the eighth and ninth grades. At this time the Salt Lake School District was experimenting with having two years of junior high and two years of high school. This meant that when he graduated from the LDS High School, in what was its last year, he was only fifteen. This, in turn, enabled him to complete three years at the University of Utah before he left for his mission at age nineteen.

The idea of wearing shoes during the summer and walking to get to places instead of riding a horse was not unsettling to the youthful

Bruce. He made friends quickly and easily, notwithstanding that by the time he got to high school, many of his friends were a year or two older than he was because of the manner in which he had been advanced in school.

While in Ann Arbor, he had enrolled in a music program and thus became the owner of a saxophone. It was a C-melody saxophone, which was not that common. The one usually used was a B-flat. After the move to Salt Lake City, he played for two years in the Bryant Junior High orchestra as the only C-melody saxophonist. "I was very poor," he confessed, "and had great difficulty telling one note from the other. I only survived in the orchestra because it was their policy to let anybody play who moved or breathed and was willing to try."

Academically he did well, but unlike Brit and Oscar Jr., he was not very athletic. He did, however, play tackle on the sophomore football team at LDS High. Apparently the team was made up of fellows whose athletic abilities equaled his. He described them as "haphazard" and "incompetent." One of the things he felt might have improved his performance would have been a pair of football cleats. Playing in street shoes put him at a distinct disadvantage. Perhaps he could have traded his saxophone for some cleats, but in any case, his destiny was not to be found on the athletic field.

He participated on the debate team, "winning and losing" in competition with other schools "depending upon who the judges were." He was the manager of the yearbook, and Bob Richards was the editor. Here a hint of the future is found in his recollection that he worked more on the editorial side than on the business side of things. Their efforts resulted in an All-American rating.

Bruce belonged to a social unit that specialized in drama. They put on a one-act play for the school, which he enjoyed. As a result, he went to the University of Utah and tried out for one of the major parts in the freshman class play. The faculty adviser was a relative on the Redd side of the family. "I have no doubt that I was by all odds the best one for the part for which I tried out, but it was perfectly clear that [my good relative] did not want me around so that I could make any comments or reports to my parents of what a jackrabbit she was. In consequence of which, I did not get the part and did not get my interests directed in that channel—which I consider to be one of the most providential things that ever happened to me. If I had gotten involved with the clique of people whose lives centered in dramatics and the applause that comes to those behind the footlights, there is no telling what bad companions I would have picked up with."

He also gave football another try—presumably with cleats—and was on the freshman football team at the U. Because he did not get significant playing time, he did not pursue football after that. That, however, may not have been as much a matter of ability as of physical maturation. Because of the years he was advanced in school, he would have been a sixteen-year-old competing with eighteen- or nineteen-year-olds. Again he accounted his lack of success as "providential." He also took classes in ROTC (Reserve Officer Training Corps) all four years at the U and graduated with a reserve commission as a second lieutenant in the field artillery. When World War II later broke out, he served as an officer rather than as an enlisted man.

Summers in Monticello

It was his family's practice to go back to Monticello during the summers. His father, who was now a district judge, was able to trade trial calendars with the judge presiding over the San Juan area. This man liked to visit Salt Lake for a few months, just as Oscar loved to return to his roots in Monticello. There the McConkie boys could work on their grandfather's farm. One summer Bruce worked for the

Blue Mountain Irrigation Company installing a culinary water pipeline.

In Monticello things were still a bit rustic, but this was much to the family's liking. The little three-room home they had left behind hardly fit a family that with the birth of William, the youngest of the brothers, now numbered eight. The older children could spend the summer sleeping under the stars with a blanket on the lawn.

Meeting Amelia Smith

While Bruce attended the University of Utah, a pretty coed at East High School, whose path he was destined to cross, was invited to join a social group known as the Quecie Club. The girls already in the club were those who had transferred from the old LDS High, which had closed down. The club was a high school imitation of a college sorority and, as such, required the inductees to eat raw liver, dress in old-fashioned clothes, be led around blindfolded, and do other such silly things, all in good humor. As was to be expected, the Quecie Club had activities designed for its members to meet and date young men. Amelia recalled that she was a part of the "wall-flower bouquet" because she did not have a special boyfriend, so others in the club would help her get dates. With this help, she remembered, she was able to meet a number of dull and boring people. It was also through the efforts of this group, however, that she met the tall, articulate boy from over on C Street.

Bruce had dated a number of the girls in this social circle and was invited to a party at the Smith home on Douglas Street, where a good-sized living room could be converted into a miniature ballroom simply by removing the furniture and rolling back the rug. All else that was needed were some records, a phonograph, and guys. Here it was that Bruce McConkie met and impressed a woman of some importance in his life—Amelia Smith's mother, Ethel Reynolds Smith. She made it a point to single him out and get acquainted with him. As they talked she took his measure and made the decision that he was the kind of young man she wanted to date her daughter Amelia. One of the things that impressed her was his indication that he had to be home by midnight because it was then the eve of the Sabbath.

Amelia's mother insisted that her daughter ask Bruce out on a date. This Amelia dutifully did but was so scared that sixty years after the experience she could still remember the phone number. She could also recount every detail of their first date. It took place on May 21, 1932, a beautiful spring evening. Amelia was a month short of her sixteenth birthday, Bruce two months short of his seventeenth. Most of the blossoms of spring had passed, and the trees had begun to leaf. Everywhere lovely flowers were making their appearance throughout the valley. The occasion was a formal dance, held, appropriately enough, at Memory Grove. Because Amelia did not have the clothes for such an event, her older sisters came to the rescue. Emily provided a light green formal dress; Naomi, her best shoes; and Lois, a pair of silk stockings (nylons were yet to be invented, as was the sixteen-year mark for dating).

Bruce arrived in his Aunt Hortense's car, a two-seater with a rumble seat in the back. After a proper welcome by Amelia's mother, her little brothers (who had hidden themselves so as to miss nothing of this historical occasion) evidenced themselves. Milton, six years of age, observed to the young man in the doorway, "Gee, you sure are tall."

"The dance could not have been a greater success," Amelia recalled. "My friend and I had seen to it that we had our dance cards well filled, and everyone seemed to be having a great time. Bruce lived up to all the nice things I had heard about him. He was fun to talk to, pleasant to be with, and friendly with everyone." All of this despite the fact that he could not distinguish between a waltz and a foxtrot. "I felt at ease," Amelia recalled, "from the time he came to get me."

After the dance they went to the town hot spot, Coon Chicken Inn, where you could get a hamburger and a malt. They had chocolate malts at the cost of fifteen cents each. Other friends joined them, including Amelia's brother Joseph and his date.

Forever after, Amelia remembered it as "a wonderful evening from start to finish." They returned to her home at midnight. Bruce walked her to the door, thanked her for inviting him, and said, "I will see you again."

When she turned on the light in the bedroom, she caught a glimpse of herself in the mirror. There was "a big glob of chocolate malt down the front of Emily's formal dress, and a nice long run down the length of Lois's silk stocking." One would think she might have lost one of Naomi's shoes, but she didn't.

Amelia recalled, "The summer after the dance in Memory Grove was filled with plenty of work around home and a lot of baby sitting," which she did for her sister Emily as well as some of the neighbors. Through the grapevine she heard that the McConkies had gone to Monticello for the summer.

It was not until the middle of October that Bruce and Amelia met again. Amelia had accepted a last-minute date with a fellow she had no interest in for the dance at the U after the football game. The surprise came when she discovered that they were going with Bruce and his date. The situation was awkward for both Amelia and Bruce, but it had a happy ending. Amelia's dance card filled up quickly, so she danced with a number of different fellows, and Bruce also asked her to dance. "I learned," Amelia said, "that he had been in Monticello all summer helping his grandparents with their farm."

"The next time I saw Bruce's date for that night," Amelia recalled, " she remarked that as soon as Bruce realized who my date was taking to the dance, he became very quiet for the rest of the evening. Then through the grapevine I learned he had tried to get my date to trade more than one dance but he wouldn't. Apparently the fellow I was with knew Bruce had had his date for that dance for some time, since she was a very popular girl, and had by then really wanted to ask me but honored his commitment. Less than two weeks later I got a call from him inviting me to go with him to another dance. From then on we only dated each other.

"Bruce usually came up and went to Church with me, on Sunday, or I went with him to his ward. This particular night he had not been able to get the family car for our date, but he often had to resort to using the streetcar to come see me or perhaps take me someplace. We thought nothing of that because in the 30's there were lots of people who were not able to afford cars. Streetcars ran frequently and cost very little so it was no problem.

"Dad's conference assignment that Sunday was close enough that he got home around 10 P.M. Bruce and I were listening to the Tabernacle organ broadcast with Alexander Schreiner when he came in. It was one of our favorite radio programs. We continued talking until about 11:30 before Bruce decided it was time for him to get home. 'Wait a minute,' I said. 'I'll see if Dad will let me take you home.' Dad was in his room looking at the newspaper. He looked at me and asked, 'What can I do for you?'

"'May I take Bruce home so he won't have to take the streetcar?'

"Dad handed me the car keys and reminded me, 'Drive safely.' When we got to Bruce's house we kept on talking until I realized it was past midnight. 'Wow, I better get home or Dad will be worried.'

"As I neared the house I saw Dad out in front walking around. 'Oh, oh,' I thought, 'he has been waiting for me. He'll probably say something about me taking so long.'

"I drove into the garage and headed for the kitchen door. Then Dad spoke. 'It is such a beautiful night you can see the stars very clearly. See,' he said, pointing toward the north, 'There is the Big Dipper, and over there is the Little Dipper. And that bright star is one of the planets.'

"Dad had a great interest in the stars. He had a small telescope he loved to use. He would even quote from the scriptures about them some of the time. That was why he had such a special interest in them. The moon was not quite full but it would be in a day or so. 'Well, it is time we went in and got to bed.' I thanked my lucky stars that night."

CALLED TO SERVE

About a month after his nineteenth birthday, Bruce talked with his bishop, Clarence Neslen, about his going on a mission. In that interview he expressed his desire to serve in England. Following the procedure of the day, he was given a recommend to be signed by the stake president and a form for a physical examination. During the meeting of the priests quorum that morning, he, as the assistant to the bishop in the priests quorum, was asked by the bishop to assign one of the priests to speak in sacrament meeting. Sacrament meetings were held in the evening at that time, and they normally lasted an hour and a half. His call for a volunteer did not elicit so much as a pair of eyes to meet his own. He took the assignment himself.

There were two other speakers in the meeting that evening: Don B. Colton, president of the Eastern States Mission, and Winslow Farr Smith, president of the Ensign Stake. Both men indicated in their remarks that they were very positively impressed by the testimony of the young priest who had spoken before them. President Colton observed that if mission presidents could choose their own missionaries, he would be pleased to choose Bruce McConkie. Bruce's mother, ever spiritually sensitive, thereafter expressed her feeling that her eldest son would be called to the Eastern States Mission.

The following Tuesday, August 29, 1934, Bruce met with two members of the stake presidency, who interviewed him together and gave him much counsel and direction. President Winslow Farr Smith promised him that he would be blessed if he worked hard, always remembered who he was, conducted himself like a missionary, avoided all that was shady, and kept himself free from sin. George J. Cannon, a counselor in the stake presidency, added, "You are never too far away to call on God."

Bruce then met again with Bishop Neslen, who was to submit his missionary papers to Church headquarters. The bishop told Bruce that he would ask Brother Reynolds to assign him to England, which greatly pleased Bruce. Harold G. Reynolds was the bishop of a neighboring ward and also the secretary to the missionary committee. He was a son of George Reynolds of the Seventy, which made him an uncle to Amelia.

The normal excitement and suspense followed. "My call," Bruce said, "was dated September 6th [1934]. I received it [Monday] September 8th. It was for the Eastern States [Mission]. Mother was right." No effort was made to disguise his disappointment. "Bishop Reynolds called my father and said, 'Someone told me Bruce wanted to go to England. My impression is to send him to the Eastern States. What is your pleasure?' 'He will do just as you say,' replied Oscar W. McConkie. 'Follow your impression.'"

Time can temper the spirit, and within a few days the conviction came that "the right place to serve is the place to which you are called." The vantage point of years and the belief that there is a Spirit that directs the destinies of men combine to make it evident that no other mission could have shaped Bruce McConkie as well for what lay ahead of him than the mission to which he was called. The Spirit he came to know in the Sacred Grove, in long hours on the Hill Cumorah, and at the place of the Church's organization in Fayette, never left him. The experience of standing on the same soil from which the seeds of the Restoration originally sprang forth deeply rooted the significance of these events in the soul of a man who would yet bear testimony of the prophetic call of Joseph Smith throughout the nations of the earth.

Endowed with Power and Promise

After Bruce received his call to serve as a missionary, his father ordained him an elder. On Friday, September 12, he and his parents went to the temple, where, in the language of scripture, he was "endowed with power from on high" (D&C 38:32).

On Wednesday, October 17, the eve of his entering the mission home, he received a father's blessing. The blessing is a remarkable commentary on both father and son. In it, Bruce was charged to magnify his calling in humility and righteousness that he might have power to teach and to draw men's hearts to the truth. He was warned that he would be confronted by the power of the adversary and that Lucifer would make special effort to overthrow him. Only in humility and strict obedience would he find safety. Indeed, he was told that Satan would seek his life because he had been called and ordained before the foundations of this world were laid "to come forth in this generation, when wickedness is ripe upon the earth, to effect God's purposes in the redemption of mankind." He was specifically charged to be obedient to the whisperings of the Spirit, to those who would preside over him, and to the word of the Lord as it had been revealed. "It shall be given you to become strong like unto prophets of old, and you shall lead your brethren in the fight for righteousness against the enemies of truth," who, he was told, would "flee before you, and shall tremble and quake in your presence."

Of the premortal life he was told, "You were a leader there," and he was assured that he would be a leader here. "The day will come," he was told, that "all men who know you will look to you for counsel and for the witness of the truth, for through your faithfulness you shall become a chosen vessel, exalted among your brethren in the holy order of the priesthood of our God." He was promised that his heart would be filled with understanding, that he would be given wisdom beyond the bounds of the earth, and that it would be given to him to comprehend the mysteries of the kingdom. He would be blessed with many revelations, and many things would be understood and taught by him that would remain mysteries to those who had not paid the price in obedience that would be exacted of him.

He was to go forth in the strength of the priesthood, relying on truths learned in the household of faith from which he came. He was counseled to "fear no man" but to reverence the power of God. "I charge you to so clothe yourself with power," his father said, "that the adversary shall be subject to your will." He was promised the gift of healing, for he would raise the sick and open the ears of the deaf and the eyes of the blind. In his ministry, the elements would obey his command, and it would be necessary for him to be prudent in that for which he importuned the heavens. He was instructed to fill his soul with charity and love, to learn patience, and to endure.

"Counsel not the Spirit, but rather seek its counsel," he was told. When the Spirit whispered, he was to "act and do so immediately." He was further directed to be unashamed and fearless in declaring repentance and in doing all that the Lord commanded him. He was promised the blessing of a choice family over which he would preside through the eternities. "Look forward to the future with great pleasure and hope . . . for you shall be numbered in the army of the Lord which is clothed upon with power and righteousness."

Bruce's mother recorded the blessing in longhand as his father delivered it. In this she would have been aided by the slow and articulate pattern of speech common to both father and son when they spoke in the name of the Lord. From those notes Oscar typed the blessing and often recalled to his grandchildren that when he reviewed his expression to the effect that all men would look to his son for counsel and for a witness of the truth, he felt that he might have been too strong and that perhaps he should modify the expression. "But the Spirit forbade me," he said, "and commanded that I leave it as it was."

This blessing marked one of the defining moments in the life of Bruce Redd McConkie. The placing of his father's hands on his head marked the end of his youth and the beginning of his manhood. He was now enlisted in the army of the Lord.

On Thursday, October 18, Bruce entered the mission home, which at that time consisted of two large old homes on State Street just north of the Beehive House. He remained there until the next evening, when he was forced to return home because of illness. Aching eyes and head, a cramping stomach, and inability to keep food down were diagnosed as intestinal flu. He was confined to bed for a week. During that time his skin turned yellow, as did the whites of his eyes, and it became evident that he had jaundice.

According to Bruce's journal, Sunday, October 21, was his missionary farewell, which was held without him. Lee A. Palmer, first counselor in the bishopric, who had been very active in laboring with the young men of the ward, made a few remarks, as did his father, Oscar. The main speaker was Joseph Fielding Smith, who took as a text Doctrine and Covenants 4, the Lord's law of service, a revelation given to the Prophet in behalf of his father, Joseph Smith Sr. Elder Smith said that a missionary should read this section once a week during his entire mission. He also commented on the "worth of souls," as noted in Doctrine and Covenants 18.

Nearly six hundred people were present at the farewell, and more than one hundred dollars was donated to help defray Bruce's missionary costs. Sister J. Reuben Clark, who was close to the family, took down the proceedings in longhand, and Louise Farr made notes

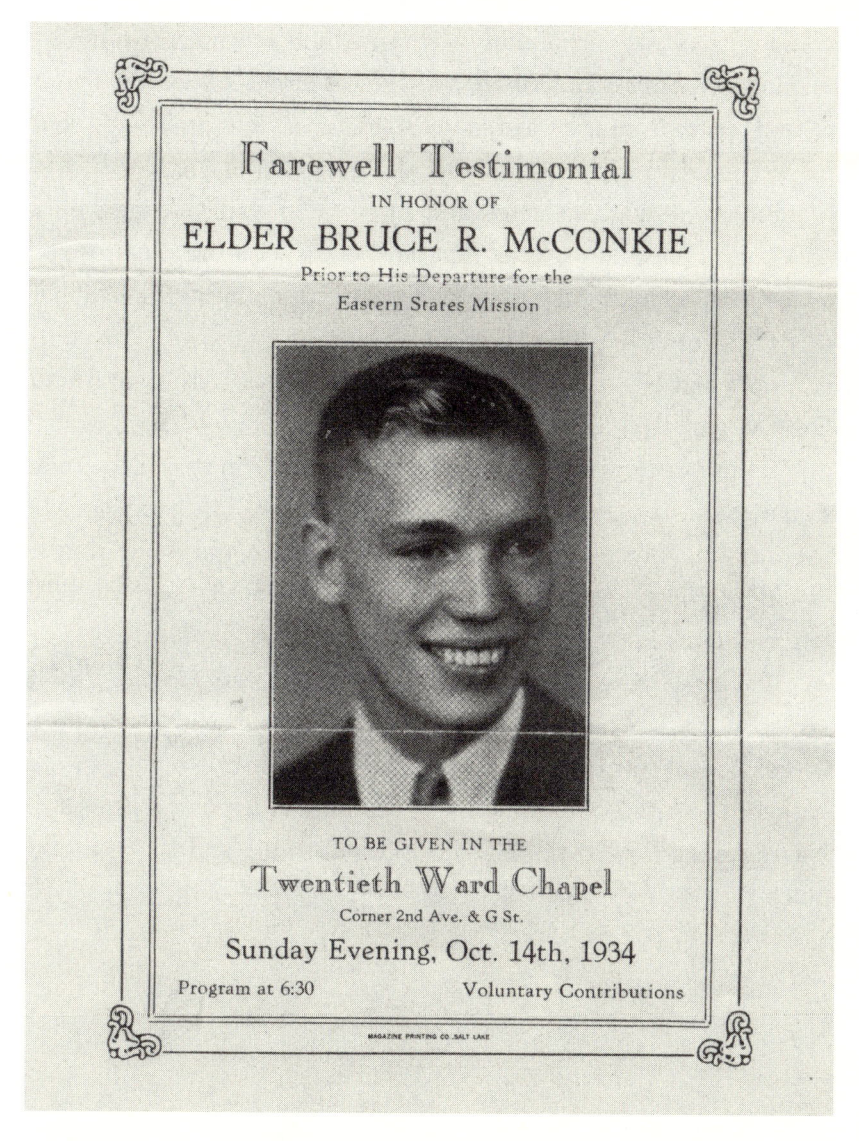

Farewell Testimonial
IN HONOR OF
ELDER BRUCE R. McCONKIE
Prior to His Departure for the
Eastern States Mission

TO BE GIVEN IN THE
Twentieth Ward Chapel
Corner 2nd Ave. & G St.
Sunday Evening, Oct. 14th, 1934

Program at 6:30   Voluntary Contributions

in shorthand, so that Bruce would have an account of what was said. After the meeting, President Winslow Farr Smith and George J. Cannon went to the McConkie home and administered to the ailing elder. In that blessing President Smith promised the young missionary that he would go with his group to his assigned mission.

By Wednesday, Bruce was well enough to get out of bed so he

could receive his patriarchal blessing, which was given to him by Nicholas G. Smith. In that blessing he was promised he would both go and return from the mission field in safety. He was also told that he would bring others to know the gospel, be a leader in the Church, be a judge in Israel, and those older than himself would seek counsel from him. Later that day he was set apart as a missionary by Joseph Fielding Smith, who repeated the same promises. That night his group left from the train station in Salt Lake. The companion assigned to him in the mission home was his close friend Elder Wayne Richards.

"There were many people at the train station to see the missionaries off," recounted Amelia. "We did get to kiss goodbye. My friends and Wayne's girl went to a movie to try and forget that it would be a long time before we saw each other again. But we wrote letters. Postage was very reasonable at that time."

"I said goodbye to my family and Amelia," Bruce wrote. "[My] last image of Amelia [was] an image which will stay with me forever. I was in [the] train door and she on the platform. No words were spoken. We just looked. She was so pathetically sad and beautiful. I shall never forget it. She's so wonderful to me and I love her so much."

6

SERVICE AS A MISSIONARY
1934 TO 1936

Spent a quiet and peaceful afternoon and evening in company with Moroni on Cumorah. Alone on a Sacred spot with my thoughts and the Spirit of the Lord.

—Bruce R. McConkie

Young Elder Bruce McConkie was first assigned to labor in Pittsburgh, Pennsylvania. The work was slow and unproductive, reflecting as it generally does the spirit and attitude of the missionaries. When others didn't have the enthusiasm to pursue the work, he went tracting alone, a practice acceptable in that day. In January 1935 he attended his first mission conference. President Don B. Colton asked the missionaries to share their testimony and give a report on the work. Bruce noted in his journal, "All the elders expressed satisfaction but myself, and I gave the truth." Subsequent events suggest that his mission president was impressed with his commitment to the work.

The Cumorah Campaign

On April 24, 1935, Elder McConkie received a letter from President Colton assigning him to work in the Cumorah District from May 1 to July 24. As the *Church News* reported, with the completion of the monument to Moroni on the Hill Cumorah, an intensive missionary campaign was to be conducted in western New York. Before the dedication of the monument, a group of about forty missionaries was formed to take the message of Mormonism to every home within twenty miles of Palmyra. This would be the most thorough preaching of the gospel in that part of the country since Oliver Cowdery, Samuel H. Smith, and Parley and Orson Pratt canvassed the area in 1830.

Elder McConkie was delighted with the assignment, and three days later he and Elder Hansen hitchhiked through dust and rainstorms to Erie, New York. They attended church on Sunday and stuck out their thumbs again on Monday morning to get rides to Buffalo and then to Rochester. Because of the lateness of the hour, they took a Greyhound bus to Palmyra. There they met the other missionaries who had been chosen for this assignment. Brief instructions were given by President Colton, and the missionaries were bedded down on army cots in the basement of the Palmyra chapel. The next day the missionaries were taken to Cumorah, the Sacred Grove, and the Smith home.

To determine companionships, the missionaries each chose a number between one and one hundred, and those whose numbers were closest to each other were designated as companions. Bruce was paired with J. Wesley Perry, who had been appointed a district leader. Elder Perry explained his companionship with Elder McConkie as a result of choices made in the premortal life. For his part, Elder McConkie thought Elder Perry to be "a prince of a fellow" and wholeheartedly concurred. Immediately they went in search of a place to live. Suitable quarters were located in Canandaigua at 151 Pleasant Street at a cost of fifteen dollars a month. Having secured a place to sleep, they headed out into the country to tract.

Service as a Missionary, 1934 to 1936

In company with missionaries whose zeal matched his own, Elder McConkie found a new delight in the work. Generally he found the people to be more courteous than they had been in Pennsylvania. The first Saturday he and Elder Perry were there, Elders Inman and Luckau visited Elders McConkie and Perry at their apartment to tell them they had received a permit for holding street meetings.

"With my heart missing a few beats," Elder McConkie recalled, "Elder Perry and I accompanied them to town where we met four lady missionaries (Sisters Jones, Tew, Nielson, and Bollschweiler) and we all listened to the Salvation Army Street Meeting. They had musical numbers, duets and harmonica solos etc. and supposedly good speakers. I doubt if outside of the missionaries there was one interested person. No one paid any attention at all to them and my heart sank a few feet of additional misgivings when we went up to the corner of Coy St. and Main Street and the eight of us sang 'The Spirit of God like a Fire is Burning' and 'How Firm a Foundation' and Elder Luckau began by giving a very pointed and dynamic talk. In the course of the meeting four elders and Sister Neilson spoke and we sang 'High on the Mountain Top.' I spoke on 'Joseph Smith as a Prophet of God' for ten minutes or so. Our meeting surpassed beyond measure that of the Salvation Army; people listened to us and at one time we had perhaps 150 people listening; our audience changed a dozen times."

Pamphlets were distributed, a copy of the Book of Mormon lent, and an invitation to speak to the Exchange Club received. After that, Elder McConkie looked forward to street meetings with excitement.

The next Saturday they were refused a permit for a street meeting on the pretext that it might cause a traffic jam. Instead, the missionaries were given a permit allowing them to preach in the park at a spot where it was doubtful anyone would ever find them. A few

Bruce with new glasses, 1935

weeks later, they obtained a permit for a meeting in front of a Baptist church. They drew a good crowd there and had another successful meeting.

On June 21, 1935, he wrote: "This is MY AMELIA'S nineteenth Birthday and I can't resist recording in my Journal what an angel of a girl she is. To me she has always been an inspiration toward greater heights, a perfect companion and associate, and a sweetheart of infinite goodness and tenderness. She it is whom I dearly love and I believe that she was predestined and foreordained to be my companion and helpmeet for this probationary state and for the eons and eternities to come. Of all the girls she most nearly perpetuates the graces and goodness of my mother. And I ask God's blessings on her and us—now and forever and ever."

The next two and a half months passed quickly as the missionaries busied themselves calling on as many homes in the vicinity of Cumorah as they could. They found many people interested and had the opportunity to do a good deal of teaching. One measure of their effectiveness was the opposition they engendered. A series of anti-Mormon lectures was held at the Bethel Mission, given by a woman evangelist by the name of Fry. Her efforts were like those of a thousand others who create a straw man using untruths and then proceed to beat it up. Her efforts resulted in a loss of membership in the Bethel Mission.

The Dedication of the Cumorah Monument

The Hill Cumorah monument was dedicated on Sunday morning, July 21, by President Heber J. Grant. Additional services were held that afternoon and on the following Monday and Tuesday. One of the sister missionaries present recalled, "It was one of the most spiritual and remarkable experiences of my entire life. At the dedication, there was a roof over the speakers' stand, since there was no building there, and President Grant stood under this canopy. He was an imposing sight as he raised his hands and offered the dedicatory prayer, near the closing of which he emphasized emphatically the very presence of Moroni himself in our midst. President Grant told us that Moroni had come to accept the offering of this monument on this hallowed hill."

On Sunday afternoon the missionaries held a baptismal service at which twelve people were baptized. Elder McConkie baptized three of them. At year's end, President Colton reported that "over a score of converts" had been baptized in the Palmyra District during the last six months of 1935 and a new branch of the mission organized at Canandaigua.

Immediately after the baptismal service, the missionaries returned to the Hill Cumorah for a meeting at which some local dignitaries spoke. Among the speakers was Judge S. Nelson Sawyer, the mayor of Palmyra. He told of growing up in the area and knowing many people who had known Joseph Smith. He spoke of the spirit that had prevailed for many years in which nothing kind was said either of the Prophet or of the Mormon people. "I was born into an atmosphere of prejudice." It was, he said, "simply in the air they breathed." He related an experience in which he had made some rude and slighting comments about Joseph Smith to a couple of Mormon missionaries. They flushed, he recounted, but controlled themselves. One of them responded by saying, "Mr. Sawyer, if you could go back to Jerusalem at the time of Christ, you would hear people say the same things about Jesus Christ that you are now telling us about Joseph Smith."

Those words stung the judge's heart and caused him much reflection. He then apologized to those present for what he had said about Joseph Smith. He said he had come to realize that just as there are two sides to all other issues, so there could also be two sides to the stories he had been told about the Mormons as he grew up. That spirit of prejudice that had once prevailed in this area, Judge Sawyer concluded, was now almost entirely gone.

These remarks, combined with the first baptisms in that region in more than a hundred years, reflected a long-awaited return of the Spirit of the Lord to a place that had been very hostile to the Church in its infancy. No blessings are given to either a people or an area for rejecting the gospel or those who come in the name of the Master. If the words of the Lord to Moses on Mount Sinai are to be trusted, such a course can result only in the visiting of the iniquities of the fathers upon their children "unto the third and fourth generation" (D&C 98:28). So it was that missionaries representing the third and fourth generation of Latter-day Saints returned to the Palmyra area to lift from it the curse of darkness its inhabitants had brought upon themselves.

In his remarks the next day, President David O. McKay also noted the change in spirit that had come to the area. "I congratulate you on having the scales of prejudice removed and that you look at him [Joseph Smith] with a certain degree of pride," he said.

Service as a Missionary, 1934 to 1936

Because of the weather, evening services were shortened to a few musical numbers and the lighting ceremony, which had a powerful effect on those present. All lights were turned off. As people sat in complete darkness, the sound of trumpets came from Cumorah, playing "An Angel from on High." The lights were then turned on in what Elder McConkie described as "a blaze of celestial glory" on the forty-foot granite shaft with the nine-foot bronze figure of Moroni at its top. Though not usually given to much descriptive writing, he noted: "The shaft shone forth with a greater illumined brilliancy than anything I have previously gazed upon. The light seemed to fade into a halo of mist of transcendent beauty around the angel proper, which to my mind added another touch of higher than earthliness to him. I know of no more beautiful or sacred feeling than that which enlivened my very being as I stood enthralled gazing at the Hill." Hundreds of tear-filled eyes matched his as he walked through the crowd that night.

The dedication gave the young elder a chance to shake hands with a number of the Twelve and other prominent leaders in the Church. These, he recorded in his journal, are "valiant servants and soldiers in the gospel cause," of whom there are "no greater men on earth." He made particular note of having met and visited with George S. Romney and Abel S. Rich, both mission presidents. He recorded also that he met Earl J. Glade, an executive at KSL Radio who would serve three terms as mayor of Salt Lake City, in which capacity he would influence Bruce McConkie's destiny.

On Tuesday, July 23, Rudger Clawson, president of the Quorum of the Twelve Apostles, presided over the afternoon meeting. Members of the First Presidency had gone into Rochester to speak on a radio program. While Elder Melvin J. Ballard was addressing the congregation, rain began to fall. When it became apparent that the storm was becoming too severe for comfort, President Clawson stepped up to the podium, said, "Let us pray," and prayed for the rain to cease. "Whether it was proper or not matters little," noted Elder McConkie. "The fact remains that it was very impressive and gave an exhibition of complete, childlike faith. The rain stopped not, but we continued the meeting albeit under conditions of some discomfort.

"At the evening meeting David O. McKay spoke on 'Our Message to the World.' President Grant [for health reasons] had declined to speak and was sitting in the audience. However, when President McKay finished his inspirational talk President Grant went to the stand and spoke to us.

"By far he gave the best talk I have ever heard him give. It was inspired beyond question. He quoted verbatim whole pages of the D&C and then told concerning his call to be one of the General Authorities. It was my first hearing of the story and it included his vision of the council in heaven at which he and Bro. Teasdale were chosen. One of the best speeches I have ever heard."

In the providence of heaven, it is particularly interesting that Elder McConkie was so deeply touched by President Grant's remarks. In a future day, similar events would precede his own call as an apostle. President Grant told how Eliza R. Snow, who was speaking in tongues (with Zina D. Young interpreting), prophesied that he, then a young child playing on the floor while the sisters sat together in a Relief Society meeting, would be called to serve as an apostle. Notwithstanding that prophecy, when he was called to the apostleship, Heber J. Grant struggled for some time with feelings of inadequacy about his call. He told of an experience he had while he was riding horseback through an Indian reservation in northern Arizona. He stopped to commune with the Lord, and as he did so a vision was opened to him of a council in the heavens. There he saw the Savior, Joseph Smith, and his own father, Jedediah M. Grant. He saw that the heavenly council was concerned with the two vacancies that existed in the Quorum of the Twelve, which had not been filled during the general conference just ended. It was determined in the council to send a revelation to correct that, naming him and George Teasdale to fill those vacancies. He learned, further, that his call resulted from a conversation among his father, the Prophet Joseph Smith, and the Savior.[1]

On Wednesday, July 24, a missionary assignment meeting was held, followed by farewells. Fourteen of the missionaries present had completed their missions and were returning home. The Seneca District was created by President Colton with Elder Perry as the district president and Elder McConkie as his companion. This meant Bruce would not be returning to Pennsylvania, an assignment he had not enjoyed nearly as much as he did the labor in the Palmyra area.

Twentieth Birthday: A New Resolve

July 29, 1935, was Elder McConkie's twentieth birthday. In his journal, under the title of "Resolutions of Obvious Necessity," he listed with considerable amplification the following resolutions:

> To be more loving.
> To seek all good gifts, including faith, wisdom, knowledge, humility, meekness, and soberness.
> To repent of my "multitudinous sins and imperfections" and labor to obtain the godly attributes listed in D&C 4.
> To live worthy of the trust placed in me by my family and the Church and as a representative of the Savior.
> To obtain the wisdom of the scriptures and live in harmony with them.
> To keep all the commandments.

In regard to other matters, he resolved to

> Develop all my talents
> Acquire *"speaking genius"*
> Walk straight
> Smile more

> Be less boisterous
> Be more amiable and courteous
> Study more
> Budget time more effectively
> Be discreet in action
> Not try to be the center of attention
> Avoid conceit and self-centeredness
> Obey all mission rules

The serious tone and the length of the list of his personal resolutions, given here in abbreviated form, suggests the seriousness of Bruce's nature and a measure of his personal expectations that must have reflected in some measure the blessing given to him by his father.

The Life and Times of Beelzebub

Elder Perry and Elder McConkie spent the next few days in search of a good used car. At that time missionaries were not precluded from owning cars, and they felt that too much time was being lost simply getting from one place to another on the country roads where no system of public transportation existed. A 1929 Ford was purchased for one hundred dollars; the license plates were an additional six dollars. Elder Perry's letters say "we" purchased a car, and it immediately became district property, with the pair of missionaries who needed it the most using it. Justifying the purchase, Elder McConkie noted in his journal that it was "absolutely essential and necessary for the effective and expedient and adequate work." We can hope that less gasoline was necessary to fuel it than the verbiage used to justify it. In truth, the car was helpful, but it hardly revolutionized missionary work in the Palmyra District. Repairs and flat tires were routine, and before long the car was named "Beelzebub," though on occasion it was also referred to as the "Gospel Chariot."

It was the hope of the missionaries that the car would run on faith rather than on gasoline and that it would respond to the direction of the priesthood rather than the principles of mechanics. Apparently this did not prove to be the case. In any event, fourteen months and seventeen thousand miles later, Elder McConkie wrote in his journal:

"Thur. Sept. 10th To Port Henry and Ironville where tracted all day long. On return trip ran off road and wrecked car.

"Fri. Sept. 11th Sold car for junk, got $22.50. Highwayed home."

Acquiring the Spirit of Cumorah

One special assignment that fell to the missionaries of the newly created Seneca District was to meet those who visited the Hill Cumorah monument and answer their questions. That task was given at least twice to Elder McConkie, prompting the following entries in his journal:

"Spent a quiet and peaceful afternoon and evening in company with Moroni on Cumorah. Alone on a Sacred spot with my thoughts and the Spirit of the Lord."

"Spent the day in companionship with Moroni on Hill Cumorah. Beautiful day and night."

Presiding over the Seneca District

On September 14, 1935, a letter came from President Colton assigning Elder Perry to be the district president in Hudson and Elder McConkie to succeed him as district president in Seneca. This meant that Elder McConkie would direct the activities of the missionaries laboring in the Palmyra and Elmira areas. A natural fruit of this labor was the formation of friendships that would last a lifetime, and though the missionaries lost themselves in the work, they didn't lose their sense of humor or adventure. Elder Dennis Flake later recalled with some pleasure the night he and Elder McConkie hoped to find a member who would put them up for the night. Failing to do so, they went to a car lot, found a vehicle with its doors unlocked, and bedded down there. On another occasion he recalled hitchhiking with Elder McConkie and getting a ride with a man who was quite intrigued with the Mormons, though he had never met one. He asked them rather seriously how many wives they had. Elder McConkie replied, "Well, we're still young. We only have three each." The man was stunned, and neither missionary said anything to disabuse him of this misinformation. When Elder Flake asked the district president if he wasn't a little concerned about leaving such an impression, he was told, "Goodness no! Tomorrow morning we will meet the men he works with when they come off their shift. Think how much more interested they are going to be after he has told them we each have three wives."

About a week and a half after his appointment as district president, there arrived in the district a sister whose gospel understanding and competence as a missionary made her a favorite of Elder McConkie. In his journal he noted that Sister Carol Read "is going to be an excellent missionary." It was not uncommon at that time for an elder and a sister missionary to team up together to go tracting or to teach at cottage meetings. Out of their mutual respect for the competence of each other, Elder McConkie and Sister Read on occasion tracted and studied together.

On one occasion, when Elder McConkie stopped at her lodgings, he noticed a picture of a young man. Learning that it was a picture of Sister Read's fiancé, he picked it up, faced it to the wall, and said, "You'll never marry him. You're going to marry Elder Dennis Flake." Sister Read, who had no idea who Elder Flake was, was rightly offended by this episode. Shortly thereafter she met Elder Flake—and it was love at first sight for them both. Elder Flake, realizing the potential problems associated with the feelings

Service as a Missionary, 1934 to 1936

he had for this young woman from Idaho, contacted President Colton to explain his interest in one of the sister missionaries. President Colton asked, "Which one?" Elder Flake said, "Sister Read." President Colton enthusiastically responded, "That's the one I would have picked, too!" Elder Flake was transferred to Hudson.

In his journal Elder McConkie recorded, "Discovered, not to my regret, that Flake and Read had fallen completely in love and had pledged their lives to each other. They make a wonderful couple and are much in love." After their missions, the two married, sank their roots in Boise, Idaho, and raised a marvelous family of ten children. Their six sons each served a mission, Dennis Jr. serving under President Bruce McConkie in Australia. To date, three of their sons have served as mission presidents.

Having foretold their marriage, Bruce McConkie was regarded as a prophet in the Flake home. He stayed there twice while on conference assignments in Boise. One of these assignments came after the Flake home had burned to the ground. Son Lawrence recalled, "I remember my Mom bemoaning to Elder McConkie the loss of many family treasures in the fire, including some great letters he had written while in the mission field. Some were addressed to 'Ye Elders of Israel' or to 'The Sisters of Zion.' Rather than giving any sympathy, he said, 'Carol, those letters may be the very reason your house burned.'"

Shortly after he was called to the First Council of the Seventy, Elder McConkie had a conference assignment in California. At the end of the conference, while he was shaking hands with the Saints, a man whom he had never met shook hands with him, saying, "You don't know me." Elder McConkie replied, "Yes, I do. You are the man who was going to marry Carol Read." "Yes, and you are the man who ruined my marriage," he replied with a laugh. This fellow, whom Bruce had recognized from the picture Sister Read had had in her apartment years before, then said that he had no hard feelings, that he had married a wonderful Latter-day Saint woman, and that they were very happy.

THE DESIRE TO BECOME A GREAT SPEAKER

The growth that comes to those who lose themselves in the service of the Lord is in itself something of a miracle. This miracle repeats itself in the life of every faithful missionary and is readily apparent to those who know them when they leave and see them again upon their return. The process can be expedited when the missionary actively seeks the gifts of the Spirit. Bruce McConkie wanted with all his heart to develop into a powerful speaker. His efforts to do so, and their results, are traceable in his missionary journal, notwithstanding its brevity.

The opportunity for missionaries to speak came frequently in the small, struggling branches that made up the Eastern States Mission and with some degree of regularity in street meetings. Bruce's journal entries generally consisted of a brief mention of the topic he addressed, the number of minutes he spoke, and his evaluation of his efforts. His first speech as a missionary was a ten-minute talk that received a rating of "poor." Two years later, the last such entry in his journal reads, "1 hr 30 min on God in night meeting." The story that unfolds between those two accounts includes entries outlining his progress from his "heart missing a few beats" at the announcement that the missionaries would be holding a street meeting to entries that bespeak his complete confidence. The early part of his journal contains a good number of entries that read like this:

"Gave poor speech in Sun. night meeting no preparation."

"Spoke in Pittsburgh in evening on necessity of Church affiliation. Did poorly."

"Gave a very very poor exposition of baptism at a North Side Cottage Meeting."

"Spoke in evening at meeting on assigned subject of 'after death, what?' for 23 minutes. Poor speech."

"During my speech [at a street meeting] I received the only boo of the evening and a few cat calls."

Elder McConkie's assessment of his speaking abilities and the assessments given by his companions were not always the same. Describing their second street meeting, Elder Perry wrote, "Last nite (Saturday), we held another street meeting. They moved us up in a section of town that had the least traffic of pedestrians, so we wouldn't block it. But, just the same we got quite an attentive crowd, especially after my companion, Elder McConkie raised his loud voice—I think he was just made for a street meeting—he had listeners even on the opposite street. I was the last to speak in the meeting that lasted from eight until ten."

Imperceptibly, a transition took place in the talks he gave as young Elder McConkie grew less conscious of himself and more dependent on the Spirit. "Gave, under inspiration, one of my best speeches. Had big crowd as many as 200 coming at one time." And again, "When I arose to speak I didn't know what to say, but began on my regular speech, after making a couple of points my mind went blank and I honestly couldn't think of the other points on my outline and of necessity I began on the Articles of Faith in general and for some reason emphasized 'organization' and 'authority' and above all else those things were what one investigator needed. . . . I was surely led in my speech to that subject that was requisite for him." Of a street meeting he said, "Was first speaker at street meeting and harangued for 36 minutes on a dozen different subjects and no one especially listened which didn't worry me much. Total meeting was 55 min." Again, "Fair street meeting. Spoke for 46 minutes on the Plan of Redemption. Probably didn't accomplish much but was good experience for me. Longer by far than the total other speakers."

In the concluding months of his mission he wrote, "I had the floor for 57 minutes. Just as hard and strait as the Lord gave me capacity I preached 'the only true and living church upon the face of the whole earth.' Using D&C 1 & 76 & 1 Cor 1 and Luke 10 and so on. Afterwards the people did not manifest a great desire that we remain in the City. Woe unto thee Elmira for if the preaching done in thee had been done in Tyre and Sidon honest souls would have flocked to the standard. I felt the definite impressions of the Spirit to leave after the meeting ended."

Elder McConkie's efforts to develop himself into an able speaker did not go unnoticed by his fellow missionaries. The spirit of it became contagious, and it appears that all the missionaries in his district became infected by it. In a letter home, Elder Perry observed, "We certainly have been having a time around here the last few days. It's been decided for every one of us to stop murdering the English language. Elder McConkie has had quite a responsibility. He seems to be the leader in speaking clearly—and thus when we try to run words together, he has quite a job.

"The word 'jist' for 'just' has certainly got a strong hold. Sister Taylor swears she'll 'just' not use 'jist' anymore. Elder McConkie bought a six-dollar dictionary for his birthday, and since then, there certainly has been a fever going around of a larger vocabulary, clean enunciation, and proper usage of words. So, as I say, it looks as though McConkie has his hands full—but I'm hoping a lot of good comes out of it for I certainly like to hear good English, especially in speaking."

Carol Read noted in her journal: "Pres McConkie has a marvelous vocabulary and perfect diction. He speaks every syllable and chooses his words so that his sentences are well nigh perfect. But I love to correct him on 'who' & 'whom' and 'have got.'" To that she added, "He's a splendid fellow, so big, so young, so very wise. My, he knows his scriptures." In another entry two weeks later, Sister Read observed, "I would rather go with Elder McConkie [on speaking assignments] than any other, I believe, for I always learn a great deal from him. He has not only a marvelous understanding and knowledge of the gospel but an equally marvelous command of English. And his enunciation is almost perfect. Since it is the custom among the missionaries here to correct each other I correct him at every chance—more on grammar than enunciation. It is fun and beneficial to us both."

It was the custom of people from the small towns and villages in the area to go into Palmyra on Saturday night. To take advantage of this, the missionaries decided to hold an open-air meeting in the city park. "The meeting began," recalls Sister Leatha Hair [later Christensen], "with Elder McConkie standing tall as he was, on the corner in the park. I remember his opening words were, 'Hear ye, hear ye, the Lord God has spoken!' He went on to expound on the scriptures and Gospel principles, particularly the Book of Mormon, and spoke in a very enthusiastic, convincing, and spirited manner.

"I was the next speaker, but when Elder McConkie noted my five-foot-four height wasn't commanding the attention of many people, he brought a wooden crate from a nearby alley and told me to stand on it. This worked all right, except that I was pretty cautious about raising my voice too high and falling off the crate. Elder McConkie assured me that if I fell it wouldn't be very far."

The man could preach, but he couldn't sing. Sister Hair noted that at a party for the Palmyra Branch, Elder McConkie and his companion Elder Richard Smith were announced as a musical number. This was someone's idea of a joke, which everyone thought was funny, but the two elders got the last laugh by accepting the invitation and actually singing. "Their rendition of their favorite hymn was barely recognizable and they sang all seven verses." The good news, stated Sister Hair, was that in the ensuing sixty-plus years she never again heard them sing nor heard any other song sung that badly.

Palmyra District, summer 1936. Bruce is in the back row. President Don B. Colton is in the second row, second from right

She also recalled that they all enjoyed teasing Elder McConkie about the girl waiting for him back home. He had mistakenly referred to her as "My beautiful Amelia" to one of the elders. The expression was passed around, so he was frequently asked how things were with his "Beautiful Amelia."

JOURNAL ENTRIES, 1936

If the brevity of the entries in Elder McConkie's missionary journal in the second year of his mission suggests an increase in his missionary activity, it was indeed a very busy year. Two entries during the early part of the year are of special note:

"Thursday May 21—1936 '4' anniversary of my first going with Amelia my dearly beloved whom I love in truth. And feel the assurance that I shall ever.

"Tues. May 26, 1936 Elder George Albert Smith of the Quorum passed thru and visited with me for about five minutes."

Under President Colton's direction, a number of creative things were being done to soften the feelings of the people in the eastern states toward the Church. One of these was a quartet of elders who traveled throughout the mission putting on programs to win the hearts of people through song. Undoubtedly they made some friends for the Church; nevertheless, the impression they left on the president of the Seneca District was not entirely positive, as suggested by the following notation in his journal: "Ran into Mission Quartette . . . doing a good work, but think they are the only pebbles on the ministerial beach."

The Pageant and the Albany District

Following on the heels of the dedication of the monument on Cumorah in July 1935, the year 1936 witnessed the first Hill Cumorah Pageant. All available missionaries had roles in the pageant, except Elder McConkie and Elder Flake, who were invited to park cars. "Assignments," Bruce observed, "were made by ability." The pageant was followed, as the dedication had been the previous year, with a mission conference and the announcement of new assignments. Bruce was assigned again to be the president of the Seneca District.

Joseph Fielding Smith Visits

Late Monday night, September 15, 1936, a car carrying President Colton, Elder Joseph Fielding Smith, and others pulled up to the old Joseph Smith home in Palmyra. Their party was lodged there that night. The next morning at the breakfast table Sister Carol Read had a delightful visit with the grandnephew of the Prophet. In her journal she recorded that Joseph Fielding Smith had come to the mission home while she was there and that she had then thought him stern and distant. She commented, "I used to tell McConkie what I thought of his 'father-in-law,'" but then noted

The Bruce R. McConkie Story

that Elder Smith was not at all as she had supposed. Having shared conversation with him at breakfast, she now described him as "the dearest man, kind and talkative and cheerful."

"I even asked him about Amelia," she continued, "and as he had already mentioned her engagement to a 'young man out here' we got to talking about McConkie too. This afternoon before they left I showed him some of the pictures that came—one of Elder McConkie. He also read my message to the Primary workers in this month's *Progress*, and said it was 'Very good.' Boy! Oh, I'm so thankful for having met him. Just think, at breakfast yesterday morning President Colton asked him to lead us in family prayer, and what a wonderful prayer he gave—prayed for the Authorities and missionaries etc—just as any one else does."

Three days later Elder Smith, President Colton, and Elder Wayne Richards arrived in the same car at Port Henry for a conference. For the previous two days Elders McConkie and Peterson had been tracting the area to invite people to attend. The meeting was held in White Church with ninety people. "Three of us spoke," recorded Elder McConkie, meaning himself, President Colton, and Elder Smith. "Excellent meeting," he added.

The next day Elder McConkie joined President Colton's traveling party as they made their way across the Adirondacks to Syracuse. Much of the time was spent with the elders asking questions of Elder Smith and soaking up the things he shared with them. Sunday found them in Canandaigua, familiar territory for Elder McConkie, where he was called on to speak. He took up the subject "Truth," and Elder Smith discoursed on the plan of salvation. More than one hundred were in attendance at this branch that had been created a little over a year before. That number included several investigators. A baptismal service followed, at which Elder McConkie baptized four people.

Another meeting was held that afternoon at Palmyra. It and the meeting held that night at Rochester got an "Excellent" rating in Elder McConkie's journal. The next day Elder Smith met with the missionaries in the Sacred Grove. At seven o'clock that evening Elder Smith shook hands with Elder McConkie and wished him well as the young missionary returned to his lodgings in Canandaigua and his future father-in-law continued his mission tour.

In a letter to his daughter Amelia dated September 20, 1936, President Smith noted, "At Fort Henry, Northern N.Y. on the shore of Lake Champlain, [Friday] afternoon I met the finest missionary in the Eastern States mission. He is a young man with light hair, quite tall and with a deep voice." In another epistle home he noted that this same young man would "be with us all day today, when our public meetings are at an end. He spoke briefly at one of our meetings and made the most intelligent talk I have heard from any missionary. I wonder if you know what his name is? I think they call him Bruce at home. He wanted to know how you are so I think you may know him."

On September 22, Elder Smith wrote home saying, "I met B.R.Mc. at Fort Henry, N.Y., in the Adirondacks. He spoke at our meeting there [Friday] night and made a very excellent talk, the *best* I have heard from any missionary. He was with us from Fort Henry all the way to Palmyra, three days. I was with him for 7 meetings and four days. He is a very outstanding young man—*so there*. I will tell you what he had to say when I get home."

7

Marriage to Amelia and the Death of Bruce Jr.
1937 to 1941

Father told us that the baby would have a great work to do where he was.

—Amelia Smith McConkie

At the end of the second year of his mission, in October 1936, Elder Bruce McConkie, at the request of President Colton, extended his mission for six weeks to travel, without a companion, from town to town throughout the mission, teaching investigators and missionaries. Then, with Elder Wayne Richards, who had been his companion on the way to the mission field, and Elder Richard L. Smith, a Cache Valley boy, Bruce—his mission now completed—headed toward Salt Lake City. The three traveled by car so they could visit notable Church history sites along the way. Their mode of transportation was sufficiently unreliable that only an approximate arrival date could be given those who awaited them at home.

The Missionary and Old Feelings Return

Sometime during the day of Monday, December 7, Bruce appeared on the doorstep of the McConkie family home on C Street. Though

Marriage to Amelia and the Death of Bruce Jr., 1937 to 1941

Bruce, Oscar Jr., James and William, Brit, Vivian and Oscar, and Margaret, about 1938

he was obviously pleased to see his family, it was also obvious that he couldn't wait to see Amelia. It was his hope to catch her by surprise. What he didn't know was that his mother was in league with Amelia. While he bathed and spruced up, she quietly called her future daughter-in-law to give her proper warning. Then, feeling a bit guilty, she convinced her son that he should call and announce his visit.

Had there been any doubt about their feelings, the reunion affirmed that the old sparks still burned brightly. "He looked great," said Amelia. "It was wonderful to see him again!" Predictably, his arrival was also of considerable interest to her young brothers. Douglas hid behind the couch in the living room to assure his place in this long-anticipated event. He was caught, however, and banished to wherever it is little brothers go while waiting to grow up.

As Christmas approached, Bruce had some important shopping to do. As it happened, Amelia and her sister Julina were downtown shopping at the same time. It was their plan to go to their father's office when they were finished and ride home with him. Having made his purchase, Bruce also headed for the office of Joseph Fielding Smith. His bride-to-be recounted, "While we were shopping, Dad's secretary, Ruby Egbert, reported to him that Bruce McConkie was there to see him. Dad, who thought very highly of Bruce and was happy to see him, welcomed him accordingly. After a few pleasant comments between them, Bruce showed him the ring he had just bought for my Christmas present and asked if it was all right for him to give it to me for Christmas.

"Yes, now get out of here," he said. He, of course, wanted to help keep Bruce's secret and get him out of the building before the girls returned. Laughing about it later, Bruce said, "When I asked Joseph Fielding Smith if I could marry his daughter, he said yes and then abruptly scooted me out of his office." Knowing the girls would take the elevator, Bruce slipped out of the building using the stairs.

The giving of that ring made Christmas 1936 a very special Christmas indeed for Bruce and Amelia. Both families were delighted with the formal announcement that Bruce and Amelia were engaged.

After New Year's Day in 1937, Bruce resumed his studies at the University of Utah. He and Amelia both graduated the following June, Bruce with a bachelor of arts degree and Amelia with a bachelor's degree in bacteriology and pathology. Bruce became a member of Delta Phi, the returned missionary fraternity, and was ordained a seventy on February 28 by Rufus K. Hardy. He was immediately called to serve as an instructor in his seventies quorum and also taught the M-Men and Gleaner class.

Hopes and Dreams

Bruce and Amelia hoped to marry in the fall of 1937, but their doing so depended on his being able to get some kind of a job to support them and pay his tuition. This was a particular concern because jobs were very hard to come by at that time. He was grateful when he got back his old job driving an ice delivery truck for Hygiea Ice. Though electric refrigerators were available, many people and stores still depended on ice to keep perishables cold.

The truck Bruce was given to drive was as dependable as spring weather. The only way it would start after having been stopped for any measurable period of time was if he popped the clutch while the truck rolled down a hill. This was easily done on C Street, which is on a hill. It was not so easily accomplished on Douglas Street, where the Smith home was and where Bruce and Amelia lived during the first years of their marriage. There, Bruce would park the truck at night at the top of the hill on a nearby vacant lot. Next morning, he would give the truck a push from the dashboard and jump in while it rolled down the hill, which really looked more like a seventy-foot cliff. He would pop the clutch, give it a little gas, and slam on the brakes as he brought it under control and maneuvered it out onto the road. His bride, who oversaw this ritual each morning, would stand at the top of the hill with her heart in her throat, praying that the truck would not turn over and that their unborn child would not be left without a father.

In the summer of 1937, Bruce attended summer camp with the ROTC in Wyoming, and Amelia went to see her sister Lois in Chicago. This trip fulfilled a promise her father had made to her when she was a little girl. She had often walked with her mother or older sisters from their home, which then was near what is now West High School, to the Union Pacific train station in Salt Lake City, either to see her father off on an assignment or to welcome him home. As with most children, trains were a source of fascination for her, and she always begged her father to take her with him. On one of those occasions she elicited an "all right" from him, and because his word was his bond, the promise was as good as gold. Because it was July and there were no conferences, it was decided that they would go to Chicago to visit Lois and her husband, who

Graduation, June 1937. Above: Oscar McConkie, Joseph Fielding Smith, Amelia, Vivian Redd McConkie, and Bruce. Left: Amelia

was in medical school there, and see their new baby. Amelia's mother was not well enough to make the trip, and her brothers Lewis and Reynolds had summer jobs, so she, her father, and her brothers Douglas and Milton were the only members of the family to go. Describing the train trip, Amelia recalled:

"At night the boys shared a bunk, but Dad and I each had our own. When bedtime came the Porter made up our beds. It was not a very restful night because it seemed rather noisy, and the train seemed to do nothing but move back and forth to let other trains pass that were going in the other direction. It seemed like we got a little jolt each time the train cars bumped into each other from changing tracks so the other trains could go by. Finally things became very peaceful and then we seemed to be traveling very quietly. In the morning we learned there had been a flood in part of the country we were to travel through and we had not moved at all. We had been in Evanston all the time!"

Marriage to Amelia and the Death of Bruce Jr., 1937 to 1941

Young Amelia

Still, the trip was a wonderful memory for each of them, though the best part, at least for her father, was that he had kept his promise to a little girl and fulfilled a dream for her. That little girl was, however, quite pleased to get home, for other plans were in the making.

She and Bruce had chosen October 13 for their wedding. The date was his mother's birthday. That way Amelia could always remind her husband that their anniversary was approaching by saying simply, "Bruce, do you remember that your mother's birthday is coming up?"

On August 26, Amelia's mother, Ethel Reynolds Smith, passed away after an illness of some length. Amelia was the oldest child still living at home. Her brother Lewis had received his call to serve as a missionary in Switzerland and was readying himself to leave. Her younger brothers, Reynolds (sixteen), Douglas (thirteen), and Milton (ten), needed some supervision, and her father needed someone to prepare meals and look after the home. She assumed that responsibility, which proved to be a blessing for her and Bruce. After their marriage she continued to perform this labor in exchange for the use of the makeshift apartment in the basement where she and Bruce began married life.

WEDDING AND HONEYMOON

October 13, 1937, was a beautiful sun-filled autumn day in the Salt Lake Valley, a day perfectly suited to a wedding. At ten o'clock that morning Bruce Redd McConkie called at the home of Joseph Fielding Smith to escort his youngest daughter, Amelia, to the Salt Lake Temple, where her father would seal them as husband and wife for time and all eternity. Joseph Fielding Smith met them as they ascended the steps to the large east doors of the temple, where brides and grooms traditionally have their pictures taken today. He opened the door, took them in, and had them fill out their wedding certificate. They then separated to change clothing and were escorted to the sealing room at the southeast corner of the celestial room, where most of the marriages took place at that time.

A few members of both families were there to greet them. Bruce's father, Oscar, and Amelia's brother Lewis, who was leaving the next morning for his mission to Switzerland, acted as witnesses. Amelia recalled, "Characteristically, Bruce paid attention to every detail. Almost fifty years later he could remind me that we were married at 11:22 A.M., in the Salt Lake Temple, by my Father, on the 13th day of October 1937."

In countless talks yet to be given, Bruce would tell his listeners that "the most important single thing that any member of this Church does in this life is to marry the right person, in the right

Marriage to Amelia and the Death of Bruce Jr., 1937 to 1941

place, by the right authority."[1] He never preached a principle that he didn't live.

Neither ever doubted that this was a marriage planned in the heavens. Bruce often surprised people by stating in sermons on marriage that he never prayed about marrying his wife. The thought to do so no more occurred to him than the idea that he ought to pray to confirm his own existence. The obvious simply needed no confirmation. It might be noted that the intertwining of their destinies was hinted at in Amelia's patriarchal blessing, given two years earlier, when she was told it would be her privilege to raise her voice in testimony in many lands throughout the world. There were few men she could have married whose circumstances would have afforded her that opportunity. Because of the office that Bruce would hold, she would teach and testify of the restored gospel in forty different nations.

Bruce and Amelia at the time of their marriage

After the ceremony Amelia changed her dress and waited some time for her husband to show up. "While doing so I sat with Dad at the table, where the wedding certificates were filled out by those officiating," she remembered. "Dad was to perform another ceremony shortly. Standing before him was a man with his daughter who was to be married. As Dad signed the papers, the man turned to the bride and said, 'Joseph Fielding Smith will perform your ceremony,' whereupon she began to cry.

"'What is the matter?' my father asked, somewhat concerned.

"'I wanted one of the Apostles to do it,' she moaned."

That may well have been the only time in their forty-eight years of marriage that Bruce was late. He had misplaced his locker key. It tickled his bride to think that he had been so nervous. All present at the wedding ceremony having now left, they did likewise. "As we walked toward South Temple on the east side of the Temple Block, we saw his parents standing on the corner waiting for the light to change. We joined them," Amelia said.

"'Mother and I were just going to the Lion House to get a little lunch,' his father said. 'Would you like to come with us?'

"Bruce quickly told them yes, and we went along.

"I don't remember ever having been to the Lion House before, and aside from the delicious-looking slice of pumpkin pie I had put on my tray, I can't remember what else we had. But then, that was the only thing I had reason to remember because when I put my fork in it to have a taste the whole thing slid off onto my lap."

Amelia recalled being very impressed with the number of people who stopped to acknowledge Bruce's parents. Among them was President Heber J. Grant. He was the first person to whom she was introduced as Bruce's wife.

The events of their wedding were unpretentious. There was no wedding dress, as such was not required for the temple ceremony, and the newlyweds chose not to impose the effort and expense of a reception on their families. Amelia knew that her father did not like receptions and that he would feel especially awkward without his wife at his side. No photographs were taken. Times were austere, and neither family was in a position to give the young couple much to get started with, beyond the expression of their love and best wishes. That afternoon Bruce's mother found some roses still in bloom in her garden, so she made the bride a corsage. Two of Amelia's sisters put on a dinner for both families at the Smith home

Bruce and Amelia

that evening. The next morning the newlyweds left in Aunt Tennie's car for a three-day trip to Bryce and Zion National Parks.

The Calm before the Storm

In the lull before the storm of war broke, Bruce completed his law degree and found time to regularly read the scriptures with his bride. Immediately following their marriage, they started to read the scriptures together. Amelia used a Bible given to her by her father when she was fifteen. It contained this inscription, "With love and the hope that the principles of truth contained in this record may be faithfully studied." Their practice was for her to read aloud from this Bible while Bruce carefully noted the changes found in his copy of the Inspired Version, or what is known today as the Joseph Smith Translation.

They began with the Old Testament, which they completed on July 24 the following year, 1938. They then read the New Testament. Notes in Amelia's Bible indicate that they reread the New Testament four more times by the summer of 1942. The dates listed suggest that they read the other standard works the same number of times between those readings. For them to have kept up this reading schedule during the law school years is especially impressive. This practice apparently continued until Bruce was called to the First Council of the Seventy in October 1946. At that point it was replaced by the demands of four children and the pressures of his office. Yet the seeds sown in that study would bear much good fruit.

STUDYING LAW

As a law student, Bruce had two professors who made a concerted effort to belittle and ridicule him and ensure that his experience as a student was as uncomfortable and distasteful as possible. One eventually became a United States district judge for Utah. Attorneys who argued cases in his court remember him as having a strong anti-Mormon bias, often treating members of the Church cruelly while being extremely liberal in judgments rendered against Gentiles. Dad felt that he was singled out in class because of who his father was and because of his known loyalty to the Church.

Bruce graduated with his bachelor of laws degree in 1939 and ranked third out of seventy-five on the bar exam. In June 1967 his degree was upgraded to juris doctor, eliciting from him the remark, "I have always claimed to believe that Ph.D.s and academic doctorates of all kinds were valued at a dime a dozen; now, with inflation, some of them seem to be free for the asking." Though not enamored with men of supposed learning, he highly prized education, even mentioning in a conference talk his hope that his sons would earn doctoral degrees.

CHALLENGES

Once when Joseph Fielding Smith's conference assignment was in Springville, Utah, thus allowing him to return home after the

Saturday meetings, he asked his new son-in-law if he would like to go with him. Bruce, who loved to hear Elder Smith preach, couldn't pass up such an opportunity. He also knew that it would provide an opportunity to "talk gospel" with his father-in-law as they drove to and from the meeting.

As they were nearing their destination, Elder Smith said, "Bruce, I am going to leave you a little time after I speak so you can talk, too."

"Yes, sir," came the startled response.

During Elder Smith's remarks, his young traveling companion searched his mind to find some suitable expression. As Elder Smith made a particular point, Bruce would think of other scriptures he could cite to continue the development of the idea being presented. Every time this happened, however, Elder Smith referred to the scripture Bruce had thought of. Finally he realized there was nothing he could do but let the Spirit direct what he said when it came time for him to speak. He did so, and he bore a fine testimony with which President Smith was quite pleased.

"Bruce came home feeling quite awed about that experience," his bride recalled, "but then isn't there an old saying about great minds running in the same channel?"

JOSEPH FIELDING SMITH REMARRIES

On April 11, 1938, in a wedding that set a lot of tongues wagging, Joseph Fielding Smith married Jessie Ella Evans. Jessie, at age thirty-five, was a year younger than Elder Smith's eldest daughter, Julina, and but three years older than his second daughter, Josephine. He was sixty-one. She was a delightful and outgoing woman, every bit the social butterfly who did much to temper the sternness that was a part of his nature. As a young woman she had been asked to become a contralto with the Metropolitan Opera. Hers was a prayerful decision that included a careful rereading of her patriarchal blessing. That blessing promised that her name would be heard at home and abroad because of her ability to entertain but that success would come in the service of the Lord. In that counsel she found her answer. She came home and joined the Tabernacle Choir.

She was always known to the family as Aunt Jessie, following the practice of an earlier generation in which children in polygamous families referred to the wives other than their mother by their first name and as "Aunt." She and Joseph Fielding Smith were married by President Heber J. Grant, who, as he concluded the ceremony, said, "Joseph, kiss your wife."

"He said it like he meant it, and I have been doing it ever since," Granddad recalled.

Aunt Jessie was the county recorder and stayed on in that position until the elections in November, when someone else filled the post. This meant that Amelia and Lois, who was living in the Smith home with her two children while her husband completed medical school, continued to take care of the home. In truth, running a household and cooking meals was not Aunt Jessie's forte, and there was never any serious thought that she would assume those responsibilities. She traveled constantly with her husband, continued on with the Choir, and generously shared her musical talent, singing in as many as twenty-eight funerals in a single month.

BRUCE JR.

Early in September 1938, Bruce became ill. When his parents learned about it, they sent their doctor to see him, that being a day in which doctors made house calls. It was determined that he had pneumonia, which without modern antibiotics could be quite serious. The doctor thought it wise to put him in the hospital. His recovery was slow, and Amelia turned the running of the household over to her sister Lois so she could spend time with her ill husband.

Marriage to Amelia and the Death of Bruce Jr., 1937 to 1941

When Bruce was well enough to be discharged from the hospital, he was taken to his parents' home so his mother could continue to look after him. Meanwhile, Amelia was about to exchange places with him at the hospital: Bruce Jr. had given notice that he was about ready to join the family. Amelia, uneasy about going to the hospital, had determined she was not going until visiting hours were over. She simply did not want to meet anyone she knew while she was looking pregnant and feeling so terrible. When her father got home from the Church offices and learned what was going on, he went to the McConkies' home to give whatever support he could.

While they waited, Judge McConkie did as he always did—involve everyone in a great gospel discussion. It was about nine o'clock when Amelia finally consented to go to the hospital. It would be another three hours after she was admitted before the child was born. Bruce's parents and her father all remained with her. She remembered only that her father and Judge McConkie sat with her during that time, lost in a gospel discussion. Bruce Jr. was finally born at 12:42 A.M., September 9, 1938.

"By morning," Amelia said, "I was already planning the baby's future. My room was on the east side of the hospital and I could hear the school bell ringing and the voices of children on their way. I even had decided what kind of clothes he would wear and how smart he would be for his age. Things hadn't been so bad after all." It was a couple of days later before Bruce's doctor would allow him to visit his wife and newborn baby. Amelia said, "He seemed overwhelmed to have a son."

At that time, mothers were kept in the hospital for ten days after giving birth and were not allowed to get up until the ninth day. The cost for this lengthy hospital stay was fifty dollars for a private room, and the doctor's bill was less than that. Upon Amelia's release from the hospital, Vivian McConkie insisted that the new mother, the new baby, and Bruce come to her home so that she could nurse all of them. When Vivian had given birth to her children, new mothers had been kept in bed for three weeks. All of this changed with World War II, when hospital beds were at a premium.

After leaving the hospital, Amelia was afflicted with a breast abscess. The problem spread to her joints so that she could hardly walk or use her hands. Twice it became necessary for the doctor to lance the abscess. As soon as her body began to heal and she was able to care for herself, Amelia insisted that they return to their own home, where they enjoyed the privacy of their apartment. A couple of weeks later, about the middle of October, she and Bruce sat in the living room with her father and Aunt Jessie, listening to him tell about the book he was just completing on the life of his father, President Joseph F. Smith. Among the stories was that of President Smith's daughter Mercy Josephine ("Dodo"), who died at the age of three. President Smith wrote: "The morning before she died, after being up with her all night, for I watched her every night, I said to her, 'My little pet did not sleep all night.' She shook her head and replied, 'I'll sleep today, papa.' Oh! how those little words shot through my heart. I knew though I would not believe, it was another voice, that it meant the sleep of death and she did sleep. And, Oh! the light of my heart went out. The image of heaven graven in my soul was almost departed."[2]

Amelia recalled that as her father told the story, she sat looking at her infant son, thinking, "I don't know how I would ever stand it if he were to die."

The Death of Bruce Jr.

About two weeks later Amelia took the baby with her to prepare breakfast for her father and Aunt Jessie. She sat down in the living room to look at the paper. The baby was sleeping soundly, yet making a little noise. Her father entered the room with his hat and coat on to say goodbye before leaving for the office.

"Listen to my baby snore," Amelia said.

Joseph Fielding Smith walked over to the baby, looked at him and listened, and then turned to his daughter and said, "This baby is sick." Without another word, he took off his hat and coat, walked over to the telephone, and called his brother Silas, the family doctor. He was at the hospital, operating, so they had to wait for him to return the call.

The two of them waited together for more than two hours before the call came. Silas suggested that they call a pediatrician. Joseph Fielding said, "No, I want you to come." It was another hour before he arrived. After examining the baby, he told them that he was very sick. Dr. Smith gave Amelia and her sister Lois instructions and left. Their father reviewed the instructions with them and finally left for the office. Bruce became very concerned when he learned of the situation after returning from classes at school.

The next morning Joseph Fielding stayed home until his brother had again come to check the baby. Dr. Smith felt that the situation had worsened and that more care was needed than could be given at home. Joseph Fielding readied the car, and arrangements were made to take the baby to the hospital. Bruce cut class to be with his wife and baby. A priesthood blessing was given. Oscar and Vivian were notified, and the vigil of faith began. Joseph Fielding joined them at the hospital as soon as his duties permitted.

That afternoon it was decided that the baby should be given a name and a blessing. Joseph Fielding Smith was voice, and Bruce and his father assisted. For an hour or so the nurses kept watch on the baby, and then Uncle Silas took over, checking his heart and temperature regularly.

After a time Joseph Fielding spoke up and said, "Silas, I feel that the baby is no longer with us."

"It has been a while since I have been able to get a heartbeat," he responded.

The Bruce R. McConkie Story

All present began to weep. Amelia asked to hold him for a little while, and she was permitted to do so. After a few minutes, the nurse said, "I will have to take him now."

It was the anniversary of Joseph Fielding Smith's marriage to Amelia's mother, Ethel Reynolds.

Oscar McConkie noted in his journal: "November 2, 1938, Bruce Redd McConkie Jr. died about the hour of 7:45 P.M., at the L. D. S. Hospital, Salt Lake City. Monday morning he was ill, and he died on Wednesday. His case was fully presented to the Lord. A short service was held at Amelia's father's home, where her father spoke. Jessie Evans Smith sang a couple of numbers. A member of the bishopric of their ward opened with prayer, and Bishop Ed. Q. Cannon [from the McConkies' ward] offered the benediction. I spoke for a few minutes at the service. J. M. [James Monroe] Redd Jr. dedicated the grave at the City Cemetery.

"He was a beautiful baby. At the service, obviously under the direction of the Spirit, Bro. Smith told of the Prophet Joseph Smith saying that some spirits were too pure to go through this life, that they had advanced so far in the Spirit World that their only need was to obtain a body and then go back for the work they had to do. He said this was one of those spirits and I knew that it was so.

"At the hospital, when the baby was born and all his grandparents were looking at him, he opened his eyes and looked at us as an adult would do. Then, at his bed just before he died, as we stood around in contemplation of death, he opened his eyes and looked at us as an adult would do. Then he raised his eyes to the top of my head and carefully examined me from the top of my head to the soles of my feet. Then when he had completely surveyed me, he closed his eyes, not to open them again. It was a searching experience that I have only had that once."

Not until the baby was gone did Amelia learn that her father had fasted and prayed from the time he knew the baby was ill until after he left them. "When we returned from the cemetery my Father sat in his comfortable leather chair and with Bruce and me and Jessie and my sisters Lois and Julina sitting close by, he talked about what would happen with Bruce Junior when he got into the Spirit World. He was no longer a baby, he explained, but a full grown spirit, who had a great work to do on the other side of the veil until the time of the resurrection.

"Father told us that the baby would have a great work to do where he was. We also learned that he was as an adult there, but when the resurrection comes he will come forth from the grave as the baby we buried. At that time, if I have died before the resurrection comes, Bruce and I would be able to raise him and teach him the truths that we want him to know, until he grows to manhood. If the resurrection should come before I die, I would not be able to touch him, as I would not be in the same state he was, but I would have the right to tell who was to take care of him, what I wanted him to be taught and do."

CONTINUING ON IN FAITH

Shortly after these events, Amelia secured a temporary job working for the Genealogical Society. "I was hired to help in the office. The work would only last 6 months, but it would be a big boost to us. Car fare was not a problem since I could usually go to work when Dad did and also come home with him." When that job ended in mid 1939, "I had another project," Amelia said. "We were preparing to welcome our second child in March."

This time Bruce was at the hospital, and they welcomed a beautiful baby daughter into their family. They named her Vivian after her grandmother McConkie.

The basement apartment in the Smith home would welcome yet another child a year later. He would be honored to hold his grandfather Smith's name. It was during this time that one of the differences between Bruce and his father-in-law became apparent. Bruce was gifted with the ability to lie down almost anywhere and fall asleep immediately, waking up twenty or thirty minutes later completely refreshed. Not infrequently, in the evening while he was tending the children and Amelia was at Relief Society or some like place, the hardworking law student would fall asleep on the floor in the company of his books. It mattered not how loud his children cried, Bruce could sleep soundly through it. He explained this as the blessing of a pure conscience. President Smith, on the other hand, never missed hearing even the quiet sobbing of a child. So it was that he walked the floor with his grandchildren for many an hour while their father slept soundly.

After Law School

Bruce was admitted to the bar January 8, 1940. In an attempt to start his own practice, he shared an office in the Boston Building in downtown Salt Lake with three fellow law school graduates. Theirs was not a partnership; rather, they scheduled the use of the office when they had a client to meet with. Because none of them had any established clients, they had to survive on cases assigned to them by the court. In February 1940 Bruce tried his first criminal case, doing so in his father's court. "[He] did well," Judge McConkie reported.

Bruce was fortunate to be offered the position of city attorney when there was a change in that department. He accepted, and for a year or so he and Amelia enjoyed a steady, albeit nominal, income. On June 19, 1941, Bruce and Amelia purchased their first home, at 1980 Michigan Avenue.

8

THE WAR YEARS
1942 TO 1946

Righteous men are entitled, expected, and obligated to defend themselves; they must engage in battle when there is no other way to preserve their rights and freedoms and to protect their families, homes, land, and the truths of salvation which they have espoused.
—Bruce R. McConkie

Perhaps no family in our nation escaped the difficulties associated with World War II. The times called for courage and sacrifice, and a generation weaned on the Great Depression proved themselves equal to the challenge. Word of the safety of a loved one brought with it immense relief, and reunions, even as brief as they often were, brought joy deepened by a keen sense of the danger in which they lived and the uncertainty of what the morrow might bring. Bruce's brothers Brit and James both found themselves in the thick of the fight in Europe; Amelia's brother Lewis was involved in dangerous assignments in Africa.

Oscar McConkie, who struggled with the premonition that James would not return from the conflict, received a call at his office on September 11, 1944, from someone identifying himself as a reporter for the *Salt Lake Telegram*. The speaker asked the worried father if he could confirm the report they had received that one of his sons had been killed in combat. When he said he had received

Clockwise from left: *Brit, William, Margaret, Oscar Jr., James, Oscar Sr., Vivian, and Bruce*

no such report, he was assured that the report was authentic. Oscar said nothing about the phone call until after letters had been received from both Brit and James dated after September 11.

On December 19—Aunt Jessie's birthday—in 1944, Joseph Fielding Smith received word that his son Lewis had been killed in an airplane explosion. His service had been a secret assignment, so little is known about where he was or what he was doing. A few weeks earlier, a strange set of circumstances had kept him off a plane he was scheduled to be on; he learned later that it had gone down. Father and son had worked out a code that escaped the censors so Lewis could let his father know where he was. In this instance, it is known only that he was on his way back to his headquarters in Nigeria when his plane, believed to have been sabotaged, exploded in the air. The loss was very difficult for his father, who had seen in Lewis characteristics that suggested that he would be a very able leader in the Church. With Lewis's death, Joseph Fielding Smith seemed to draw his son-in-law Bruce more closely to him and savor the opportunities to tutor him in gospel principles.

A measure of the seriousness of the times is that the April 1942 general conference of the Church was not held in the Tabernacle as usual but rather in the Assembly Hall and the upper room of the Salt Lake Temple. The general membership of the Church and the public were not invited. Attendance was limited to general authorities and to presidents of high priest quorums and stake presidencies. (The responsibilities of stake presidents and presidents of high priest quorums were organized differently then from the way they are today.) The Sunday morning and Monday morning sessions of the conference, however, were broadcast by KSL Radio. Two other sessions were held in the upper room of the temple, one of these being a three-and-a-half-hour testimony meeting. The concluding session, held Monday morning, consisted of Church business, the addresses of two speakers, and the reading by President J. Reuben Clark Jr. of a lengthy statement from the First Presidency dealing with questions and challenges facing the Saints on account of the war. Except for this statement and an address given by Elder Albert E. Bowen the preceding day, the content of the talks differed very little from that which is usual for a general conference. The central message of the conference was that ultimately answers and direction must come from personal revelation and testimony.

At the conference it was made plain that losing the war would mean losing our liberty and hence our right to worship. Loyalty and patriotism were thus expected of all who shared the blessings of liberty. "The despot always seeks to put religion down," observed Elder Bowen. "The rise of Hitler in Germany heralded assaults upon the church. His Minister of Religion said, 'Adolph Hitler is the true Holy Ghost,' and the Minister of Culture declared, 'We must proclaim a German Christ, not a lamb of God.' In Russia the line was the same, 'What is worrying us is not that Christianity is dying in

Russia, but that it is still surviving,' said the Commissioner of Justice. 'The natural transition,' said another, 'is to bring about the death of all religion.'"[1]

Military Service

For the next four years life continued to be lived with a sense of impending danger. Although Bruce traveled a great deal in connection with his military service, he was blessed to live at home. His brother James, on a mission over Germany, left his seat to help a comrade only to return and find a hole had been blown through it. Their attempt to make it back to their base in England was unsuccessful, and he had to parachute to safety. Brit was wounded in Belgium—shrapnel in his left shoulder—but when he was released from the hospital, he refused his leave and returned to fight under General George S. Patton. He distinguished himself for bravery in the Battle of the Bulge, in which he was wounded again.

Little is recorded about Bruce's military service. At the University of Utah he had enrolled in the reserve officer training program, graduating with a commission as a second lieutenant in field artillery. He was called up to active duty on March 5, 1942. At his induction physical, it was discovered that he had suffered with polio as a child. The polio had gone undiagnosed, but it manifested itself in the bearing of his shoulders. He also failed the eye test and could have been excused from military service, but he pleaded his case and was assigned to military intelligence at Fort Douglas, a twenty-minute walk from his home on Michigan Avenue. He served at Fort Douglas for the duration of the war.

What is known about his military service is that he traveled extensively throughout the western states and was involved in briefing governors and mayors on security matters. His association with Governor Earl Warren of California was such that when they met many years later, the governor knew him by name. It is also known

The War Years, 1942 to 1946

Lieutenant Colonel Bruce R. McConkie with young Joseph and Vivian

that he wrote something of book length, which was classified as top secret. When he was later asked why he never received any Church assignments in Eastern Bloc countries, he replied, "Are you kidding? The KGB have a dossier on me two inches thick." A request for a copy of his military record was met with the explanation that it had been destroyed in a fire at the National Personnel Records Center in St. Louis, Missouri, on July 12, 1973.

Bruce was awarded the American Campaign medal and the World War II medal. At the time of his discharge on February 26, 1946, he held the rank of lieutenant colonel. He was one of the youngest men in army intelligence to hold that rank.

In Defense of the Faith

At the end of February 1945, a letter from the headquarters of The Church of Jesus Christ of Latter-day Saints arrived at 1980 Michigan Avenue in Salt Lake City. The letter was addressed to "Captain McConkie," though the occupant of the home was a lieutenant colonel. The letter, a stinging rebuke, bore the signature of the general superintendent of the Sunday School. It began with the announcement that Brother McConkie had brought unwarranted charges against the author of the Sunday School manual and the General Sunday School Superintendency at a recently held conference of the Bonneville Stake. "We are informed," the letter stated, "that you charged that the manual contains false doctrines." Such charges, it noted, had "no value unless the critic points out what particular doctrines in the manual are contrary to the teachings of the Church." Further, the letter continued, "You were asked, we are informed, to furnish specific evidence and you refused to do so. We think it entirely unfair and misleading for you to make these statements before a group of Sunday School teachers. We think you should point out specifically what these false doctrines are."

The letter noted that the charges were "decidedly damaging" to the superintendency and "false so far as facts are concerned." The concluding line of the letter stated, "We are sending copies of this letter to our advisers of the General Authorities and to Elder Joseph Fielding Smith, chairman of the Publications Committee." The bottom of the letter noted that copies of it had also been sent to David O. McKay, Stephen L Richards, and John A. Widtsoe.

A letter advising David O. McKay, second counselor in the First Presidency, and three members of the Quorum of the Twelve of Bruce's reported inappropriate conduct at a stake conference doubtless caused him considerable embarrassment. Nevertheless, it was necessary for the Gospel Doctrine teacher to respond, and respond he did—in a seven-page, single-spaced typewritten letter under the date of March 1, 1945.

The letter began: "Your letter of 24 February 1945 relative to purported objections of mine to the present Gospel Doctrine lessons has been received.

"The report that was made to you was in error. I did not make any of the charges or statements contained in your letter either as you have written them or in substance, nor did I say anything that could be construed or interpreted to mean what I am quoted as having said, except that I did say that in my opinion there were doctrines in the manual which are contrary to the teachings of the Church. With respect to this statement, I did point out what are in my opinion two specific instances of these doctrinal errors, and I will repeat them in writing below. I also made one other point to which your letter does not make reference, and which I will also repeat in writing below. However, some of the substance of the statements attributed to me was made by another Gospel Doctrine class teacher who participated in the discussions. No person present made any derogatory statement about the author of the manual and the General Superintendency was not even mentioned.

"Dr. William M. McKay conducted the class discussion for the Gospel Doctrine and Gospel Messages group. He began by asking for any comments or problems that the class would like to bring up. I led out in a discussion on the merits and demerits of the manual. He requested that I make my objections in writing to you. I indicated that I did not think I would do so, for I had no desire to reach forth and steady the ark.

"The statements I made to Dr. McKay were these: 1. That in my opinion the manual contained doctrinal statements contrary to the teachings of the Church; and, 2. That in my opinion the manual as a whole was written from the perspective of worldly knowledge and the wisdom and philosophies of men, rather than from the viewpoint of latter-day revelation and the gospel, and that in consequence of this it was not designed to instill and encourage that faith in the hearts of the Latter-day Saints that it otherwise might have done."

Even a cursory examination of the manual evidenced justification for concern about its spirit and content, Bruce observed. On page 2 of the eighty-four-page manual, under "Acknowledgments," the sources used were cited. They were twenty-one in number, and all came from secular authors. These sources were quoted liberally throughout the manual. No Latter-day Saint sources were mentioned in the acknowledgments, and such sources were rarely used in the lessons. The tone of the manual was that of a teacher who was very conscious of his superior knowledge and the need to liberate his students from childish and naive notions about Christ and the Bible. Moreover, the lessons avoided teaching doctrine, preferring to center attention on cultural, historical, and ethical matters. While the "Gospels as Literature" or the "Literary Characteristics of Mark" might constitute the heart of the lesson one week, the next week would follow with the "Humanitarian Teachings of Luke" or "Conflicting Stories" found in the New Testament. With very little editing the manual could have been used in either a Catholic or a Protestant Sunday School class. Although the scholars of the world were liberally quoted, the standard works, Conference Reports, and the teachings of the living prophets were strikingly absent.

The manner in which the New Testament came together was described as "survival of the fittest in the fierce competition for popular approval," with the appended observation that its authors "made no claim for their works to be regarded as scripture." Christ was portrayed as uncertain about his role as the Son of God and thus in need of forty days in the wilderness for the "task of adjusting his mind and spirit." His success in converting publicans and sinners, the manual suggested, ought properly to be "attributed to the assistance of this worldly wise, apostolic convert," Matthew. As to the matter of miracles, the manual asserted, history has shown "that events that were regarded as miraculous in one age are found to be the result of natural causes by a later, more scientific age." Thus, references to casting out devils were simply the healing of the "mentally deranged." From beginning to end, the manual consistently slanted every matter involving faith in favor of scholarly or intellectual explanations.

There was no shortage of illustrations of "bad doctrine" in the manual. Bruce's copy had scores of question marks in the margins and places where he had written an emphatic No! to identify his concern about a particular statement. Indeed, this manual alone is a persuasive argument for the current system of various Correlation committees reviewing Church publications in an effort to assure orthodoxy.

"In my opinion," Bruce wrote, "the manual is written from the perspective and viewpoint of a sectarian church and not from the standpoint of latter-day revelation. It appears to be a scholarly approach based almost wholly upon the philosophies of men and the notions they have gained by research. It does not present, except occasionally and in a very incidental manner, the doctrines and view of the Church on the matters considered. In analyzing material written from this perspective it is difficult to put one's finger on specific statements and say that this or that is wrong, but by reading the lessons and the manual as a whole the impression is conveyed that the New Testament activities were the result of the wise acts of men rather than the result of the inspiration of God revealed to them by the Holy Ghost. In my judgment this is a far more serious objection than the one that there may be statements found in it which do not conform to the accepted teachings of the Church on particular subjects." The chief illustration of this point was the representation of Christ as a great moral teacher rather than as the Son of God.

Concluding his written response, Bruce stated: "I have and will scrupulously avoid any act or statement that will bring discredit upon the General Superintendency, the General Board, or upon the Stake or local Sunday School personnel. I have intended none in the past and in my judgment have brought no such discredit upon any Sunday School worker. There are few if any persons in the Church who have more respect for the General Authorities than I do, or who more assiduously avoid any taint of evil speaking against the Lord's anointed.

"I regret that you sent copies of your letter to your Sunday School advisers and others of the General Authorities without first having referred the matter to me. If you had been fully and correctly advised, I do not think you would have attributed the hearsay report to me. In view of this I am taking the liberty of sending copies of this letter to President J. Reuben Clark, Jr., and President David O. McKay, to your Advisers, and to Elder Joseph Fielding Smith, Chairman of the Publications Committee, to two other members of this Committee, and to Dr. McKay, who conducted the class discussion in the Bonneville Stake." Copies were sent to President J. Reuben Clark Jr. and to Elders David O. McKay, Joseph Fielding Smith, Stephen L Richards, John A. Widtsoe, Marion G. Romney, and William M. McKay.

Although there is no record that the General Superintendency of the Sunday School chose to respond to this letter, two others did. One was Marion G. Romney, then serving as an assistant to the Quorum of the Twelve, who indicated that he had read both letters carefully and appreciated receiving them. The other was J. Reuben Clark Jr., who noted, "I deeply regret that the Gospel Doctrine course is amenable to the criticisms which you have labeled against it, but a cursory examination of it does not give me basis for disagreeing with what you say." In private conversation Joseph Fielding Smith discussed the matter with his son-in-law, affirming complete agreement with him. Elder Smith directed Bruce to send a copy of this correspondence to Harold B. Lee, who was not among those who had received a copy of the letter from the General Superintendent of the Sunday School.

The War Years, 1942 to 1946

This experience constituted the introduction of Bruce McConkie to a number of men prominent in the Church, and if nothing else came of this incident, it served to acquaint them with a young seventy who was well grounded in gospel principles and an articulate defender of the faith.

ENDING OF THE WAR AND NEW BEGINNINGS

In August 1945, Bruce was given the only furlough he had received since his induction into the army in March 1942. He and Amelia decided to take a little trip. Bruce's sister Margaret and her husband, Bill Pope, agreed to watch the children. The chosen destination was Yellowstone National Park.

Amelia recalled, "One of our stops on the way was in Idaho Falls to see the newest of the Church's Temples. To our delight we discovered they were having an open house, before it was to be dedicated. We got in the line to go through and as we were waiting to get in, to our surprise and delight my sister Julina Hart, came with a group of Primary Children from her ward in Rexburg, Idaho. She was serving as the Primary President at that time, and so we were able to join with her group and go through the Temple with them. Needless to say she had no idea we would be there but it was a very special experience.

"We decided to stay in a motel there that night and in the morning continue on our way to Yellowstone. As we continued on our trip the next day, when we got to West Yellowstone we were surprised to find a good number of people in front of a good size lodge blowing horns and making a lot of noise, also dancing around and seemingly having a great time. Then to our great delight we learned that Germany had surrendered and World War II, in Europe, had ended. Germany had finally been beaten. What a glorious day it was for everyone. We really enjoyed the rest of our trip."

Our Faith and the Constitution

During his service in the army, Bruce wrote twenty articles on the Constitution of the United States that were published in the *Deseret News* between March 19 and April 10, 1945. The articles, which appeared under his name without reference to his military rank, were both readable and instructive. They considered the genius in the division of power among the legislative, executive, and judicial branches of government and the necessary limits that must exist on each of these branches of government. They showed how the American system of government is not a democracy—for the freedom of minorities is always in peril of the majority in a pure democracy—but rather a representative and constitutional republic. These articles showed how war might necessitate a limiting of the personal freedoms the Constitution guarantees but reminded readers that those freedoms must be immediately returned at the war's end.

The "miracle at Philadelphia," or the story of the framing of the Constitution, Bruce asserted, was followed by another story of equal or surpassing drama. This was the story of its ratification by the states. It will be remembered that the Continental Congress had called upon the state legislatures to send delegates to Philadelphia to revise the Articles of Confederation. The delegates were convinced by James Madison, the Father of the Constitution, that the salvation of our nation rested in their willingness to revise those articles out of existence. Having moved so boldly from their commission, they knew the legislatures that had sent them would likely refuse to ratify the document they had created. Thus, they called for the people to choose delegates to a special convention to either ratify it or reject it. It was agreed that should nine of the states ratify the Constitution, it would thereby be in effect among those nine.

In Massachusetts the vote was 187 for ratification and 168 against. In Virginia, the home of Washington, Jefferson, and

Madison, the vote was 89 to 79 in favor of ratification. The New Hampshire convention was delayed so that men of a more favorable mind-set could be elected, and even then the resolution passed by only ten votes. In New York the matter was headed for certain defeat until news arrived that New Hampshire and Virginia had voted to ratify. Even then, New York ratified it conditionally, with a resolution calling for a second constitutional convention to draft a more acceptable document. Eight of the states that ratified the Constitution did so with the understanding that a Bill of Rights would be added by amendment. Rhode Island and North Carolina chose not to enter the union at that time.

Bruce wove these and other facts of American history into his appeal for the return of Constitutional liberties restricted during the war years. His love of the Constitution had been planted deep within his heart by his father, who cherished that document and its principles as he cherished life itself. As the father declared that all true prophets would stand in its defense, so the son declared that America was "discovered, colonized, and made into a great nation so that the Lord would have a proper place both to restore the gospel and from which to send it forth to all other nations." The freedom to worship provided by the Constitution, Bruce constantly maintained, was "essential to salvation," whereas civil control of religion was "Lucifer's way of enforcing an enduring state of apostasy upon all who were subject to such control." There was no question in his mind that the Founding Fathers of this land were raised up in the providence of a wise God to perform a labor that will bless all who love truth and desire that which is right.

The importance of the Constitution to the Restoration cannot be overstated. At the 1942 October conference, President J. Reuben Clark observed: "You and I have heard all our lives that the time may come when the Constitution may hang by a thread. I do not know whether it is a thread or a small rope by which it now hangs, but I do know that whether it shall live or die is now in the balance." He identified the Constitution as part of our religion "because it is one of those institutions which God has set up for His own purposes . . . set up so that this Church might be established, because under no other government in the world could the Church have been established." After quoting Doctrine and Covenants 101:77–80 relative to the Constitution, President Clark continued: "I suppose you brethren will all know, but I will recall it to your attention, that the Constitution of the United States is the basic law for all of the Americas, or Zion, as it has been defined by the Lord."[2]

WRITING FOR THE DESERET NEWS

In March 1945 President David O. McKay met with Oscar W. McConkie to inquire whether his circumstances were such that he could accept a call the following year to serve as a mission president. There was no hesitancy on Oscar's part in assuring President McKay that he would be able to do so. Oscar hoped that Bruce, upon his release from the military, would take over his law practice. The timing would have been almost perfect because Bruce was discharged from the military a little more than a month before the First Presidency announced his father's appointment. Nevertheless, Bruce had decided not to return to practicing law. One of his strong dislikes was working with the criminal element as city prosecutor. Instead, he hoped to obtain employment as an editorial writer for the *Deseret News*. The newspaper offered him a job as a reporter, which he accepted.

This was a great disappointment to his father, who lost his law practice while he served as a mission president. In fact, his father might have choked when Bruce became a newspaperman. As a city councilman, Oscar had had negative experiences with the press. He observed, "When the truth is spoken, at the judgment bar of God, the press will have full representation in hell."

Bruce's career with the *Deseret News* was short-lived. This may have been due, at least in part, to his doing his job so well. Unbeknownst to him, on July 29, 1946 (Bruce's thirty-first birthday), Earl J. Glade, mayor of Salt Lake City, wrote to Church president George Albert Smith:

"So impressed have I been, during the past several months, with the fine representation the *Deseret News* enjoys in the person and work of Bruce R. McConkie, that I desired to make it a matter of record.

"Entirely at my own instance, it seemed to me I should convey to you how satisfying it is for me, as mayor, to feel that I can repose with absolute safety, the most important of confidences with Bruce and know that he, as a newspaper man, will be guided only by the utmost discretion.

"Although he is doggedly persistent and unrelenting when there is a desired objective in the offing, he always observes the proprieties. This moves us to do every honorable thing we can to help him.

"Bruce's fine legal mind makes us want to counsel with him. We highly value his judgment.

"Added to these traits of good sense, competence and ability, are those other priceless loyalties in personal conduct which we of the church so dearly treasure. How truly well our great institutions might serve us and the world if we all, and our youth especially, would only fully measure up to our well known standards: Bruce does.

"I know how hard Brother Mark E. Petersen is working to establish in the *News* one of the world's most distinctively excellent newspapers, and one fully worthy of the church. In my humble opinion, outstanding young churchmen of the fine leadership qualities of Bruce R. McConkie, can be of great help in winning this objective.

"As one who takes pride in the achievements of our own institutions and our own young people, I am happy this morning to send you this observation and this word of commendation."

It is not to be expected that President George Albert Smith would have remembered a brief visit he had had with a young missionary in Palmyra, New York, a decade earlier, so this letter may well have been his introduction to Bruce. Nor is it to be expected that Mayor Earl J. Glade would remember that he too had met and visited with this young man eleven years earlier at the dedication of the monument on the Hill Cumorah.

9

CALLED AS A SEVENTY
1946 AND 1947

Mother and I did not ask the Lord to put you in the First Council; we just told him you were available if He wanted you.

—Oscar W. McConkie

As Bruce McConkie, a beat reporter for the *Deseret News*, left the City and County Building on Tuesday, May 28, 1946, he crossed to the west side of State Street and headed north, back to the Deseret News Building. In doing so, he passed a relative of his wife by the name of Jensen, who stopped him to inquire if he had heard about the death of John H. Taylor of the First Council of the Seventy. Bruce indicated that he had. His questioner then congratulated him on being the one who would succeed Elder Taylor in that office. This kind of experience repeated itself many times in the next four months as October conference approached.

This was long before members of the First Council of the Seventy were ordained high priests, as they are today, so it was expected that vacancies in that body would be filled by someone holding the office of a seventy. At that time, Bruce was a seventy, serving in the seventies presidency of the Bonneville Stake. This fact, combined with his growing reputation as a strong speaker and one who knew the scriptures, made him—among those who speculated on such things—a viable possibility, despite his being only thirty-one years of age.

The closer they got to conference, the more frequently Bruce and Amelia were told by friends, acquaintances, and even strangers that Bruce was going to fill the vacancy among the Seventy. All he or Amelia could do was either to deflect such observations with what would likely have been thought to be false modesty or to use humor. They chose humor. The frequency of such statements got to the point that when Bruce went home in the evening he would say to Amelia, "Well, we got [number] votes today." Even his fellow reporters and the photographers at the *Deseret News* insisted on taking his picture so they would be ready for the news release when the call was made.

After months of dismissing the possibility that he would be called to such an office, Bruce began to get the sense that it might be true. This feeling was strengthened when Henry Smith, editor of the Church section of the *Deseret News*, asked to interview him to get the biographical data for a story announcing his call, if it became necessary. Bruce declined. Henry insisted, saying it had been hinted to him that the new Seventy might be one of several men, and he thought, in wisdom, that he ought to interview each of them. He had the files of a number of men on his desk before him. In fact, he had already been told of the Brethren's decision, and this was part of his ploy.

"I do not know if it was inspiration," Bruce said, "or just the psychological effect of what had been going on all these weeks before the conference came," but the idea started to form in his mind that he would be called.

October Conference 1946

The first day of conference passed without the general officers being sustained. The second day passed in like manner. Sunday morning, the final day of conference, came and went without their being sustained. "I was home," Amelia recalled, "alone with the children and listening to Conference on the radio. I was as interested as the rest of the Church to know who would really be called to fill that vacancy."

About half an hour before the final session of conference began, the phone rang. Amelia answered it. "The unmistakable voice of President David O. McKay inquired, 'Is Bruce R. McConkie there?'"

She answered, "I am sorry. He is not here. He is at Conference in the Tabernacle with the *Deseret News* reporters."

"Thank you very much," came the response.

"Then for the first time," she said, "I began to wonder if there was some truth to the rumors that had been going around. I checked to see if four-and-a-half-month-old Mary was still napping peacefully and the other children occupied. Then I turned on the radio again and practically glued my ear to it. It was almost the last item on the Conference agenda that day, before the General Authorities were sustained."

Bruce was standing at the press table in the Tabernacle. As the conference proceeded, he took notes of the talks, from which would be written the press account that would appear in the *Deseret News*. A few minutes before the two o'clock session of conference was to begin, Joseph Anderson, clerk of the conference, walked down the pulpit stairs, leaned over the banister, and whispered in Bruce's ear, "President McKay would like to see you."

Bruce recalled, "I knew instantly what was wanted, and so felt somewhat overwhelmed as I followed Brother Anderson back up the stairs. President McKay was standing on the top platform. He said: 'Come with me, I want to talk to you.' I followed him out into the room marked General Authorities. We went in, passing Elder A. E. Bowen coming out, who smiled, shook my hand, and said, 'Hello, Bruce,' and then President McKay locked the door.

"He took me by the hand, led me over to a chair, had me sit down, and still holding my hand, he sat on the edge of a small table, and said:

"'Brother McConkie, I have been delegated by the First Presidency to interview you. Your name will be submitted to the Conference this afternoon to fill the vacancy in the First Council of Seventy. Do you know of any reason why you cannot serve?'

"'No, sir, I do not,' Bruce replied.

"'Are you morally clean?' he asked.

"'Yes, sir, I am.'"

In rapid succession a series of questions followed, each allowing only enough time for a quick response:

"You have a testimony of the gospel?"

"Yes."

"You know that Joseph Smith was a prophet?"

"Yes."

"Are you in harmony with the General Authorities of the Church as at present constituted?

"Yes."

"You are the unanimous selection of the First Presidency, the Council of the Twelve, and the First Council of the Seventy," President McKay said. And then he added, "It is the voice of the Lord. You go back to your place; we will not go out together."

Bruce responded, "Thank you very much, President McKay. I will go out and go down the stairs and come up alone at the press table."

He had to force himself to concentrate on the talks being given throughout the session so he would have the necessary notes to report on them for the newspaper. The names of the general authorities were not presented for a sustaining vote until all who had been invited to speak in that session had done so. After concluding remarks by President George Albert Smith, President McKay presented the names of the general authorities for a sustaining vote. When he came to the First Council of the Seventy, he read six names: Levi Edgar Young, Antoine R. Ivins, Richard L. Evans, Oscar A. Kirkham, Seymour Dilworth Young, and Milton R. Hunter. Then he paused and with some emphasis said, "Bruce R. McConkie."

After the sustaining vote was taken, a letter from Church Patriarch Joseph F. Smith to the First Presidency was read, suggesting that his health was such that he could not continue functioning in that office. His release was announced, and the official business of the conference was concluded.

After the amens, people immediately began to crowd around Bruce to offer their congratulations.

Oscar McConkie, who had been sitting with the mission presidents, went over to his son, took him by the hand, and kissed him. Oscar did not say a word. A few moments later Bruce's mother, whom he had not previously seen at the conference, walked up to him. She was crying. "I kissed her," Bruce recalled, but "she did not speak." He then went up to the second pulpit where five members of the First Council were assembled. Each congratulated him. Levi Edgar Young was not present because of illness.

Matthew Cowley, who had been called to the Twelve in the October conference of the previous year and who had spent much time in bed with heart trouble since that time, said, "Don't let it get you so emotionally upset that it puts you to bed."

Joseph F. Merrill said, "I knew it was to be you, but I couldn't say anything when I talked to you the other day."

Joseph Fielding Smith came down and congratulated and kissed him. Bruce then went up to the top pulpit, where Aunt Jessie greeted him and kissed him. She was crying.

President George Albert Smith approached him. Bruce put out his hand and said, "I am Bruce McConkie." President Smith said,

"We have a lot of work for you to do. You will have to be good to live up to all the good things I have heard about you."

Bruce responded, "With the help of the Lord, I will."

President Smith indicated that Bruce would be notified when he would be set apart. Bruce went back into the general authorities' room to have his picture taken by the *Tribune* photographer and to give reporter Clarence Barker his biographical information. The last general authority he saw as he left the Tabernacle was Bishop Marvin O. Ashton. Bishop Ashton passed away that same night.

Bruce walked north on State Street to where he had parked his car and drove through City Creek Canyon to his home. There he was greeted by Amelia and the children. "She was thrilled," said Bruce, and she conveyed messages of congratulations from his bishop and stake president. Many others also phoned.

Shortly after conference was over, Joseph Fielding Smith and Aunt Jessie stopped by. He was delighted with Bruce's call and told his daughter that "he knew nothing about it until Bruce's name was presented to the Twelve and First Presidency for their approval."

"What do I do now?" Amelia asked.

"Just keep your feet on the ground," her father replied.

Bruce talked in the Monument Park Ward that evening on the subject of testimony and then taught the study group he and Amelia were members of on the subject of the Judgment.

It was midnight before he and Amelia got to bed. Both were overwhelmed but profoundly grateful for the opportunity that had come to serve.

Taking Up the Mantle

Early the next morning, Bruce went down to the *Deseret News* office to type up his account of President George F. Richards's conference talk. Mark E. Petersen indicated his pleasure at Bruce's call and told him that the First Presidency had directed that he continue

Called as a Seventy, 1946 and 1947

First Council of the Seventy, October 1946. Back: Elders S. Dilworth Young, Oscar A. Kirkham, Milton R. Hunter, and Bruce R. McConkie. Front: Elders Antoine R. Ivins, Levi Edgar Young, and Richard L. Evans.

to write editorials for the *News*. He offered to take Bruce with him on his stake conference assignment that weekend.

Bruce also spent an hour with Antoine R. Ivins, who gave him much practical advice and showed him his office in the Church Office Building (now called the Church Administration Building).

On Monday evening, October 7, 1946, a person could buy a copy of the *Deseret News* from a newsboy in downtown Salt Lake City for five cents. Although the headline that day announced the death of Bishop Ashton, Elder McConkie's call to the Seventy was the lead story on the front page. The article noted that he was not only the youngest general authority at the time but also the youngest man to be called to the First Council of the Seventy since B. H. Roberts's call in 1888. The writer's math was a little off, as Elder McConkie was actually four months younger than Elder

Roberts was when he was called to that office. Bruce was described as a "man of imposing appearance" who had been "prominent and active in many community affairs," an accolade normally reserved for obituaries. The lead editorial welcomed him to his new office, stating, "He is humble, he is strong, he is a splendid student, he is a powerful speaker."

On Tuesday, Bruce moved his books into office 204 in the Church Administration Building. He met President J. Reuben Clark that day across the street at ZCMI. President Clark said, "Maintain your stability and your orthodoxy." He added, "I am happy for you and for your father, and the Lord will bless you."

President Clark and Oscar McConkie were close personal friends and both members of the Twentieth Ward. Often they would meet and walk together to and from their downtown offices, a distance much too short for the length and breadth of their discussions.

On Wednesday, Bruce visited with his parents before they returned to their assignment in the California Mission. His father said, "Mother and I did not ask the Lord to put you in the First Council; we just told him you were available if he wanted you."

On Thursday, Bruce met for the first time with the Council of the Seventy in the temple. About eleven o'clock, President Clark knocked on the door and asked President Levi Edgar Young if the Seventy would come to meet with the First Presidency and the Twelve so that Elder McConkie could be set apart.

Nine of the Twelve were seated in a semicircle in front of the First Presidency. President David O. McKay and three of the Twelve were on assignment or ill. President George Albert Smith spoke for about twenty minutes on various subjects. He counseled obedience and prayer with promises of eternal life and joy. He said that when any man present wrote anything as doctrine, great care should be taken to be sure it was correct, and that if there was any doubt, it should be left unwritten. He gave this caution because people would think that what they wrote was the voice of the Church.

President Smith then said he had not had opportunity to talk to Bruce and asked him if there was any reason that he should not be ordained. Bruce responded, "No, sir, there is not."

President Smith instructed Bruce to continue writing for the *Deseret News* and told him that what he wrote would be subject to much greater criticism than it had been previously because of his new calling. He also charged him to strive, along with Mark Petersen, to have faithful Latter-day Saints working there.

"Seated in that council meeting, I felt the calm and joy of the Spirit of the Lord as I have never felt it," Bruce recounted. "It seemed as though President Smith was speaking the word of the Lord, or even as though the Lord himself was there before us telling us his will."

Bruce R. McConkie was then set apart by President George Albert Smith. All seventeen general authorities present stood in the circle. President Smith expressly "ordained" him and set him apart. He promised him joy and blessings through service. Some discussion followed the blessing in view of the word *ordain*, because apparently Levi Edgar Young and S. Dilworth Young had been ordained and the others only set apart. President Smith said that men were ordained to the First Council of the Seventy because it was a lifelong job but that they were set apart to their position of presidency in that quorum. President Clark explained that in giving such a blessing "it was the intent that counted."

On Friday, President Clark called Bruce to his office to instruct him. He told Elder McConkie that he had never heard him speak but that he had heard from his own family and others that he was a good speaker. The Church needed good speakers, he said. He applauded Bruce's interest in the gospel and counseled that on many matters there was more than one opinion and warned against forcing his views on others. This did not apply, he said, to matters of the so-called higher criticism and added that Bruce was entirely right on the matter of the Sunday School manual, which was full of higher criticism. He also told Bruce that he would "get sat on": where he was wrong, he should correct himself; and where he was not, he should not worry about the rebuffs. As to Bruce's writing, President Clark counseled him to be plain and to avoid, in the language of Elder James E. Talmage, the "witchery of words."

That weekend Bruce attended his first stake conference as a general authority with Elder Mark E. Petersen, in Blackfoot, Idaho. This was a good learning experience for the new member of the First Council of the Seventy. On the way home they stopped in Pocatello, finding Elder Joseph F. Merrill of the Quorum of the Twelve in need of a ride back to Salt Lake.

Some months later, when he received his copy of the October 1946 Conference Report, Bruce put his name on the outside cover, read it, and underlined a single sentence in the talk given by Elder Harold B. Lee: "I came to a night, some years ago, when on my bed, I realized that before I could be worthy of the high place to which I had been called, I must love and forgive every soul that walked the earth, and in that time I came to know and I received a peace and a direction, and a comfort, and an inspiration, that told me things to come and gave me impressions that I knew were from a divine source."[1]

So it was that Bruce McConkie was drawn into the life and labor that would be his for nearly forty years.

The next week he filled a conference assignment with S. Dilworth Young, traveling to Malad, Idaho. On Wednesday of that week he set apart missionaries for the first time—thirteen in number, one of whom was his younger brother Oscar, who would serve in the New England States Mission. At the recommendation of Oscar's stake president, Bruce also ordained him a seventy.

Called as a Seventy, 1946 and 1947

Through the years he set apart thousands of missionaries. Each received a blessing tailored by the spirit of revelation to his or her own particular needs and circumstances.

At a report meeting that week, President George F. Richards of the Twelve told Bruce it was all right for him to attend conferences with someone else for a few weeks, but that was all. President Richards said they wanted him to be "a work horse, not a dog under the wheels."

The following weekend he accompanied Elder Spencer W. Kimball to the Timpanogos Stake conference in Pleasant Grove, Utah. William Walsh joined them, representing the Welfare Committee. Bruce was excused from the afternoon session to substitute for President McKay, who was ill, at a meeting in the University Ward in Provo. The meeting honored six members of the ward who had served in general board assignments. He spoke for fifty minutes on what would become his favorite subject—celestial marriage. Of his experience with Elder Kimball, Bruce said, "It is a joy to travel with him; he is an apostle indeed. He is a man of great inspiration and humility, and he also has a keen sense of humor." He noted that Elder Kimball was "one of the most devoted men I have ever met."

The next week Elder McConkie soloed for the first time, in the East Millcreek Stake. The stake president was LaMont Gundersen, who impressed Elder McConkie as being a man of ability, integrity, and devotion. The spirit of the conference was one of testimony and expression of gratitude for the blessings of the gospel. President Gundersen told the congregation in the concluding session that in his opinion it had been the best conference ever held in that stake.

On November 7, Elder McConkie, according to appointment, met with President George Albert Smith for about twenty-five minutes. This was the first real meeting between the two men. Bruce was given general instruction relative to his duties and was told that when he spoke or acted to be sure he was right and then go ahead. Most of the instruction centered on Bruce's being an editorial writer for the *Deseret News*. President Smith expressed concern over an editorial Bruce had written about the actions of a city judge. (What President Smith would not have known, and Bruce would not have said, was that he had appeared before this judge a number of times as the city prosecutor and had been treated unfairly.) "Because she slipped once, we should not overlook all the good she has done," President Smith said, and instructed him to go and make things right with her. "It takes a big man to say 'I'm wrong,'" President Smith said. As they parted, Elder McConkie assured the Church president that he "would follow his counsel in all things."

In his biography of George Albert Smith, Francis Gibbons remarked about this meeting: "In selecting Bruce R. McConkie as Elder Taylor's successor, the Prophet came close to crossing the barrier of nepotism about which he was so sensitive. Elder McConkie's wife, Amelia, is one of the daughters of President Joseph Fielding Smith, which made the new General Authority a quasi cousin of President George Albert Smith. However, because of the remoteness of the relationship and the lack of any blood ties, only President Smith's most ardent detractors would accuse him of nepotism on this account. And, there is an implication that President Smith was unaware that Bruce McConkie was married to a Smith, or, at least, that the Prophet's prior relationship with him was not close. 'Bruce McKonkey came in office,' President Smith wrote on November 7, 1946, 'and I talked to him about his responsibility.' The Smith clan was sufficiently large that the Prophet could not have been expected to know all the in-laws of the various branches of the family, nor the correct spelling of their names. But even if a case for nepotism could be made here, one might ask, 'so what?' As it turned out, this obscure young man eventually became a member of the Twelve and one of the most prolific writers in the Church, exerting an influence far beyond that entailed in his ecclesiastical callings."[2]

RETURNING TO HIS ROOTS

In November, Elder McConkie had a conference assignment in the Mount Graham Stake in eastern Arizona. At that time the most convenient way to get there was by train, which required his going first to Los Angeles. He left Salt Lake at midnight on Thursday evening and arrived in Los Angeles at 4:15 the next afternoon. He was met at the train station by his father and mother and youngest brother, William. They took him to the mission home for dinner and returned him to the train station to catch an eight o'clock train for Bowie, Arizona. "Mother told me to get my eyes examined and buy a new hat," he noted. "Dad said after my call he said to President Smith: 'I am glad you have taken Bruce under your wing,' and President Smith replied, 'When the Lord really wants a man, he finds a way to get him.'"

He arrived in Bowie at 2:20 the following afternoon and waited an hour for the local train to Safford. When the conference was concluded, he went on to El Paso, Texas, to visit the mission headquarters. He spent Thanksgiving Day there writing editorials for the *Deseret News*. Friday he left for a stake conference in Colonia Dublán, Mexico. On Monday he visited Colonia Juárez, which he was particularly pleased to do because his great-grandfather Lemuel Hardison Redd was buried there, and his grandfather George W. McConkie was buried not far from there, in Colonia Pacheco. They were both among those who had sought refuge there during the persecutions over plural marriage.

Of the stakes in the colonies, Bruce noted: "Members of the Church there are somewhat isolated from the world and do not have the influences to combat that are generally found elsewhere.

In consequence of this and because of strong leadership the Stake is outstanding in all activities, and probably leads the Church in most. For instance, their sacrament meeting attendance is 67 percent as compared to a Church average of 20 percent, and all Aaronic Priesthood activity for those under 21 is 70 percent as compared to a Church average of 38 percent."

Work Habits

The new member of the First Council of the Seventy responded to President George F. Richards's challenge to be "a work horse, rather than a dog under the wheels" with what might seem excessive zeal. On February 2, 1947, four months after his call, Bruce spent time with his family, that being the first day he had taken off after his ordination besides Christmas and New Year's Day. "Otherwise it has been seven days a week every week." Not infrequently he was, at least to his knowledge, the only man in the office building. Traveling was time consuming and tedious. Air travel had not come into its own, so the rule of thumb was this: If you are going east, you take the train; if you are going west, you take a car. Conference assignments were organized so that the Brethren could share rides. The one going to the most distant point would drop the others off along the way and then pick them up on his return. When he traveled by train, Bruce used the time to write editorials for the *Deseret News* and to study the scriptures. Every minute was captured and put to work.

First Conference Talk

Friday afternoon, April 4, 1947, Elder Bruce R. McConkie spoke for the first time in a general conference of the Church. He bore a powerful testimony of Christ, of the Prophet Joseph Smith, and of George Albert Smith as the living oracle of the Church. He noted that the source of testimony must be the revelation of the

Holy Ghost and that such a testimony comes to all who abide the law upon which testimony rests. To receive a testimony of the saving principles of the gospel, he said, we must first desire to know the truth; if we do not desire it, it will never be manifest to us. We must then study the principles of the gospel, for "the Lord does not pour a testimony into a vacuum."[3] We must also live the principles involved if we are to come to the knowledge of their truth, and we must seek the confirmation of those truths through prayer.

Elder McConkie concluded his remarks with an expression of appreciation for his call to the First Council of Seventy and the opportunity to labor with the Saints. In a statement that would become common to him, he declared, "There is nothing in this world that I would rather do than have the privilege of preaching the gospel and of devoting such time and abilities as the Lord may bless me with to the building up of his kingdom."[4]

He was satisfied with his effort. He recorded: "I used no notes whatsoever; not a scrap of paper in front of me. Bore my own testimony; considered the principles by obedience to which any person can gain such a testimony." It also pleased him that when President J. Reuben Clark spoke to an overflow meeting of seventies in Barrett Hall that evening, he quoted Bruce's statement about the Lord's not pouring a testimony into a vacuum.

Attendant to this conference, a meeting of general authorities, stake presidents, and bishops was held Monday morning in the upper room of the Salt Lake Temple. The meeting lasted from 9:30 A.M. to 2:00 P.M. The Twelve passed the sacrament, and the First Presidency spoke. Elder McConkie described it as the "most blunt meeting" he had ever attended, as instruction was given on such matters as giving temple recommends and handling moral transgressions. In all he described the conference as the most edifying he had ever attended and spoke of his renewed desire to grow spiritually.

Between sessions of conference, Bruce was in his office working

Elders Milton R. Hunter, A. Theodore Tuttle, Paul H. Dunn, S. Dilworth Young, Hartman Rector Jr., Bruce R. McConkie, and Loren C. Dunn

on editorials for the *Deseret News*. On Sunday, he shared the lunch Amelia had made for him with her father. That evening he and Amelia hosted his family, including his grandmother Lucinda Redd, at dinner. He was back in the office that evening by seven, where he worked until 10:15 P.M. on a conference editorial and articles on the new general authorities who had been called, so he could meet the deadline for Monday's paper.

As to stake conferences, the pressure was as constant as a mortgage payment. At a dinner one evening, he and Amelia sat beside Joseph L. Wirthlin and Thorpe B. Isaacson of the Presiding Bishopric. They talked about their experiences at stake conferences. Bruce asked, "Are the first ten the hardest?" Bishop Wirthlin responded, "No. The hardest conference is always the one coming up."

Along with his duties as a Seventy, which included his writing editorials for the *Deseret News*, came an endless array of invitations to speak. Bruce's natural inclination was to accept more of these than he should. That was in part an expression of his sense of duty but also part of his innate drive to develop the ability to think on

Called as a Seventy, 1946 and 1947

Elder McConkie served for twenty-six years as a member of the First Council of the Seventy

his feet, rely on the Spirit, and speak with power and effect. Following the pattern established in his missionary journal, he occasionally evaluated the talks he gave. One such note reads: "Sunday, Dec. 29, 1947. Came down to the office and worked for several hours in the morning. Attended a 5 P.M. sacrament meeting in the Marlborough Ward where I spoke for 65 minutes on What Think Ye of Christ. I had no inspiration. Never have I labored so hard to bring forth some light on gospel principles. I just couldn't tune myself up with the Spirit.

"At 7 P.M. went to my own Ward, the Monument Park, where I spoke for 45 minutes on the Testimony of Christ, and was able to tune myself up so that the Spirit was with me.

"This Sunday has witnessed to me the need for continual reliance on the Lord in my sermons, because unless the Spirit is with a speaker, no matter what he may say it will not carry over into the hearts of men as it otherwise would."

During the first twenty-five years of their marriage, Amelia and Bruce found little time to vacation. The best they could do was to pack the children in the car and take them along occasionally on a conference assignment. In the fall of 1946, Bruce was assigned to a stake conference in Monticello, an assignment that inevitably became a family event. He was, I am sure, delighted, as this would be the first time in ten years that he had been back to the home of his youth. The plan was, of course, to stay with his grandmother Redd.

Though but seven years of age, I remember the trip, as it was the first I had ever been on. Not having had much experience traveling in a car, I got quite car sick on the way down, adding to everyone's pleasure, but I had the good fortune of falling asleep for most of the return ride. I remember how pleased I was to wake up and discover that sleep had excused me from the tedium of a journey that otherwise gave new meaning to "endless and eternal" for a little boy.

While at Grandmother Redd's, I was told not to get into the wheat silos, which I did anyway. When asked about it, I gave an answer that was somewhat short of the truth. I got caught when Mother insisted I take a nap. I lay down on the living room couch, and grain came flowing out of my pockets. Mother, Grandmother McConkie, and Grandmother Redd were all present, and I could not have been more embarrassed had the three of them caught me naked. Mother said, "Well, I think we know where you have been." To my relief, nothing else was said about the matter.

There were a lot of matters about which little was said. My father made no effort to enshrine Monticello as the place of his youth. He did not take us around to tell us where various things happened during his growing-up years. It would have been both fun and interesting had he done so, but such things were not an issue

Called as a Seventy, 1946 and 1947

with him. He spoke little about himself or his personal experiences. He was a man with a message, and he did not want the message confused with peculiarities about the messenger. Such details as his shoe size or where he grew up were matters he considered of little importance; what was important was a testimony that Joseph Smith is the great revelator of Christ for this dispensation. Without a testimony of Joseph Smith, he often said, no one can have a testimony of Christ that leads to salvation. Indeed, in telling the story of Bruce McConkie's life, should we wander far from its central purpose, our understanding of the man would be something like that of the child who, preoccupied with the pebbles on the beach, fails to consider the ocean and its tides.

10

THINGS GREAT AND SMALL
1948 TO 1961

Who am I to tell someone how to hold a high council meeting? I've never been to one. I just teach doctrine.

—Bruce R. McConkie

When Mark Lewis joined the Bruce McConkie clan in June 1948, he was welcomed by Vivian (eight), Joseph (seven), Stanford (four), and Mary (two). Things were getting a bit crowded in the little home on Michigan Avenue. The solution was a move to the country, or at least that's what we kids thought it was. In 1948 anything more than three miles from downtown Salt Lake was considered rural living. The mascot for Granite High on Thirty-Third South was a farmer, and to venture much farther toward Provo made you a Jordan High beet digger. So it was that we took up country living in a two-story home at the bottom of Lambourne Avenue on about Nineteenth East and Thirty-Second South.

Our new home came with a number of problems about which the seller had been less than forthcoming, but it had two redeeming features. It was a great place for playing hide-and-seek, and the neighborhood was full of good kids to play with. Here three more children eventually joined our ranks: Rebecca, Stephen, and Sara.

Things Great and Small, 1948 to 1961

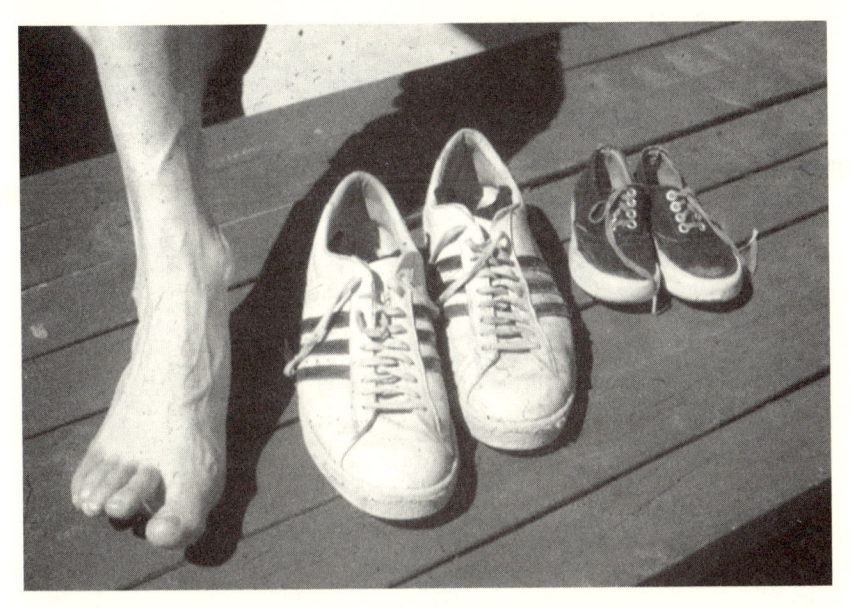

Things great and small

Here Mother was called as Relief Society president—a position from which, as we recall, she was never released—and Dad had a good seven-and-a-half-mile walk to work. We had a garden area the size of a building lot with irrigation rights and numerous fruit trees: peach, apricot, pear, and plum trees in the backyard, and apple, almond, and walnut trees at the side of the house or in the front yard. What we didn't have was a big old cherry tree, but the Harts, who lived just up the street, had several of them and didn't mind us kids taking what we needed for survival.

THE NEIGHBORHOOD GANG

Two houses and a vacant lot up the street from our home was the home of the Rudds, who moved there in 1956. They had a large family like ours, and soon a number of friendships were formed. The father, Glen Rudd, was the kind of guy who loves people—it did not matter what age, size, or color; if he met you, he was going to make a friend of you. The mother, Marva, though quiet and shy by nature, was a darling lady. It wasn't long before the heads of our households were fast friends. Other than their relatives and the people my parents met within the various study groups they belonged to, they had no social life. This, however, was all about to change.

Across the street from the Rudds were the Palmers, and up the street two more houses with both a pool table and the cherry trees were the Harts. Behind the Harts' home on a cul-de-sac leading off Thirty-Third South were the Paulsens. Like the Rudds, they all had large families, and whatever spare time that jobs and Church allowed them, they were together. A trust developed in this group so that Dad could be himself without the concern of being quoted or constantly asked questions or becoming the source of stories to be passed on to others. Glen Rudd recalled, "Many people thought Bruce was stiff and a bit arrogant, a kind of know-it-all, but he wasn't. He was one of the sweetest, kindest individuals you could ever meet; he just didn't know how to relax at the pulpit. Away from the pulpit he was wonderful. He would come to our house and just visit for an hour on a day when we were all home. I remember one day my wife was out in the kitchen and he came in, went in on the front room floor and lay down—he nearly stretched from wall to wall—and kicked off his shoes and started yelling, 'I'm starving to death! I'm hungry! Marva, Marva, help a hungry man,' so she'd take him a drink of something and he'd say, 'More, more.' He'd lie there, kick his feet, and shout. At first Marva wasn't sure what to think, but she quickly realized that he was just a big kid.

"He became the ringleader in organizing the neighborhood," Glen continued. "In the summer when the evenings were long, we would often have spontaneous parties or get-togethers. Once on Memorial Day, about five o'clock in the morning—Marva and I were sleeping soundly—the doorbell started ringing. We could hear someone pounding on the door, yelling like crazy. Marva said, 'That's either Bruce McConkie or some drunk.'

Things Great and Small, 1948 to 1961

Bruce and Amelia in a less formal moment

"We got up in our pajamas and ran to the door, and there were Bruce and Amelia. He pulled me outside and said, 'Come on, we're going to Finn Paulsen's for breakfast.' We wanted to get dressed. He said, 'No, just come as you are.' Finally he condescended to allow us to dress, and off we went to rouse the others in the neighborhood before presenting ourselves at the Paulsens', who of course had no idea we were coming. A wonderful breakfast would follow. Everyone got a chance to host such a breakfast or late night dinner."

This group enjoyed doing things together so much they vacationed together in the summer. Colter Bay, near Jackson Hole, Wyoming, and Bear River, in northern Utah, became favorite spots. When Finn Paulsen became the president of the stake, the group invited his counselors and their families to join them. They, too, had large families, so one summer at Colter Bay there were 110 in their group. When their campout included a weekend, Dad would always be the Sunday speaker.

"We had a big backyard," Glen recalled, "and lots of yard parties and the whole neighborhood—eight or ten families—would come. I remember we had a hula hoop contest, which Bruce and Amelia were determined to win, but they just weren't any good.

"I used to have terrible migraine headaches," Glen said, "and Marva would call for Bruce when I was really down. I was at his house one day and we were just talking when I began to get really sick. I got so I couldn't see and couldn't walk so Bruce took me home. Then I got violently ill. I began to perspire and was terribly sick. I remember he gave me a blessing, and I was just soaking wet. He put me in the car and took me to the doctor. He stayed in the doctor's office. I had already taken what pills I had. When I got to this doctor's office, he gave me a drug that I had a bad reaction to. The doctor and Bruce spent more than half an hour holding me on a table while I perspired. I lost ten pounds in this attack. Bruce said, after it finally left, 'I thought you were going to die.' He always was worried about my health, and so was Finn. I was having these really vicious headaches about once a month or maybe every three weeks, and they worried a lot. I outlived both of them and have never felt better. I realized what a very compassionate, sweet, lovely man Bruce was when he would come to the house and spend sometimes an hour or two with my wife trying to help me through some of those bad times.

"Bruce loved his wife," Glen continued. "I've never seen a man more affectionate to a wife than he was. He liked to have her by him all the time. Because of them, Joseph Fielding Smith and Aunt Jessie were out here at our house a lot and down at Bruce's and Amelia's. She would play the piano, and they would sing for us."

Mickey Hart, who owned a music store in Sugar House, wrote music that Aunt Jessie sang. Often when we wanted her to sing, she would have one of us kids run up the street and get Mickey to come down and play for her.

Glen Rudd remembered an occasion when he, Bruce, and Finn Paulsen, who was the stake president at the time, were together at a fathers and sons outing. As they stood looking at the various mountain peaks, Bruce pointed to the highest and said, "We ought to climb that."

"You can't do that," Glen countered.

"Sure we can," came the immediate reply.

"I'll bet you a T-bone steak dinner that you can't get to the top of that mountain," Glen retorted.

"Within five minutes, Bruce and Finn were off," Glen recalled. "They didn't have hiking boots, a canteen, or anything but the crazy confidence that they were going to get to the top of that mountain. I was worried sick. I figured that if anything happened to them it would be my fault. Finally, I saw them halfway up that mountain, and they took something with them, so they could signal me. I spent one of the worst mornings of my life waiting to see if they were going to get to the top of that peak without killing themselves. Finally I saw them waving from the top of the mountain. It took them three hours to get up there and three hours to get back. Here I was with all these kids on the outing, and they went up there. It was the highest peak we could see.

"When they came back, I tried to talk myself out of the bet, but Bruce said, 'No, sir, we're going out to dinner. We're going to take our wives, and you're going to pay for it.'

"A night was chosen, and we and our wives went to the Hotel Utah, where they ordered the biggest steaks on the menu. I paid through the nose."

When I was about nine or ten, I went with Dad and Elder Milton R. Hunter on a conference assignment to the Little Big Horn Stake in Wyoming. We spent the night en route in a cabin at

Bruce and Amelia

Yellowstone Park. The only source of heat in the cabin was a wood stove. The catch was that the Forest Service forbade visitors to gather wood. Visitors could, however, purchase wood from them. The cost was 75 cents for the amount of wood that could be carried in one arm. This annoyed both men, but neither of them wanted to be cold all night. They decided that Elder Hunter would stack as much wood as possible onto one of Dad's arms. They went about their task with some zeal. It was something of a sight to see Elder Hunter standing on his tiptoes reaching up to place the last few logs on the top of the pile Dad was holding. The two of them felt quite proud of themselves when they saw the astonished look on the ranger's face as he took their three quarters. The next morning they still had a good stack of wood left. It irked the two of them because they realized that the Forest Service would simply reclaim it and sell it again.

THE DEATH OF HIS BROTHER

In July 1953 James Jr., the son of Dad's brother James, contracted polio and became dangerously ill. James Sr. gave him a blessing rebuking the disease. Nevertheless, his life seemed to hang in the balance for some days. Granddad Oscar McConkie, who could not remain idle on such matters, boarded a plane for the first time in his life and made his way to Minneapolis to add his faith to that of his sons. The extended family united themselves in fasting and prayer and the blessings given were honored. James Jr. enjoyed a miraculous recovery.

Within days it was discovered that James Sr. had been attacked by the same vicious disease. Again the united prayers of the McConkie and Wirthlin families ascended to heaven, and again Oscar made his way to the bedside of an afflicted son. Great spiritual energy was expended, and blessings of faith were given. Indeed, three faithful priesthood holders had each in turn laid their hands on James's head and given the promise that his life would be spared. His father sought in blessing him to affirm that promise, but the Spirit would not consent. Days of wrestling with the Spirit followed, and finally permission was granted by the Spirit to give a blessing with such a promise. Still James's life hung in the balance, and the doctors despaired.

Notwithstanding the blessings and promises given him, James McConkie passed away on Friday, August 21, 1953. As my grandfather related the story to me, in the very instant in which James passed away, by the authority of his priesthood Oscar commanded the spirit to return to its body. Subsequent to this, while importuning the Lord on the shores of Lake Harriet, Oscar heard the Spirit speak to him, saying, "James has never disobeyed you. He will not do so now, but I need him." "Take him," was the response. Within the hour he was taken.

Realizing that in his prayers he had not asked the Lord that His will be done, Oscar now did so. He then went before the Lord and formally "revoked every promise" he had made and withdrew all of his petitions to the Lord and those made by others in James's behalf if they did not conform to the Lord's will. "I asked only," he said, "what was in accordance with the divine will."

James McConkie was a man of musical genius. He had earned a master's degree in music at the age of nineteen, received his doctorate in the same field from Columbia University in New York City, and spent two years at the Sorbonne in Paris. He was professor of music at the University of Minneapolis at the time of his death at age thirty-five. As a young man, he had been promised by his father in a father's blessing that he would write the greatest music ever written.

Not understanding how James's death accorded with the promises that had been given his son relative to the music he would write, Oscar returned again to Lake Harriet, where he was told, "You have misunderstood, for you have supposed that all these things should come to him while he lived upon the earth. But behold, all men must die." He was also told that James would not lose any of the blessings that he had been promised.

At James's funeral, Henry D. Moyle of the First Presidency said that James died and went to the spirit world, where he was told of the promises that had been given him at the hands of the priesthood. He was told that those promises would be honored if he wanted them to be, but there was a special need for him there. Oscar noted in his journal that his sons Bruce, Brit, and Oscar Jr. had each independently told him the same thing. He mentioned this to Elder Harold B. Lee, who after a night of prayer and deliberation, affirmed that it was the case. In his remarks at the funeral, President J. Reuben Clark spoke with some feeling and said, "The Lord never allowed our faith to interfere with his work." President David O. McKay also spoke briefly, saying that he had never been at a service in which the veil was so thin. He wept repeatedly and affirmed the verity of what the other speakers had said.

A seal was placed on these events some years later at a general conference when the congregation stood to sing a hymn. At that time a vision was opened to Dad in which he saw his brother James leading a great choir in what he understood to be a conference of the Church in the world of spirits.

A Missionary Son

I left home after graduation from high school to attend Brigham Young University. One of the motivating factors was to get away from my dad's haircuts. I had never been to a barber in my life—Dad had some gifts, but I didn't think cutting hair was one of them. I took a lot of good-natured ribbing from my classmates at Olympus High every time he got the clippers out. Now when I see kids running around with their now-fashionable bowl haircuts, I realize he was just ahead of his time.

Before the end of my freshman year at BYU, I started to get a sense that I was going on a mission that summer. This was a time when missionaries were not being sent out at age nineteen. I had just turned nineteen. People asked me, "Now, what are you going to do this summer?" I would answer, "Oh, I'm going on a mission."

Actually it was Mother, not Dad, who first planted in my mind the idea of going on a mission. While I was just a little guy playing with the neighborhood kids, I learned that they were getting an allowance. I wasn't. I immediately marched home to make my demands on Mother. "I want an allowance," I announced.

"What's an allowance?" Mother innocently asked. With great patience I explained the concept to her. I was obviously convincing, because she got her purse and gave a nickel to me. I was proudly marching out of the house to show my newly obtained wealth to my buddies when Mother called me back. She said, "I'm going to give you another nickel," which she did, and then she had me put one nickel into my bank. "From now on," she said, "we will have you save half of all you earn for your mission." I had no idea what a mission was, but I knew that if it was important enough to save half my earnings for, it must be important.

When I arrived home from BYU in the spring of 1960, Dad said, "Now, son, get out and get a job." I replied, "Dad, I want to go on a mission." He said, "You can't go on a mission." I insisted, "I want to go on a mission." He said, "Get out and get a job." That was on a Friday; the missionary committee met on Tuesdays. Tuesday morning at ten o'clock he called me at home and asked, "Would you like to go on a mission?" I said, "I'd like to go." He said, "When can you be ready to go?" I answered, "Oh, by the end of the week." He replied, "I'll arrange it." Dad told me later that he'd talked to President Henry D. Moyle, who headed the missionary committee, and told him, "I've got a nineteen-year-old son who's just as smart as any of these twenty-year-olds, and I'd like to send him on a mission." President Moyle said, "Send him!"

Dad wanted to make sure I was processed and everything taken care of by the next Tuesday so President Moyle could not forget his promise. Within twenty-four hours I had interviews with my bishop, stake president and a general authority, which was the requirement in those days. I met with Elder S. Dilworth Young, who was famous for his interviews. No stones were left unturned. He inquired about every possible transgression, reaching back to the premortal life. The only thing I could think of to confess to was having helped myself to the neighbor's cherries. To this he responded, "Cherries don't count." Afterwards, he went to my father's office and reported to him. Then I had my physical—all within a twenty-four-hour period. Within a week, I was in the mission home.

In the meantime, a number of people became involved in the question of where I ought to be assigned. Glen Rudd, who worked in Church Welfare and often traveled with the Brethren to their conference assignments, had been a close friend of our family over the years. I had worked in his yard many times, and he'd spent a lot of time telling me about his experiences as a missionary in New Zealand. Now he said, "Joseph, how'd you like to go to New Zealand?"

I said, "Oh, that'd be wonderful."

He said, "I'll arrange it. I'll be with President Moyle on a conference assignment Sunday. I'll be with him until 1:00 A.M. Tuesday morning, and I'll tell him to send you to New Zealand."

On Saturday we went to visit my grandfather Joseph Fielding Smith to announce that I was going on a mission. As we approached his door, my father said to me, "Be very careful what you say to your grandfather."

"Why?" I asked.

"Because he doesn't approve of nineteen-year-old missionaries" was the response.

When the talk started about my going on a mission, Aunt Jessie said, "How would you like to go to Japan?"

I didn't want to go to Japan, but I didn't know how to tell her. So I said, "That'd be fine."

She started working on Granddad to see that I was sent to Japan. All of a sudden he got a stern look on his face, and everything stopped. Time stopped, people stopped breathing—the whole world stood still—and he looked at me very seriously and said, "Young man, how old are you?"

I smiled and said, "Well, Granddaddy, I'm in my twentieth year." (I'd learned that approach from reading the Joseph Smith story.) He smiled and nodded his head. The clock resumed its ticking, all present began again to breathe, and the world commenced once more to rotate on its axis.

Dad described what took place in the missionary meeting that Tuesday morning. He explained that they knelt in prayer and then sat down. Somebody read the names, and President Moyle snapped off the mission to which they would be assigned. When they came to my name, there was a pause. Dad said it was silent for a minute

Joseph Fielding Smith with grandson Joseph Fielding McConkie about the time of young Joseph's mission call

and a half by his watch. Finally, President Moyle turned to him and said, "Somebody told me at one o'clock this morning to send this boy to a particular mission, but I cannot remember who it was and I cannot remember what mission it was that they wanted him sent to." Then he added, "North British Mission."

President Moyle continued: "I had been told there was a disagreement between the boy and his father as to where he wanted to go." My father said, "No, he has said that he will be happy to go wherever he is sent, but since I have known that he could go, there has been only one mission that has entered into my mind. That is the North British Mission."

President Moyle said, "We will send him to the North British Mission."

The North British Mission was presided over by Bernard P. Brockbank. He was the man my father wanted me to serve under. The mission included Scotland, and I had some marvelous experiences there under the direction of President Brockbank. Those experiences prepared me for the time some years later when I returned with my own family to preside over that mission.

Conference Assignments

Glen Rudd eventually served as mission president in Florida, as a member of the Seventy, and as the president of the temple in New Zealand. In the course of his experiences in those capacities and in the Church Welfare Department, he traveled with about seventy different general authorities and came to know many of them well. Of President Joseph Fielding Smith he said, "I traveled with him quite a few times. He was a lovely sweet man. Of all the men I traveled with, Joseph Fielding Smith was the easiest to please. He never wanted anything. I don't think he knew how to worry. He didn't have any worries. If we were late getting somewhere, it just didn't bother him. I would get nervous. I went with him to Pocatello, to Sacramento, to Kanab, to New Mexico, to Ogden, to Murray, to California, and two or three places in Salt Lake, and I loved to go with him. He was so considerate, so kind, yet people never ever saw the real Joseph Fielding Smith, just as they never got to know the real Bruce R. McConkie."

Elder Rudd traveled on a number of occasions with Dad. "I talked to him about loosening up and changing his way with people so that they wouldn't be scared of him, and he got so he could. He really tried. I think he realized he was not perceived by the people as being a warm individual, and he wanted that. Bruce had a great personality, but his training and experiences in the first few years in the Seventy made him appear pretty aloof. I saw Bruce mellow and change. When he finally was put into the Quorum of the Twelve, he became one of the most popular men among the Twelve, and everyone who really knew him loved him, but when he stood at the pulpit, he was stiff and rather straight. He had a style of preaching that was strictly Bruce McConkie, but it didn't expose the real man. Behind the pulpit he had only one thing on his mind and that was to teach people about the Savior and about the Church.

"I went with him to a conference in Colorado. We had a wonderful time. I said, 'Bruce, today don't be your usual self. Try something different. Give them a lot of interesting little stories, anecdotes, and even humorous things.' He said, 'Okay, I'll try to please you,' but when he stood up, he was the same old Bruce. I never worried, however, because there was a mellowing, and people who listened to him were always taught. He was a teacher."

Describing Bruce McConkie as a conference visitor, Elder Rudd observed, "He had been a seventy, never been in a bishopric, never been on a high council, never been in a stake presidency, never been in a position of leadership until he was made a general authority, so he did not attempt to teach priesthood leaders how to run their wards or stakes. He just taught them the gospel, because, as he told me time and again, 'Who am I to tell someone how to hold a high council meeting? I've never been to one.' He said, 'I just teach doctrine.' As he moved along, he was asked questions and learned enough from different stake presidents and was able to give good advice, but he never went out with that in mind. He went out to tell them what he knew, not things he didn't know. That is the mark of real integrity. He never apologized for being inexperienced. He just very honestly said, 'I've never had that experience, President. You know more about that than I do.'"

Later, when Elder Rudd was on the Church Missionary Committee, he was assigned to tour Bruce's mission in Australia. "We had a great time," he said. Bruce told him, "This is the first time in my life that I've been in a position where I can make decisions. I'm the president of the mission and I call men to positions—I call men to be branch presidents and district presidents—and I preside. I can do things now. When I go home, I will have learned what I should have learned years ago."

The challenge of teaching bishops and stake presidents how to do their job without any personal experience to draw from was not unique to Bruce McConkie. None of the First Council of the Seventy at that time had experience in those callings. Each of them had been called from the ranks of the seventy. None of them had been bishops or stake presidents. None of them had administrative experience in the Church. Rather than pretend to have experience on such matters, Dad made it his practice in the leadership sessions of stake conferences to teach doctrine rather than administrative procedures or leadership skills. In this behavior he was completely consistent. As a mission president, he would put a young missionary with mechanical skills and experience in charge of all the cars in the mission and rely entirely on his judgment. The same was true regardless of the field of knowledge. He respected others' knowledge. Age or position had nothing to do with it. At the same time, he was not about to act as if there was some uncertainty in his mind about principles he fully understood.

Ordained a High Priest

On Sunday, June 11, 1961, President Henry D. Moyle ordained Bruce Redd McConkie to the office of high priest in the Melchizedek Priesthood. That evening at the conclusion of the general ession of the sixty-second annual MIA conference in the Tabernacle, President David O. McKay said: "This morning four members of the First Council of Seventy were ordained high priests and the other members of the First Council of Seventy will be so ordained. Under the direction of the Twelve Apostles, the First Council of Seventy go to all parts of the world to set in order the affairs of the Church. That means ordaining high priests, setting apart presidents of stakes, high councilmen, setting apart presidents of high priests quorums, etc. and doing other things necessary for the advancement of the work. The First Presidency and Twelve recently agreed that the First Seven Presidents of Seventy under appointment by the Twelve, should have power to set in order all things pertaining to their assignment; and this is an official announcement that they are so authorized."[1]

For many this seemed a revolutionary step because of an incident that had taken place in the days of Joseph Smith. The following is recorded in the *History of the Church* of a meeting held in the Kirtland Temple on April 6, 1837:

"Another subject of vital importance to the Church, was the establishing of the grades of the different quorums. It was ascertained that all but one or two of the presidents of the Seventies were High Priests, and when they had ordained and set apart any from the quorum of Elders, into the quorum of Seventies, they had conferred upon them the High Priesthood also. This was declared to be wrong, and not according to the order of heaven. New presidents of the Seventies were accordingly ordained to fill the places of such of them as were High Priests, and the *ex-officio* presidents, and such of the Seventies as had been legally ordained to be High Priests, were directed to unite with the High Priests' quorum."[2]

Growing out of this statement, the precedent had become that of calling men who were seventies to serve in the First Council of Seventy. President McKay's announcement caused sufficient concern among many that Elder Harold B. Lee said at general conference, "What might have been contrary to the order of heaven in the early 1830's might not be contrary to the order of heaven in 1960."[3] In a letter to me while I was serving as a missionary in Scotland, Dad explained his ordination as being the way that President McKay had chosen to give the First Quorum of Seventy the authority to reorganize stakes and do other tasks that until that time had needed to be performed by a member of the Quorum of the Twelve. Dad suggested that this delegation of authority could have been accomplished by granting the Seventy keys or in some other way. In fact, as he would yet learn, President McKay's approach was consistent with the original intent of the heavens and responded more perfectly to the needs of the Church than the conveying of keys to a Seventy would have done. In the future, those called to serve as general authorities would be high priests who brought with them the administrative experience that Dad wished he had been able to bring with him.

What happened in 1837 was that Joseph Smith responded to pettiness on the part of some priesthood holders in failing to establish the order of heaven. From February 1835, when the seventies were first called, to April 1837, there was great agitation and continual bickering among the seventies and high priests about which office was the greater and which had precedence over the other. Describing these conditions, President Brigham Young said: "This dissension has come between the Seventies and the High Priests in consequence of some poor, miserable, beggarly whiners who craved after power, and who did not know what to do with the authority they already possessed. Some of these high priests would go to Joseph saying: 'Brother Joseph the Seventies, are they ordained to as high authority and power as the High Priests? Are the Seventies equal to the High Priests? Brother Joseph, it cannot be so, it must not be; the High Priests must be the greater, and they are first.' Now, even to this day there is contention, and I do not know but even among the first Elders of Israel, there may be argument as to which should come next if anything were to happen to the First Presidency and the Twelve, the High Priests or the Seventies."[4]

In the hope of ending this contention, Joseph Smith on April 6, 1837, released from the First Council of the Seventy the five brethren who had been ordained high priests before they were ordained seventies. These brethren were told to take their places with the high priests. There is no record that any quorum members other than these five presidents were handled in this way. All other quorum members, without reference to any prior ordinations as high priests, apparently continued to serve as seventies. These five were the only ones ever released for that reason.

As Dad later explained after reading the full account of what Joseph Smith did that day, it appears that the statement about a seventy not being a high priest was an erroneous conclusion drawn by an unnamed clerk in taking the minutes of the meeting. Likely what the Prophet actually said was that it was against the order of heaven for the brethren to bicker and contend as to their priesthood prerogatives. This conclusion is in harmony with the actions of the Prophet. Acting "according to the visions and revelations" given to him, he installed as quorum presidents five other brethren who had previously been ordained high priests. The release of these brethren and their replacement appears to have been done because of personality difficulties and not because of principle.

President Brigham Young, who was conversant with the entire situation, made an express point of correcting the concept that high priests could not be ordained seventies. In 1877, he said that the Prophet had directed, both at the time of the ordaining of the members of the First Council of the Seventy and on subsequent occasions, that brethren ordained as seventies should *also* be ordained high priests. President Young explained the 1837 release of high priests from the presidency of the First Council of the Seventy as follows:

"I know some of you might say, 'Did not Brother Joseph take high priests out of the quorum of seventies and place them in the high priests quorum and put others in their places?' Yes, but what did he do this for? I can tell you—it was to satisfy the continual teasing of ignorant men who did not know what to do with authority when they got it, and I think most of those high priests who were so anxious upon this subject afterwards apostatized."[5]

Responding to questions about why members of the First Council of Seventy had been ordained high priests, President McKay said at the 1961 October conference: "It should be sufficient for you who have the Spirit of the Lord to know that the work today is required of those members of the First Council of the Seventy which needs the High Priesthood. They do not join the high priests quorum, but they are sent out by the Council of the Twelve Apostles to set in order the Church in the stakes and missions, and they should be given authority to set apart a president of a stake, a high councilman, a bishop of a ward, which requires the High Priesthood."[6]

So it was that as Bruce McConkie labored to grow up into his office, the Church in like manner struggled to grow up into an understanding of the proper role of the office of a Seventy. In a future day it would be his lot to help in that struggle.

11

THE MORMON DOCTRINE SAGA
1958 AND 1966

I've never seen a man in the Church in my experience that took our criticism—and it was more than criticism—but he took it better than anyone I ever saw.

—Henry D. Moyle

The book *Mormon Doctrine*, written by Bruce R. McConkie, is one of the time-honored classics of Mormon literature. Few books can match it in endurance or number of copies sold. Perhaps few books, except the scriptures, can match it in the frequency with which it has been quoted in talks and lessons by those seeking to teach gospel principles. And perhaps no book save the scriptures themselves has been surrounded by more myth and lore. In recounting the *Mormon Doctrine* saga, I have confined myself to matters upon which I am competent to speak and have used a question-and-answer format because that seems the most natural way to respond to the kinds of questions I have been asked most frequently.

Question: What was all the flap and fuss about *Mormon Doctrine*, anyway?

Response: The first edition of *Mormon Doctrine*, released in 1958, caused something of a stir by directly identifying Roman Catholicism as the "great and abominable church" spoken of by

The Mormon Doctrine Saga, 1958 and 1966

Nephi in the Book of Mormon. The authoritative tone of the book was also a concern, with the question being asked, "What right does Bruce McConkie have to speak for the Church?" The book came in for some criticism because of the strong language in which it denounced marginal practices among Latter-day Saints, such as card games in which face cards were used and family reunions that were held on the Sabbath.

Question: Is it true that President David O. McKay banned the book?

Response: In January 1960, President McKay asked Elder McConkie not to have the book reprinted.

Question: How is it, then, that the book was reissued?

Response: On July 5, 1966, President McKay invited Elder McConkie into his office and gave approval for the book to be reprinted if appropriate changes were made and approved. Elder Spencer W. Kimball was assigned to be Elder McConkie's mentor in making those changes.

Question: Is this generally known?

Response: I don't think so. I don't know how people would be expected to know this.

Question: Haven't you heard people say that Bruce McConkie had the book reprinted contrary to the direction of the First Presidency?

Response: Yes, but if they would think about it, that assertion does not make much sense. The publisher was Bookcraft, not Bruce McConkie, and Bookcraft was always very careful to follow the direction of the Brethren. It could also be noted that *Mormon Doctrine* was reissued in 1966, and its author was called to the Quorum of the Twelve in 1972. It takes a pretty good imagination to suppose that a man who flagrantly ignored the direction of the president of the Church and the Quorum of the Twelve Apostles would be called to fill a vacancy in that body.

Whatever faults one might want to attribute to Bruce McConkie, no one who knew him could question his integrity or his discipline, particularly where matters of priesthood direction were concerned. Never in my life have I known a man who was more disciplined or obedient to priesthood direction. Bruce McConkie would have died a thousand deaths before he would have disregarded the prophet's counsel or that of the Quorum of the Twelve. He was a man who, when assigned to speak in general conference for fourteen minutes and thirty seconds, would not have thought to speak fourteen minutes and thirty-one seconds. He took a stopwatch with him to conference and timed himself by it. For that matter, he made it a practice to watch carefully what other speakers did. When individuals went to him with concerns that fell outside the bounds of the authority or responsibility explicitly given to him, he simply refused to hear what was being said. He followed counsel and minded his business. I have never met, nor do I expect to meet, a man more disciplined to the order of the priesthood. To suppose that he would reject the counsel of the president of the Church or the Quorum of the Twelve is to completely misrepresent the man and the truth.

Question: How do you know President McKay directed your father to reprint *Mormon Doctrine*?

Response: My father told me that President McKay had so directed him. In addition to that, I am in possession of handwritten papers by my father affirming that direction.

Question: Did the first edition of *Mormon Doctrine* cause embarrassment to President McKay?

Response: Yes. The Catholic bishop in Salt Lake City, Bishop Hunt, communicated to President McKay his displeasure with the book and what it said about the Catholic church.

Question: What was Elder McConkie's reaction to that criticism?

Response: He agreed that what he had written did not facilitate

The Mormon Doctrine Saga, 1958 and 1966

good relations with our Catholic neighbors. He stated, "It wasn't smart on my part." He had no reluctance in making the changes he made in the second edition of the book.

Question: So, at least originally, the First Presidency had concerns about *Mormon Doctrine?*

Response: Yes. One of those concerns was the title itself. There was some question about what business a Seventy had declaring the doctrine of the Church. It is interesting to note, however, that no suggestion was ever made that the title of the book be changed.

Question: Would it be fair to say that the First Presidency gave your father a good horsewhipping for some of the things he wrote in *Mormon Doctrine?*

Response: I think their concern was not as much with what he had written as that he had done it without seeking counsel and direction from those who presided over him. This was back in a day before the Brethren did much writing, and there was no established review system for what they did write. As to their giving him "a good horse whipping," I think we can be confident that they were not shy in voicing their feelings. I have been told that when he met with the First Presidency, my father was invited to be seated but chose to remain standing. I also know that it was his practice (because he told me I was to do the same) when you are getting scolded, you offer no excuses—you just take it. After the experience President Moyle observed, "I've never seen a man in the Church in my experience that took our criticism—and it was more than criticism—but he took it better than anyone I ever saw. When we were through and Bruce left us, I had a great feeling of love and appreciation for a man who could take it without any alibis, without any excuses, and said he appreciated what we said to him."

Question: So what kinds of things were omitted from the second edition of the book?

Response: In a number of instances, the first edition of *Mormon*

Doctrine reached beyond the stated purpose of the book—the declaration of the doctrines of Mormonism—to include denouncing various Christian heresies. Entries included the veneration of Mary, or Mariolatry, penance, transubstantiation (the notion that in the sacrament the wafer and wine become the actual flesh and blood of Christ), indulgences, and supererogation, which is the teaching that some people perform more good works than are necessary for their salvation and thus their surplus can be sold to the wicked. This teaching provided the basis for indulgences. Because the purpose of the book was to identify Mormon doctrine, not to catalog heresies, in writing about these things, Bruce McConkie had strayed from his purpose. Hence, such subjects were dropped in the second edition.

Question: Would it be accurate to say that the kinds of changes made between the first and second editions of *Mormon Doctrine* were primarily a matter of tone? If so, would it be fair to say that the editor of the original book was asleep at the switch?

Response: The changes between the two editions center on the softening of the tone in which things were said and the selection of things that were commented on. A responsible editor would have caught these things and insisted that they be changed. Much of the flap and fuss about *Mormon Doctrine* could thereby have been avoided.

Question: So who was the editor?

Response: There wasn't one. Bookcraft was a young company in the process of establishing itself and growing up into the fine, professional publisher of Latter-day Saint books that it eventually became. George Bickerstaff, their first full-time editor, began working for Bookcraft in 1968, two years after the release of the second edition of *Mormon Doctrine*.

Question: So if George Bickerstaff, or someone with his Church sense, had been the editor at the time Bruce McConkie took the

The Mormon Doctrine Saga, 1958 and 1966

manuscript of *Mormon Doctrine* into Bookcraft, the first edition would probably have appeared essentially as the second edition did?

Response: Yes. That is one of the important roles a good editor will play. Getting a call from your editor can be like going to the dentist. It often means that something has to be pulled or filled or, at best, polished.

Question: How extensive was Elder Kimball's list of things that needed changing?

Response: There were about fifty items that Elder Kimball wanted Elder McConkie to revisit.

Question: Were these doctrinal matters in which he differed with Elder McConkie?

Response: No. They dealt with tone and with the wisdom of including particular things.

Question: How did Elder McConkie feel about the suggestions made by Elder Kimball?

Response: He was very appreciative. Elder Kimball was a wise mentor who taught him the difference between being right and being appropriate. The fact that something is true does not necessarily mean one ought to say it.

Question: Elder Kimball's list of things that needed changing sounds much less extensive than the changes that were made in the second edition. Does this suggest that a wiser Bruce McConkie did a lot of rewriting on his own?

Response: Yes, it does.

Question: It has been suggested that the treatment of the Catholic church may not have been the primary source of the criticism directed at *Mormon Doctrine* but, rather, that the standard Elder McConkie held out for the members of the Church caused some to squirm. Is that the case?

Response: I think so. It is hard to imagine that a lot of Catholics in Salt Lake City were buying a book entitled *Mormon Doctrine* and then taking offense at it. The Protestants had been saying worse things about them for four hundred years, and it was, for the Catholics, like water off a duck's back.

At the same time, marginal practices among members of the Church were addressed strongly by Elder McConkie in the first edition of *Mormon Doctrine*. For instance, birth control was described as "gross wickedness" and "rebellion against God." Card playing was called "apostasy and rebellion." Light speeches in church meetings were described as "highly offensive" to the Spirit. Elder McConkie was not very adept at tolerating the gray area between right and wrong. Even today, my experience suggests that his unequivocal stand on organic evolution is the primary reason the book has been criticized. Critics frequently attempt to give credence to their objection by finding fault with the author or the book on any count they can.

Question: What did he say about evolution in the first edition that he was directed to change in the second edition?

Response: Changes between the two editions involve only a couple of sentences. The discussion on evolution is the longest single entry in the book, and it includes a lengthy quotation by President John Taylor against Darwin and his theory of evolution. In the first edition, this quotation was introduced with the statement that President Taylor's views reflected "the official doctrine of the Church." In the second edition, that statement was dropped. Elder McConkie wrote, "How scrubby and groveling [changed in the second edition to 'weak and puerile'] the intellectuality which, knowing that the Lord's plan takes all forms of life from a preexistent spirit state, through mortality, and on to an ultimate resurrected state of immortality, yet finds comfort in the theoretical postulates that mortal life began in the scum of the sea, as it were, and has through eons of time evolved to its present varieties and state! Do those with spiritual insight really think that the infinite

The Mormon Doctrine Saga, 1958 and 1966

Creator of worlds without number would operate in this way?" The conclusion to this section in both editions is "There is no harmony between the truths of revealed religion and the theories of organic evolution."

Question: Elder McConkie was never without his critics, both in and out of the Church. To what extent do you see that criticism growing out of his uncompromising stand on evolution?

Response: It is, in my judgment, directly related. Secular writer Philip E. Johnson, in a work entitled *Reason in the Balance*, captures what is involved here: "In all the world there is no greater dogmatist than 'everybody knows.' Dogmatism is a human characteristic that grows out of insecurity. It is particularly pronounced in the case of individuals or groups that hold power positions which are threatened by criticism. Religious priesthoods have sometimes tried to protect their power by forbidding the translation of the Bible into vernacular languages or by taking a know-nothing attitude toward scientific observations that threatened traditional ways of viewing the world. In our own day the ruling priesthood consists of authoritative bodies like the National Academy of Sciences, the academic and legal elites, and the managers of the national media.

"The new priesthood, like the old ones, has a vested interest in safeguarding its cultural authority by making it as difficult as possible for critics to be heard. The modern equivalent of excommunication is marginalization, which is much more humane than physical punishment but just as effective in protecting the ruling philosophy. Those who try to challenge naturalism are confined not in a prison cell but in a stereotype, and the terms in which the media and the textbooks report any controversy are defined in a manner designed to prevent dangerous ideas from getting serious consideration. Whatever the critics of naturalism say is mere 'religious belief,' in opposition to 'scientific knowledge'; hence it is, by definition, fantasy as opposed to solid fact."[1]

In short, Elder McConkie's very certainty on this issue raised the ire of disciples of the theories of organic evolution within the Church. The controversy surrounding *Mormon Doctrine* thus provided a forum that some of them have used to marginalize one of their most outspoken critics.

Question: In the course of his ministry, did Bruce McConkie change his opinion on any doctrinal matters?

Response: Certainly. I recently received a telephone call from a young returned missionary who was frustrated about a doctrinal conversation he was having with some friends. He indicated that he had quoted Elder McConkie in support of his position, and his friends rejected what Elder McConkie had said on the grounds that he had changed his opinion on other things he had written. How, they argued, could you trust him if he changed his mind?

I told him that any man who could serve as a general authority for forty years and not improve his views on a few doctrines as a result of that experience was not to be trusted. It seems to me that Elder McConkie's credibility is strengthened by the fact that he was always anxious to grow in understanding and refine his views. In fact, as part of the preface to his *Mortal Messiah* series, he said: "As to its value, I say only that it is what it is, and it will stand or fall on its own merit; nor do I think what is here recorded is the beginning and the end. It too is but an opening door. Others who follow will find the errors and deficiencies that always and ever attend every mortal work, will correct them, and, building upon whatever foundations then exist, will write greater and better works on the same subject."[2] This expression reflects the attitude of a lifetime. He never had any difficulty with the idea that he was wrong on something, and he was always anxious to change when he discovered that to be the case.

Question: Do you know how your grandfather Joseph Fielding Smith felt about the book?

The Mormon Doctrine *Saga, 1958 and 1966*

Response: He thought so highly of it that he kept his copy at home. He was afraid that if he took it to the office, someone might walk off with it or borrow it and forget to return it.

Question: Did Bookcraft receive complaints about the book?

Response: I asked that question of Marvin Wallin, who was managing director of Bookcraft when *Mormon Doctrine* was published. He said they never received a single complaint.

Question: What doctrinal errors were corrected between the first and second editions of the book?

Response: I do not know of a single instance in which Elder McConkie was asked to change or chose to change his doctrinal position. The second edition of *Mormon Doctrine* is a substantially better book. The tone of the book is softer, articles attacking false doctrines born of apostasy but not directly germane to Mormonism have been dropped, and eighty pages of new material have been added. No doctrinal changes were made, however. The essence of each entry remains the same.

The report submitted to the First Presidency by Elder Spencer W. Kimball indicates that he checked changes made on fifty-six pages, all of which he approved. He did not indicate a single instance of doctrinal disagreement with what was written. Again, I know of no single instance in which the doctrine announced in the first edition differed from that of the second edition. Much was changed by way of tone: Things were simply said more appropriately, but the same things were said.

Question: Are there entries in *Mormon Doctrine* that are particularly revealing about its author?

Response: Yes. One of the most revealing expressions in the book is found under the heading "Sermons." In the first edition, we read: "To read a written sermon, except under very unusual circumstances, is a mockery of sacred things. There may be a few instances in which sermons may be read, just as there are a few formal occasions when prayers may be read, as for instance at the dedication of temples. On some radio and television broadcasts written sermons may be appropriate, and there is no impropriety in little children reading written talks. But in the absence of some compelling reason for making an exception to what the Lord has commanded, a written sermon does no more than bear record that the preacher has neither the knowledge to draw on, the faith to rely on the Spirit, nor the ability to attune himself to the spirit of inspiration."

The standard suggested here reaches well beyond the maturity level of many Latter-day Saints. The expression represents a personal standard that typifies the desires of a man who sought to become a great preacher of righteousness. In his missionary journal, the occasion of each talk he gave is noted, along with its length and content, and his evaluation of it. As a student at the University of Utah, he frequently spent his time while walking from campus to the family home on C Street mentally organizing and giving talks to himself. When he traveled by car as a general authority, he rarely turned on the radio. He was not interested in being entertained. For him, this was a good time to continue the practice of assigning himself topics and seeing how well he could develop them in his mind or what kind of a talk he could give to an imagined audience. Nevertheless, membership in this Church does not require one to be a great speaker. To one is given one gift, and to another, another.

Question: Elder McConkie dedicated the book to his father, Oscar W. McConkie. Do you have any idea what your grandfather McConkie's feeling was about the book?

Response: He told me that he "so prized his copy of *Mormon Doctrine* that if John the Revelator came and asked to borrow it" he would tell him, "'Nothing doing. The book is not leaving my house. You can sit down and use it here, but you can't leave the house with it.'"

The Mormon Doctrine Saga, 1958 and 1966

Question: As your father looked back on his life, would he have done anything differently as far as *Mormon Doctrine* is concerned?

Response: He did observe on a number of occasions that, perhaps, in writing the book he had done too much for its readers. "It may have been better for them," he said, "to have been required to find answers for themselves."

Question: Do you think he remained pleased with the work?

Response: Yes. Once, after I had been reading Brigham Young's sermons, I said to him, "No one in the Church has ever spoken on the breadth of subjects that Brigham Young did." With a smile, he responded, "Have you ever read *Mormon Doctrine?*"

12

The Australia Years
1961 to 1964

Being a mission president is the best job in the world.
—Bruce R. McConkie

We were a one-car family, and that car was temperamental, choosing for itself when it would and would not work. Bruce's normal practice was to take the bus to work or, if he got an early start, to walk the nearly eight miles to his office so Amelia could have the car for the myriad things necessary in running a household. At day's end, when he was ready to come home, Bruce would call and give her the route he intended to walk so that she could meet him and pick him up. He loved the fresh air and exercise.

On February 9, 1961, he called as usual: "I will go up South Temple to Thirteenth East then head out to Twenty-Seventh South . . ." Having passed the point at which she normally expected to find him, Amelia started to worry. She was convinced she had missed him by the time she was driving along South Temple. To her relief she finally spotted him just a little over a block from the Church offices.

She pulled over to the side of the road, put the car in park, and

The Australia Years, 1961 to 1964

slid over. He climbed in behind the wheel and continued west to the first intersection, made a right turn, and headed up State Street toward the capitol. He said nothing. Passing the capitol, he continued up toward Ensign Peak. Finally reaching the trail that leads to the top of the mountain, he stopped the car and said, "It's a beautiful evening. Wouldn't you like to climb the peak and look over the city as the sun goes down?"

It was obvious something had happened, and it looked like it would require climbing Ensign Peak—mud, patches of snow, and all—to find out what it was. When they reached the top, they sat together on a rock near the flag pole. It felt good just to be together. For a while they looked out over the valley. The moment etched itself into Amelia's memory: "Fluffy white clouds catching the reddish glow of the setting sun were floating lazily over the shimmering lake. We were captivated by the city lights as they began to twinkle like fireflies in the darkening sky," she noted in her journal.

Bruce pointed out landmarks as they soaked in the scene. Then he pulled an envelope out of his pocket and handed it to her. "Just after I called you, I got a call from President Moyle," he explained. "He wanted me to come down to his office and see him."

From the envelope Amelia took out a one-page letter, noting first the Church letterhead at the top of the page. It was addressed to her husband. The first line read: "We are pleased to extend to you a call to preside over the Southern Australian Mission of The Church of Jesus Christ of Latter-day Saints." The letter consisted of four paragraphs of instruction and was signed by David O. McKay, J. Reuben Clark Jr., and Henry D. Moyle.

"Australia," she thought. "Why, I have never so much as been on an airplane, and we have six children still at home." Vivian was married, and I was in Scotland on my mission. Then perhaps Amelia remembered the promise of her patriarchal blessing, given years before, that she would have opportunity to bear her testimony throughout the nations of the earth.

Bruce said, "A couple came out of President Moyle's office just before I went in. Finn and Sara [Paulsen] are going to Brazil." While a hundred questions raced through Amelia's mind, Bruce reminded her that they were to say nothing, not even to family members, until the public announcement had been made.

The Journey Begins

At 5:15 on the morning of their departure, Thursday, July 20, the phone rang. It was Bruce's father. He asked his son to come down to his home so that he could give him a father's blessing. When Bruce had asked President Henry D. Moyle if he was to be set apart, he was told no. The explanation was that he held the office of seventy, which embraced all the necessary authority for him to preside as a mission president. So that morning, Oscar W. McConkie—with the same faith and the same spirit of prophecy that had been his twenty-eight years before when he gave his son a blessing prior to his departure to the Eastern States Mission—laid his hands on Bruce's head once again to give him a father's blessing. In the earlier blessing he had said to him, "You will lead your brethren in the fight for righteousness against the enemies of truth," and they will "flee before you, and shall tremble and quake in your presence." Now he assured his son that "the time has come to enlarge the foundations for a great work in Australia. Your readiness was primed beforehand. Some will say in amazement: 'He is a friend of God,' and they will thank God 'upon every remembrance' of you." Bruce was admonished to keep first things first and not to concern himself with problems that might develop at home. "The Lord is here also," he was told, "and we know how to reach him." The parting of father and son was very emotional, for Oscar had been in poor health for some time and did not expect to see his son again in this life.

Later that morning Bruce and Amelia and six of their children were "waved on their way" by a host of friends and relatives at the Salt Lake Airport as they boarded a plane for San Francisco. An hour and fifteen minutes later they touched down at the San Francisco International Airport, claimed their luggage, and took a bus downtown, where they hailed two taxies to take them to Pier 32 to board the *S.S. Canberra*, which was to take them to Australia.

At the pier, porters immediately took their bags on board, but when they attempted to board themselves, they were met by a harbor guard with "a little authority" who would not allow them to pass. Because this was the maiden voyage of the *Canberra*, special security precautions were being taken. The fact that their tickets were in order did not matter to him, nor did their letter from the Peninsular and Orient Steamship Company affirming their passage. Providentially, Ed Burgoyne of Murdock Travel Agency, who had booked their accommodations, happened by at just that moment. He and his wife had boarded the *Canberra* in Vancouver, British Columbia, and were on their way to Long Beach, California. He went on board and got each one a visitor's pass. Thus all were able to board the ship, which was not leaving until Saturday, as visitors. They could stay both nights as long as they didn't do so as passengers. The logic of this experience would serve them well.

The *Canberra*, which was to be their home for the next three weeks, was a floating palace. The McConkie children counted fourteen decks, or stories, in their exploration. They discovered lounges, a cinema, bars, stores, four swimming pools, deck space for games, two libraries, reading rooms, two ballrooms, and special rooms for private parties. The ship was nearly a city block in length and weighed forty-five thousand tons. It had a crew of nearly a thousand

and accommodated twenty-three hundred passengers, along with enough liquor to float the ship. A carnival atmosphere was maintained day and night.

The McConkies spent Friday, July 21, in San Francisco, visiting the zoo, the planetarium, and the aquarium. On Saturday, Amelia's sister Lois and her husband, Bill Fife, drove in from Sacramento to bid them farewell. At 4:00 P.M. they were on their way, sailing under the Golden Gate Bridge and heading toward Long Beach Harbor. They spent Sunday in Long Beach, where they attended church, and Bruce spoke in sacrament meeting. Monday they relaxed and played on the beach. Friends stopped by to bid them farewell.

From Long Beach they sailed to Hawaii, arriving on July 28. They spent a day touring Oahu and then sailed to Wellington, New Zealand, where they arrived fifty-three hours late on account of a storm at sea. Winds between ninety and a hundred miles an hour had created waves like mountains. Their view from the ship's fourteenth deck was spectacular, giving them the feeling of watching scenes in a movie. "It seemed like the whole sea was pouring down on a small ship."

At Wellington, they visited the mission home, having arrived at the same time as Fred Schwendiman, the new mission president there, and his wife, Lillian. A program that evening welcomed the new mission president and bade farewell to the president being released. Elder McConkie endorsed President Schwendiman's call and the new missionary program that was being instituted.

Their next stop was Sydney, where they arrived on August 10. There, too, they visited the mission home. At this point Elder McConkie, eager to be in the harness, left the family and flew to Melbourne. The *Canberra* would not arrive in Melbourne until noon on Saturday, August 12.

Great plans had been laid by the mission staff to welcome their new president with a steak dinner. Unfortunately, they forgot to

President and Sister McConkie in Sydney, Australia, 1961

tend the steaks and so greeted their new president with a billow of smoke instead. President McConkie observed that they really didn't need to "offer burnt sacrifices just for him."

The Other Side of the World

To Bruce and Amelia, visiting Wellington and Sydney and arriving in Melbourne made it seem that they were stepping back fifty years in time. Melbourne, a metropolitan area made up of a number of smaller municipalities, had the appearance of a single city. The mission home was in a suburb called Toorak, in the city of Prahran. Across the street was the city of Malvern. Kooyong Road, on which the mission home was located, was surfaced on the Toorak side of the street but not on the Malvern side. Toorak was posh, with large homes and even mansions, but the mission home was not large enough to accommodate the McConkie family, and a lot of doubling up had to be done. Twenty months later they moved into a new mission home on 1216 Burke Road in the same city.

In Melbourne, milk was still delivered by horse and buggy, and it came only in pint bottles. The Australian (or imperial) pint,

The Bruce R. McConkie Story

The McConkie family in Australia. Back: Stanford, Mary, Rebecca, and Mark. Front: Stephen, Bruce, Amelia, and Sara

however, is about 20 percent larger than the American pint. Cars were driven on the left side of the road. Supermarkets were unknown in Australia at that time, so Amelia shopped at a fruiterer for fruit, a grocery store for other foods, a fish market for fish, and so forth. Central heating was unknown, even in church buildings. If you got cold, you put on a sweater; if you were still cold, you put on a coat. Tradespeople felt free to walk into your home unannounced and make themselves comfortable. In a letter home Amelia noted, "Our baker came in once and had a shave and on another occasion asked to use the toilet. A truck driver in the dirtiest clothes you ever saw came in and made the same request. We had guests at the time. If we don't keep the front door locked we have people walk in and wander about at any time. A few mornings ago the Elders came to see if I knew we had someone sleeping in the sick room. I was greatly surprised and a little suspicious that they were playing a joke on me because they had such silly grins on their faces. Believe it or not we had a real live 'Goldilocks' who had crept in during the night and decided that 'this bed was just right.'

"I asked Bruce why she would come here and he told me she probably had a revelation and the voice of God had told her to come. He said he would take care of her because after all a lone woman, or for that matter any woman, had no business in the Elders' living quarters. So he took care of it by having me get her up and out. But sure enough when I asked her what she was doing in our house she revealed that God had told her to come as she had no accommodations for the night. We understand that she now has some for quite some time in the Park Royal Mental Hospital."

THE NEW PRESIDENT

The missionaries felt a measurable sense of anticipation as they waited to see what life would be like under the direction of a general authority with a reputation for sternness and discipline. Their previous president had taught them to work hard—they led all missions in the Church in proselytizing hours per week—while he kept them at arm's length. Collectively they were holding their breath. Could a normal mortal survive under the leadership of Bruce R. McConkie?

Elder Jay R. Eastley wrote: "President McConkie, his imposing height and low voice notwithstanding, soon proved to be love personified. Yes, he expected consistent dedication to the work, and he requested diligent study and effective application of the 'new' proselytizing lessons. But the tone of our missionary efforts began to change. We worked 'smarter' and with increased love, under his direction. We began to see that President McConkie was as approachable as he was brilliant, that he genuinely cared about each missionary, that he not only tolerated occasional mistakes, but expected them in the spirit of innovative finding and teaching."

When Elder Eastley was transferred to the mission home, where he would serve for eight months as an assistant to President McConkie, he met the president in the living room, sitting on the floor playing with his children. He was to observe that his mission president consistently took time for his wife and family.

Once, when the McConkies "were quite new in the mission and missionaries were still unsure as to how to read them," wrote Elder Eastley, "an enterprising elder named Sam Hales ordered several dozen kangaroo skins from an Aussie wholesaler. He laid them out side-by-side near the sidewalk surrounding one of the chapels on a morning when President McConkie had scheduled a zone conference there. Elder Hales had anticipated selling the 'roo skins to attending missionaries at a tidy profit, I suppose. To his surprise, President and Sister McConkie came out of the building without warning and began to view the merchandise. They said nothing, just walked around 'inspecting' the skins. Elder Hales got very nervous, assuming that he was in deep trouble, and that the President would certainly reprimand him and shut down his operation. After what seemed an interminable time to everyone present, President McConkie in his deepest bass voice boomed out, 'Elder Hales . . . ?'

"'Y-y-yes, president?' replied Hales, expecting the worst.

"'How much is this one right here?'

"All the missionaries gasped with relief. I think President and Sister McConkie purchased several, thereby giving the green light to others to do likewise. It simply was one example of the down-to-earth attitude manifested by President McConkie. He felt that missionary work and enjoying life were not mutually exclusive pursuits."

The Australia Years, 1961 to 1964

Getting Things Going

One of the first things that the new mission president did was to establish what were called "Share the Gospel Nights." These were held in the districts for which he was responsible. Members were encouraged to bring their nonmember friends and acquaintances. These meetings followed the format of a general session of stake conference: one or two short talks or testimonies, a musical number, and then President McConkie would take the balance of the time. Typically he would speak for forty-five minutes or an hour. At first these talks were something of a shock to the Australian Saints. He did not entertain them; he taught them. They were not used to hearing the gospel preached without stories or faith-promoting rumors, nor had they ever heard anyone speak for that length of time on a gospel subject. As the Saints' understanding of the gospel grew, so did their love to hear it preached. With that, their love for the man who preached it grew also.

About a month after their arrival in Australia, President McConkie was invited to be part of a television program called "At Random," an Australian version of "Meet the Press." This program featured "men of the cloth" discussing the question "Can the Christian churches unite as one?"

When Bruce arrived at the television station, he learned that the other panelists would be a Catholic priest, a Methodist minister, and a Jehovah's Witness. The producer and his assistant screened him for an hour and a half. He told them about the Eleventh Article of Faith, agency, and how all men are our Father's children. The TV people feared that he was too mellow and would not provide the conflict necessary for good ratings. Right up to airtime they prodded him not to be too agreeable.

They soon discovered that their fears were unfounded. The Catholic and Methodist quickly united in desiring to distance themselves from the Jehovah's Witness and the Mormon. They suggested that the discussion center on the historical basis for unity. Bruce captured the moment and refused to let it go. "Now, gentlemen," he said, "everyone believes in Christian unity in principle, but let's talk about how to bring it about and upon what we shall unite. Instead of agreeing we should unite organizationally, let's talk about what the truth is and then of course everyone will want to unite on principles of truth. Let's talk about what kind of a being God is, about the principle of revelation, about visions and miracles, about whether God speaks today through living prophets, about priesthood, and the necessary ordinances of salvation." He identified virtually every distinctive doctrine of Mormonism before he was interrupted by the Methodist minister, who said, "Anyone could come here and proselyte for his particular belief. I suppose you would even want us all to unite on the Book of Mormon?"

The Book of Mormon being about the only thing he had not mentioned, Bruce thanked the Methodist for bringing it up and explained what it was and how it went hand in hand with the Bible. Unable to counter his well-reasoned statements, the Catholic and the Methodist tried to steer the program away from his challenges by attacking the Jehovah's Witness. The best they could do, however, was to ridicule him for the way the Jehovah's Witnesses annoyed people as they went from door to door and, in doing so, they ended up praising the Mormon missionary system.

Bruce concluded by pointing to the Catholic priest on one side of him and the Methodist on the other, saying, "Now, on this side we have a representative of the fallen apostolic faith and on the other side we have one who represents those who rebelled against them but lacked priesthood authority. And here [pointing to himself], in the middle, we have the restored gospel of Christ in all of its magnificent glory, having the Lord's legal administrators who are authorized to baptize the faithful."

After the program ended, the participants retired to a room to remove the make-up that had been applied for the telecast. As Bruce was leaving this room, his new Catholic and Methodist friends came into the room arm in arm. Bruce simply said, "Well, brethren, until we meet in the unity of the faith, cheerio," and walked out.

The program sparked the zeal of the members, who were gaining greater confidence in the message that was theirs. They realized their new mission president was going to leave his mark on Australia.

Baptizing

The commission of a missionary is to teach, testify, and baptize. Common to missionary work is people's resistance to being baptized. Satan simply doesn't want people baptized, and virtually every time missionaries commit an investigator to take this step, all hell breaks loose. Thus it was no great surprise to President McConkie that dotting the landscape of his mission were an unusually large number of "dry-land Mormons," that is, people who attended church regularly and participated in other activities but who had not been baptized. So he commenced a campaign to immerse these people in the waters of salvation. He knew that the first thing he had to do was to get his missionaries over any squeamishness they had about challenging people to be baptized. To that end he introduced a "Testify and Challenge" program in which the missionaries would approach the fence-sitters, testify of the truthfulness of the gospel, and state that they knew the person they were testifying to also knew the gospel was true. The missionaries then announced that a baptismal service had been planned and that the person they were addressing should be baptized at that service. Bruce knew that it was important for him as the mission president to set the example, and he had no hesitancy whatever in doing so. Whether it was over the pulpit or in personal conversation, he never missed the chance to extend to those to whom he spoke the invitation to be baptized.

One challenge that the missionaries faced was the negative attitude of priesthood leaders toward their proselyting methods. It seemed that some bishops viewed every convert as a potential less-active member and then labored to prove themselves right. There were those who constantly told the missionaries to "go slow." Some even advocated meetings in which no mention of the gospel would be made at all.

President McConkie observed that one of the prideful boasts of Australians was that they did not live under pressure, as did the Americans. Their way of life, as a matter of pride and national tradition, was to take things easy—not to rush, not to work hard or long, and not to make any great personal sacrifices.

In an epistle to family members at home, he reported on a district conference held at Perth. Sunday morning, he said, a youth testimony meeting was scheduled. None of the district presidency showed up. The meeting was marvelous with more than one hundred youth in attendance, many of whom bore sweet and good testimonies. After the ten o'clock session, President McConkie talked to a twenty-year-old nurse who knew the Church was true but was holding off being baptized in the hope of influencing her mother. Two sister missionaries had taken her to visit with him, hoping he could influence her to be baptized right away rather than postponing indefinitely. After a fifteen-minute conversation, she agreed to be baptized the following Saturday.

Of that experience he wrote: "The minute I said, '*next Saturday*,' I knew perfectly well I had made a mistake and should have said, '*today*.' The missionaries were perplexed. They had had her scheduled to be baptized Monday, and I had set it up for Saturday." He overheard their conversation and told them, "I made a mistake. Her baptism is to be *today* and *not* Monday." Then, turning to the nurse, he said, "We are baptizing you at 4:45, just 15 minutes after this session ends."

She said, "Oh, I can't. I want my friend to be here."

"That's all right; we'll send for your friend and bring her here to see it." She agreed. Then President McConkie turned to the elders and said, "We have a mission rule requiring us to baptize even numbers. You go and get someone else for this afternoon's service." The elders did just that with a young man they had spoken to earlier that day.

In the afternoon session of the same conference, just before getting up to speak, President McConkie leaned over to the district president and asked, "Are there any people here who have been investigating for a long time and who know the Church is true but who won't be baptized because of tithing or the Word of Wisdom or some other prejudice?" He answered, "There are two: 'Brother' Bancroft and 'Brother' Thurnbur."

"I talked for 50 minutes on baptism, and told why it was necessary. For texts I took the account of Paul and Silas baptizing the jailer and his family; the account of Peter on the day of Pentecost; and what the Lord said about baptism to the Nephites in the 27th chapter of Third Nephi. I also read what Amulek had to say about procrastinating the day of your repentance until the end as it is found in the 34th chapter of Alma. I talked with greater plainness than is my wont and with considerably more emphasis, telling just exactly what was wrong with people who would not respond to the call, 'Who's on the Lord's side,' who would not take Joshua's pledge, 'As for me and my house, we will serve the Lord,' and many other things. I could see a man who was there for the first time, a guest of a member of the district presidency, who had every right to be driven away by the kinds of things I was saying; and I could read the thoughts of the district president and one of the counselors and knew they thought I was tearing the district apart and driving people from the Church and from baptism, which only made me take a more affirmative stand.

"Finally, I decided that if Wilford Woodruff could preach a sermon and then have people come up for baptism, I could too, if the Lord would take over for me like I knew he had done for Wilford Woodruff. So I announced there would be a baptismal service as soon as the meeting was over and that there were a number of people in the congregation who should be baptized and that I expected them and the Lord expected them to respond and come into the Church. The Spirit was present and people's hearts were touched.

"I sat down and the choir sang and the prayer was said. I turned to the district president and said: 'Who is there in the congregation I can talk to and get baptized?' He answered: 'There on the second row is "Brother" Bancroft and his daughter.' I had watched Sister Bancroft keep her head buried with her hands and had supposed she was thinking that I was driving her husband finally away.

"There was room for one person on the bench by where the Bancrofts were sitting. I went down and took it, put my arms around the girl, leaned over to her father, and said: 'I guess you know that you two are the ones I have been talking about.' He said: 'Yes, and my daughter is ready to be baptized.' I had seen them whisper together as I came down. I said: 'Fine, you come with me.' I took her by the arm and led her out to the room where the baptismal clothes are stored, got one of my lady missionaries, and escorted her over to the dressing room. She was shaking and visibly upset, scarcely able to control herself.

"I went back in to her father and said: 'You're next. Come on.' He refused. His wife walked away and with tears in her eyes said to me: 'John's ready, I know he is. He has been attending church for years, keeps all the standards of the Church, and has been a dry-land Mormon.' I said: 'Brother Bancroft, your wife just told me with tears in her eyes that you are ready for baptism.' He bristled: 'Oh, she did. Well, I'm not.' I said: 'And furthermore, I say you are and that you are going to be baptized. Now you come with me peaceably or I'll get one of these elders to help me carry you out.' He refused. I put my arm under his, lifted him slightly off the floor and marched him down the aisle of the chapel, across the amusement hall, out through the patio, and into the room where the baptismal clothes are stored. All the way out he kept saying, 'I am not joining the Church; I won't be baptized; you can't force me; it doesn't matter what my wife thinks; I'm not joining the Church.' I simply assured him verbally and physically that he was. When we got into the room with the clothing, someone was already handing items to the other young man, and I asked 'Brother' Bancroft what size pants he wore. He did not respond. I held a pair up to him and said, 'These will fit you,' and put them over his arm, and then asked for his shirt size. He said: 'Sixteen,' and with that single word agreed to join the Church. With his clothes, I marched him across the foyer to the dressing room. Since he had been around the Church for years, people began flocking around to shake his hand. I said: 'You folks please leave us alone and do not interfere.'

"By this time a couple of hundred people were aware of what was going on and so they congregated in the outside patio to watch. I marched Brother Bancroft over to the dressing room, took him in, and said: 'Get dressed.' He had given up and began taking his shirt off. I said: 'I've got someone else, but I'm posting a guard at the door.'

"Well, by this time the stage was set and so the elders who had contacts at the conference who they thought should join the Church began taking me from one to the other, and in each instance after five or ten minutes' conversation and a little gentle persuasion, one after another agreed to join the Church, until we ended up with nine baptisms—not one of whom had come with the slightest intention of being baptized.

"What we did may seem strange, but it was the right thing

under the circumstances, and the Spirit was with us. The missionaries were amazed and so were the members; these things just couldn't happen, so they thought, among Australians, who everybody keeps saying cannot be pushed or told what to do. . . .

"One of the striking things was how grateful all who were baptized were after the event. Any hesitancy beforehand was forgotten. All expressed appreciation and were pleased beyond measure to be in the Church and to have the decision behind them. They just needed the right setting, the outpouring of the Spirit, and someone with enough foolhardiness to tell them this was it and there was no turning back."

Thirteen people were baptized by the end of that district conference. The week before, the same thing had taken place in a conference at Hobart, with eight being baptized there.

Some years ago when I was in Alberta, Canada, speaking on a Know Your Religion program, a young man came up after one of my talks and introduced himself to me. He was Bruce Bancroft, son of the man whom Dad had urged to be baptized. His father was sufficiently grateful that he named his son Bruce after Dad. He thanked me for my father having baptized his father.

Sister Bancroft later acknowledged that as President McConkie concluded his talk, she prayed in her heart, "Heavenly Father, if this is your only true church, let President McConkie come down right now and tell my daughter so."

At another youth missionary testimony meeting in Tasmania, five nonmembers spoke; four of them committed themselves to baptism. The fifth badly wanted to join but could not get permission from his parents. Some easily obtained their parents' or spouse's consent to their baptisms, but for most it was not so easy. In Adelaide the missionaries baptized a young woman who, though of legal age, acted against her parents' wishes. When the missionaries had gone to visit the father, he told them to get out. The district fasted and prayed for the Lord to soften his heart, and then the elders went back to talk to him. He blew his top, as expected, but within forty-five minutes they had him on his knees, praying. Sister McConkie met the man and his wife at the chapel and said, "They seemed very friendly."

For others, even the prayer of the righteous was of no avail. Amelia recalled coming home one evening, after dropping the older kids off at Mutual, to the smell of tobacco in the mission home. Though the door to the living room was closed, she had no difficulty hearing what was going on. A woman was screaming at President McConkie, accusing him of a host of vile and unspeakable things. Then she heard the woman's daughter calmly apologize for her parents' behavior. The girl explained that all she could remember about her home life was drunken brawls and fights. She told her mother that if she would study and pray, she'd guarantee that she would join the Church in three weeks.

When the family finally left—threatening to sue the Church as they did so—Bruce turned to Amelia and said, "I entertained the devil tonight." Much that these people had said and done, including the smoking, had been planned before they came. He was, however, very proud of the young woman, and not long after her baptism he called her to serve as a missionary.

Bruce took great delight in sending Australian youth on missions within his mission. Many of them were terrific, and these missions developed and strengthened leadership. Consequently, many young converts eventually found themselves serving in the mission field. One young man who was a chain smoker and on his way to becoming an alcoholic was converted and called by the mission president to labor as a missionary. The change in his life was nothing short of miraculous. His family members, who were willing to attend his missionary farewell, were totally amazed by the change in his life. This young man was also possessed of a delightful sense of humor. Amelia recalled, "When I saw him in Adelaide during a light rainstorm he could not help but comment on the 'Catholic Rains.' This puzzled me until he explained it was *just sprinkling*. He also revealed that "the largest church in Australia is *me-own church*." That was the polite refusal the elders frequently got on the doorstep: "I've got me own church, thanks."

His Mission Companion

About four months after their arrival in Australia, Amelia suggested to her husband that just because he had not been set apart was no reason she should not be. Dad was in full agreement and gave her a wonderful blessing. He blessed her as "a helpmeet, a guide, a comfort, and a light" to him. He also set her apart to serve as the president of the Relief Society of the Southern Australia Mission and conferred upon her every gift and grace appertaining to that office. He blessed her with the gift of testimony, by which, she was promised, many souls would be brought into the kingdom. She was also granted the assurance of health, peace of mind—freedom from anxiety and uncertainty—and the spirit of love for all with whom she would be called to labor. She was promised that she would be a recipient of the choicest blessings of an Eternal Father.

On December 23, 1961, her husband wrote the following letter to her:

"Amelia darling—

"It seems to me it has been longer than usual since I wrote you a letter to remind you of my feelings toward you. If there has been a single day of our married life on which I have failed to tell you I loved you—such was not intended. There has been no day on which I have not had a feeling of deep appreciation and thanksgiving that you are mine.

"You have made this life a foretaste of what our association will be together forever. I preach and believe that the concept of eternal continuance for the family unit is the noblest view of life and its purpose that ever entered the heart of man. To think that you are mine now and will continue so to be endlessly with an increasing bond of love and affection between us, is something that overwhelms me with gratitude.

"I love you for yourself and all the attributes and characteristics you have. I love you because of Bruce Jr., Vivian, Joseph, Stanford, Mary, Mark, Rebecca, Stephen, and Sara. I love you for your faith and devotion to the truth, for the fact that you love the Lord and keep his commandments, for the example you set for me, for the good and bettering influence you have been and are in my life, and for all the reasons I have told you over and over again.

"Before we came to Australia, I told you we would be closer here in the mission field than we had ever been before. That prediction is now and yet shall be fulfilled. I enjoy being with you; want to have you around me all the time; and find your companionship both delightful and satisfying. Thanks for everything.

"As Ever—
"Your husband
"P.S. I love you."

Teaching the People

President McConkie rarely made formal preparation for the talks he gave. He would honor a request to speak but felt no obligation to confine the Spirit to someone else's topic. He did, however, prepare himself to speak specifically in response to the falsehoods being perpetuated by a Protestant radio ministry in Perth. In his talk one night he told of the time two ministers of one of the largest and most powerful Protestant denominations came to a stake conference to hear him preach. Recounting that experience he said:

"After the meeting I had a private conversation with them, in which I said they could each gain a testimony that Joseph Smith was the prophet through whom the Lord had restored the fulness of the gospel for our day and for our time.

"My message was the same. Taking the Book of Mormon as their guide, they must read, ponder, and pray in order to gain a witness from the Spirit as to the truth and divinity of this great latter-day work.

"I told them of my prior experience with their two colleagues and how one of them had refused to read the Book of Mormon, saying that they had experts who had read the book and he had read what the experts had said.

"I then said, 'What is it going to take to get you gentlemen to read the Book of Mormon and find out for yourselves what is involved, rather than relying on the views of your experts?'

"One of these ministers, holding my copy of the Book of Mormon in his hands, let the pages flip past his eyes in a matter of seconds. As he did so, he said, 'Oh, I've read the Book of Mormon.'

"I had a momentary flash of spiritual insight that let me know that his reading had been about as extensive as the way he had just flipped the pages. In his reading he had done no more than scan a few of the headings and read an isolated verse or two.

"A lovely young lady, a convert to the Church, whose father was a minister of the same denomination as my four Protestant friends, was listening to my conversation with the second two. At this point she spoke up and said, 'But Reverend, you have to pray about it.'

"He replied, 'Oh, I prayed about it. I said, "God, if the Book of Mormon is true, strike me dead"; and here I am.'

To this Bruce responded, "But you have to have faith."

Spirit of the Mission

Monthly training meetings for the missionaries usually lasted eight to ten hours with President McConkie using most of the time for gospel instruction. He also communicated with his missionaries in a monthly publication entitled *The Harvester*. The publication always began with a letter from the president and was followed with instruction on the how or why of missionary work. It was for *The Harvester* that he wrote the "Missionaries' Commission," which has been memorized by missionaries throughout the world.

My Commission

I AM CALLED OF GOD.

My authority is above that of the kings of the earth.

By revelation I have been selected as the personal

representative of the Lord Jesus Christ.

He is my Master and he has chosen me to represent him; to stand in his place; to say and do what he himself would say and do if he personally were ministering among the very people to whom he has sent me.

My voice is his voice, and my acts are his acts; my words are his words, and my doctrine is his doctrine—for I am his agent.

My commission is to do what he wants done, to say what he wants said, to be a living, modern witness—in word and in deed—of the divinity of his great and marvelous latter-day work.

And he that receiveth me, receiveth him, while he that rejecteth me, rejecteth him that sent me.

How great is my calling!

Along with the "Missionaries' Commission," President McConkie also wrote what he entitled "My Mission," which is as follows:

My Mission

I AM A MISSIONARY.

My blessings are above those of the kings of the earth.

In my hands I hold the pearl of great price.

Mine is the same gospel taught by Paul, the same plan of salvation preached by Peter, the same saving truths which sanctified Enoch and Elijah.

I rejoice in the same priesthood held by Abraham and Melchizedek.

It is my right to see visions as did Nephi; to teach and testify as did Alma; to entertain angels and work miracles as did Nephi the Disciple; to receive revelations as did Joseph the Seer; to walk daily in the light of the Spirit as did Wilford Woodruff; to enjoy all of the gifts and graces which that Holy Being, who is no respecter of persons, always pours out upon those who love and serve him.

How great are my blessings!

Both statements are vintage Bruce McConkie. The compelling desire to live so that he might see visions, entertain angels, work miracles, receive revelations, walk by the Spirit, and enjoy all spiritual gifts was very real with him. He believed it a mission president's responsibility to teach his missionaries that such experiences were possible and that they were to live for them, and he believed it was for him as their leader to do precisely that as well. His life evidenced that he did so.

Special Visitors

The McConkies shared their experience in Australia with a surprising number of special visitors—surprising because of the distance of their mission from Church headquarters. Among them were four apostles who would yet preside over the Church, sisters who were members of general boards of the Church and for whom President and Sister McConkie had great regard, and some of their dearest friends. These visitors both contributed to the mission and were enriched by it. Hulda Parker, a general board visitor, was sufficiently impressed with the "Testify and Challenge" program that she took its spirit and its principles home with her. She described her experience as follows:

"I remember our conversations at the dinner table, and I think it was probably the McConkie style. It was definitely a gospel discussion, and the one thing that he was emphasizing at that time in his mission—and they were getting a lot of baptisms from it—was to have his missionaries seek out people on their records who always wanted to continue to be friends with the missionaries but never seemed to be ready for baptism. 'You have been acquainted with the Church and you have had the missionaries calling on you, some of them for as much as ten years; it is time for you to be baptized. We are going to have a baptism on such and such a day, and we will expect you to be there to be baptized.'

"Anyway," Hulda continued, "he so impressed me with that. At the time I was substituting part-time at home for the investigator class in our ward, where I had just had an experience with a nonmember Dutchman who had immigrated with his wife some forty years earlier. His wife and three children had joined the Church and were all active in it. This man was a good man, but he had never quite got to the point of joining. Just before I left to go on this trip to Melbourne, I had challenged him to read the Book of Mormon and pray about it and ask the Lord if it was true. Much to his amazement, and to mine, he told me he would do it.

"I explained this to Elder McConkie, and he said, 'When you get back, you challenge him to baptism.' I said, 'The way you have been doing it down here?'

"He said, 'Yes, that man should be baptized!'

"When I got back, I went to my bishop and explained to him what Brother McConkie had told me. He said, 'All right, Sister Parker, go ahead and do it. I'll back you.' He checked ahead of time to see when the next stake baptism was, and he told me to challenge him and to tell him the bishop was in his office and to come and talk to him and they would do all the paperwork.

"I went to the investigator class that morning, and there was

Brother _____. As he went out of the class, I said, 'Brother _____, the bishop is upstairs in his office waiting for you. There is a stake baptism on such and such a night, and we feel that you are now at the point you need to be baptized.'

"He just about died. I thought he was going to have a stroke. But he had read the Book of Mormon like he'd promised, and he had prayed about it. I asked him how he felt about it. He said, 'I know it is true. I now know the Prophet Joseph Smith is indeed a prophet.'

"I went ahead with that. That poor man was shaking. I took hold of his elbow and said, 'Come on, let's just go right on up here.' We had to go upstairs and wind around to where the bishop's office was. I didn't know whether that man was going to get up the stairs or not. But we got there and knocked on the door. I said, 'Bishop, here is Brother _____.'

"He said, 'Fine. Have him come right in.' We went in and shook hands, I stepped out and waited about 20 minutes, and then he came out and said, 'Sister Parker, I am going to be baptized on such and such a date. I can hardly wait to go home and tell my wife. She really won't believe me after all these 40 years. She really won't believe me.'

"I said, 'She will probably collapse in tears,' and that was just exactly what she did. He called me back in about three or four days and said, 'My family would like me to be baptized on my birthday, and that is about a week sooner than the date we had set.' His baptism was pretty exciting to me."

One of the first general authorities to visit the mission was Sterling W. Sill. He was a consummate businessman. In fact, when I graduated from the Y, he called my father twice in an effort to get him to talk me out of teaching seminary and instead to sell insurance for the New York Life Insurance Company. While in Australia he gave Dad a lecture on how to approach people for donations. At the conclusion of his visit, when Mom and Dad were taking him back to the airport, he quizzed Dad to see what he had learned. Dad said, 'Well, let me see,' and immediately applied all the techniques on Elder Sill that Elder Sill had taught him. Dad concluded by saying he wanted him to get out his checkbook right there and write a check—and he didn't want it to be for anything less than four figures. The fifteen-hundred-dollar check he received as a contribution to the mission suggested that Dad had been a pretty good student.

When Glen Rudd visited as part of his assignment with the Missionary Committee, he was delighted to see how his old friend had learned to handle what Elder Neal A. Maxwell has called "administrative awkwardness."[1] He was delighted with the way Bruce had solved a problem involving his branch clerks, each of whom needed an adding machine. "I decided to buy ten adding machines," Bruce explained. "I then discovered that they were $100 each and that was $1,000. As a mission president, I didn't have the authority to spend $1,000 without going through Salt Lake and all manner of red tape. I got hold of the man who was going to sell me these ten machines and told him I couldn't buy them because I didn't have full approval from Salt Lake."

The man said, "Well, I'll help you any way I can." When Bruce got back to the mission office, he realized that he had authority to spend up to a hundred dollars. So he "got hold of the salesman and said, 'Can you sell me those machines at $99?'

"He said, 'Yes,' so I made ten separate purchases at $99 each. I got my machines without troubling Salt Lake."

If it needed to be done, Bruce McConkie found a way to do it—and without bothering Salt Lake. He must have been something of a legend, because twenty-five years later, when I attended the orientation for new mission presidents, Thomas S. Monson told us we did not need to call Salt Lake every time we had a problem. "Why," he said, "when Bruce McConkie was in Australia, he called Salt Lake only three times the entire time he was there."

Bruce had a situation in one of the districts he was responsible for in which he found it necessary to call a high priest to serve as an elders quorum president. When Elder Ezra Taft Benson toured the mission, a conference was held in this district. Elder Benson was fielding questions in a leadership meeting when a disgruntled soul in the back of the room asked, "Elder Benson, did you know that President McConkie made a high priest the president of an elders quorum?" Elder Benson said, "I'm sorry. I can't hear the question." The question was repeated. Again Elder Benson said, "I'm sorry. I can't hear the question." When the man repeated his question for the third time and for the third time President Benson said, "I'm sorry. For the life of me, I can't hear that question," the man, finally getting the message, quietly sat down.

Two other visitors were Sister Belle S. Spafford, general president of the Relief Society, and Sister Eileen Dunyon, counselor in the general presidency of the Primary. When Bruce got the word that they were coming to Australia, he received permission from Church headquarters to have these two women visit with people in the mission as well as in the stakes. Just before Sister Spafford was to leave Salt Lake, her husband passed away, and it looked for a time as if her visit would be cancelled. The First Presidency encouraged her to go ahead with her plans, however, because they felt that doing so would help her adjust to her loss.

The day they arrived, Bruce and Amelia met them at the airport. After a welcome by local members of the Church, the McConkies took them to the mission home, where they would stay. Bruce sensed that Sister Spafford was weighed down with some troubling concerns, so he sat up and talked with her for some time. Amelia said, "When morning came and we had breakfast, Sister Spafford came down looking greatly refreshed and at peace.

"She thanked Bruce for talking with her and listening to her the night before and explained that because of his counsel, she had seen her husband in a dream and he had told her how she was to solve the problem that had been troubling her. From then on as we toured the mission she seemed perfectly at peace and was able to give valuable instruction and counsel to the various stake and branch people in the mission areas."

Amelia also recalled that Sister Spafford was not only very effective with Relief Society women but also set an example worthy of emulation. "I watched and listened to her speak with awe and admiration. Repeatedly she managed to give the sisters exactly what they needed as well as discerning needs they did not express.

"On one occasion I was sitting by her on the stand before a meeting began. She looked out over the congregation and noticed a very faithful and good woman sitting near the front of the room. She turned to the stake president and informed him that this sister had a very serious problem in her life and she needed help. This turned out to be true, and the stake president was able to give the needed help.

"When the stake Relief Society president in the Perth Area asked Sister Spafford if she would like to do some sightseeing while she was there, her answer was a quick, 'No, but if you have any sisters in the hospital or with some other health problem I would like to visit them.' This resulted in a special treat for some of the handicapped women in the Church in that area. Her perceptive insights and loving example were an inspiration to me as well as the people of Australia."

When Bruce received word that Elder Gordon B. Hinckley would be traveling to Melbourne, the members were greatly excited about the prospects of having an apostle visit them. Bruce worked through the multitudinous details that planning such a visit requires

President McConkie with Elder Gordon B. Hinckley in Perth, Australia

and rearranged schedules so he could include all the meetings Elder Hinckley had requested.

"It was not long before he received word that Elder Hinckley's plans were changed and he would be coming on a later weekend. Accordingly, Bruce notified all the parties involved with the conferences and began making new plans. The ramifications of changing plans in Melbourne spilled over into Adelaide, causing him to make changes there, too. "We are now on plan B," he announced.

All seemed to be going well and the time was drawing near for the big event in Melbourne when Bruce got another call, saying that Elder Hinckley had to change his plans back to the original date. "This means that we are back to plan A and I will not be able to attend the Melbourne Stake conference," Bruce informed Amelia. "It's too late to change the Adelaide schedule again, so I'll go there and you will need to stay here."

At the last moment, they were notified of yet another change in Elder Hinckley's plans, and this time it meant there would be no

The Australia Years, 1961 to 1964

priesthood leaders available to pick him up at the airport. So Sister McConkie and Sister Davis (the wife of the stake president) set out on that rainy Sunday morning with plenty of time to get to the Melbourne Airport.

The scheduled flight was to arrive at 9:15, but the sisters learned it would be delayed until 10:05, which meant they would be late for the morning conference session. At about 9:10 the thought occurred to Amelia to check the other airline's schedule and see when it would arrive from the city Elder Hinckley was traveling from. The two women raced down to the other end of the airport on the chance that Elder Hinckley would be on that plane instead of the one scheduled to arrive at 9:15. He was.

Amelia recalled, "We did manage to get Elder Hinckley to the church moments after they had started the meeting, only to discover someone else had taken our reserved parking spot in front of the chapel. We let him out, found another parking space, and then Sister Davis and I dashed into the women's rest room to take advantage of it before proceeding into the meeting since we were already late—and another few moments would not make much difference. A seat was reserved for us down in the front where some of my children were already sitting, and I quickly made my way down there. As I sat down and crossed my legs at the ankles, I discovered I had walked the length of the chapel with about two feet of bathroom tissue trailing behind me, stuck firmly to the heel of my shoe. What a grand entrance that had been.

"In the afternoon session Elder Hinckley unexpectedly called on me to say a few words, and I felt more than a little unprepared and nervous. After the meeting was over, one of the good sisters in attendance consolingly told me, 'You sounded as confused as I would have been if I had been in your place.' Not exactly the confidence booster I might have chosen, but it was the next intended compliment that really made me chuckle: 'You have a way of

Bruce and Amelia with Joseph Fielding and Jessie Evans Smith in Australia

touching people's hearts even if you are not as intelligent as your husband.'"

To those at home Amelia wrote: "It isn't surprising that Bro. Hinckley is ill, the way he tears around on jam-packed, tight schedules, with little rest." He was the junior member of the Quorum of the Twelve at this time. She added, "People here really did enjoy him." Neither the schedule he keeps nor the love people have for him has changed.

The Melbourne Saints were also thrilled to have Elder Joseph Fielding Smith as a conference visitor. In addition to his conference assignment, he met with missionaries, local members, and investigators and presided over a special program to dedicate the new mission home. The home had already proven to be a great blessing to the mission with its separate missionary quarters, family quarters, office space, kitchens, entertaining areas, and guest rooms.

Amelia recorded, "No sooner had we returned from the airport with our guests than a female reporter and a photographer arrived from the *Melbourne Herald* daily newspaper to interview Dad and

Aunt Jessie. The reporter made it clear that Aunt Jessie was the only one she wanted to interview because of her reputation as a vocalist. She completely ignored the men. The rest of us discreetly kept our distance.

"We had a memorable family home evening in which Dad taught us a lesson and let everyone ask questions. Aunt Jessie sang, and then Dad joined her in singing their famous duet, or do-it, as he called it. Then Dad set Mary apart for her mission, and ordained Stephen a deacon, though he was a couple weeks shy of his 12th birthday."

Teaching the Missionaries

President McConkie loved to teach his missionaries, he loved to be outside, and he loved climbing mountains. He found these three loves to be quite compatible. For instance, one day in Hobart, Tasmania, he told the missionaries, "We will hold our meeting on the top of Mount Wellington," a tremendous mountain that overlooks the city and the bay. "They did not realize I was serious, at first, but after I told them that all great men—Moses, the brother of Jared, Nephi, and so on—climbed mountains; they consented. So while it was scarcely dawn we assembled at the foot of the mountain and spent a good many weary hours climbing to the top. Much good gospel instruction was given to the missionaries on that mountaintop."

In another setting, he drew upon that experience to teach the principle of revelation. "On the top we found some television relay stations. Since we were there, we gained permission to be shown through. There was a very bright young man who, using language that we did not understand, but speaking with a tone of authority, explained in detail the things that were involved in relaying television broadcasts. I was totally unable to comprehend or understand what was involved, but I knew that the thing did take place.

President and Sister McConkie after a zone conference

"That night, down in the valley again—two of my young sons were with me—we stayed in a room where there was a television set. They tuned the wave band of that set to the broadcast that came from the top of the mountain. We saw and heard and experienced what had been described to us in words.

"The same thing applies in radio. If we had a radio here today and tuned it to the proper wave band, we would hear the symphonies that are being broadcast into this building. Or if we looked on television we would see in effect the visions that are coming forth in a similar way. Now in the same sense, if at any time we manage to tune our souls to the eternal wave band upon which the Holy Ghost is broadcasting, since he is a Revelator, we could receive the revelations of the Spirit. If we could attune our souls to the band on which he is sending forth the visions of eternity, we could see what the Prophet saw in Section 76, or anything else that it was expedient for us to see. It would all happen by compliance with law, by conformity to the eternal principles that God has ordained.

"Now I am not able to explain how this takes place. I know that the laws exist; and like the young man who explained the television broadcast without really knowing how the pictures go through space, I also can state, as one having authority, that these things do take place in the spiritual realm, and that it is possible to receive revelation and direction and guidance in our personal affairs.

"This, I think, is the sort of thing that we ought to desire above all else. If we are spiritually inclined, I think that we want to know what the Lord would have us do—we would like to have the direction that would enable us to govern and control properly in all the affairs of our lives."

A Time of Rejoicing and Sorrow

May 13, 1962, was Mother's Day in the United States. President and Sister McConkie were in Perth holding a missionary training meeting. That afternoon, they joined the Saints and the missionaries of the Perth Branch for what turned out to be a highly spiritual testimony meeting. Forty-four people, including themselves, bore witness of Jesus Christ and his gospel. After the meeting, fourteen people were baptized. It was, they felt, a grand way to celebrate Mother's Day.

Before the baptismal service ended, someone handed Bruce a note. He read it and then silently left the room. "Afterwards when I saw him," Amelia said, "I could tell by the look on his face that there was something seriously wrong. 'What is the problem?' I quietly asked. In response he simply handed me the note and I read, 'Elders Johnson and Denney killed in train car accident, 6:30 PM, near Ballarat.'

"I was stunned, and unable to control the tears. Elders Johnson and Denney were two of our finest elders and were the district leaders where they were assigned to labor in the Victoria area. Bruce thought it best not to say anything at that time for fear of dampening the spirit that was present at the meeting. With heavy hearts we tried to appear normal as we joined those eating the food so graciously prepared for those who had been at the chapel most of the day. As the final meeting resumed, Bruce was not able to get his mind and feelings off the tragedy. He spoke with great feeling and power, telling those assembled that since none of us know when our time would come, we should get on the Lord's side of the line now. Many, touched by the spirit there and their love for these two Elders, wept."

At the conclusion of that meeting, a young investigator asked to be baptized. Her mother, who was not a member of the Church, thanked Bruce for what he had taught.

A Visit to the Bush

Australia was an adventure, and Bruce and Amelia thrived on it. Amelia's description of a visit to Kalgoorlie illustrates her enthusiasm. They arrived by plane, a Cessna with four seats. From the air, the town "reminded me of a good old Western cowboy scene," Amelia said, "with its one hotel, and several bars, a few homes, and perhaps a place or two where one could eat." President and Sister McConkie had come to meet with the small branch of Saints there.

The elders met them as they got off the plane. Since they had three hours before their meeting was to start, they toured the town. As one would imagine, this didn't take long, so a "tourist special" was suggested—a visit to the Bush to see how the primitive Aborigines lived.

Amelia wrote, "Drink, apparently easily available, had more than one native sprawled out on the side of the road covered with the stickiest horde of flies I have ever seen. One cannot imagine the dreadful plague flies can be until they have met the sticky, determined little pests this country breeds. They seem to prefer going for your nostrils, mouth, or eyes, and it isn't unusual to see someone with their back completely covered with them. You simply could not brush them away."

Such a visit required a souvenir or two, so the group stopped while the mission president dickered with an Aborigine over a few handmade boomerangs. All of a sudden, the fellow he was talking to got a very agitated look on his face. He was looking past Bruce at another Aborigine, who was hollering as he ran toward them with his spear raised, ready to throw. The natives quickly scampered out of the way. The elders, in much alarm, were anxious to get their mission parents back into the car. Bruce, camera in hand, was snapping pictures as fast as he could. He even got a good shot of the tall, thin, black man readying himself to throw a long spear in his direction. "Just as we got into the car I turned my head back to see the angry man let an arrow fly into the tents right where we had been standing," Amelia said. The group left with some dispatch.

A little farther down the road, they saw a group of about ten Aborigines and stopped to see if they could get some pictures. "Four of them were drinking, flies so thickly encrusted on their faces that you could not see their eyes. Another three were curled in awkward positions on the gravelly ground fast asleep. The others were just happy enough to be friendly. Elder Clawson paid them a few shillings, and Bruce got his pictures."

The Australian Experience

When President McConkie received word that his fellow Seventy Marion D. Hanks had received a call to serve as a mission president, he sent him a telegram: "Congratulations on receiving the choicest assignment in the Kingdom!" Bruce repeatedly said, "Being a mission president is the best job in the world." He loved it. As a mission president, he could make decisions and exert leadership. He could make a difference.

At the same time he felt pressure to succeed. The office he held brought with it a high level of expectation. At that time, there were only sixty-four missions in the Church, and their numbers in baptizing were published, compared, and talked about. Some missions were posting remarkable numbers of baptisms. Where this was the case, the numbers being posted generally consisted of youth baptisms or, as their critics called them, "infant baptisms." Many of those baptized disappeared faster than the morning dew. Still, baptisms were the standard by which the success of a mission president was measured in many quarters. Bruce's challenge was not simply to baptize more people but to *convert* and baptize more people. He did this successfully, and baptisms increased markedly each year, so that when he left the mission, four times as many people were being baptized as when he came. But, he said, "Our greatest achievement was the saving of delinquent missionaries, and our next greatest the delegation of authority to local leaders so as to prepare Adelaide and Perth (and Hobart in due course) to become stakes."

Australia is a big place, and big suited Bruce McConkie just fine. He loved the country, and he loved its people. He was up consistently at 5 or 5:30 in the morning—field glasses in hand—out bird-watching with his wife or leading his missionaries to the top of mountains where their zone conferences would be held. And he memorized the 104 lines of the poem "The Man from Snowy River" so he could quote it to his missionaries as he drove them to the airport after they had completed their missions.

13

FAMILY TRADITIONS

True greatness is found only in the family.
—Bruce R. McConkie

The McConkie family traditions likely differed little from those of other Latter-day Saint families. Morning scripture reading had not been invented yet, so our day began with breakfast, which was always the same—whole wheat mush. Mother ground the wheat in an old coffee grinder. With eight children in the family, we had store-bought cereal as a holiday treat. Eggs, bacon, and the like had apparently not been discovered. We always had family prayer. I don't think my father ever offered a prayer in which he did not pray that his sons would go on missions and his sons and daughters would marry in the temple. The thought that anyone would do otherwise simply never occurred to us. Dad held up as his ideal a grand old patriarch in our stake by the name of David A. Broadbent. As I recall, he had twelve children, all of whom married in the temple, and the family filled twelve missions. My father thought that was perfect. I think it was not by chance that all eight of his children married in the temple and that among their number eight missions have been served.

Such Was Life

After breakfast Dad would kiss Mother good-bye. This was something of a ritual. They would go into the hall, where Mother, who stood about five foot six, could stand on the first step of the stairs to more comfortably bid farewell to her six-foot-five husband. Sometimes they got a bit carried away in this ritual and put Dad in danger of missing his bus.

Before Dad came home, Mother would end her work for the day, change clothes, and "doll herself up" for him. They enjoyed taking walks together in the evening. Dad liked to lie on the floor in the living room to read the *Deseret News*. He had a special interest in the editorials. Any of the older children who were unwise enough to get caught were conscripted into scratching his head while he read the paper. This duty was regarded as a step beyond torture and, as such, became the source of all manner of very creative complaints. Dad held firmly to the position that it was an absolute requisite to the development of character and strong hands.

More dreaded still were his haircuts, which may also have aided in the development of character as they always elicited a good deal of teasing by friends at school. The haircuts Dad gave us constituted an eloquent refutation of the notion that practice brings improvement. Rather, they evidenced the fact that to practice doing something poorly aids in developing the ability to do it even worse the next time. In fairness, it ought to be noted that his haircuts were a strong source of motivation for his sons to go on missions and to go to Brigham Young University rather than to live at home and go to the University of Utah. Having cut our hair, Dad would invite Mother to cut his. She didn't do much better than he did, which didn't bother him in the least. He was simply devoid of vanity. So

Family Traditions

Bruce with grandson Joseph Jr., son Joseph, and son-in-law Michael Pinegar

what if he looked as if he had been scalped with a dull knife when he stood to give a talk at general conference? It was the message that counted, not the appearance of the messenger. I heard Mother telling him once that he had holes in his socks and he simply could not wear them to conference. "If I can't keep their eyes off the holes in my socks," he said, "I don't deserve their attention."

We were the last family in the neighborhood to get a television, and then we got one only because a neighbor gave it to us. I don't think my father ever watched it. In fact, I have no recollection of my father sitting in front of a television set. By contrast, Mother used to say it was useless to visit her father, Joseph Fielding Smith, on Wednesday nights because he enjoyed watching the Wednesday night boxing. For that matter, I am not sure my father ever turned on a car radio, either. The time that other people spent listening to the radio he chose to spend planning and organizing talks. This is not to suggest that he did not know how to relax or that he did not believe in healthy recreation. He was a birder and enjoyed getting out with his binoculars to see what interesting birds he could find.

Dad with some members of his mountain climbing club. Clockwise from top: Stanford, Mark, Sara, and Stephen

He became a lapidary and brought home stones from the many places his conference assignments took him. After his children were married, he filled his garage with equipment so he could cut and polish stones. He made some very beautiful jewelry. I told him I thought it a wise course, for if heads ever rolled at 47 East South Temple, he would have something to fall back on. "Funny," he said.

Dad was an avid hiker, and whenever a free Saturday presented itself, he would turn us out of the sack early with his watch cry, "Come on, great men climb mountains." And so we climbed mountains. When he felt he needed special direction from the Lord, out came the hiking shoes and off he would go to the kind of places that yielded much of heaven's instruction to prophets and righteous men in ages past. While hiking Mount Olympus, a mountain that towers majestically above the Salt Lake Valley, I dislodged a stone about twice the size of a basketball. As I moved to avoid its fall, I saw that it was going to hit Dad, who was a few steps behind and below me. His head was turned so he did not see it coming. Things happened so quickly I didn't have time to warn him, but some unseen power did. That power snapped his head toward me so that the stone flew over his shoulder close enough to his cheek to shave that side of his face. Neither he nor I questioned that we had shared the companionship of someone from the unseen world that day.

Mother was a magnificent cook. Her bread and rolls were the envy of the neighborhood. She spent most of her adult life as a Relief Society president, and thus we knew that when we came home to a house filled with the aroma of freshly baked bread, it was certain death to touch the loaves destined for neighbors or someone in the ward whose circumstances merited them. By contrast, Dad's skill in the kitchen was limited to opening the refrigerator and turning the stove on and off. When Mother went to the hospital to bring a new member of the family into the world and Dad was left to do the cooking, he would get out a big pot and empty the contents of the refrigerator into it, warm it up, and serve it. We had a special name for these meals, which we will not preserve for posterity. Suffice it to say we were always especially happy to welcome Mother home again.

Mother saw that our home was filled with good music, and Dad saw that it was liberally stocked with good books, most of which dealt with either the history or the doctrine of the Church. After we started going off to school, he would frequently complain that whatever the book was he wanted, one of his children had taken it. There was something about his complaints that seemed to suggest he was quite pleased that his children had sufficient interest in such books to take them. The importance of learning was something that was caught, not taught. Children generally learn to love what their parents love. In our home, gospel understanding was highly prized.

Participation in high school athletics was greeted with tolerance rather than excitement. Mother was even less interested in such things than Dad, who referred to the high school as the Athletic Club. Practices typically ended sometime after dinner, which caused some consternation for Mother. One night when I returned home, she said in an exasperated tone, "Daddy, you have to talk to that boy." He responded with a cheerful, "Hello, Joseph," and returned his attention to the evening paper. In my senior year of high school, when a knee injury prevented my playing basketball, I joined the debate team instead. When Dad learned about this, he held a one-man parade, marching from the kitchen down the hall through the living room to the dining room and back to the kitchen. Around and around he went, marching and singing, "My boy is going to use his brain, my boy is going to use his brain."

Dad's enthusiasm was generally reserved for such events as a son receiving a mission call. His praise was evoked only by things that mattered. The first time an article of mine was published, he wrote me a letter in which he commended my craftsmanship, the illustrations I'd used, and the way the chain of thought developed the idea. The article wasn't that important, but the encouragement was.

We children did not get an allowance, but we were expected to help around the home. As to money, we learned that when babysitting or cutting lawns, the rule was that half of everything we earned was to be saved for our missions. In fact, virtually everything we earned was saved for that purpose.

In our home there was no pretense about being religious. My father and both grandfathers were great spiritual men who thought and spoke about the gospel constantly, yet they did not wear their religion on their shirtsleeves. There was nothing phony, contrived, or just for show in what they did, never a thought to impress others or to suggest in any way that they were something they were not. They did not bribe their children to read the scriptures or nag them

Family Traditions

about religious duties. They simply loved the Lord and loved the scriptures, and their children and grandchildren, who loved them, caught that spirit and sought to imitate that example. We understood that the Lord came first simply because we never saw Him or His principles given second place.

Dad hoped that his children would come to love the gospel as he did. It was not his nature to engage us in gospel conversations as his father did; still, he never tired of answering our questions and always treated them respectfully.

Generally, if you got a gift from Dad, it was a book. Each was carefully chosen and always included a note on the inside of the cover or on the first page. For instance, the book he gave me the first Christmas after my return from the mission field contains this inscription:

> To: Joseph F. McConkie—
>
> The most important single thing that any Latter-day Saint ever does in this world is to marry the right person, in the right place, by the right authority—
>
> Dad & Mother

In other words, he thought I ought to be looking for a wife. He was giving me that counsel for Christmas, and the book provided the opportunity.

The letters Dad wrote usually came at Mother's prodding. Exceptions were letters written to commend something he thought well done or to counsel on matters that concerned him. Missionary service and calls to positions of responsibility generated wonderful letters of counsel. While our missionary companions got newsy letters from home, we got the modern equivalent of the epistles of Paul.

Many of the important lessons we learned from Dad came from the rich teaching moments that only the vicissitudes of life can provide. He taught what he knew. He did not teach us to throw a baseball, dribble a basketball, bait a fishhook, or shoot a rifle. He did not teach us how to fix a car or do anything else mechanical. All of this has something to do with the principle that you cannot teach what you do not know. He did, however, teach us to work, and he taught us that sweat, blisters, and a sore back were an important part of a well-rounded life.

Priesthood Authority and Blessings

My father had a profound respect for priesthood authority. As a newly ordained deacon, I walked with him from the Church offices to the Tabernacle for a general priesthood meeting. Of course, we met a number of the Brethren along the way. As my father introduced me to them, the tone of his voice said as plainly as he would have said it in words, "I have great respect for these men."

When his children asked him gospel questions, they learned that answers did not come easily. We always had to prime the pump. Our question to him would evoke a series of questions in return, questions that measured our understanding and the effort we had made to find an answer. The answer we got was a measure of his confidence in us. I had conversations with him in which he freely shared what he thought, only to hear him say "I don't know" to the same question when it was asked by someone he judged to be spiritually immature.

The same principle applied in the giving of blessings. In some homes, the father gives each of his children a blessing as they start each new year of school. That was not done in our home. The blessings I received were on such occasions as missionary and military service or marriage. Rich in the outpouring of the Spirit, these blessings were recorded, and they are in counsel and prophecy the equal of the blessing given me by an inspired patriarch. The first of such blessings my father gave me attended my being set apart as a missionary. In that day missionaries were all set apart by general

Family Traditions

authorities while they were in the Missionary Training Center, which was across the street from the Church offices. On the day we were set apart, all the missionaries then in the Training Center were assembled in the auditorium in the Church Office Building. The missionaries were divided into groups of ten or twelve and sent to the office of one of the Brethren. I was among those sent to the office of Elder Bruce R. McConkie. I remember my excitement as I waited to be set apart. I also remember how distinctively different each blessing was. As each one was set apart, I wondered if I would be next. When the others in my group had been set apart, they were excused. I sat, wondering if my father had forgotten me. After their departure, he arranged his Dictaphone to record the blessing and then both set me apart as a missionary and gave me a marvelous father's blessing. It was one of the most meaningful spiritual experiences of my life.

I shared a similar experience with my brothers on the eve of my leaving for Vietnam. We were having a family night with my parents, and Dad suggested he had in mind giving Stanford and Mark a father's blessing, not having done that previously. While distinctively different, both blessings were remarkable. I would have loved to lay claim to the promises given to either one of them. As I listened, I offered a silent prayer that Dad would see fit to give me a blessing also. Having finished those blessings, he then turned to me and suggested that I might also be in line for a blessing. Again, the blessing given was different from the others. It was tailored to my circumstances and needs and answered perfectly the matters of greatest concern to me in handling my responsibilities as a Latter-day Saint chaplain in a combat zone. The principles announced in that blessing constituted a compass that guided me through a lot of difficult situations. I have since learned that these same principles work just as well in civilian life.

It was the practice of the Church in our growing-up years for young people to give two-and-a-half-minute talks in the opening exercises of Sunday School. Given that there were eight children in our family, it seemed like one of us was always taking his or her turn as a two-and-a-half-minute speaker. Generally the speakers chose their topic. That was not the case in our family. Dad made the choice for us, and it was always the same. Our talk came from the First Vision and centered on our bearing testimony that Joseph Smith was a prophet. We used to fuss and act a little embarrassed that our family only knew one subject to talk on. Dad remained unmoved. With the passing of the years, we have all come to see the wisdom of his purpose in having us speak repetitiously on that subject. Lay the foundation of your understanding right, and everything else fits nicely and naturally into place.

The Extended Family

In that day people knew how to visit. Each week we visited both sets of grandparents. As we did so, the conversation always turned to gospel subjects. My father could not get together with his own father or my Granddaddy Smith without the conversation turning immediately to a gospel subject. There was no small talk about the weather or rehearsing of recent sporting events, nor was there even concern about political or national matters. The thing of greatest interest to these men was the gospel, and they never missed an opportunity to discuss it. Mother and Dad belonged to a couple of groups that met monthly—both centered on gospel study. Grandmother McConkie was a very strong matriarch who insisted that her married children meet frequently to study the gospel together. Granddad McConkie generally gave direction to these gatherings. If anyone showed up without his scriptures, he was sent home to get them.

Dad followed this same tradition with his married children. The scriptures were always the source of his instruction. He did not use

Family Traditions

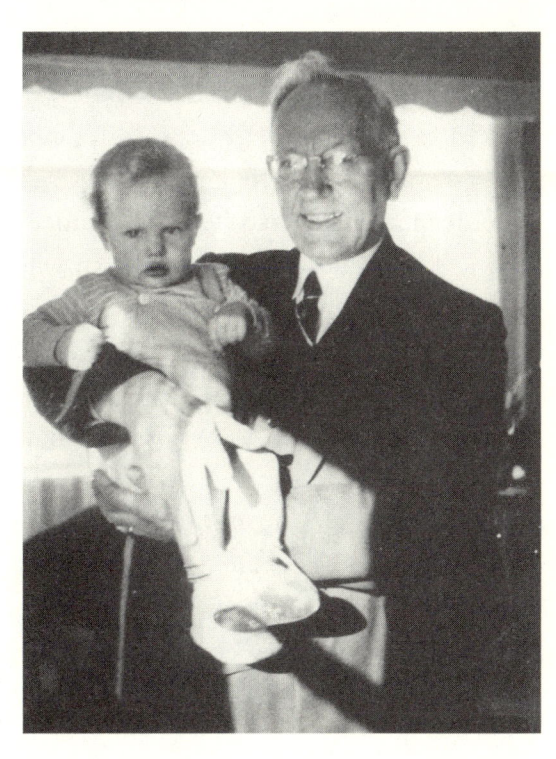

*Joseph and his
grandfather Smith*

himself or his experiences as the source of his teaching. He was very guarded about his own experiences and rarely told the experiences of others. While taking him to the airport one Saturday morning, I shared a frustrating experience from the previous evening. I had told what I thought were a couple of faith-promoting experiences to the members of a temple preparation class I was teaching. Each story was countered by someone who was supposed to be there to encourage the others who were preparing for the temple. When I shared my feelings of frustration with Dad, he said simply, "Did it ever occur to you that you don't teach gospel principles with stories?" What he was telling me was that although we generally expect the emotion of our stories to carry the burden of changing people's hearts, we are better off to let the principle stand on its own and leave it to the Holy Ghost to bear witness of it.

After his own father began to have trouble with his health, Dad became very conscious of watching his weight and getting proper exercise. When we lived on Lambourne Avenue, he frequently walked to the Church Offices in the morning, a distance of just under eight miles. He took up jogging at the age of sixty-five. On a Saturday morning when he had a chance to run, he would take a dime to call home and then head in whatever direction he felt inclined to. He would run until he was tired and then call Mother to come and get him. On occasion he ran distances of fifteen—and in one instance eighteen—miles. Dad secretly wanted to run a marathon and liked to go to Liberty Park to watch the runners finish the annual *Deseret News* marathon each July.

After the death of Aunt Jessie, Joseph Fielding Smith moved in with my parents. This was difficult for Dad, because he knew there would be some who thought he courted special favor with his father-in-law. Nothing could have been further from the truth. Because of this, however, he steadfastly avoided being alone with Granddaddy Smith. I think it annoyed Mother a little, and it caused some awkwardness, but knowing how strongly Dad felt about the matter, she accepted it.

Of Holidays and Such

On Christmas morning, we got up, dressed, made our beds, and had something to eat (in our mother's vain hope that it would keep us from stuffing ourselves with Christmas goodies). Then we lined up on the stairs according to age and waited for Dad to go into the living room to turn on the Christmas tree lights and see if Santa had really come. His manifestation of surprise invariably assured us that Santa had not forgotten us.

About mid-morning, Granddaddy Smith and Aunt Jessie would arrive. Everyone would be hugged and kissed—by the man others thought of as a stern apostle—and then he would give each of us a new silver dollar. After their visit, we all jumped into the car to visit

Family Traditions

our McConkie grandparents. The last of those visits was particularly memorable. It took place on Christmas Day 1965. Granddaddy McConkie had been ill for some time. At the conclusion of our visit, he said he had something very important to tell us. We all gathered around, and even the young ones were quiet.

I don't remember all that he said that day, but some of his words I will never forget. "I am about to die," he began. "I don't know yet what my assignment will be in the spirit world, but this much I do know: when I die I will not cease to love you; I will not cease to be concerned about you; I will not cease to pray for you; and I will not cease to labor in your behalf." In April of the following year he died. He was taken to the hospital on a Saturday night. Dad had a local stake conference. In the leadership meeting that evening, he did something he had never done in any of the other thousand or more leadership meetings he had spoken in. He, not knowing why, chose to be the first speaker rather than the last. As he concluded his remarks and was about to sit down, someone gave him a message about his father's condition. He was able to excuse himself and immediately joined the family at the hospital.

It does not seem that long ago that our family spent our last Christmas with my own father. Because he was coming down to Provo on Christmas Day to speak to the missionaries at the Missionary Training Center, we invited him and Mother to join our family for Christmas dinner. There was nothing Dad loved to do more than take the scriptures and tell the story of the birth of Christ. He wanted to speak to the missionaries for a couple of hours but knew that his strength was very limited. That was the last meeting I attended with him. None of us realized the seriousness of his situation. He spoke for an hour and then sat down. The missionaries sang and special musical numbers were rendered while he rested. He then stood and spoke a second hour. We left immediately after the closing prayer. Dad wanted to shake hands with the missionaries, but he just didn't have the energy.

We returned to our home. Dad immediately lay down on the floor to rest and asked if I had a sweater he could borrow. In my closet I found a sweater he had given me for Christmas more than twenty years before. I had never worn it. The sleeves were too long. Why I had kept it all those years, I don't know. I suppose I hoped my arms would grow. I took the sweater to Dad and said, "Merry Christmas." The fit was perfect. He lay back down on the living room floor and fell comfortably asleep while my wife and daughters completed the preparations for dinner.

Christmas dinners are always good in our home, but this one was especially so. As we ate, we took turns unwrapping treasured memories, laughing, and crying together. That evening when Dad left, he kept that sweater. It was wrapped tightly around him. He never cared about gifts. No one could ever figure out what to give him. In recent years I had made it a practice at Christmas to present him with a manuscript I had written and ask him to review it for me. That seemed to please him more than any other kind of gift I could have given him.

Still, there was something special in my being able to return that sweater to him. In some unspoken way, it seemed to represent my desire to return to him all that was warm and good that I had received from him.

14

"What Was It Like?"

I would never brag about my children. If they are worth bragging about, someone else will do it for me.

—Bruce R. McConkie

What was it like to have Bruce R. McConkie as your father?" and "What was it like to be the son of an apostle?" are questions I have been asked a thousand times over, and perhaps they deserve a written answer. It seems to me that two observations ought to be made. First, I would not suppose that the experiences I had in the home in which I was raised differ greatly from the kind of experiences anyone else has who is privileged to have parents who love the Lord, strive to keep his commandments, and endeavor to live up to the covenants they made with him in exactness and honor. We are members of the same Church, hear the same doctrines taught, fill the same assignments, have the same concerns and sorrows, and rejoice in the same things. Second, the love and respect children feel for their parents stands independent of offices or callings that their parents may hold. The love and respect children have for their parents has nothing to do with how well known or how little known their parents are. The love and respect a child has for his parents is the result of experiences they share together. The newborn, whose birthright includes some of the wisdom of heaven, has no interest in the social or financial standing of his parents. Whether the parents are rich or poor, of high standing or low, are looked up to or away from, matters not to their children. How children are taught and what they are taught to love is the extent of their concern. Children simply don't grow up thinking, "Well, I would love Dad or Mom more if only they held a more prominent position in the Church."

Of this I am sure: my father's ability to call down the powers of heaven, his knowledge of the gospel, his love of God, and relentless pursuit of gospel truths were not appended to an office or calling. No office added to them, and no office could take from them. It is for the man to make the office, not the office to make the man. The same principle is, of course, true for women. True, there is a mantle of spiritual power to which one becomes a rightful heir in certain offices, but it is obvious to all that the mantle does not wear well with those unworthy or unprepared to wear it.

The doctrine that my father espoused was that "true greatness is found only in the family." Such was the standard by which Bruce McConkie expected to be judged, and by such a standard his children and his wife feel no awkwardness in placing him among the great patriarchs of all dispensations.

A Tribute to Fathers

A few years ago, I was invited to speak in a sacrament meeting devoted to paying tribute to fathers. Each speaker who preceded me described how his father had taught him to catch a baseball, ride a horse, hunt deer, or change the oil in a car. As I listened to them, I realized that I had no such stories to tell. My father never threw a ball to me, never took me hunting or camping, nor did he have any idea how to change the oil in a car. We didn't even go to church together because he was gone virtually every Sunday on conference assignments. He was not present when I received any of the offices in the Aaronic Priesthood nor any award in Scouting. He did not teach me how to drive nor how to tie a tie, nor was he around when I learned, by rather painful experience, how to shave. He never took me to a baseball or basketball game, nor did we ever go to a movie together. In short, we simply were not a recreationally minded family.

Among the other things he did not teach us was patience. When we worked with him in the yard or on some home improvement project, he expected us to read his mind or to be able to quickly find things that were never where they were supposed to be. Such gifts are rarely found in children or any other conscripted labor. They did not manifest themselves in his children, nor have I learned that any trace of them has been found in his grandchildren.

What, then, did we do together? We dug a root cellar and a septic tank, we painted the house and shingled the roof, we built shelves, and we tiled the basement floor. When he came home in the evening and I wasn't working, the first thing he would say was, "Mother, isn't there something Joseph can be doing?" He was gone so much that it was my mother who taught me how to plant a garden, pull weeds, and irrigate. Yet, of my father it must be said he was simply fearless where sweat and calluses were concerned, particularly if they were mine.

So it was that when it became my turn in that sacrament meeting to speak of lessons learned and experiences shared with my father, my memories were confined to administering to the sick, listening to him instruct priesthood leaders when he took me with him to his Saturday meetings, hearing the gospel taught with power and clarity when he fulfilled all the promises to speak he had made at Christmastime, listening to remarkable gospel conversations that he had with his father-in-law, Joseph Fielding Smith, and his own father, Oscar W. McConkie, and, of course, with the passing of years, sharing in the same kind of conversations with him. In it all, I came to realize that the Lord has his own system of compensation, and that as a kid growing up, maybe I hadn't missed out on too much that mattered after all.

AGENCY

It was an unusual Sunday that found Dad without a conference assignment and hence at home. It was on one of those Sundays when I was in my early teens that I took occasion to see how the doctrine of agency worked. When it came time to leave for church, I announced that I had decided to exercise my agency and not attend church that day. Dad assured me that I had agency, which in our family meant that I could go to church willingly or I could go unwillingly. The choice, he said, was mine. Then he added, "Now get your coat on. You don't want to be late."

Some years passed before I understood the principle involved. When I was baptized, I chose to be an agent for Christ. As His agent, that is, as one committed to represent Him, I had already made the decision of whether I would attend my meetings or not. The covenant I had made assumed the responsibility to attend meetings and fill assignments. Properly understood, agency is the right to act, the right to do our duty. It is not and cannot be the source of excuse for refusing to do the same.

PAY THE PRICE

The most important thing our father taught his children was that, like everything else of worth, gospel knowledge comes only with a price. For instance, when I received my mission call, he said, "Now, son, what I want you to do is to read the Book of Mormon and report." So I read the Book of Mormon and reported. Then he said, "Now, son, what I want you to do is to read the Book of Mormon and report." So I read the Book of Mormon and reported. Again he said, "Now, son, what I want you to do is read the Book of Mormon and report." By this time I was in the mission field. I read the Book of Mormon once again and wrote to report. I received a letter back that said, "Now we've laid the foundation. You are ready to begin your study of the Book of Mormon." Then he began to tutor me in the meaning of the book.

He Encouraged and Taught

Some years later, when I was in Vietnam, I received a letter from Dad indicating he had taken occasion to read my master's thesis and was quite pleased with it. The thesis dealt with Joseph Smith's concept of God. He told me that he had gone to one of the major Latter-day Saint book publishers to see if they would be interested in publishing it. They looked at it and said, "We don't see this kind of thing as marketable, but we figure that somebody who could write it could write something we would publish. Have him come and see us when he gets back."

When I returned from Vietnam, I made an appointment to see them. We talked, and I was invited to write a book on my experiences in Vietnam. The suggestion was made that I prepare an outline and write a first chapter. They would look at it and see what they thought.

A few weeks later I returned to these same men with a first chapter and an outline in hand. They looked at what I had done and again said, "This isn't marketable." The difficulty was that I was writing from the point of view of the "establishment." In that era, defending the "establishment" wasn't the thing to do. So the suggestion was made that I go back and write it from a different perspective. I was told that it was a perfectly legitimate literary device to manufacture dialogue if it represented what was said. I was also told that if I wanted to say some things I was a little uncomfortable with saying, it was a perfectly legitimate literary device to use a pen name. It was back to the drawing board.

I wrestled with the invitation I had been given and finally sought counsel from my father about it. I remember distinctly what he said: "You will yet write books, and when you do, you be sure that they are worthy of your name." End of interview. End of discussion.

This was a father talking to a son who had never received anything better than a C+ in an English class. If my father had said, "Someday you will write a paragraph that will be published," I would have had a hard time believing it. He didn't say that, nor did he say, "You will yet write a book." He said, "You will yet write books," and then charged me to make sure they were worthy of my name. Since that time I have written or co-written twenty-four books, and I believe that all of them meet the standard set by my father.

I threw out the Vietnam material. I decided if I could write, it would have to be about something else. Then the idea came that I could write a biography of my grandfather Joseph Fielding Smith, who was then president of the Church. That was a little audacious for a kid my age, but I went back to the publisher with the idea, and they were excited about it. So I wrote a book on the life of President Smith, which sold very well and opened the door for me to write other things.

Get Your Own Answers

A lesson common to each of Bruce McConkie's children was that the answers we received to questions we asked were always in direct proportion to the preparation we had made. He never just answered a question. He would always ask "find out" questions first. He wanted to know what we had done by way of preparation. His answers were an expression of the confidence he had in you. Usually you had to prime the pump—he didn't just volunteer information. You had to almost twist his arm and prove that you were hungry to learn.

There was a point, however, when I asked a question and the answer was, "Look, junior, you have the same sources available to you that I do to me." That was his way of saying, "It's time for you to be weaned. I've taught you how to get answers. Now, you go get your own." With that, the nature of our relationship shifted. Thereafter, I would say to him, "I've been struggling with this question. I've done this and this, and I've determined that," and then we would talk on those terms. It has since dawned on me that in doing this we were following the pattern for getting answers that the Lord gave in Doctrine and Covenants 9, which instructs us to study things out in our mind, make our best conclusions, and then seek confirmation from the Spirit. I don't think Dad always knew the answer to my questions when we began this kind of exchange. It was exhilarating to explore and discover things together. Further, I never felt intimidated in those matters on which we chose to disagree.

It has been said that a teacher has succeeded when you no longer need him. Dad taught us how to get answers for ourselves rather than having us develop a dependency relationship on him. Had he done that, the well of our understanding would have dried up when he passed away. Perhaps the most important thing he taught us was how to keep the waters of everlasting life continuously flowing into that well.

Don't Drink below the Horses

As an extension of the idea that we are capable of getting our own answers and are responsible to do so, Dad added a bit of cowboy wisdom. "Don't drink below the horses," he would frequently tell us. In the providence of heaven, every child of God has claim upon the love of our eternal Father, the right to petition him in prayer, and equal claim upon his direction. All who are baptized are given the companionship of the Holy Ghost and thus the right to personal revelation. No one is required to "drink below the horses," that is, to rely on the spiritual experiences of others. The heart of the gospel centers in the verity that all are invited to drink at the fountainhead.

BUILDING ON THE RIGHT FOUNDATION

Before he wrote his *Messiah* series, Dad made it a point to read everything that Elder James E. Talmage had read on the subject. He asked Sam Weller at Zion's Book Store to find copies of a list of long-out-of-print books. While returning from a conference assignment, he was reading one of those books while waiting for a plane and discovered some material by a sectarian scholar that harmonized perfectly with the restored gospel. As he boarded his flight, he met Marion G. Romney, then a member of the First Presidency, who was also returning from an assignment. He said, "President Romney, I have got to read this to you. This is really good stuff," and proceeded to share his newfound treasure. When he was finished, President Romney said, "Bruce, I have to tell you a story. A few years ago I found something that I thought was remarkable confirmation of Mormonism written by one of the world's great scholars. I read it to J. Reuben Clark, and he said, 'Look, Marion, when you read things from the great scholars of the world and they don't agree with us, so what? And when you read something like that and you find they are right on the mark and they agree with us, so what?'"

My father thought that a good lesson. We err when we seek confirmation for our doctrines from the world.

YOU'RE AS SMART AS ISAAC, AREN'T YOU?

I didn't get married as early as Dad thought I ought to, and he let me know he was concerned. Our conversations sounded like a missionary's interview with an overanxious mission president. He'd say, "Son, don't you think you ought to have a goal? How many dates do you think you should have each week?"

As a returned missionary, I was subject to a draft board that felt obliged to see that all returned missionaries had the opportunity to serve in Vietnam, and they made that opportunity available to me. While being processed by the Church to serve as a chaplain, I was in summer school at Brigham Young University. Dad called me one afternoon to tell me there would be a delay in the process of getting my name cleared with the government so I could receive my commission. The delay would mean that I would be drafted and go to boot camp, and when things were cleared with Washington, I would be taken out of boot camp and sent to the officers' training course. When he finished the explanation, I said, "Oh, no."

He said, "Well, I know you are disappointed."

I said, "You don't know the half of it."

He said, "There's a girl involved."

I said, "Yes."

He said, "Marry her."

I said, "Dad, I've only known her for a week and a half."

He said, "You've heard the story of Isaac and Rebekah, haven't you?" (You remember the story in Genesis 24:67—they met, walked into Sarah's tent, were married, and loved each other.)

I said, "Yes."

He said, "Certainly you're as smart as Isaac, aren't you?"

I said, "Yes." I proved it by marrying the girl in question, who has since proven herself in faith and in works a worthy counterpart of Rebekah of old.

Being Competent Witnesses

The McConkie children were taught to assume responsibility for what they believed. In a question-and-answer session with the

BYU religion faculty, Dad illustrated this principle by explaining how he went about writing his six-volume *Messiah* series. "Before I wrote *The Promised Messiah*," he explained, "I read the standard works from cover to cover and elicited from them everything that dealt with the promise of a Messiah. I organized this material and then wrote the book." Then he said, "Before I wrote *The Millennial Messiah*, I read the standard works as if I had never read them before and elicited from them everything about the millennial Messiah. I organized this material and then wrote the book."

This process stands in rather sharp contrast to the usual practice, in which if someone intends to write a book on either of these subjects, he or she first seeks a research grant, hires a research assistant, and commences to see what everyone of importance in the past has had to say on the matter. A compilation of quotations is then assembled, organized, and called a book. What Dad was saying was that we ought to drink from the fountainhead rather than simply rehearse what others have said. To further illustrate the point, he said, "I would never quote another man unless I could first square what he said with the scriptures and unless he had said it better than I could." He added, "Last week I quoted Parley P. Pratt for the first time in my life. I did it because I could square what he said with the scriptures and because he said what I wanted to say better than I could say it."

Too often in the Church, we fill our assignment to teach a particular principle by quoting an authority while at the same time excusing ourselves from the responsibility to first assure ourselves that the quotation squares with the scriptures. Dad's concern was that this practice could lead to spiritual atrophy because it shifts the responsibility for pondering and praying to someone else and thereby makes us dependent on the someone else rather than on ourselves. I think that is what he was trying to teach me when, as a young man, I took on a number of my McConkie uncles in a gospel discussion. They are all strong-minded and articulate men. I knew, however, from previous conversations that Dad agreed with the position I was taking. When I turned to him for support, he sat silent and then quietly slipped out of the room. It was for me to sink or swim. I later learned that Mother, who overheard the conversation from the kitchen, said to him, "Don't you think you ought to go give your son some support?"

He responded, "No, he is doing just fine." I interpreted that to mean that I must learn to stand on my own.

"Teach What They Should Have Asked You to Teach"

After my return from military service in Vietnam, I received a number of invitations to speak at firesides. Concerned that I was being invited to entertain with faith-promoting stories rather than to teach gospel principles and, moreover, that those stories might appreciably improve with continued telling, I asked Dad what I should do. His counsel was to accept the invitations to speak and then "have the good sense to speak on what they should have asked you to speak on in the first place."

Taking Personal Responsibility for What We Believe

We err in supposing that knowledge and wisdom are inherent in a particular office or position. Similarly, no office can bestow faith. The virtues of a particular office are those that the one holding it brings to it.

While reading the biography of a man of high standing in the Church, I was troubled about attitudes the author of the book attributed to him. In some instances, these differences were on matters I understood to be fundamental to our faith. I mentioned this concern to my father, who observed, "Everyone is responsible for what they believe and what they choose not to believe. No office can excuse them from that responsibility."

I was reminded of the example of my grandfather Smith. Every year for years he was invited to a Christmas open house by a man for whom he had great love and respect. He never accepted the invitation because the open house was always held on Sunday, and he did not believe that activity to be a proper observance of the Sabbath. That the man was a prominent Church leader made no difference to him.

The Measure of Orthodoxy

Dad was very much of the opinion that the measure of a person's spiritual maturity is found in his or her loyalty to the Prophet Joseph Smith. For him, the revelations of the Restoration were the key which unlocked the meaning of the Old and the New Testaments. They were the key by which one came to know Christ and his gospel. He told his missionary sons that it was easier to convert someone to the Book of Mormon than it was to bring them to an understanding of what the Bible was really teaching. For him, to study the Bible without the aid of modern revelation was the same as denying that we had living prophets, the priesthood, or the gift of the Holy Ghost. He was fully convinced that this principle unlocked more to our understanding of the Bible than anything else we could do.

Defining Greatness

During my graduate studies, I was bombarded with statements about the greatness of various men. In my judgment, some of these so-called great men did not merit the accolade. Hence the question to my father: "What do you think constitutes true greatness?"

There was no hesitation. His answer was immediate and couched in a little impatience that a question with such an obvious answer would be asked. "True greatness," he declared, "is found only in the family."

THE SPIRIT OF REVELATION

One of Dad's favorite texts for a family home evening was 2 Nephi 31. He used this passage to illustrate the necessity of planning, and then faithfully following, a course that will lead us back to the presence of God. During one of these lessons, I asked several questions that slowed down the flow of ideas—to the annoyance of my siblings. My questions reflected the kind of questions I was being asked as a teacher, and I was interested to see how Dad would respond to them. At one point, I asked how he could teach a particular principle with such confidence. I noted that when I did the same thing, my colleagues objected, telling me that I was going beyond the period that ended the sentence. He replied, "If you can't go beyond the period that ends the sentence, you don't have the Spirit; and if you don't have the Spirit, you shouldn't be teaching."

That idea is both bold and vintage Bruce McConkie. It suggests that a gospel teacher not only has the right to interpret scripture but, as directed by the Spirit, can expand on it. I am sure there are many who would be uncomfortable in granting teachers that much latitude. Certainly, it would be hard not to suppose that at some point someone might misuse such authority. It could be noted, however, that his bold statement is not nearly as bold as granting agency to all the children of men or giving the priesthood to all worthy males in the Church. That both agency and priesthood have been misused does not argue for doing away with either.

On another occasion, Dad suggested to me that all scripture is given with sufficient ambiguity that those desiring to misconstrue or misuse it will be able to do so. This, he held, was very deliberate on the Lord's part, for the way we interpret scripture becomes a measure not only of our understanding but also of our spiritual integrity.

Following Priesthood Authority

One evening when my wife, Brenda, and I were eating dinner with Dad and Mother, he got up, went to the refrigerator, and poured himself a glass of buttermilk.

This surprised me, as I had never seen him drink buttermilk before. Teasing, I asked, "Isn't drinking buttermilk one of the first signs of apostasy?"

He responded that he had never liked buttermilk, but one of the senior members of his Quorum saw to it that Dad was served buttermilk when the Twelve had a meal together after their Thursday temple meeting, and he had developed a taste for it.

I then asked, again in jest, "How do you discern between unrighteous dominion and the proper use of priesthood authority?"

His immediate response: "You don't!"

I have come to learn that those who constantly question that which they are asked to do will always question that which is asked of them. Those who do not constantly question always seem to carry with them a rich portion of the Spirit.

Dating Standards

There was no topic upon which Dad would rather preach than that of eternal marriage, especially if one or more of his own children were present. He took some considerable interest in those whom his children dated. My sister Vivian told a fellow who asked her out once that he would have to have a temple recommend to date her. I answered the door on the appointed evening and took him into the living room to meet my father. I then went out to the kitchen, where Vivian was waiting. I said, "He's not going to pull out a recommend." She said, "Just wait. He will." After a few minutes of small talk, the young man handed Dad a letter from his bishop attesting to his worthiness. Dad, acting as if this were routine, carefully read the letter and asked a few follow-up questions. Only at this point did Vivian have the mercy to make her appearance. I don't think anyone ever bothered to tell the young man that the recommend was not really necessary. But there was never a question in anyone's mind about the kind of friends we were to have or the kind of people who were acceptable for us to date.

Perspective

It was a family tradition that after his sons received the priesthood they would attend general priesthood meeting with Dad each year in April and October. This was always a special experience because it was one of the few occasions when we were able to attend a meeting together. I remember asking Dad before one of those meetings who was going to talk. His response was, "Peter, James, and John." There was no question about what he was telling me. The First Presidency were going to speak, and that was the same to him as if he were going to hear Peter, James, and John do the preaching.

Missionaries Are Blessed

The first letter I received from Dad as a young missionary read in part as follows: "Throughout the revelations the Lord takes frequent occasion to mention great blessings that will attend missionary work—almost always the blessings are promised to the missionary, not the convert. It is assumed that the convert will gain blessings, because the reception of the gospel always brings such. But the one especially and particularly blessed will always be the one sent to carry the message."

He then reviewed what my grandfather Smith had said about Doctrine and Covenants 4 at my farewell, emphasizing the passages that promise faithful servants that through their service, they would lay up in store that they perish not but bring salvation to their own souls. When I asked a missionary who served under my father in

Australia how he had motivated them, he said, "He just told us that we were there to work out our own salvation."

Wearing a Blue Collar

To a son struggling in choosing a profession, Dad wrote: "It is certainly not important whether people have a white collar or a blue collar job. It is just as important to work with your hands as it is with your mind." He further cautioned, "Don't try to choose the thing that will make life easy. Look for something that will make life hard."

As to measuring people's success by their income, he held that the amount of money people had was usually the result of accident or chance, and it mattered little. Character, he maintained, was eternal.

Following Counsel

Often in responding to a question about why he was doing a particular thing, Dad would say, "I just do what the Brethren tell me." His natural propensity was to be accepting and obedient, not to challenge and question what he was asked to do. When he preached, he always sought to obtain the mind of the Lord and teach only as the Spirit directed. He said it did not make "the snap of the fingers" difference to him what the doctrines were or what the Lord wanted taught. His responsibility as the Lord's agent was simply to find the course the Lord wanted him to follow and then follow it.

In that same spirit, when President Kimball told the Saints they ought to grow a garden, Dad did not suppose that members of the Quorum of the Twelve Apostles were excused from that instruction. Dad and Mother were living in the house on Dorchester Drive at the time. The yard provided no natural place for a garden, so he created one. This meant tearing out a beautiful old hedge at the cost of some scratches and sore muscles. It meant the loss of a wonderful little shady spot and also any privacy in the backyard. On the other hand, it provided the opportunity to follow the direction of the prophet, which for Bruce McConkie was reward enough.

Balance Even in Gospel Study

Dad prized gospel study, yet he was keenly aware of the necessity for balance. It was not surprising that Mark—who had spent three of his teenage years in the mission home in Australia either associating with missionaries or following his father from one teaching assignment to another—gained the desire to be able to teach those same principles with the power and conviction his father did. Concerned that his son might spend time studying the gospel to the neglect of his other studies during his freshman year at Brigham Young University, Dad assigned his older brother and roommate, Stanford, to see that Mark spent a balanced amount of time studying for his classes.

Doctrines and Their Fruits

Occasionally, before I went off to college, when Dad had a local conference, he would take me as his companion for the Saturday leadership meetings. Often during those meetings he would respond to gospel questions. A commonly asked question was whether the Father, like Christ, had been a savior on the world in which he experienced his mortal probation and if there was a special strain of savior Gods?

To this question Dad, in a deep, modulated tone, would always respond, "What earthly good could possibly come from teaching such a thing?"

For Elder McConkie that question constituted a sure standard by which supposed doctrines could be discerned. If a doctrine was good, its fruits would be good; conversely, if a doctrine was bad, its fruits would be bad. In this instance, the implication of such a teaching was that an elect few within the family of God abided, as it were, by a different standard or law than the rest of us. The great difficulty in this teaching is that it negates the Savior's life as an example to be emulated because it reasons that he lived by a different set of laws than the rest of us. Because such a chain of thought does not engender faith, the question is, Why teach it? Thus the test for good doctrine is this: Does it produce good fruits?

I Will Know

When my grandfather Joseph Fielding Smith passed away, Dad was asked by the First Presidency to speak at his funeral. Because I had written a short biography of him, Dad sought my help in preparing that talk. I shared with him some stories that I thought might be appropriate. One of those stories dealt with the birth of my grandfather Smith and his receiving his father's name. His mother, Julina, the first of Joseph F. Smith's plural wives, had given birth to three daughters. Meanwhile, sons were born to two of the other wives, and each asked for her son to be given his father's name. President Smith refused, saying that right belonged to Julina as the first wife. She pleaded with the Lord to give her a son, promising that if he did so, she, like Hannah of old, would consecrate his life to the Lord's service. Finally, after ten years of marriage, Julina gave birth to a son, the tenth child of Joseph F. Smith. He was named for his father and often was spoken of by his mother as the "tithing child" of the Smith family.

I told Dad I had a reservation in telling the story, that being that my only source was Aunt Edith Patrick, who was eighty-three years of age when I interviewed her. Having just completed a master's degree in history, I was concerned that historians would not consider her account reliable. At the funeral, I sat next to my brother Mark, to whom I said, "I am a little concerned about something Dad might say today." He responded, "Yes, I know. Dad told me. He said, 'What Joseph doesn't understand is that I will know.'" Experienced in listening to and responding to the Spirit, Dad knew that when he came to that point in his talk, the Spirit would affirm or constrain as appropriate. The Spirit affirmed, and the story was told.

To some it is given to know that Jesus is the Christ, and to others it is given to believe on their words (D&C 46:13–14). In like manner, to some it is given to recognize the promptings of the Spirit with perfect surety. Bruce McConkie had that gift. It irritated some, who viewed his confidence in the realm of spiritual things as arrogance. People of this temperament were never reluctant to write and share their discomfort with him. It was his choice not to accommodate their feelings or make any concession to their criticism. He had seen what he had seen, and he knew what he knew, and he was not about to act otherwise.

15

THE NATURE OF THE MAN

Tell them to warm up the tar. I'm coming to speak.
—Bruce R. McConkie

When gospel principles were involved, there was never any question where Bruce McConkie stood. He could not be numbered among those who tempered or moderated their tone to accommodate the moment. For him, the course was sure, the response certain. The darts and arrows of his detractors only added to his confidence. His reasoning was simple: Joseph Smith's name was to be had for good and evil among all the peoples of the earth, and if he was to echo the same doctrines with the power of the same Spirit, then surely he could not expect other than the same treatment.

My father called me several days before a Brigham Young University devotional at which he was to speak. He had been assigned by his Quorum to address a matter that would offend many. "Tell them to warm up the tar," he said. "I'm coming to speak."

The Nature of the Man

Having the Right Enemies

Criticism followed Bruce McConkie like a shadow. He expected it and measured himself by it. "The measure of a man," he explained to his children, "is not found in who speaks well of him but who speaks against him. It is just as important to have the right enemies as it is to have the right friends." He was an agent of the Lord. "Agents represent their principal. They have no power of their own. They act in someone else's name. They do what they are told to do. They say what they are authorized to say—nothing more, nothing less." As the Lord's agent, he delivered the Lord's message. If people were offended with him for having done so, so be it. Scripture refers to Christ as the "messenger of the covenant." In rejecting Him, they rejected the covenant He brought. It could be no other way. Surely it is self-deception to feign offense with the messenger when the offense lies with the message.

In a general conference of the Church, he said: "What I am saying is what the Lord would say if he were here." He was strongly criticized by some for the audacity of that statement. Ironically, what preceded it was his testimony that each man who had stood at the head of the Church was the man chosen of the Lord to be his agent. Those who were offended with the testimony of Bruce McConkie were also those who would take offense with what the prophets of whom he testified had said and done.

Bruce never wanted to give a talk or write so much as a paragraph that did not give offense to the prince of darkness. The praise of others was not a source from which he chose to drink. "Have in mind also that it really does not make a particle of difference to any of you what we teach. I often think as I go around the Church and preach in various meetings that it just does not make the snap-of-the-fingers difference to me what I am talking about. I do not care what I talk about. All I am concerned with is getting in tune with the Spirit and expressing the thoughts, in the best language and way that I can, that are implanted there by the power of the Spirit. The Lord knows what a congregation needs to hear, and he has provided a means to give that revelation to every preacher and every teacher."

As to the matter of our sustaining the living prophet, many were troubled when the Lord allowed President David O. McKay to lose his vigor some time before his death and then to have the same thing happen with President Spencer W. Kimball and President Ezra Taft Benson. I asked my father why he thought the Lord kept these men alive as long as he did. He pondered the question for a moment and then said, "Whenever the prophet ceases to be a vigorous voice, all the wolves come out to bay. Perhaps this is the Lord's way of allowing the wolves to identify themselves."

HIS NATURE

Bruce McConkie had no interest in style or fashion. Surely he was not without faults, but vanity was not one of them. He wore short-sleeved shirts and had no idea what a "power tie" might be. Mother was his barber for years, and when she scalped him, he laughed at her concern and reminded her that "it would probably grow back." He relaxed in clothes that were well worn and comfortable. He seemed to have a propensity for socks with holes in them. He didn't care for suits and ties and never put one on unless he was going to a meeting or to his office.

When he received a stake conference assignment, he never wrote ahead with a list of special requirements for his comfort. He knew wherever he went that whatever was given him would be the best they had. Surely that would be enough. He consciously sought to put people at ease and was not critical when priesthood leaders made procedural mistakes. His purpose was to help, not to criticize. A man called to be a stake president at the age of thirty-six wrote: "As doubtless you have done with the scores of others in similar circumstances, you calmed my wife and me in a kind, warm and humorous way. Your wise words have helped immeasurably as we have faced the responsibilities you gave to us."

A brief note from Elder Carlos E. Asay, dated September 4, 1984, simply said, "I don't know how I can survive without a weekly exposure to your warm personality and wise counsel. I have become accustomed to your cheerful attitude and direct approach, even when heavy problems have been considered. I believe few men within the kingdom exemplify the Christlike virtues which I see in you."

Elder McConkie did not seek to draw attention to himself and felt no need to dominate discussions. When his extended family gathered, engaging gospel discussions were inevitable. For the most part, he sat silent and often had to be prodded to say anything. On one such occasion, his Aunt Hortense said, "Bruce, it's a wonder your children learned to talk, having never heard anyone do so at home."

When asked about his reluctance to say much around his extended family, he expressed concern about being misquoted and about having sacred things sensationalized. There were very few people with whom he dared shed his office and truly be himself.

In teaching, he rarely shared personal experiences. When he was presiding over a priesthood training session in St. George, his brother Oscar, who at the time presided over the Arizona Mission, which included St. George, joined him. In talks given in the Saturday meetings, Oscar used instances from his elder brother's life to illustrate various points. Though the people enjoyed this, his elder brother did not. That evening, "Bruce called me aside," Oscar recalled, "and told me that if I made so much as one reference to him in another talk, I would not be called on to speak again."

When Bruce McConkie stood to speak in the name of Jesus Christ, and that is what he believed he was doing, he had no interest in being cute or funny. He followed the example of his mentors

Oscar W. McConkie and Joseph Fielding Smith. Generally, if either of these men said something funny when he spoke, it was unintentional. If people laughed, these brethren were offended. They were not storytellers and did not feel that the declaration of the gospel and light-mindedness were compatible. Both of these men spoke at my missionary farewell when I was a young man. In my remarks, I made a number of what I thought were clever quips. Afterward, I overheard someone tell my grandfather McConkie that I would make a fine missionary. "Well," he said loud enough for me to hear, "if he can preach the gospel as well as he does nonsense, he will be fine."

These were not humorless men. To be with them was always a pleasant experience, but each of them took preaching the gospel to be a serious thing. Though Dad could be quick with a clever retort, his humor was usually more ponderously clever, as evidenced in his poetry or carefully planned pranks. An instance of each of these kinds of humor still had Mother laughing decades later. While they were staying in a foreign hotel, Mother complained that "the toilet paper was so thin it was just like using your hand." "I wouldn't know," Dad responded. While they were in Australia, Mother pleaded with Dad to replace his worn and dirty ties. The next morning he showed her one of them and innocently asked if she thought he ought to throw it away. She grabbed it, said yes, and put it in a wastebasket. The next morning he repeated the same ritual. This went on for four days before Mother realized he had been giving her the same tie each morning.

Of Mountains, Birds, and Rocks

While presiding over a mission in Australia, Dad noted in a letter to his mother: "Amelia and I have become bird watchers. She got some binoculars for Christmas, plus a bird book. Since then, every morning, at 5:00 or 5:30 or so the two of us have traipsed off to the paddock, marshes, river banks, and such, which adjoin our property and have begun to pick out the different kinds of birds. I am happy to report that this morning there was added to our list of birds identified: a Red-Kneed Dotterel, an Eastern Swamp Hen, and a positive identification, at last, of a White-faced Heron. This is pretty good for one day. Nearly all birds, incidentally, look much better than even the fanciest pictures of them in books."

A letter written a couple of years after their return from Australia notes his continued interest in getting outside and enjoying nature. "We had a remarkably fine time at Colter Bay. The really alert were up early and went out to Ox Bow Bend on the Snake River, where we saw great blue herons, sand hill cranes, pelicans, and a belted kingfisher, not to mention a moose calf suckling its mother, a muskrat swimming across the river, and other beauties of nature."

After helping his youngest daughter, Sara, with an assignment for a geology class, Dad also became a rock hound. The two-car garage of their home on Dorchester Drive was converted into a rock shop. Soon it was filled with rocks, a rock saw, a buffer, a polisher, and everything else necessary for him to make anything from bookends to tie tacks.

As occasion would afford, he and his mountain-climbing friend Finn Paulsen would team up to see what they could find. The two men shared some remarkable experiences together. "We were up Salina Canyon," Dad recalled, "on a ledge along the side of the mountain, digging into a vein. We were digging in the pocket which was about a yard deep under an overhanging cliff.

"We'd started at opposite ends and we worked toward each other. We'd come to the point where we were right together and we were so close that I could no longer use my crowbar, so I was going to move back and start over again.

"As I stood up to move back, and as he laid down again, the

whole cliff caved in and a couple of tons of rock came tumbling down.

"One rock about 18 inches or two feet in diameter came down where my head and shoulders had just been five seconds before. It came so close to my head that I felt it go through the top of my hair.

"At that same instant, Finn Paulsen, still lying on his side where he'd been, without knowing why, just started to roll. The cliff came so close to him that it caught his trousers where his legs were but he got out from under it.

"Neither one of us had a scratch on us. All we lost was his chisel which was under two tons of rock."

Music

Bruce McConkie had the ability neither to carry a tune nor to tell the difference. "When I was a young teen, between eleven and fourteen," Vivian recalled, "Dad asked me if I would like to go with him to his stake conference assignment on Sunday. The conference was in Logan, which was a two- or three-hour drive. Dad happened to be what we always called 'tone deaf.' Some people have tried to insist that there is no such thing, but he could not carry a tune or even approximate one. His voice seems to slide about in his throat. On our homeward journey, he sang hymns much of the way. He knew all the words to all the verses of an hour's worth of hymns, none of which could be recognized by their tune or any tune at all. I would occasionally say, 'It goes like this,' and try to give him the pitch. 'That's what I sang, wasn't it?' he would say, and go on with something unrecognizable. It was interesting to hear the words sung out of their usual habitat and be forced to center attention on their meaning."

He frequently capitalized on his inability to carry a tune when teaching how our premortal life affects who and what we are in our present estate. To illustrate that he was "playing hooky" when he

The Nature of the Man

should have been in a premortal music class, he would simply sing a few lines from a Church hymn. His efforts were most convincing and quite humorous. In this demonstration, he also gave everyone present a chance to laugh at themselves, for we all came into this world with an interesting collection of both abilities and inabilities. What he could not do with music, he did with words, expressing his plight this way:

MUSICANA

When once I dwelt in realms of light,
Where music could be read by sight,
I was so blind I could not see,
Nor did I know what ought to be—
Alas, Alas, I cut the class,
And failed my music test to pass;
And so to me sweet strains of song
Now seem like some resounding gong.

"To say that Bruce did not like good music," Amelia said, "would not really be true. He even had a saxophone at one time and played in the Junior High orchestra. He claims that it was not because he was any good at it but that he was the only person in school at that time who had a saxophone." This account leaves the origin of his possession of the saxophone as something of a mystery, as he was the oldest child in the family and thus would not have inherited it from an older sibling.

In the Eastern States Mission, where he served, the missionaries used to speak in street meetings. To begin these meetings, they would usually sing a few hymns. In his first experience at such a meeting, he stood by a sister missionary who had taught music in school. When they finished their first hymn, she said, "Elder McConkie, either stop singing or go down to the other end of the line." He did both. "From then on," Amelia recalled, "he would sing only when he was alone or when he and I were in the car going someplace."

Though his inability to carry a tune made him reluctant to sing, he knew the Church hymns well and could quote all the verses of most of them by heart. Once while traveling with Amelia he suggested a contest. He would sing the second verse from one of our Latter-day Saint hymns, and she would have to identify it. When she could not name the hymn, he would teasingly say, "Oh, I'm ashamed of you."

"When he was not home," Amelia recalled, "I generally had the radio tuned to the BYU classical music station, which I thoroughly enjoyed, but knowing it was not his idea of real beautiful music, I would turn it off while he was there. To be fair, he did not care for the so-called popular stuff either."

When he was called to the First Council of Seventy, he received tickets for concerts that were being held in the Tabernacle. Mother generally got someone else to share the tickets with her. Then came the day when a really famous orchestra was scheduled to play at the Tabernacle, with a world-famous conductor. Hence the following experience.

"I'll get one of my friends to go with me, if it is all right with you."

"No," he said, "I'll take you."

"But you don't have to. I know there is someone close by who would enjoy going."

"No, I'll take you."

So it was that he went to the concert. As the evening progressed, Bruce spent all his time jotting down ideas he had for the book he was writing. Knowing he was simply making the time pass and was utterly miserable, Mother couldn't enjoy the music, either. Finally the concert was over, and as they left, he said, "I'll get you a

The Nature of the Man

stereo and all the records you want if you never ask me to go to one of these things again."

So the deal was made, and Dad got Mother her stereo and records to go with it.

All this is not to say that Dad was totally without appreciation for music. At Christmastime one year, he came home with the entire set of Handel's *Messiah*. Then he put the records on to play. He lay on the floor with his scriptures and the script that came with the recordings, and he spent the full four hours of *Messiah* thoroughly enjoying himself.

While the love of music was not natural to him, the power of its message was, as evidenced in his poem "I Believe in Christ," now a favorite Latter-day Saint hymn. He also wrote a fourth verse for the hymn "Come, Listen to a Prophet's Voice," which was included in the 1985 edition of the LDS hymnal. The words, which suggest his own spiritual quest, are as follows:

> *Then heed the words of truth and light*
> *That flow from fountains pure.*
> *Yea, keep His law with all thy might*
> *Till thine election's sure.*
> *Till thou shalt hear the holy voice*
> *Assure eternal reign,*
> *While joy and cheer attend thy choice,*
> *As one who shall obtain.*[1]

STUDY HABITS

I have frequently been asked how Bruce McConkie or Joseph Fielding Smith studied the scriptures. To the best of my knowledge, their method was the same: It consisted of not having a method. If either of them were to be asked, I am confident they would assure the questioner that the secret to scriptural mastery is not to be found in some system of scripture marking, or anything like unto it.

The great and grand key was the frequency, intensity, and consistency with which they studied. Simply stated, they paid the price. For instance, Dad had a score of loose-leaf binders full of scriptural notations and analyses of every doctrine he found in his study of the Book of Mormon. He always studied with purpose.

Dad was remarkably well read. Rarely did I ask him about something I had read that he was not familiar with. He could not read a book without marking it up. After reading a book, he would record the date when he finished reading it and write a brief review of the book. At the end of a book on the history of ancient Israel by a noted secular scholar he wrote:

26 November 84

> 100% Anti-Christ
> 75% Anti-Jewish
> 50% Pro-Baal & Pro Canaanite
> Of questionable historical accuracy
> Highly speculative
> Unreliable
> Written with a bias intent to foster unbelief
> Not objective in any sense
> Almost pure hog wash
>
> —BRM.

Of a book written by a Latter-day Saint writer, he said in part, "Much that is said in the book is true. The book is in fact one of the best illustrations I have ever seen of the old adage: The more truth an error contains, the more dangerous it is." He then went on to note a number of the dangers found in that particular work.

He read with interest New Testament apocryphal works and recorded his assessment of them. For instance, of the *First Epistle of Clement to the Corinthians*, he wrote the following:

7 August 1980

This contains much wisdom and good counsel, the same

The Nature of the Man

being patterned after Holy Writ and what is found therein. It also contains many errors which an inspired theologian would not have made. It is not inspired writing—BRM.

Of the *Epistle of Mathetes to Diognetus*, a missionary tract with an apologetic tone, he wrote:

> 18 August 1980
> Some expressions about Christ and Christians are of surpassing worth. The reasoning about idols and idol worship is excellent. Some nonsense is also set forth—BRM.

Of the *Epistle of Polycarp to the Philippians*, an exhortation to be worthy and loving, full of Christian virtues, he wrote:

> 18 August 80
> A sound and edifying document, not pure scripture, but well expressed commentary thereon. It contains good counsel—BRM.

Of the *Epistle concerning the Martydom of Polycarp*, which recounts events related to Polycarp's being sentenced to be burned, he wrote:

> 18 August 1980
> Splendid Fiction! Aside from a few general comments about martyrdom in general, there is not a word of truth in it—BRM.

In response to a question about why he read secular writers, he said, "I read this stuff because it makes me mad and that helps me write with greater strength and power than I otherwise might."

When and How He Wrote

People often asked Dad when he found time to write. Mother's answer was, "On my time." He made good use of his holidays, days off, and other opportunities when he was free from assignments.

"More correctly, however, the answer should have been all the time," according to Mother. "Although he was a fun-loving, normal, well-balanced, and interesting person, he seemed to have the gospel on his mind all the time. Unlike other wives who would keep flowers in vases, mine were well supplied with pens and pencils, and pens could be found in the drawers and on the tables and many other places. Especially a shirt pocket with a bit of paper.

"You see, they had to be available so when a thought came it could be promptly recorded, even if it came in the middle of the night or the middle of a daughter's performance at a piano recital, for, as he said, he had to write when the inspirational juices were flowing.

"Then those thoughts were organized, and outlines made, and when he began to write on the typewriter, he seldom had to change a word.

"Thus after he was gone, we found innumerable notes, written on the spur of the moment. Written on any available paper, and filled with thoughts for books, or sermons, or articles, or whatever.

"People were always asking him questions; therefore the subjects he chose to write about were chosen because he felt a need for them. He wrote to instruct, to edify, to lift the members of the Church, and he was not in the least upset by those who were critical. He did not care about what they had to say as long as he felt it was what the Lord wanted said."

Preaching with Faith

Bruce McConkie wanted to be a great speaker, and he consciously worked to become such. As a young missionary, he set the standard in his mission for good diction and was called by his mission president to extend his mission for six weeks to fill a "speaking mission," in which he went from town to town to preach.

People came to recognize the discipline and organization in his talks, which they attributed to the training he received in law school. If this was the result of his legal training, we are left to wonder why so many who have had the same training show little evidence of it when they speak. The more probable answer rests in his habit of assigning himself gospel subjects to organize and speak on as he walked to and from the campus while he was a student at the University of Utah. He followed the same practice of assigning himself subjects and speaking on them when he had to drive long distances to attend stake conferences as a general authority.

Being Truer Than True

Mother, it seemed, was always a Relief Society president and of course was always coming home with new ideas to aid in her campaign to perfect the family. I remember one evening when Dad was lying on the floor reading the paper and she was reciting a litany of things they ought to be doing. Dad's response to all of it was a loving "Amelia, relax."

Dad always sought a balance in spiritual things and that included time to relax. Spiritually, the path of safety is the path of tried and proven orthodoxy. It is not found in extremes, however pious they may appear. In instructing his family, Dad consistently warned against becoming "truer than true," that is, against becoming overzealous about any particular facet of the gospel. "Fanaticism in one area makes it a short step to fanaticism in another," or, to paraphrase him, nuttiness in one area makes it a short step to nuttiness in another. This, he would tell us, is the kind of stuff that cultists are made of. All virtues are members of the same family, and all must learn to get along harmoniously with each other. When one virtue seeks to outshine another or is practiced in neglect of another, an imbalance immediately occurs, and we can easily get off course.

When a food faddist cornered Dad at a stake conference to

advise him that there were people in that stake who ate both ham and chocolate, he responded, "You have no idea how widespread that problem is. Why just last Thursday after our Temple meetings the First Presidency and the Quorum of the Twelve ate a meal together in the Temple and were served both ham and chocolates."

Getting to the Heart of the Matter

In responding to our questions, Dad was usually good for a zinging one-liner that really drove his point home. When asked why the Lord allowed the apparently untimely death of a prominent Church leader, he responded, "It is the Lord's church, and he runs it." To a member of the family who had a propensity to improve stories and tell too much, he warned, "The Lord doesn't reveal himself to blabbermouths." To a son perplexed over the actions of someone who should have conducted himself according to a higher standard, he said, "Junior, it's not who you are in the kingdom that counts; it's how well you keep the commandments." To children who were looking to get out of a tough task, he would say, "Life never was intended to be easy," or "The pursuit of easy things makes men weak."

Defender of the Faith

Elder McConkie gave two landmark addresses on the gathering of Israel. The first was given in Mexico City while he was still a Seventy.[2] This talk was quoted by President Harold B. Lee in a subsequent general conference.[3] The second was given in an area conference in Lima, Peru, under the direction of President Spencer W. Kimball. Afterwards, President Kimball stood and said: "We have just listened to Elder Bruce R. McConkie of the Council of the Twelve. He has given to us many great truths. It was a masterpiece. I hope you took many notes and then I hope you have recorded them in your minds and in your hearts. And I hope that you will watch for this article when it is published."[4]

These addresses shattered several Mormon myths about the gathering and, as was to be expected, Elder McConkie received a number of letters intended to correct him. His response to one such letter was dated October 5, 1977. It evidenced the firmness with which he taught gospel principles and his response to those who, with considerable energy, sought to oppose what he had taught.

"In your letter of September 18, 1977, you take vigorous exception to what I have preached and written on various occasions relative to the gathering of Israel and the building up of the Latter-day Zion. You quote a great many passages of scripture relative to the gathering in the United States and interpret them to mean that before the Lord comes, all of the faithful saints in all of the nations of the world will be assembled to Jackson County and its environs so that a people will be prepared for our Lord's glorious advent.

"As a matter of policy I do not engage in theological debates or discussion on doctrinal matters. In appropriate instances I do recite what the doctrine of the Church is and let it go at that. People are then free to believe or disbelieve as they choose. I have no intention now to debate any issue with you or to make any further explanations of the doctrine of gathering than have been made in the published sources to which you refer.

"Under the circumstances, however, I think it is only fair to you to state that the very reason my articles have been written and my sermons have been delivered is to correct the false impressions which many members of the Church have relative to the gathering and which impressions have been restated by you in your letter. I am sure you would be wise enough to know that I have a complete awareness of all of the passages you quoted together with a great many others that bear on the same subject. The issue is not what they mean but those to whom they apply. Both President Harold B.

Lee and President Spencer W. Kimball have taken an entirely different view of them than you have expressed. My recent article in the *Ensign* to which you refer was published under the direction of the First Presidency and the Twelve, in order to correct the views that you have written in your letter.

"It is not only the policy of the Church that Saints remain in the lands in which they live to build up the Church there, but it is also the doctrine that when the Lord comes he will find in every nation and among every people the Saints of God who, speaking every language, will then be qualified to live and reign on earth with him a thousand years. Whenever a stake of Zion is created in any part of the earth, that portion of the earth's surface becomes Zion and the gathering of Israel then consists of coming to that area. The Brazilians gather in Brazil, the British in Great Britain, the Japanese in Japan and so on. This is the doctrine of the Church. It is taught in the scriptures. I will not recite the proofs here. They are in the sources to which you have already referred.

"My counsel to you is that until and unless you come to an understanding of this doctrine, it would be wise to refrain from further discussion of it. We do not believe that the Saints will come out of all nations and gather to Jackson County before the Second Coming. We do believe that Zion will be built up in all nations before the Lord comes, and that after he arrives there will be added glorious things connected with the gathering of Israel. Many of the prophecies talk about a gathering after the Second Coming. Eventually the whole earth will become Zion.

"You stated very plainly that you thought I had misinterpreted the scriptures. Please do not be offended now when I tell you that my views are those of the Brethren and that your problem now is one of applying the scriptures you have quoted to the particular phase of the gathering of Israel that is involved in each instance.

The Nature of the Man

This is far more complex and extensive doctrine than many have supposed.

"We hope that people everywhere gradually will have the light dawn on them and know that the views that I have expressed are those that should and will prevail in the minds of Latter-day Saints. Please do not be offended at what I have written to you here. Believe as much of it as you can and if there is something you do not believe, please keep an open mind, study further, and eventually the glorious perspective that is here involved will dawn upon you."

Confidence and Leadership

While Bruce was teaching missionaries during a mission tour in Australia, a young convert, now a bishop, slipped into the meeting to listen. During a break in one of the meetings, he approached Elder McConkie, who was walking along a hallway, wanting to ask a question. Mustering all his courage, he said, "Elder McConkie, you once said . . ." Before the young man could utter another word, Bruce said, "Son, if I said it, it was true," and kept on walking.

The young man interpreted that to be "a moment of integrity," that someone could have such confidence in something he had said without even knowing what it was.

That same sense of confidence saved more than one missionary when Bruce served as the president of the Southern Australia Mission. He shared a classical illustration of this in a letter to his father: "I have had one rather interesting case recently—a young man who decided he wanted to go home and never wanted to come in the first place. He set out to get home; wrote eleven letters to his father in two days; talked four times—overseas to America in two days, and sent two cables in the same period. His father and some of the Brethren began turning handsprings; I got a cable from the

Presidency to send him home and advanced the fare; everyone was afraid the boy was going to do some drastic thing—except me.

"I didn't send him back, and he kept up his campaign. Finally I got a telephone call from one of the Brethren to find out if I knew what I was doing. I assured him I did and also talked on the same telephone call to the boy's father and told him to relax and let the mission president run the mission. As a matter of fact, it has taken me a long time to get through to the boy that he wasn't going anyplace, and that he couldn't even run away and earn the money and get back as long as I had his passport locked in my safe and he couldn't get a new one from the Consul without my approval.

"Well, I think he is going to turn out all right in due course. New Year's Eve, as part of a program, he was one of a group who sang a number that included the phrase: 'President McConkie's favorite word is No. Elder _____ will tell you so,' indicating that he is now beginning to joke about the matter and to reconcile himself to his imprisonment. I had one of those cases a year ago—the boy went on a hunger strike and lost 30 pounds in 30 days and did a whole host of other things to get out of the country. When I finally got through to him that the only choice he had was to go ahead and die, in which event I would bury him in Australia, or to start swimming, in which event the sharks would get him, he snapped out of it. About 10 days ago, in an interview, he told me how much he appreciated me, for insisting that he stay and make a man of himself. This other lad will be the same way in due course, if it doesn't kill me off first, which it won't."

Elder John K. Carmack of the Seventy shared this experience in a BYU talk illustrating the kind of boldness typical of Elder McConkie. "While Elder McConkie was on assignment to change the stake presidency during Christmas of 1983, I was the mission president visiting that stake conference. I introduced him to my traveling companion, Pastor Wally Cooper, an ordained Baptist minister in Ammon, Idaho. On Sunday after conference, Elder McConkie met Pastor Cooper and me with these words: 'Pastor Cooper, why don't you be baptized by a legal administrator?' Pastor Cooper replied, 'That is a good idea.' Elder McConkie continued . . . 'Why don't you let President Carmack, who is a legal administrator, baptize you?' Then, turning to me, he said, 'Can't you find a font open somewhere today, John?'"[5]

HIS RESPECT FOR PRIESTHOOD OFFICES

Bruce McConkie was as respectful of those who held offices that were under his direction as he was of those who held offices from which he received direction. He manifested this respect in his refusal to usurp either the dignity or the authority of another man's calling. He was not the kind of leader who had to have his hands on everything. As an apostle he desired to do only those things that were apostolic, while trusting others to labor in their own callings and offices.

In a letter of counsel to his son Mark, then a newly called bishop, he wrote: "This past weekend I was in Afton, Wyoming, dividing the Afton Stake. I had with me Brother Garth Lee, a Regional Representative. He lives in Hyrum, Utah, and we were traveling by car. In the 10 A.M. session Sunday, he said, in the course of his remarks, that when he was a stake president his high council meetings averaged 1 hour and 15 minutes in length. He was talking about how church officers should organize their time and be free to be home and spend more time with their families. As we rode back from Afton to Hyrum in the car, I said to him: 'You don't mean that you really held high council meetings that averaged an hour and 15 minutes in length? If that is true, this is the only schedule like that I ever heard of in the Church.' He replied: 'That's exactly what I mean. Some of our meetings went an hour and a half and some an hour but we averaged an hour and 15 minutes. I do not believe in long meetings and held them accordingly.'

"Then he began to tell me how he operated when he was a bishop. He said: 'There were two wards using the same building. The other bishop spent all day on Sunday in the building, and I spent only a short time. I determined that I would make my assignments to my priesthood and auxiliary officers and expect them to follow through. If they did and had any successful achievements, merit, or event, then we made a special point of praising them publicly for what they had done. If they did not achieve or failed, I talked to them privately.' Then he said, 'It wasn't very long until I had the best ward in the stake and all our statistics improved, while the other bishop who spent his full time trying to run everything himself just went along in a lackadaisical way without any particular success.'

"I thought this was an interesting comment and that perhaps you would like to hear it. I have never been a bishop and do not know many of the problems involved, but have been rubbing shoulders with bishops and stake presidents for a long time and have learned many things about their office and call from the Brethren and am strongly of the opinion that it is wise to delegate and not try and do everything yourself as a bishop. One other thing that this Regional Representative said to me was, 'I loaded everything I could on my counselors and expected them to do the work.'

"When I go out into the stakes to do something, I never lift a finger to do anything that anyone else can do. This weekend, for instance, Brother Lee and I had to choose two stake presidents. There were 12 wards in the stake, 6 going into each of the new stakes. We had the officers from each group come in one by one to be interviewed. They make their suggestions as to who they think the stake president should be and the interview gives us an opportunity to size them up and make a determination as to what position, if any, they might hold. We first met with the old stake presidency and

The Nature of the Man

I did the talking. We then met with each member of the stake presidency alone in an interview and I did the talking. Then we began our interviews with the members of the high council and the bishops. From this point on I said practically nothing. I said, 'Brother Lee, you handle all the interviews.' He had seen me set an example as to what I wanted and I just left the balance of some 35 or 40 interviews to him and I sat and listened. On a few occasions when I wanted some special information, or evaluation, I asked for it but other than that I let him do the work.

"In due course we had the two men selected who should be the stake presidents. I told them to choose their counselors and that we would interview them and if all went well call them. This was done. Then I told each stake presidency that they were to choose their own high councils and other officers including executive secretaries and clerks.

"I fixed it so I would not have to interview anyone other than the counselors, whom I had already called. Sunday morning there were 30 brethren to be interviewed between 8 A.M. and 10 A.M. so they could be called as high councilors, bishops and in other positions. I said: 'Brother Lee, this is your job. You will do all the interviewing and issue all the calls and I will go out and shake hands with the people.' This I did. There were 2600 people at conference and nearly everyone had to come through one door so I shook hands with about 2000 people as they came in. The old stake president came out and said, 'Brother Lee has so many interviews, he can't possibly get them done.' I said, 'That's his problem. He can shorten his interviews or you can go and help him. I think I'll just stay here and shake hands with the people.' That was the way we did it, and he and the old stake president got the work done. They did it as well as I could have done it anyway.

"When it came to setting people apart, I set apart each of the stake presidents and had the Regional Representative set apart the four counselors in the two stake presidencies. I instructed each stake president to set apart all of his high councilors and each one of them to ordain and set apart the new bishops in their stake. What I am saying is that I never lift a finger to do a thing in a stake that anyone else can do. I've done it all at some time or other, but see no reason why other people should not have the experience and gain the development.

"When I hold a leadership or other meeting in a stake, I deliberately confine myself to things that I think are worthy of apostolic attention. I do not involve myself in petty details. . . . When Moroni comes to visit, I think he should tell about the coming of Elijah or some general principle and not spend his time teaching how to make out a family group sheet."

Administrative Work

The operation of the kingdom of God requires a variety of gifts. Effective administrators are needed. Bruce McConkie was a teacher, not a gospel executive. Administrative meetings simply didn't excite him. It may be fair to say that he was passed over for some committee assignments because he didn't have the reputation for being an effective administrator. While that didn't bother him, his private opinion was that "running a committee is not that hard," and that the "management fellows" didn't get things done any better than he did.

Hate Mail

Hate mail was a routine part of life for Bruce McConkie. There were always people anxious to tell him that they felt he was "too rigid, too uncompromising, and too self-assured in presenting and teaching gospel principles." During one particularly productive season, he put a cardboard box in the corner of his office to collect the letters of his critics. Occasionally, he would have copies of one of these letters made and sent to his children. Knowing that people would extend themselves to say nice things about him to his children, I assume his purpose in this was to remind us that there were always others who felt differently.

He wrote an article for the *Ensign* entitled "The Salvation of Little Children." In that article he noted that the scriptures promise the fulness of eternal blessings to children who die before the age of accountability. This article and the expression of that doctrine engendered more criticism than anything else he ever wrote. One writer demanded the right to meet him in a public debate over the issue. As is usually the case, that may have constituted more of a commentary on his critic than it did on him.

THE POWER OF THE PRIESTHOOD

The gift of revelation was Elder McConkie's, and it found frequent expression in the giving of blessings, setting people apart, and in the calling of stake presidents and others. "I met Elder Stapley in Sydney to assist in the reorganization of the Sydney Stake presidency. This turned out to be a real choice spiritual experience," Dad recounted. "Both of us selected the same man to be the new stake president, each independently. It was a case of pure inspiration, and there was no question about it. No one whom we interviewed among all the bishops and high council suggested this man as their choice, although his name had been mentioned as a possible second or third choice by a couple of brethren. To top it all off, he used to be a member of the Reorganized Church, and he and his wife have only been in the Church for 15 months. This is probably the only time anything like this ever happened in the history of the Church in the selection of a new stake president. Brother Stapley had a little anxiety about what the Brethren would think, but he could not get around the fact that he knew this man should be chosen and he knew I knew it also. He had me do the praying about the matter for the two of us (after we had completed all of our interviews), and in the prayer I named the new stake president, which I had no business doing and which was presumptuous."

In future years, Dad had a somewhat similar experience in Mexico. There he called a twenty-three-year-old man to be a stake president. When he shared the experience with one of his associates, he was asked, "What in the world are you going to tell the Twelve when they learn that the man you called as the stake president is only twenty-three years old?" Elder McConkie quipped, "That's easy enough. I'll just tell them I thought I should call someone who was older than the bishops."

Apocryphal Stories

Bruce McConkie stories are legion and not all to be believed. One man created many of these stories, which he frequently shared over the pulpit. Though the stories made Elder McConkie a modern Paul Bunyan and were not told with ill intent, they were nevertheless a source of embarrassment to him. Responding to a request to verify these stories, Elder McConkie wrote: "The stories to which you refer relative to my alleged activities are totally and completely false. They did not happen nor did anything happen from which they could be inferred or assumed. I have a 'friend' who some years ago manufactured them out of whole cloth and told them in numerous places. He was doing it to humanize me. He has since apologized and said he will never again tell them and that he knew they were false. There is very little I can do to counteract them except to say that they did not occur and that I would appreciate not having them repeated."

I rarely meet anyone who had some kind of interaction with my father who doesn't have a story to tell. I have made no effort to collect such stories and generally believe about half of what I am told. My father once said that history is a myth agreed upon. Such

The Nature of the Man

stories—and again, they are generally well intended—are often myth and in some cases pure nonsense. Dad said that he never spoke in a Saturday evening session of a stake conference without hearing himself misquoted the next day in the Sunday session. As my uncle said, "I have never heard a story that I can't improve upon." I hope this volume does not seek to improve upon the truth. Truth, we are told, will prevail, and correct principles will outlive us all. It is not the purpose of this work to establish a myth about a man but rather to reaffirm the principles that made that man what he was.

16

As He Saw It

It is the practice of the Lord to give added knowledge to those upon whose hearts the true meanings and intents of the scriptures have been impressed.

—Bruce R. McConkie

Take Bruce McConkie, a modern Isaiah who refused to wrap his message in ribbons or dip it in honey, a man who carried the spirit of strong pioneer forebears, a man who echoed the call of the early Brethren, "The kingdom of God or nothing," a man who cared nothing for the world or its praise, and what kind of view do you get of the mercy of God and the hope of salvation? Just what hope does the ordinary Latter-day Saint have of meriting the blessings of heaven in the eyes of such a man? As ironic as it may seem, his views were nonetheless hopeful, positive, and filled with promise. His was a practical religion, one in which you could reach out and touch heaven, find peace, keep your covenants with exactness, and have a wonderful time doing it.

Balance and Moderation

I have in my possession a folded piece of yellow scratch paper upon which Dad had written the following phrases:

Stay in mainstream
Practice of the Church
Education—first
Church Service during School
Second Coming—how far
Decisions
Special relation: Christ
Prayer—mediator
No prayer on dates
How to choose a wife

Each phrase represented an idea he developed at a multistake fireside for the leaders of young adult stakes. The thread tying them together was that each of them represented spiritual excesses to which well-intended and faithful people are occasionally prone. His purpose was to encourage an approach to the gospel that reflected balance and moderation.

He directed the priesthood leaders to help the young members of their stakes to be well-rounded, to find the right balance between spiritual and intellectual concerns. "We don't want the pendulum to swing too far one way or the other," he said, cautioning that fanaticism or overzealousness could end up doing more harm than good. He counseled against religious fads and extremism in any form.

As to scriptural interpretation, he explained that the "practice of the Church was the interpretation of the scriptures." The Church was not out of the way and thus in need of correction. Our salvation will be perfectly secure, he explained, when we are in harmony with the practice of the Church, that is, as we follow those the Lord has ordained to lead us.

Using his own law school days at the University of Utah as an example, he said his stake president, Marion G. Romney, released him from the responsibility of serving as a stake missionary when he learned that he was a law student. In such matters, he said, bishops and stake presidents should administer with temperance.

He warned the priesthood leaders about extremism in Sunday worship. "After they have attended their meetings, and filled their assignments, let's not make it a sin for them to open a book," he counseled.

He also dispelled the prevalent idea that the second coming of Christ was imminent and that people need not make long-range plans. He said, "The Second Coming will not be in my lifetime or in the lifetime of my children, and I doubt that it will be in the lifetime of my children's children." His perspective grew out of the study he had done in writing *The Millennial Messiah*. Had he enlarged on the subject then, as he did elsewhere, he would have noted that we are assured in prophecy that Christ will not return until the gospel has been taught in every nation and among every people (Revelation 14:6–7) in their own tongue (D&C 90:11) and by their own people (Alma 29:8) and until congregations of Saints are found among all the nations of the earth (1 Nephi 14:12), presided over by people who have received the fulness of temple blessings (Revelation 5:9–10). More than one generation will be required to bring such prophecies to pass.

Too much emphasis had been placed on certain well-intended goals, Elder McConkie said, leading people to lose their balance. One such fad at the time was that of developing a personal relationship with Jesus. Noting that it was difficult to preach against such a doctrine, he explained that Jesus taught his followers to worship the Father, in his name, through the Holy Ghost. Thus, one who has the "mind of Christ" will do what Christ did, which was to worship the Father. It is a strange notion, he said, that we should single out one member of the Godhead for "a special relationship."

If we were to do so, however, he said such a relationship should be with the Father, not the Son.

Elder McConkie spoke against other practices he had noticed growing in the Church, including the giving of "special blessings." Beyond patriarchal blessings, father's blessings, and administration for the sick, he said, members should not continually seek special blessings. Such blessings tend to encourage a feeling of dependency between the member and the priesthood holder—especially if they are not related—and encourage undue reliance upon divine intervention in mundane matters.

He also discouraged the practice of young people praying on dates, saying it created an unnatural intimacy that should be reserved for marriage. Continuing in this vein, Elder McConkie said that in his opinion individuals should choose their marriage partners on the basis of personal judgment, not requiring a heavenly revelation in the matter. Though young people should seek counsel and guidance from parents and Church leaders, he continued, good judgment and appropriate worthiness can lead them to marry someone equally worthy without the agony he often witnessed. Saints should not ask the Lord to make such a decision for them, he concluded.

A Practical Gospel

When he taught, Elder McConkie sought to challenge the Saints to do better, without placing heavenly rewards beyond their reach. "You could take the expressions that I've made and say they're a little severe, or they're harsh or difficult, and hence, it's hard to gain eternal salvation," he said. But "I'd like to append to them the fact—and this is a gospel verity—that everyone in the Church who is on the straight and narrow path, who is striving and struggling and desiring to do what is right, though far from perfect in this life; if they pass out of this life while they are on the straight and narrow, they are going to go on to an eternal reward in the Father's kingdom.

"We don't need to get a complex or get a feeling that you have to be perfect to be saved. You don't. There's only been one perfect person, and that's the Lord Jesus, but in order to be saved in the Kingdom of God and in order to pass the test of mortality, what you have to do is get on the straight and narrow path—thus charting a course leading to eternal life—and then, being on that path, pass out of this life in full fellowship. I'm not saying that you don't have to keep the commandments. I'm saying you don't have to be perfect to be saved. If you did, no one would be saved. The way it operates is this, you get on the path that's named the straight and narrow. You do it by entering the gate of repentance and baptism. The straight and narrow path leads from the gate of repentance and baptism, a very great distance, to a reward that's called eternal life. If you're on that path and pressing forward, and you die, you'll never get off the path. There is no such thing as falling off the straight and narrow path in the life to come, and the reason is that this life is the time that is given to men to prepare for eternity. Now is the time and the day of your salvation, so if you're working zealously in this life—though you haven't fully overcome the world and you haven't done all you hoped you might do—you're still going to be saved. You don't have to do what Jacob said, 'Go beyond the mark.' You don't have to live a life that's truer than true. You don't have to have an excessive zeal that becomes fanatical and becomes unbalancing. What you have to do is stay in the mainstream of the Church and live as upright and decent people live in the Church—keeping the commandments, paying your tithing, serving in the organizations of the Church, loving the Lord, staying on the straight and narrow path. If you're on that path when death comes—because this is the time and the day appointed, this is the probationary estate—you'll never fall off from it, and, for all practical purposes, your calling and election is made sure. Now, that isn't the definition of that term, but the end result will be the same."

He explained that those of the household of faith were "called" and "elected" in the premortal life to obtain salvation. That is, they were foreordained to receive the ordinances of salvation and to keep their second estate. Having done so, it becomes their privilege in the eternal course of things to inherit the kingdom of God, which was what they were elected to do, and thus they have made that to which they were called and elected "sure," or as scripture states it, they have made their calling and election sure.

Views on How Many Will Be Saved

Elder McConkie's views on what portion of the premortal host who come to earth will be saved would perhaps surprise most people. Yet he was very positive on this kind of thing. He believed that the vast majority of those in the premortal life who followed Christ would be saved in the celestial kingdom. In so saying, he was not unmindful of the Savior's statement that "strait is the gate, and narrow is the way . . . and few there be that find it" (Matthew 7:14). The Savior was describing his day and ours. He was not giving commentary on the destiny of the great hosts of children who have died without reaching an age of accountability, all of whom will be saved. He was not giving commentary on those who do not hear the gospel in this life and who will accept it in the spirit world. He was not giving commentary on the great hosts who were taken into heaven as part of the city of Enoch or the city of Salem or were translated at some other time and place. He was not giving commentary on the great hosts who lived righteously for hundreds of years after the visit of Christ in the New World and in other places that the Savior visited. Most important, he was not giving commentary on the Millennium, during which there could well be far more people who would be born and "grow up unto salvation" than lived during the rest of the temporal history of the earth. Taken from such a perspective, Elder McConkie saw God coming off victorious in numbers and the greater part of the premortal host being saved.

It seemed to me that what he did in his preaching was to get heaven within our reach—make it something we could obtain—which he did without compromising the integrity of the commandments. "All faithful Saints," he said, "all who have endured to the end, depart this life with the absolute guarantee of eternal life." He also firmly believed the doctrine preached by Joseph Fielding Smith at the funeral of Richard L. Evans "that no righteous man is ever taken before his time."[1]

Bruce McConkie was a gospel teacher, not an administrator of programs and procedures. He understood the inevitability of some bureaucratic procedures in the Church's transition from a local to a worldwide organization. He saw the best solution to many of these challenges in decentralizing the decision-making process. A classic illustration centered on a stake center built in Argentina. "It is built on a lot so that the back of the building faces the street with the front facing the back of the lot," he wrote. "It is not possible to use the front entrance. By going out of the front entrance you are immediately greeted by a ten-foot brick wall. The reason the church was built this way is that the plans prepared by the Building Department showed that it should be constructed in that position on the lot, and in spite of the vigorous and vociferous pleadings of the local people, the Building Department insisted on building the building to conform with the plans made in Salt Lake on the theory that Church Headquarters knew what ought to be.

"All of this puts me in mind of the illustration told me by Brother Wells years ago which dramatizes the need to decentralize operations. It seems that two men were crossing a field. In the field was a raging bull, which took after them. One man, to escape, climbed a tree, and the other ran into a cave. The bull stood at the foot of the tree, pawing the ground. The man came out of the cave, and the bull charged him, and he went back into the cave. Then the bull returned to the foot of the tree. This happened several times. Finally the man in the tree said to his friend on the ground, 'Why don't you stay in the cave and be safe?' The reply that came was, 'You don't understand the local situation. There is a bear in the cave.'"

On Baptisms in Europe

The relatively low rate of convert baptisms in Europe and Scandinavia has been a matter of great concern to the Brethren. Elder McConkie discussed this matter at some length with Elder Busche and felt quite enlightened by his observations. Elder Busche noted that European cultures were self-contained units in which people centered their attention on nationalistic and in-group sentiments. This had the effect of excluding people from other cultures and of barring their own people from making changes in their lifestyle that conflicted with the national culture. From birth, people were conditioned to follow the traditions of their fathers. One result of this is that in the major cities of Europe, most convert baptisms came from people outside the particular culture who have moved into that city or from cultural misfits who had already been thrust out of the normal orbit of society. Various forms of the welfare state also worked against some relying on the Lord for temporal support because they knew that the government would attend to their needs.

By contrast, in the United States—a nation which has from its inception been a melting pot of all nations—we have of necessity accepted cultural differences and thus the idea that all men are created equal before the law and are entitled to be treated with respect and dignity. This creates a condition in which people feel free to exchange views and to change their lifestyles. In Europe there are state churches that are supported by taxes. Ours is a culture that allows free exchange of opinions and withdrawal from, or adherence to, different organizations at will. This simply does not exist in the nations of Europe. There has been an increasing influx of foreign workers into those lands. Italians, Yugoslavs, and others were moving into Germany, for example. The result of this would be a gradual breakdown of the long-held social structure. People would feel more free to accept new ideas, ways of doing things, and even a new religion. Nonetheless, this would be a slow and difficult process. Missionary work would not succeed in any significantly measurable fashion until social change made that possible.

An attendant problem was that the members of the Church in these areas often would not accept new members, sometimes deliberately doing things to discourage them. "In his talk to the mission presidents, Brother Busche said that when he joined the Church and went to the branch, one of the old-time members took hold of his tie and lapel and told him that he would last four months in the Church and then he would be gone."

Out of all of this, Elder McConkie concluded that the trouble in Europe was not that those nations have fewer spiritually inclined people, who under the right circumstances would join the Church, but that they live in a social circumstance that wars against new ideas. "Our problem," he said, is to find ways of breaking down these traditional nationalistic walls that have been built up so that we can get over to people the importance of what we have to say." He felt we also needed to get the members of the Church in those countries to put the Church ahead of their national instincts, so that they can fellowship people of all classes, races, and colors rather than assume that the only good people were those of their own nation.

Evolution: A False Religion

Nothing made Bruce McConkie less popular in the academic community than his open objection to the theory of evolution as an answer to the question of man's origin. His 1982 article "Christ and the Creation," published in the *Ensign* and written at the request of the First Presidency, details some of the major scriptural conflicts between the theory of evolution and the scriptures. The publication of this article was preceded by a powerful speech entitled "The Three Pillars of Eternity," delivered in 1981 at a Brigham Young University devotional. In that address he illustrated the incompatibility of the theory of organic evolution and the doctrine of the Fall.

Handwritten notes among his papers indicate he intended either to speak or to write more forcibly on this matter than he had. "Evolution," one note reads, "is not a science; it is a religion. It is not an objective analysis of what is found in a test tube; it does not involve experiments that all researchers can duplicate. It is, rather, a mass of theoretical postulates by which its devotees seek to explain the origin and destiny of man without reference to revelation."

As a preacher of the gospel, he felt obligated to question the tenets of evolution and did so, knowing he would be labeled a bigot for having done so. He noted that in true science, no offense is taken when someone attacks a tenet, because facts stand on their own.

Seeing Further

Bruce McConkie loved the gospel and always sought to teach it to the best of his understanding. He loved to expand his knowledge and thought it no shame to discover that he could improve on something that he had written or preached or that he had just plain been wrong on something. Immediately after the receipt of the revelation granting the priesthood to all worthy males, he said, "Forget everything that I have said, or what President Brigham Young or President George Q. Cannon or whoever has said in days past that is contrary to the present revelation. We spoke with a limited understanding and without the light and knowledge that now has come into the world."[2]

Those defending questionable doctrinal positions have made much of the fact that Elder McConkie changed his mind on this, that, or the other thing, and therefore, they have frequently argued, he can hardly be quoted as competent authority on the issue at hand (if, of course, he has written or said something contrary to their own beliefs). This is a mirror reflection of the evangelical reasoning that the Bible must be inerrant and infallible, for if it were to be wrong on one thing, how could it possibly be trusted on another?

On the contrary, Elder McConkie felt that if a man could serve as a general authority for forty years without learning something new and thus having to correct his views on a thing or two, that would truly be a "sad commentary." His world was big enough for different views and stable enough that no great personal trauma attended changing his mind on something.

As he felt it his right to stand on the shoulders of those who had come before and see further than they had seen, so he felt it the right and responsibility of the coming generation to do the same. At a gospel conference at BYU, at which both he and I were speaking, a member of the faculty mentioned that they enjoyed having his son on the faculty and that they felt that he made a positive contribution. Dad's response was, "Well, he better do a good job, and it is expected that he will do better than his father has done." This was a genuine expression. He expected each of his sons and daughters to do better than he had done.

When Elder McConkie changed his views on things, he made no effort to cover the paper trail. For instance, changes could easily have been made in subsequent editions of his books to align with such changes. When this course of action was suggested to him, his response was, "Goodness, no."

The following extract from a letter responding to one such issue illustrates his attitude:

"You asked about the interpretation of a passage in the 14th chapter of John with particular reference to the 16th and 17th verses. You point out that in one of my volumes of *Doctrinal New Testament Commentary*, I indicate that the verses have reference to the Lord Jesus who is the Second Comforter and in another volume I interpret them to apply to the Holy Ghost. Reference is also made to the way in which President Joseph Fielding Smith interprets them in *Doctrines of Salvation*.

"I think that I could have expressed myself better with reference to this subject, perhaps in both of the volumes where it is touched upon. However, as I reread and ponder what I have said, I see no real reason for any change. I wrote both interpretations with deliberation and an awareness that I was creating a seeming conflict, but I think the passage can be interpreted properly in both ways. I take courage in this view by the fact that the Prophet Joseph Smith took the same passage of scripture and interpreted it in conflicting ways on different occasions and said that he was doing it with an awareness and deliberately.

"On the surface this may seem to be improper but I think there is what we might call a law of dual interpretation, which properly allows us to make more than one interpretation of the same passage. One instance in which Joseph Smith did this is found in his interpretation of Malachi's prophecy about the coming of Elijah. Another is in his interpretation of the passage in Hebrews about the fact that we cannot be perfect without our dead."

The Fulness of Gospel Blessings Intended for Everyone

People who study and believe the scriptures see the world differently from those who do not. "Those who preach by the power of the Holy Ghost use the scriptures as their basic source of knowledge and doctrine," Elder McConkie declared. "They begin with what the Lord has before revealed to other inspired men. But it is the practice of the Lord to give added knowledge to those upon whose hearts the true meanings and intents of the scriptures have been impressed. Many great doctrinal revelations come to those who preach from the scriptures. When they are in tune with the Infinite, the Lord lets them know, first, the full and complete meaning of the scriptures they are expounding, and then he ofttimes expands their views so that new truths flood in upon them, and they learn added things that those who do not follow such a course can never know. Hence, as to 'preaching the word,' the Lord commands his servants to go forth 'saying none other thing than that which the prophets and apostles have written, and that which is taught them by the Comforter through the prayer of faith.' (D&C 52:9.) In a living, growing, divine church, new truths will come from time to time and old truths will be applied with new vigor to new situations, all under the guidance of the Holy Spirit of God."[3]

GIVE THE WORLD A STRAIGHTFORWARD MESSAGE

One area in which Elder McConkie's views changed markedly over the years was the manner in which we should present the message of the Restoration to the world. The more he studied the revelations of the Restoration, the more convinced he became that we will never have the success in missionary work that we should have until we as a people come to the realization that we cannot present that message independent of the testimony of Joseph Smith. That is, for instance, we cannot simply go out into the world and profess our faith in Christ; we must, rather, profess our faith in that Christ revealed to the Prophet Joseph Smith. In his judgment, to attempt to teach of Christ without reference to the Book of Mormon or without drawing upon the revelations given to us by the Prophet Joseph Smith was to offend the Spirit. "Joseph Smith is the revealer of the knowledge of Christ for our dispensation. If it were not for him and the witness and testimony he has given, we would not have more knowledge than the sectarian world has; hence, we bear testimony of Joseph Smith." Similarly, if it were not for Joseph Smith, we would have no authority to perform a baptism or to preach the gospel.

To illustrate his point, he wrote in a letter about his experience at the World's Fair in Osaka, Japan: "I went to the United States pavilion and I went to the Russian pavilion. The United States pavilion was marvelous in some very minor respects. They had the capsule that the astronauts went to the moon in and this sort of thing, and people were tremendously interested. They may have had just volumes and rooms full of modernistic art and all sorts of things that supposedly show our culture, but didn't really project any image of the United States. Not one word about the Constitution. And then I went into that Russian pavilion. Now it's godless communism; it's everything that President Benson ever said it was. Floor after floor and room after room it was just pure propaganda for Russia, and there were quotations from Lenin and all the rest. And I thought, 'These people know how to get their message over.' Now their message is false, and it is not good and it is unrighteous, but the fact is they knew how to launch a message to the world, and as far as I was concerned, the United States pavilion was just a failure.

"Well, I didn't believe a thing, propaganda-wise, that I got out of that Russian pavilion, but I went out of there knowing that they thought they had the message for the world, and at least I was impressed with that much.

"Now I'm not too impressed with the fact that we try to be very soft and very gentle in all the visitors centers and in the missionary work and in everything else, just trying to leave people feeling good. I think we've got a message, and it ought to be delivered. It's a worldwide message, and our centering should be on Joseph Smith. Here is Joseph Smith and he revealed Christ, and here is Christ, and here is salvation through this system. That kind of approach will have the effect of dividing people on one hand or on the other, but so you divide them. You divide them—you get some people who are interested. You don't make friends with everyone.

"As some of you may recall, President Clark said, 'You can't tell the Joseph Smith story without offending people.' He said, 'We don't need to be so anxiously concerned about not offending the world.' And he used the Joseph Smith story as his illustration.

"Well, of course, you can't. Jesus offended people. Now, we are not trying to offend people but he offended them by the nature of the message that he presented, and we, in my judgment, just have to more affirmatively present our message and do it in the way I think this talks about."

Being True to the Restoration

In the spring of 1984, Elder Bruce R. McConkie was invited to speak to a group of faculty members at BYU who would be teaching the Book of Mormon in the fall. The first thing Elder McConkie did was to reach into his briefcase and bring out a computer printout. "I have something here which, when I first saw it, about bowled me over," he began.

He had our attention. "I have here the results of a 'testimony survey' that was conducted at the Missionary Training Center in Provo. Elders, sisters, and older couples were surveyed as to the depth of their testimony in regard to certain doctrinal matters."

Elder McConkie indicated that the missionaries were asked to respond anonymously to ten statements of fact, statements such as the following:

1. God is my Father, the Father of my spirit.
2. Jesus is the Christ, the Son of God.
3. Joseph Smith is a prophet of God.
4. The Book of Mormon is the word of God.
5. Spencer W. Kimball is a prophet of God today.

The missionaries were asked to respond in one of four ways:

A. I know this to be true because I have received a spiritual witness of its truthfulness.
B. I believe this to be true, but I have not received a spiritual witness.
C. I do not know whether this is true.
D. I doubt whether this is true.

In a very sober tone, Elder McConkie asked: "Would you be interested in knowing which of these areas was the lowest in terms of testimony?" Everyone nodded. He said: "The lowest areas of testimony across elders, sisters, and couples were these:

3. Joseph Smith is a prophet of God.
4. The Book of Mormon is the word of God.

The effect upon the whole group was visible. It was as though someone had hit us in the stomach with a baseball bat. We were stunned—shocked, for these matters were fundamental to what the missionaries would soon be proclaiming. Elder McConkie raised his voice and said: "Something's wrong. Something's terribly wrong! Maybe it's something I've done wrong. Maybe it's something the Brethren have done wrong. Perhaps it's something we've done wrong here at BYU or in our Church Educational System, but clearly something's wrong."

And then, as though he were reasoning the matter as he stood on his feet before us, he added, "Maybe in our efforts as a Church to ensure that everyone knows we're Christian, we have gone too far. A while back we changed our missionary discussions to make our first discussion a message about Christ. It seemed at the time a good thing to do, given that Jesus is the Head of the Church. But what was the result? A decrease in convert baptisms and a decrease in the number of copies of the Book of Mormon placed by full-time missionaries from one million per year to 500,000. We are not teaching the Restoration as we ought to."

What Elder McConkie said next changed the way many of us who were present now teach. He stated: "We will never achieve the quantity and quality of converts that President Kimball and the Lord have envisioned as long as we continue to stress the similarities between us and those of other faiths. It is only when we stress the differences that we are able to make our distinctive contribution in the world and thus make our influence felt."

We read together from the Doctrine and Covenants several passages that state powerfully our need to be loyal to the Restoration and to the truths delivered through the Prophet Joseph Smith (D&C 5:10; 20:11–16, 17; 31:3–4; 49:1–4) and also of the condemnation, scourge, and judgment that still rest upon the Church because of our neglect of the Book of Mormon and latter-day revelation (D&C 84:54–61). Elder McConkie charged us, with great power and persuasion, to view all things through the lens of the restored gospel, and he promised us that greater outpourings of the Spirit would accompany gospel teaching that was Restoration-based and Restoration-centered.

For Bruce McConkie, prophets—particularly those spoken of in scripture—were examples of what the Lord expected every righteous man to be. Like Nephi, he thought it his right to "see, and hear, and know" of the things the prophets had learned by the spirit of revelation. Indeed, he thought it not only the right but the responsibility of all men to seek after such things. He likewise followed the pattern of the prophets in his teaching. That pattern, as he understood it, was to declare the truth in plainness and then to seal his teaching with the testimony that what he had taught was indeed the gospel and that it was true. While his thoughts and feelings were fastened on the heavens, he was able to keep his feet firmly on the ground. He taught a gospel that one could live; he believed in a God that one could approach.

17

A Time to Laugh

To every thing there is a season, and a time to every purpose under the heaven: . . . a time to weep and a time to laugh.

—Ecclesiastes 3:1–4

Good humor is a gift something akin to a spring day. Like a spring day, humor brings with it newness of life and the confidence that we can handle whatever obstacles lie in our path. And like a spring day, good humor has warmth enough for all who desire to share in it. Bruce McConkie loved spring, loved people, loved Amelia, and loved a little impish fun; he also had no difficulty in laughing at himself. Elder James E. Faust recalled inquiring of Dad's well-being after he had fallen off the roof of our house when he was painting it. "I urged him to see a doctor," Elder Faust said, "but he felt that wasn't necessary."

"It doesn't hurt a thing," Bruce explained, "when a McConkie lands on his head."

Having a Little Fun

Back when Dad was dating Mother, he was at the Smith home one evening when Joseph Fielding Smith returned from a conference assignment in California. Elder Smith brought with him a sack of olives, which he had harvested from an olive tree. He was quick to invite Bruce to eat a "fresh" olive, an experience he assured him he would never forget. Biting into one of the olives, Bruce experienced a taste more bitter than anything he had ever known. "Oh, my goodness," Granddaddy said, "you must have got a bad one. Here, try this one" and handed him another.

While on a mission tour in southern California, Bruce had an unfortunate experience with a pigeon. The following comes from a description of the event he sent to his friend Glen Rudd: "Today I ran into a puzzling problem. Is it true that birds can read? And if they can't, who tells them things that are none of their business? This is what happened: I stopped at San Juan Capistrano to see the old mission building constructed by that great church which is not the Lord's Church. The swallows are not yet back, but there were some Catholic pigeons around, and as it happens, I had a rather, shall we say, discomforting experience. And me with a clean white shirt put on only this morning! Now what I want to know is this: How did those pigeons know what I wrote about the Catholics in *Mormon Doctrine?*"

On a mission tour in South America, Dad caught an unintended elbow from Mother one night when she was adjusting her pillow. The next morning he discovered he had a real shiner. All day long they had to field questions about what had happened to his eye. "She did it," Dad would say, gesturing to Mother, and she in turn would flex her muscles and say, "Muy fuerte! ['very strong']."

Of his experience in Australia, Dad told this story: "Everyone recognizes Americans the minute they open their mouths. One sentence suffices, and they ask: 'How long have you been here?' I was with Amelia and another American woman in a store. The clerk asked, 'Where are you from in America?' I said, 'From Salt Lake City; we are Mormons.' He said, 'Oh, I've been to Salt Lake City.

A Time to Laugh

Always conscious of the need for good physical fitness, Bruce and Amelia encouraged their family to do likewise

Are these your wives?' 'Oh, yes,' I said, 'they are.' Then I asked, 'How come you have been to Salt Lake and aren't a Mormon yourself?' 'Well,' he said, 'I have had one wife for forty years and that is all I can stand.'"

Later, Dad had to call this man to check on the order he had placed with him. The person answering the phone asked, "Who shall I tell him is calling?" Dad said, "He doesn't know my name. Just tell him the Mormon with two wives is calling." This brought immediate attention. At the conclusion of their conversation, the fellow said, "My regards to your ladies."

"Thank you," Dad said.

Dad's missionaries recall that he often expressed his love for Mother in their presence. He told them that they could not marry the best girl because she was already taken. In zone conferences, A. J. Schomas recalls, "the two of them often kidded back and forth like newlyweds." Some years later, at a mission reunion, Mother got

The Bruce R. McConkie Story

When Elder McConkie first went to Australia, the Saints were not used to long doctrinal talks. He taught them to love hearing the gospel preached

up to speak with her coat on. It was a cold, blustery day. She apologized, noting that it was cold in the chapel. No one was very surprised when Dad got up and put his arm around her and explained that the reason she was wearing her coat was not because it was cold. "Actually," he said, "it's because she forgot to wear her girdle."

When he was a missionary in the Eastern States, he and his companion took a good tongue lashing from a man who told them he knew their only purpose was to get their woman and take her back to Salt Lake. His wife, a redhead, who had invited the elders back, stood silently in the background. When the storm of words ended, Elder McConkie said, "Well, you're right, and for that matter we lost money on every redhead we sent in the last bunch." The man broke out in laughter and invited the elders in.

FRIENDS AT THE OFFICE

Not long before he went to Australia as president of the Southern Australia Mission, Bruce wrote a tract to respond to claims to priesthood authority being made by an apostate group. He entitled his effort: *How to Start a Cult; or, Cultism As Practiced by the So-Called Church of The Firstborn of the Fulness of Times Analyzed, Explained, and Interpreted; As also Dissected, Divellicated, Whacked Up, Smithereemed, Mangled, and Decimated; or, An Essay Showing Where All Good Cultists Go.* Needless to say, the essay did not meet with approval by those appointed to approve such things. When a friend inquired about his call to preside over the mission in Australia, he explained, "Well, I have been writing again."

Among the Seventy, Bruce became particularly close to S. Dilworth Young, with whom he often matched wits. The two frequently traded places as perpetrator and victim of practical jokes. In a delightfully sardonic letter from the mission field in Australia written to Elder Young, Bruce described the ridiculous hassle they faced with government restrictions on the kind of urinals they could put in a new chapel then under construction. Of the whole experience he said, "It stinks." The problem centered on building codes that forbade the use of anything modern. Australia was required by Commonwealth attachments to Britain to use only British goods. Britain had no need to modernize the products they were selling because their buyers were required by law to buy them. Bruce wrote, "Well, when your correspondent arrived in Australia, he discovered that all urinals in public buildings were of the trough variety—an unsatisfactory collection system comparable to what Moses used in Ancient Israel three and a half millenniums ago, and which is only one step more advanced than the honey buckets of Japan. To accurately catalogue them and avoid confusion, these archaic, antediluvian, antique receptacles—which became extinct in America about 100 years ago—will hereafter be called privies." Thereupon he launched into a long and detailed account of all their failed efforts to be able to use modern plumbing.

The relatively common experience of people confusing names

and faces among the general authorities elicited the following memo, also addressed to S. Dilworth Young:

MEMORANDUM

To: S. Dilworth Young
Date: October 26, 1971
From: Bruce R. McConkie
Re: A Case of Questionable Identity
Dear Duff:

Sunday in the Torrance, California, Stake, the Stake President introduced me by saying how grateful they were to have Brother Hinckley with them and to partake of his wonderful spirit and superior counsel. Jim Mortimer, who was sitting by me on the stand, looked askance. I acted as though nothing was amiss, figuring if I pretended to be Brother Hinckley, perhaps things would go better than otherwise they could have done.

After the meeting, a devout sister approached me, grasped my hands in a grip like a vise and said, "Oh, Brother Packer, that was the greatest sermon I have ever heard in all my experience in the Church. We are so pleased that you were our visitor, and I can't thank you enough for the things you said."

Today as I walked up Second East, an oversized limousine pulled up to the curb, and the man inside it called out, "Oh, Brother Hanks, if I don't give this to you to give to your wife, my wife will kill me when I get home." I thanked him, took the package, and said, "I'll be happy to deliver it to my wife."

After more mature reflection, I think I might perhaps impose upon you to deliver it to Maxine.

Sincerely your brother of questionable identity,

A. Theodore McConkie

P. S. I am taking the liberty of sending a copy of this memo to Boyd Monson, so that he will be apprised of what a great sermon he preached.

A Time to Laugh

As to poetry I present the following with its poetic review by S. Dilworth Young.

Amelia

I am in love with my dear wife,
We live a life devoid of strife;
To us have come nine children dear,
Who bring us hope and joy and cheer.
Our home is one where peace abides,
Because we do what she decides.
   Bruce R. McConkie

I look at this and cry and cry;
This statement is a damn-ed lie.
   S. Dilworth Young

In another poetic tribute to his wife, Bruce wrote:

Poor Amelia

I am Amelia good and true;
I have so many things to do;
My work goes on and on and on,
With scarcely even time to yawn.
I wish I knew how others plan
To meet the needs of one day's span.
How can they do so many things?
And yet have time to live like kings?
I guess it must be Bruce's fault;
He always seems to call a halt
To what I need to do with vim
And take me to hunt rocks with him.

The following expression also represents his passion as a rock hound:

I think that there shall never be
An ignoramus quite like me,
Who roams the hills from day to day

And picks up rocks and sand and clay;
For there is one thing I've been told:
I take the rocks and leave the gold.
O'er deserts wild or mountains blue
I search for rocks of varied hue.
A hundred pounds or more I pack
With blistered feet and aching back.
And after this is said and done
I cannot name a single one.
I pick up rocks where'er I go;
The reason why I do not know,
For rocks are found by fools like me
Where God intended them to be.

One year for Christmas, Dad planned to give friends and family a copy of his new book *Doctrinal New Testament Commentary*, volume 3. Delays at the press precluded that, so we received the book's jacket with the following bit of verse:

VOLUME III

PREFACE
To you methought a gift I'd give—
A book that makes the scriptures live—
Until I heard that you can't read;
And then I knew there was no need
To spend on you my hard-earned cash
By doing anything so rash.

CONTENTS
And so to you I send this flap,
In which no book is found to hap;
'Tis my fond hope, which saves me coin,
That it your unread books may join,
Upon that shelf where books unread,
Remain forever as though dead.

EPILOGUE
But now to me repentance comes:

A Time to Laugh

I vow I must for all my chums,
Bequeath a book of wisdom rare,
To place within this jacket bare;
So shall it be in course of time,
As promised in this silly rhyme.
Finis

A letter from Elder McConkie to Glen Rudd:

Dear Glen:

I am totally overwhelmed to see your influence made manifest.

One day you find a mistake in the *Deseret News*, the next day they release the president of the company.

I hope you are always my friend.

The following was extracted from the *Church News*: "An active man, he walked often from his home to his office. Also, he jogged and encouraged others to exercise. When the *Church News* wrote an article about physical fitness several years ago, he readily agreed to be photographed jogging. He ran in a wide circle so the photographer could shoot a variety of pictures. As he ran, he quipped to the reporter and photographer, 'You can go home tonight and write in your journal that you had a member of the Twelve running in circles today.'"[1]

After one of his general conference talks, Bruce received a letter from a father who watched conference with his family. After the conference was over, the father asked his children to name their favorite speaker. His youngest son said it was the boxer. The father went over the names of the speakers in his mind but could not think of a name that sounded like Boxer, so he started naming the Brethren. When he got to Bruce R. the young boy said, "That's him—BruiseR McConkie." Dad remembered that letter with fondness.

On another occasion, when Dad was speaking in the Saturday

The Bruce R. McConkie Story

Bruce and Amelia at their best

evening session of a stake conference, he felt a bit queasy when he stood to speak. In the course of his talk, it became evident that his stomach was about to reject his dinner. Sensing the moment was imminent, he invited the congregation to sing a hymn, while he bee-lined to the restroom. It was obvious to everyone what was happening. When he returned, he said, "I might be the only general authority in the history of the Church who gave a talk that was so bad that it even made him throw up."

Bruce often said he played hooky when they taught the music classes in the premortal life. One night while teaching at the institute at the University of Utah, he called on Margot Butler to help him make a point. She was quite aware of his musical deficiencies. "He turned to the class and announced that he would now sing a duet with me, and chose a hymn that everyone would know. I stood there aghast. Was he really serious? He was.

"So we started. By the end of the first line, he was going along happily in his monotone, but I was sadly off-key. I couldn't go on and started laughing. He was gracious. We would try again. We did. Same thing. I laughed; the class laughed; Amelia chortled. Bruce R. was long-suffering. Two more times we started off, but he had me off the track and off the melody by the end of the first line. I can't remember the lesson he taught, but it was certainly a great example of how others can get us off the strait and narrow."

BY THE SHOVELFUL

One year when Mother and Dad went to Manti, Utah, to see the pageant, he had an unexpected reunion with one of his missionary companions, Morgan Dyering. The next day the Dyerings took Mom and Dad on a drive up in the mountains in what Mother called "an oversized jeep." When they got high enough that they could find snow, Morgan parked the jeep and pulled out an ice cream freezer. Using the snow and taking turns churning, they soon had a wonderful batch of ice cream. Bruce, who was very much into the spirit of the thing, refused to eat his ice cream from a paper cup. He chose to use the shovel instead. "I always did want to shovel it in," he explained.

Mother provided the following example of Dad's prowess in the kitchen. On an evening when she could not be home to fix his dinner, she operated on the false assumption that he could warm it up in their new microwave. "I prepared a nice dinner for him and covered it with wax paper and refrigerated it so he could warm it up when he was ready to eat. I also left a note on top of the plate of food with detailed instructions on how to warm it up.

"The instructions were quite simple, I thought, with each step clearly stated:

"1. When you are ready to have your dinner, take this plate of food out of the refrigerator.

The Bruce R. McConkie Story

"2. Open the microwave door and place the plate of food in the center of the oven.

"3. Shut the door.

"4. Push the number 3.

"5. Push the word *cook*.

"6. When the oven stops, open the door and turn the plate halfway around.

"7. Push the number 2 and then the word *cook* again.

"8. When it turns off, open the door, take the food out, and eat it."

When she got home, she found the meal she had prepared still in the refrigerator. "Why didn't you eat the dinner I fixed for you?" she asked.

"Well, I tried, but all it would do is sit there and blink at me. So I unplugged it."

"What did you have to eat, then?"

"I found a can of pork and beans and some bread and milk," was his answer.

In the biography of Spencer W. Kimball, the story is told of how Elders Kimball and McConkie, while laboring in Mexico City, "took off their suit coats in the heat while they relaxed on the chapel lawn. When it came time for the meeting inside, they playfully picked up the wrong coats and pulled them on. Elder Kimball's coat reached just halfway down the taller man's forearm. Elder McConkie's swallowed the shorter man's hands. All the missionaries around raced for their cameras."[2]

Dad's telling of the story was a bit different. According to his account, Elder Kimball, whose mind was deeply absorbed in the meeting at hand, put on the wrong coat without noticing that he was swimming in it, so Dad playfully put on Elder Kimball's coat. It took a moment or two for Elder Kimball to notice.

After having been called as a bishop, I was bragging to Dad, "In

A Time to Laugh

Bruce R. McConkie and Spencer W. Kimball exchanging jackets

our ward we've had 100 percent home teaching for the past five months."

"Well," he responded, "we have found that a bishop who has 100 percent home teaching lies about other things, too."

ARE GENERAL AUTHORITIES HUMAN?

Addressing the topic "Are General Authorities Human?" at a 1966 institute devotional at the University of Utah, Dad said, "I would like to read a couple of quotations. I know these are good quotations because I wrote them myself. The first one is under the heading 'General Authorities' in a book entitled *Mormon Doctrine*, which is reputed to have said more than it ought to have said on some subjects, and this may be one of them. After listing the general authorities, it says, 'These Brethren are all delegated general *administrative* authority by the President of the Church. That is, they are called to preach the gospel, direct church conferences, choose other church officers, perform ordinations and settings apart, and handle the properties and interests of the Church.' That is all that is meant by General Authority; it means that the administrative authority delegated overlaps local boundaries so that they administer beyond the ward or stake or the region and out in the Church generally. 'Some general authorities are empowered to do one thing and some another. All are subject to the strict discipline the Lord always imposes on his saints and those who preside over them. The positions they occupy are high and exalted. But the individuals who hold these offices are humble men like their brethren in the Church. So well qualified and trained are the members of the Church that there are many brethren who could—if called, sustained, and set apart—serve effectively in nearly every important position in the Church.'"

Having developed that point, he read on: "Though general authorities are authorities in the sense of having power to administer church affairs, they may or may not be authorities in the sense of doctrinal knowledge, the intricacies of church procedures, or the receipt of the promptings of the Spirit. A call to an administrative position of itself adds little knowledge or power of discernment to an individual, although every person called to a position in the Church does grow in grace, knowledge, and power by magnifying the calling given him."[3]

When Bruce McConkie was a boy, he would walk around with a broom handle between his elbows and his back to ensure the habit of standing straight and tall. Thus, when he became a man, he stood straight, and when he stood to speak, he made it a practice to speak straight also. He did not trifle with sacred things. On the other hand, when meetings were over and assignments filled, he was not slow to take off his coat and tie, and he relished the opportunity to enjoy friends and family. Ice cream, watermelon, or

A Time to Laugh

pie was requisite to such occasions, as were a bit of humor and a story or two.

The balance was always there—there was a time to be serious and a time to relax. He savored both.

18

CALL TO THE APOSTLESHIP

No one can listen to that testimony without knowing that the Lord has called the right man to be his new witness in this high place.

—President Harold B. Lee

"I asked the Lord," stated Elder Bruce R. McConkie in his April 1972 general conference address, "what he would have me say on this occasion and received the distinct and affirmative impression that I should bear testimony that Jesus Christ is the Son of the living God and that he was crucified for the sins of the world." He then said that he had what is known as "the testimony of Jesus," for his knowledge of the divinity of Christ was the result of personal revelation.[1]

APRIL CONFERENCE 1972

It was in this talk that Elder McConkie read the words of a poem he had written, now a favorite Latter-day Saint hymn, "I Believe in Christ":

> I believe in Christ; he is my King!
> With all my heart to him I'll sing;

Call to the Apostleship

I'll raise my voice in praise and joy,
In grand amens my tongue employ.

I believe in Christ; he is God's Son.
On earth to dwell his soul did come.
He healed the sick; the dead he raised.
Good works were his; his name be praised.

I believe in Christ; oh, blessed name!
As Mary's Son he came to reign
'Mid mortal men, his earthly kin,
To save them from the woes of sin.

I believe in Christ, who marked the path,
Who did gain all his Father hath,
Who said to men: "Come, follow me,
That ye, my friends, with God may be."

I believe in Christ—my Lord, my God!
My feet he plants on gospel sod.
I'll worship him with all my might;
He is the source of truth and light.

I believe in Christ, he ransoms me.
From Satan's grasp he sets me free,
And I shall live with joy and love
In his eternal courts above.

I believe in Christ, he stands supreme;
From him I'll gain my fondest dream;
And while I strive through grief and pain,
His voice is heard: "Ye shall obtain."

I believe in Christ, so come what may,
With him I'll stand in that great day
When on this earth he comes again.
To rule among the sons of men.[2]

Never before had he given a talk that had such a powerful effect on the hearts of those who heard it or that carried with it a greater measure of the spirit of prophecy. After the conference, President Harold B. Lee, then first counselor to Church president Joseph Fielding Smith, said to him: "Bruce, you raised the level of the whole conference." Elder McConkie confided that the Spirit had taken over and carried his message into "the hearts of people with convincing power."

This address was given in the Sunday afternoon session of conference. While listening to that session, I received the distinct impression that one of the speakers would in some way identify himself as the one to fill the next vacancy in the Quorum of the Twelve. After Dad spoke, there was no question as to who that was. Like many others, I carried the feeling of that talk with me for days afterward. Though none of his children shared their feelings with Dad, after his call he acknowledged that he was very much aware of them.

A number of people gifted with a love of music wrote to him, describing their impression that his poem should be put to music and requesting his permission to do so. Others sent musical renderings they had already made.

The Passing of Joseph Fielding Smith

Granddaddy Smith passed away quietly on Sunday, July 2, 1972. Dad was with him during the final days and hours of this life. He was "holding his hand when his pulse stopped beating," and he was invited by the First Presidency to speak at the funeral.

Dad enjoyed an unusually strong outpouring of the Spirit while paying tribute to President Smith. Many received the impression at that time that he would be called to fill the vacancy in the Quorum of the Twelve. Among their number was Marion G. Romney. Another was Spencer J. Condie, then a professor at Brigham Young University, who wrote Elder McConkie a letter dated May 10, 1973,

Call to the Apostleship

to report on another matter. In that letter he noted: "Early on the morning you were sustained as an apostle in General Conference, I was driving to the conference session with my neighbor who happens to be a stake president. In the course of our conversation, he casually asked me who I thought the new apostle would be. I shared with him the feelings which I experienced during the sermon which you delivered at the funeral of our late beloved President Joseph Fielding Smith. At that time, after you had concluded your sermon, I looked at my wife and said, 'There is the next apostle of the Lord.' The Spirit bore witness to me so very strongly that you were to be called that I had no doubts. Thus, I replied to my good neighbor that you were to be he whom the Lord had chosen."

Area Conference in Mexico

The end of August found Bruce and Amelia at an area conference in Mexico City. This was for them a great spiritual experience. Although larger groups of Latter-day Saints had assembled in open air meetings, this was the largest congregation of Church members ever assembled under one roof. At this conference the names of the general authorities were presented for a sustaining vote. It was the first time the new First Presidency, consisting of Harold B. Lee as president, N. Eldon Tanner as first counselor, and Marion G. Romney as second counselor, had been presented for a sustaining vote. The names of eleven Apostles were read, there being a vacancy in that Quorum. Dad recorded: "I, however, heard the twelfth name. It was mine." From that day he knew he was to fill the vacancy created by the call of Elder Marion G. Romney to serve in the First Presidency.

Again at that conference a distinctive and unusually powerful spirit attended his remarks. It was at this conference that Elder McConkie spoke of the doctrine of the gathering. In this talk he identified—with a plainness not theretofore heard among Latter-day

Saints—how the prophecies dealing with the gathering were describing various stages. He indicated that there was a time when Israel was to gather from the ends of the earth to Ohio, Missouri, then to Illinois, and finally to the mountains of the Great Basin. But now, the Church had entered into a new stage—also very much a part of the prophetic word—in which Israel was to root itself among all the nations of the earth where stakes would be established and temples built. It was from this talk that President Harold B. Lee quoted in the April 1973 general conference to affirm that doctrine.[3]

A Preparatory Spirit

After his call to the Quorum of the Twelve Apostles, which came in the October conference, many people observed to Elder McConkie that they had known beforehand that he would be called. They added that a witness to that effect came to them when they heard him speak in the April conference, or at the funeral of President Smith, or in the conference in Mexico City. The Spirit of the Lord was clearly preparing the way so that there would be a spirit of acceptance when the call came.

Why would such a preparatory spirit be necessary? My brother Mark shared a story that may help to answer that question: "In San Diego I met Bob Daynes, whom Dad called to be a Patriarch when Brother Daynes was only 36. Of his call, he said he thought Dad really wrestled with it, to be certain it was right. Brother Daynes also told me that he had had a witness of the Holy Ghost in the conference before Dad's call to the Twelve that Dad would be called. He reported that many others he knew had had the same experience, and wondered why. I suggested that because of the long-term impact that Dad would have on the Church, even long after his death, because of what he has contributed to our understanding of the gospel, perhaps the Lord wanted many people to have the additional witness that his call was inspired, so that in turn they would have greater confidence in his teachings."

Bruce's brother Oscar approached that question differently. He noted that his experiences as "a McConkie" were often not unlike those known to his older brother. Illustrating the point, he shared what Elder Marion G. Romney had said to him in calling him to serve as a stake president. Elder Romney said, "Now, Oscar, when you speak, make sure you are right, because the way you say it is going to make people mad anyway." Uncompromising, plain, direct speech was characteristic of Oscar McConkie Sr. and is very much evident in his children and grandchildren. Faults they may have, but there is little chance you will be uncertain where they stand where gospel principles are involved.

THE CALL

During the first week of October 1972, the meetings normally held in the Temple on Thursday were held on Wednesday to accommodate additional conference meetings. Wednesday afternoon Bruce was invited to President Harold B. Lee's office, where President Lee put his arms around him by way of greeting and said, "The Lord and the Brethren have just called you to fill the vacancy in the Council of the Twelve." Bruce responded, "I know. This is no surprise to me. I have known it for some time." President Lee also indicated that he had known for three months. The two men visited together for about thirty minutes.

In his biography of President Lee, Brent Goates noted the following from President Lee's diary: "Today while fasting, I went to the most sacred room in the temple. There for an hour I prayerfully considered the appointment of a new Apostle. All seemed clear that Bruce R. McConkie should be the man. When I told my counselors they both said that from the first they seemed to know also it was to be Elder McConkie.

The Bruce R. McConkie Story

"When I talked with Brother McConkie he related an experience he had at the recent Mexico City area conference. When the General Authorities were sustained, following the reading of Elder Marvin J. Ashton's name (the eleventh Apostle in seniority), he heard his own name spoken. Since that time he had wrestled with this forewarning in the temple for a long time, and seemed to feel, as President Grant had expressed himself when he was called, that he 'seemed to see' a council of the Brethren on the other side, where they were advocating his name."[4]

In his conversation with Elder McConkie, President Lee said that he "had argued" with the Lord about the matter. Realizing that he had been more open than he wanted to be, he said, "I should better say 'counseled with the Lord,' and he made it very plain who he wanted." Later, Bruce's brother Oscar reminded Bruce of the story about Heber J. Grant indicating to Melvin J. Ballard that he had wanted to choose someone else and the Lord told him no. Elder Ballard had been hurt to learn that he was not the prophet's choice. "Didn't that hurt your feelings?" Oscar asked. "Are you kidding?" Dad responded. "I would much rather know I was the Lord's choice!"

When I saw Dad after the solemn assembly in which he was sustained, the first thing I asked him was, "Was your call the same as Heber J. Grant's?" Interestingly, Oscar had asked him the same question. His response was, "Yes." He indicated that he knew by revelation that his call came in large measure to honor his father. During Elder McConkie's first speech as an apostle, Amelia did not hear the voice of her husband as he spoke but the voice of his father. I think, however, that his call came not just in honor of his father but also in fulfillment of promises given to faithful progenitors reaching back some generations, for the promise given them as a reward for their faith was that righteous men and women would come of their loins and that prophets would be among their number.

That our generation is blessed by the deeds of those who went before us is not simply a matter of family pride. It is an eternal principle. As Dad said so often, "Salvation is a family affair," and it centers in the idea that we are not alone and that "root" and "branch" are indeed inseparable. These are principles to which all families have equal claim. In describing his call to the apostleship, Elder Spencer W. Kimball wrote: "I thought of my Father and Mother and my Grandfather, Heber C. Kimball, and my other relatives that had been passed from the earth for long years and wondered what part they had had, if any, in this call, and if they approved of me and felt that I would qualify. I wondered if they had influenced, in any way, the decision that I should be called. I felt strangely near them, nearer than ever in my life."[5]

"God Gave Him Another Heart"

Notwithstanding that Bruce knew the Lord had called him to serve as an apostle, the call brought with it an emotional shock. The anticipation had been humbling; the reality was overwhelming. He immediately took refuge in prayerful scripture study. In so doing he found particular comfort in promises given of the Lord to Saul after he was called to lead the nation of Israel: "The Spirit of the Lord will come upon thee, and thou shalt prophesy with them, and shalt be turned into another man. . . . And it was so . . . God gave him another heart" (1 Samuel 10:6, 9).

In his address at the funeral of President Smith, Bruce had mentioned that he had never known a man with a more "sharply defined sense of duty" or greater desire to "do everything expected of him."[6] On such matters the men were equals. Bruce McConkie never left an assignment unfinished. What could be done tomorrow, he did today. Yet he sensed there was more that he could do in extending himself and the spirit of the sacred office with which he had been entrusted. With all his heart he now sought the ability to do that. Some have said that indeed he received both a new heart and a new spirit as he assumed his new call.

As to Offices and Callings

There is an inherent danger in centering undue attention on the importance of offices and callings. Salvation is not found in offices, and a preoccupation with them can be self-destructive. Dad was very sensitive to this danger and took great pains to warn his family against such a danger. He recalled that when President J. Reuben Clark was changed from first counselor in the First Presidency to second counselor, President Clark reminded the Church as a whole that what matters is not "where one serves, but how."[7]

Dad explained that when there is a vacancy in a bishopric, a stake presidency, or among the general authorities, there are those in the ward, stake, or Church generally who begin to speculate and wonder whether they ought to be called. Some of them obviously pray to the Lord and ask to be called and then think that when someone else is called, the best man has not been chosen. He pointed out that "there are usually many men who could fill any position, who could take any vacancy that arises and do it honorably and well, building up the kingdom and furthering the work. But some individual has to be called to do it. It is certain that whoever is called thereby becomes the Lord's anointed, and even if the Lord would have preferred someone else, yet the one called is entitled to inspiration, and if he seeks to magnify his calling to the full, he will come off triumphant in the work assigned."

The great lesson is that it does not matter what position we have in life. What does matter is how we keep the commandments. "The family unit and working in the cause of righteousness are more important than any position. Service is essential to salvation, but the place where we serve is not."

Call to the Apostleship

Years before, Dad was assigned to attend a quarterly conference in the Assembly Hall on Temple Square. In one of the meetings, Dad spoke about magnifying one's calling in the priesthood and thereby working out an inheritance of exaltation and receiving all that the Father hath—this in accordance with the statements in Doctrine and Covenants 84 on the oath and covenant of the priesthood. George F. Richards, president of the Quorum of the Twelve Apostles, followed Dad and spoke on the same general theme. One of the things that President Richards said was, in substance, there are many in the Church who hold no position at all who in eternity will have higher positions than many of the Council of the Twelve. Furthermore, he said that he did not have the slightest doubt that there would be a realignment of Church positions and responsibilities in the life to come. People who were not called to leadership positions in this life could well be called to such positions in the spirit world. He also foresaw a future day when the organization we now have will no longer exist. The only promise that we have about apostles and prophets in the scriptures, for instance, is that they are going to continue until there is a unity of the faith, meaning that some time during the millennial era, apostles and prophets will no longer be needed. That is because every man will be converted, and there will no longer be a need for special witnesses to bring them to the truth. This will also be because everyone will know all of the doctrines, including all of the future, and there will be no occasion for prophets to foretell it.

Elder McConkie held that what was of eternal moment was the family organization, the patriarchal system, which goes from father to son. The thing that counts will not be what position someone held in the Church in any dispensation but, rather, how he lived and whether he is entitled to exaltation and his place in the patriarchal order.

The Quiet Workings of the Spirit

In the April 1977 general conference, Elder McConkie spoke in the Saturday morning session about the Latter-day Saint view of Christ, reciting His position and status in the plan of salvation and what He has done to redeem mankind and make eternal life available. The session was broadcast, so it was timed for music and sermons. Elder McConkie's concluding words were, "He is truly God's Almighty Son in whom we shall rejoice both now and forever."[8] As he sat down, without further announcement the Tabernacle Choir began to sing the words he had written, "I Believe in Christ," to music composed by Rhea B. Allen. It was as though the words of the hymn were a continuation of the sermon just preached.

After the meeting Dad told Jerold Ottley, the Choir director, and Oakley Evans, manager of the Choir, that he was very flattered they would sing his number as he concluded speaking. Brother Ottley said they had not known what he was going to talk about but chose the number because they were certain something would be said about Christ in that session. Dad observed, "As it turned out, it was better than if it had been planned and programmed."

19

AMONG THE NATIONS
1968 TO 1982

I can compare going around the Church . . . as a member of the First Council of the Seventy and now . . . as a member of the Council of the Twelve. There is a very marked difference in how much people pay attention to what I say . . . because of the office that I hold and the esteem that people have for this office.

—Bruce R. McConkie

The Church increased in membership more than sevenfold during the time Bruce McConkie served as a general authority. In 1946, at the time of his call to the First Council of the Seventy, the Church had 592 full-time missionaries with convert baptisms that year numbering almost 5,000. By the time of his death in 1985, the number of full-time missionaries had increased by 27,000, and the number of convert baptisms was just under 193,000. The travels and responsibility of the Brethren had increased in like manner during those years.

AMONG EVERY NATION, KINDRED, TONGUE, AND PEOPLE

When Bruce was a young general authority, the common practice was for two or three of the Brethren to share rides to their assigned stake conferences, the one going to the most distant point dropping the others off along the way and then picking them up on the return trip. By the time Bruce was called to the apostleship, most traveling was done by air. He and his associates logged hundreds of thousands of miles a year. Crossing multiple time zones and waiting in airports became a way of life. The growth of the Church could almost be measured by the number of miles he and his colleagues traveled, with each trip proving to be an adventure of its own. During the twenty-six years he served as a Seventy, he attended more than 900 stake conferences. Upon discovering that Bruce had had no Sundays without a conference—something not true of any of the other Brethren—S. Dilworth Young, his senior president, investigated the matter. He discovered that through a bookkeeping error, no page had been made to record any time off for his faithful colleague. That was promptly corrected. In addition to the twenty-six months he served as a young missionary in the Eastern States Mission and the three years he spent presiding over the mission in Australia, he had as a Seventy spent the equivalent of five years on mission tours. During that time, together with his years of service as an apostle, he may well have spoken at more than 1,500 stake conferences.

Supervising Church Affairs in the Far East

From July 1968 to July 1971, Bruce, still a member of the Seventy, supervised the missions in Asia under the direction of Elder Ezra Taft Benson of the Council of the Twelve Apostles. During this period Bruce and Amelia made four trips to Asia and held three seminars with the mission presidents and their wives. Amelia described these as "the most interesting experience we have ever had." Describing the first trip, Amelia said, "We landed in Japan to be treated like real celebrities with banners, songs, and flowers. Oh yes, and people! On the way to church the next day we got a look at Mt. Fuji—a very rare experience for Tokyo, as the sky is usually too hazy to see the mountain. At church someone called me 'Sister Smith,' so I knew for sure we were with our own people and felt right at home.

"When Brother Benson arrived a couple of days later and got in a huddle with the two Japan mission presidents, the next play was changed," she recalled. "Instead of Korea and all of Japan as we had planned, we went to Vietnam, Singapore, and the Philippines, finishing up with a mission presidents' seminar in Hong Kong. That's how we got to see Joseph. It's also how we got to have some wonderful experiences with many people who could teach us many things about humility, faith, loving, and giving. Half the world's population is in these missions, and miraculous things are happening.

"Singapore was opened for missionary work last May, and Bruce was the first General Authority to speak at a meeting for members. More than 60 people were there. He was the first to visit Clark Field in the Philippines since my father dedicated that land for missionary work in 1955. The countries and people are fantastically interesting. Someone said they were lands of great contrast, with the ultimate in wealth along with the ultimate in poverty—the ultimate in beauty which contrasts with the ultimate in filth. We came to love all these people, people who welcomed us so warmly, and we gave what we could, which in Bruce's case was much, as he gave them a better, clearer, more meaningful understanding of the gospel, and as a consequence more faith and more hope for an eternal life."

During this trip my parents' path crossed with mine as a result of an unusual set of circumstances. I was serving as an LDS chaplain in Vietnam at the time. There were three districts of LDS servicemen in Vietnam, which were under the direction of President Brent Hardy of the Hong Kong Mission.

We were holding a servicemen's conference at Long Binh, where I was stationed. Hundreds of LDS servicemen had come from one end of the country to the other. As I remember it, we were meeting in a large hangar. Our district president and beloved friend,

Chaplain Farrell Smith, was waiting for Elder Benson's plane at an airport near Saigon. He was to bring him and President Hardy to our meeting as soon as they landed. My assignment was to speak until Elder Benson arrived.

When the door finally opened, to my surprise it was my father who stepped through it, followed by Chaplain Smith and President Hardy. Dad moved quickly down the center aisle and bounded up the steps to the pulpit where I stood. Somewhat stunned, I extended my hand, which he took, and then pulled me into his arms. As my father kissed me, tears streamed down my face, and an audience of battle-hardened soldiers, I am told, also lost the fight to control their emotions.

Lieutenant Colonel Rulon P. Madsen recounted that event in the *Improvement Era*. He wrote: "Father and son shook hands, then, in the presence of the entire conference, embraced each other with a kiss of love. Many respectful, homesick men beheld that tender scene with tear-filled eyes.

". . . As I think of it even today my eyes moisten with tears. It was the sweetest and most humble greeting I have ever witnessed. I was filled with joy for both of them, moved by the open expression of such outstanding love between father and son. No doubt many others sat through the remainder of that conference considering, as I did, the basis of so wonderful a relationship, and praying that as fathers or sons we might, through the gospel of Jesus Christ, build such love between us and our dear ones at home.

"It was an experience none of us will ever forget."[1]

Dad told me that earlier that morning, as he stood in line at the airport in Hong Kong, Elder Benson had turned to him and asked, "Bruce, where are you going?" My father rehearsed his itinerary, and Elder Benson said, "We're trading tickets." He then handed his tickets to Dad and took Dad's in exchange. Elder Benson had been advised that it would not be wise for someone with his high profile

Among the Nations, 1968 to 1982

Bruce in Vietnam between meetings

to travel to Vietnam. Dad, in company with W. Brent Hardy, left immediately for Saigon. Mother was taken back to the hotel in Hong Kong and left the next morning to meet Dad in Saigon.

"It was in the afternoon on a Sunday," Mother recalled, when she and Elaine Hardy boarded a plane for Vietnam. Needless to say, both women were quite uneasy about going into a war-torn country without their husbands. Much to their relief, they were met at the airport by a faithful elder, who took them into the city and got them situated at their hotel.

I had no idea my father would be walking through the door that day and have thought many times since how grateful I am that when he came I was at my post doing my duty. After the servicemen's conference, we visited LDS men in various evacuation hospitals. We administered to a number of them. That experience was

A surprise reunion in Vietnam, 1968: Bruce, Amelia, and Joseph

the best lesson on faith and priesthood that I ever had. When Dad laid his hands on their heads, he spoke as one having authority. His purpose in Vietnam was to give blessings, and that is precisely what he did. In the name of the God of Israel, he commanded bodies to mend and organs to function. In effect, his language was "take up your bed and walk."

The next morning I was among those who escorted Dad and President Hardy back to Saigon, where both men met their wives. Mother was quite pleased to see us. I took a lot of teasing about it, as there are not many soldiers whose mother comes to check up on them in the middle of a war.

We left the women in Saigon and spent two days meeting with various groups of LDS servicemen. This was made possible by what we called our Mormon Airlines. The Lord saw to it that we always had military pilots with access to either helicopters or fixed-wing planes who could take us to wherever our soldiers could get together. Major Ray Young, an Army pilot, who could fly by radar or the Spirit, as necessary, was the pilot of our little fixed-wing aircraft on this trip. During the middle of our second night out, we had the opportunity to see how quickly we could move to bunkers to avoid incoming artillery fire.

In October 1969 Dad and Mother again accompanied the Bensons on a tour of the Asian missions. After a mission presidents' seminar in Manila, their group—which in addition to the Bensons included Wilford W. Kirton (general counsel for the Church), W. Brent and Elaine Hardy (from the mission in Hong Kong), Brother Harding (of the Church Building Department) and Carlos and Lavon Smith (who were to take over missionary work in Singapore)—were scheduled to go to Djakarta, Indonesia. At this time there was a small branch in Indonesia. The primary purpose of their visit was to determine whether the time was right for the Church to formally enter that country and whether it should be dedicated for the preaching of the gospel.

They arrived at the Manila airport for their international flight less than an hour before the flight was scheduled to leave. President Hardy wanted to ship a half dozen boxes of copies of the Book of Mormon to Djakarta and said, "Let's get group baggage." He took everyone's tickets and passports and went up to the counter to make the arrangements. There was no trouble in getting the boxes added to their baggage; however, it was discovered by the representative of Garuda Airlines that the Bensons did not have visas to admit them to Djakarta. It was now forty-five minutes before the plane was to depart. The week before, the airline had been fined a thousand dollars for carrying someone to Djakarta without a visa, so the firm ruling was that the Bensons could not go. Elder Benson immediately phoned the American ambassador in Manila, who phoned the American ambassador in Djakarta, who, within the short time available, made arrangements to get him into the country with a visa.

Representatives from the Canadian embassy met them upon their arrival in Djakarta and accorded them VIP treatment. After the women had been taken to the hotel, the men were taken to a males-only affair related to a royal wedding. There they were able to meet the diplomatic corps of the country.

Before leaving for Djakarta, Elder Benson had received permission from the First Presidency to dedicate Indonesia for missionary work if he felt so impressed. Visits with government officials, the local branch members, and the mission presidents who were traveling with him helped bring him to the conclusion that the time had come. That morning Elder Benson held a meeting in an upper room of the hotel. Those attending sat in a circle, and each was invited in turn to express his feelings about dedicating Indonesia. Dad sat on Elder Benson's left and was the last to speak. All spoke affirmatively. After they had done so, Elder Benson said, "I have been praying to the Lord that if it were not proper for the land of Indonesia to be dedicated to the preaching of the gospel, that he would hedge up the way and prevent it from being done." Dad later joked with him, "Yes, Brother Benson, even to the point of not having a visa so that you could get into the country."

Carlos Smith was assigned to find a suitable place for the dedication, which was scheduled for the next day. The morning of the dedication, the Saints were greeted by rain. Mother described the place chosen by her cousin Carlos as "beautiful" and "pristine." To get there they had to climb a hill covered with banana trees to a lookout point overseeing a valley of rice fields and terraced cornfields. The decision was made to go forward with the service, despite the rain. As the opening prayer was being offered, the rain stopped in a circle around those present, and the clouds parted enough for the sunlight to shine down on them. President Benson offered the

Among the Nations, 1968 to 1982

dedicatory prayer, and Elder McConkie made a few remarks. Others spoke briefly or offered prayers. When the last amen had been said, the clouds closed in and the rain fell once again.

The occasion was deeply touching. Elder Benson's voice cracked with emotion as he spoke. Among those present was a high government official whom Elder Benson had met when he visited the United States on agricultural business. That man requested baptism.

En route home from Asia, Bruce and Amelia stopped in Tehran, Iran, where they visited mosques, the market place, and museums, including one housing the plates of Darius. They also spent five days in the Holy Land. They walked through the old city of Jerusalem, "crossing without question many times the paths and standing in the areas where Jesus and the Ancient Apostles walked." They observed life in many instances much as it would have been two thousand years before, though Bruce thought it might have been "better organized and arranged" in that ancient day. He wrote:

"We stood on the Mount of Olives, visited the garden of Gethsemane, crossed the brook Kidron, stood upon Mount Zion, walked along the wall of the City, saw the Wailing Wall, visited the place where the Catholics say the crucifixion took place, and also the garden outside the city where the Protestants suppose that it occurred. The Protestant site is believable. There is a tomb there supposedly like the tomb in which Jesus was buried. It is somewhat of a hill and could well be the place of a skull meaning that on the hillside there are configurations in the rock which look like a human skull.

"We also rented a car and traveled from Hebron on the south to the Sea of Galilee on the north, visiting Abraham's burial place as also Isaac, Jacob, and Sarah. We went to the City of Nazareth, traveled across the plain of Armageddon, walked around the Sea of Galilee and an old synagogue area that dates back to the first century if not the actual time of Jesus. We stood on what is probably the mountain where the Sermon on the Mount was delivered. It was a rich experience and gave many insights into scriptural expressions. Nazareth is 'a city set on a hill that cannot be hid,' for instance. The many walls in the Judean hills in which olive groves are planted show branches growing over the wall. There is much progress because of modern agriculture and the like, yet portions of the area are now as they were anciently."

THE MORMON PAVILION AT EXPO '70

In September 1970, after the mission presidents' seminar in Osaka, Japan, Bruce and Amelia and Brent and Elaine Hardy visited the World's Fair, which was being held in that city. The Mormon Pavilion, with the film *Man's Search for Happiness*, had proved itself one of the most popular exhibits. Mission president Edward Y. Okazaki and his wife, Sister Chieko N. Okazaki, were their guides. At the Mormon Pavilion, Amelia observed a beautiful little Japanese girl standing in front of the statue of Christ and trying to pose in the same way. "That created," she said, "a very touching picture."

After they saw the film at the Mormon Pavilion, the group set out to visit some of the other pavilions. They were pleased to meet a number of former Japanese missionaries who were employed as guides at various exhibits because of their fluent Japanese and English. When they came to the Christian Pavilion, Bruce said, "Come on. Let's go inside and see what the opposition has."

As they entered, they were handed a pamphlet announcing the theme of the pavilion as "Holy Emptiness." To dramatize the theme, the cathedral was empty except for a few benches and an organ in the center. An organ recital was given each day, and they had arrived just in time for it. The organist was immediately identified by the missionaries as a Mormon elder. Amelia said, "Let's get him to play some Mormon hymns." She and the two elders went over to talk to him while Bruce and the Hardys walked through the back of the cathedral.

In a few moments the elder was playing "Come, Come, Ye Saints" and "We Thank Thee, O God, for a Prophet." People began to assemble to listen. At the same time the pavilion director was on his way to see what was going on. Learning that some Mormons were in his building, he immediately approached Bruce and Elder Hardy. "Are you Mormons?" he asked.

Bruce responded in the affirmative.

"Well," the director began, "I had not had an opportunity to visit your pavilion until the other day when I went in to see that film you show, and I want you to know that it made me furious."

"Is that so?" Bruce said. "Why?"

The man's face and neck got redder. "I did not take occasion to look up the director of the pavilion and register my protests, but since you are Mormons, may I tell you?"

"Certainly," was the response.

He then expressed his displeasure with the film *Man's Search for Happiness* because it portrayed a continuation of the family unit and the conscious identity of the human soul after death. He explained that he had been in Japan for eighteen years as a Lutheran minister teaching at a Lutheran school. "All these Buddhists by instinct think that the family unit exists after death. I have spent eighteen years of my life trying to knock this idea out of their heads and then I see this film that destroys all my work, and I would like to know if this is really what Mormons believe."

Bruce said, "Sir, you are very perceptive; that is precisely what we believe."

After some discussion of this matter, the pavilion director inquired about the Apostasy. He said, "I get the idea that you Mormons think you are the only true church."

Elder McConkie shaking hands with President Reagan at the Church Offices, September 1984

"I assured him," Dad said later, "that he was catching the vision of what was involved."

Then the pavilion director said, "I wouldn't mind so much if your missionaries spent their time preaching to Buddhists, but I can't understand why you preach to the Christians. At the school where I teach, your elders come and pass out literature to my Christian converts. I would like to know why you do this and can't operate like other churches do." In making these expressions, he was getting quite exercised, so Dad "took off the kid gloves," as he said later. He answered, "Reverend, I am delighted to answer your question. The reason that our missionaries come and teach your people is that we think it is just as important for a Lutheran to be saved as it is for a Buddhist." To this he added the story of the First Vision, after which they parted.

The missionaries remained behind for a few minutes, and the director said to them, "I really didn't want to talk to him; I just wanted to talk to you."

"My reaction to that," Dad said, "was that if I were a Lutheran minister, I wouldn't want to talk to me either."

Laboring in South America

For about seven years, Elder McConkie's assignments took him primarily to South America. His six-foot, five-inch frame made him something of a giant among these people. It was common for little children to run up and place one of their feet at the side of his to measure the difference. President James E. Faust recalled such an experience during a lunch break at one of their training conferences: "I said to Elder McConkie, 'Bruce, let's go across the street and I'll buy you a shoe shine from one of the little boys with a shoe shine box.' When Bruce put his size 15 shoe on the shine box, the little shine boy's eyes opened wide. He took his rag and measured from toe to heel on Brother McConkie's shoe and then he held it up to look at it. He began to shine the shoe. In a moment or two he measured again, as if he could not believe the first. He stretched the shine rag from the toe to the heel. He held it up again [and looked at it]. He proceeded to shine. A third time he measured. He had never shined size 15 shoes before in his life and possibly never would again. Naturally, I paid him double."

Elder Faust continued: "The first mission presidents' seminar I ever attended, I conducted as a new Assistant to the Twelve in Buenos Aires. I was anxious, nervous and a little bit scared. Elder McConkie was my first contact in the Twelve. Sensing my feeling of inadequacy, Bruce said in an off-hand way to my Ruth: 'I wish I had Jim's experience in the Church.' At that time he had already been a General Authority for 30 years. This was so typical of his sensitive concern for others.

"At that seminar he and I had a simultaneous, instantaneous, remarkable revelation. We were given at the same time to know by the Spirit that an obscure Seventy from the Mexican border, attending the seminar, serving at the time as a mission president in Santiago, would be called as a General Authority in three weeks. That man was Elder William Bradford.

"Finn Paulsen, one of my missionary companions, and Bruce were fellow rock-hounds. They were together when their lives were spared in a miraculous way, which has been reported. Perhaps it was on that occasion when they found the special stones from which Bruce personally made beautiful polished stone brooches which he and Amelia gave to our mission presidents' wives in South America.

"Bruce was a colorful personality. One time in Buenos Aires we were admiring some of the beautiful leather articles made in Argentina. There happened to be some well-tailored sheepskin coats hanging on the rack. We urged Bruce to try one on but he was not very hopeful that they could find a coat big enough to fit him. By some minor miracle the shopkeeper brought out a great sheepskin coat that fitted Bruce perfectly. Amelia urged him to buy it and he did. That night after the meetings of the seminar were over Bruce and Amelia went for a walk down Florida Street. Bruce put on his new sheepskin coat and paraded down Florida Street among the well-dressed Argentines. Now that was a sight, Elder Bruce R. McConkie wearing his sheepskin coat, standing a full head above the other people, walking down that fashionable street."[2]

When the McConkies returned from one of their many visits to South America, Amelia observed that her patriarchal blessing had said she would proclaim the gospel in many lands, "but so far we have not seen many places." "Well," Bruce answered, "I am supposed to be a witness of Christ in all the world but so far I am the Archbishop of South America."

At his next meeting with the First Presidency and the Twelve,

Sara Tanner and Amelia in Tahiti, March 1976

when he reported to them in their temple meeting, Bruce told them about that conversation. President Spencer W. Kimball was surprised to know that Bruce had been going to South America so frequently and also that he had rarely had a Sunday without an appointment taking him away from home.

The next year Bruce's appointments took him to other countries, but the year after that, he was sent back to South America again.

Visiting the Islands

From April 15 to May 2, 1977, Elder McConkie visited among the Polynesians in Hawaii, Tonga, and Samoa. He found this to be a pleasant experience, in part because it was the first time in years of traveling that he had had any free time to work on various projects. During these two weeks, as part of his assignment on the Scriptures Publication Committee in preparation for a Latter-day Saint edition of the Bible, he wrote 250 chapter headings, beginning in the middle of Isaiah and continuing through the Old Testament and into the book of Mark in the New Testament. He also wrote drafts of a number of conference talks.

Bruce and Amelia at the Vatican, August 1977

Visiting Saudi Arabia

In November 1978, Bruce and Amelia were given a rare opportunity. He was assigned to go to Dhahran, Saudi Arabia, where the Church had more than six hundred members, mostly from the United States and Canada. These expatriates were working for oil companies or in related occupations. The Saudi government allowed the Saints to hold a district conference once a year, but tourists were not permitted in Saudi Arabia. Only a few non-Muslim male visitors were allowed to enter, and they were not usually allowed to bring their wives because it was felt that the appearance of foreign women would have a negative effect on Saudi women. Nor were the teenaged children of employees of the oil companies allowed into the country because of their decadent influence on Saudi youth. They had to remain with friends or relatives at home or be enrolled in boarding schools.

Among the Nations, 1968 to 1982

Ernest A. Weeks, the district president, who worked as a school superintendent for the younger children of the expatriate Latter-day Saints, and members of the Church in the oil company arranged for Bruce and Amelia to enter the country. They left Utah a few days early so that they could stop in London on the way to visit the museums and art galleries. Bruce was particularly interested in the Bible collection in the Natural History Museum, which is simply unmatched in the world, and he also wanted to study the Egyptian collection in the British Museum. They visited St. Paul's Cathedral and other tourist attractions as well. From England their journey took them to Germany, where Bruce presided over a stake conference in Düsseldorf, and from there they headed to Saudi Arabia.

Bruce and Amelia had been warned that they could not bring their scriptures or any other religious items into the country. They were told of instances in which people's scriptures were stolen from their luggage or soaked in water or otherwise ruined. Modest dress was of course required of all women allowed into the country. They arrived in Dhahran on a Tuesday and were immediately taken to pay their respects to the consul official who had approved their visas. They were then taken to meet the LDS people working there. The following day had been declared a holiday because the Saudi king had returned from a successful medical visit to England.

The Church members who had arranged the McConkies' visas also arranged two remarkable sight-seeing trips for them. On Tuesday they were flown out into the Rub al Kali desert, the largest sand desert in the world. Oil workers were flown into this place for a twenty-eight-day work period and then replaced with another crew. As they flew, Bruce and Amelia saw an occasional oasis and a few camel trains wending their way across the desert, as Amelia said, "like little toy trains." The pilot called the area over which they flew the Main Street of Saudi Arabia.

On Wednesday they were taken by helicopter for some hours

along the Arabian Gulf, flying over the oil refineries, and offshore drilling rigs. They described the experience as "mind boggling." They saw oil pipes like those in Alaska, except these were larger. There were always at least two, side by side, and sometimes three or four. Frequently the pipes were crossed by others going in another direction. The pressure, they were told, was so great that the oil did not need to be pumped; instead, pipes were just sunk into a well and the oil flowed readily. Some of the pipes ran to the Gulf, where oil tankers were waiting to be filled directly from the wells. They were told that a single pipeline transported about three hundred fifty million dollars' worth of oil a day.

Upon their return, Bruce and Amelia were taken from the compound into Dhahran, where they discovered that women could not drive a car. Out in public, women were always veiled. They carried their families' fortune with them as gold bracelets and necklaces. They also learned that people held in jail were not provided food. Friends outside the jail had to take it to them. Alcoholic beverages were not allowed in the country, and joining any non-Muslim religion was an offense punishable by death. If a person was caught stealing, his hand would be cut off. The Saudis practiced plural marriage, a man being allowed four wives. Some of their kings had had hundreds of wives, marrying them four at a time and then divorcing them. The word of the monarch was their only law.

On Thursday, Bruce presided over a series of conference sessions. People attended from all over Saudi Arabia, Kuwait, and Yemen. Many traveled more than a thousand miles by air. Their number included many with significant experience in Church leadership. Some 350 people attended the meetings, which was more than half the number of Saints in the region. Testimony was the theme of the meetings. After the conference, Bruce and Amelia left for Athens, Greece, where they spent the night before heading to Stuttgart, Germany, for another stake conference.

Among the Nations, 1968 to 1982

A Visit to China

In May 1983 Bruce and Amelia were invited to join June and Dallin Oaks, who was then president of Brigham Young University, as chaperones of the Young Ambassadors for their trip to China. It happened that the BYU group became a kind of voodoo doll for the Chinese officials to stick with pins in an attempt to square accounts, as they saw it, with the United States government. A few weeks before the group was to leave, a Chinese tennis player had defected while in America. This was very embarrassing to China, and in retaliation, the Chinese threatened to cancel the trip. Only at the last minute was permission granted for the BYU group to make the journey. This concession was extended because BYU was a private institution and agreed to pay for all expenses, including the dinners at which they were to be honored and given gifts of appreciation. Nevertheless, the group was deliberately given second-class treatment, which was in marked contrast to their treatment in earlier visits. They experienced such things as deliberate delays and unduly thorough checking at customs, second-class hotels, and hosts of inferior social status.

Bruce and Amelia both talked in the first sacrament meeting the group held in China. After doing so, they learned from Church members from the American and Canadian embassies that the meeting had likely been bugged and they could expect to have all that they had said be refuted by their guides in the next few days. This proved to be the case. The next day, when they visited the Great Wall of China, the guides made a deliberate effort to isolate and question each of them. Bruce was able to elude them. Amelia was not. She was asked a host of questions about her husband, his position on the board of education for BYU, his Church position, and so forth. The guards also asked to have their pictures taken with her. Bruce assumed that they were building a dossier on him and that if he sought a visa for China again, it would be denied.

Bruce with a guide in China, May 1983

The Temple Dedication in Santiago, Chile

Bruce and Amelia were delighted to be among those invited to be a part of the dedication of the temple in Santiago, Chile. This was especially so because he had visited that land so frequently in years past and was well acquainted with many of the Saints there. At an area conference held some years earlier, Bruce had promised a future day when there would be a temple in that land.

The dedication took place September 15–17, 1983, with President Gordon B. Hinckley presiding and Elders Boyd K. Packer and Bruce R. McConkie participating. Three sessions were held each day with a break between. Each session was filled to capacity. Many in attendance came from some distance and at considerable sacrifice. Some borrowed a suit from others who had attended a previous session. Some wore shoes whose soles had been mended with newspaper. But they all were neat and clean, with love for the Lord

Bruce and Amelia in Lima, Peru, January 1977

and gratitude for the opportunity to be there shining in their faces. In one session, when it was time for the Hosanna Shout, two lovely little girls sitting by their parents carefully took the pieces of white tissue they had kept in their pockets and very carefully smoothed them out so they could participate.

On the final day of the dedication, President Hinckley said to Amelia during the lunch break, "Amelia, how would you like to speak in the session this afternoon? Marge and Donna will also be speaking."

These three women may well have been the first in our (or any) dispensation to speak at a temple dedication. President Hinckley again called upon Amelia to speak at the dedication of the Mount Timpanogos Utah Temple in 1996. President Hinckley must have figured she was a veteran by then, because he just called her out of the audience without warning.

20

THE NATURE OF HIS MINISTRY
1946 TO 1985

You were called to be a work horse, not a dog under the wheels.
—President George F. Richards

It may be inevitable that a lay church—one with a constant influx of new members coming from a great variety of backgrounds and one in which there will always be a good number of people who are in the process of growing up into a particular office or calling—will be afflicted by "false spirits," including excessive zeal, religious fads, doctrines of devils, and doctrines of men. One of the duties resting on the general authorities of the Church, and particularly on the Quorum of the Twelve Apostles, is to protect the Church from such deceptions. Few men have come to the office of apostleship better prepared for such a responsibility than Bruce R. McConkie. He was seasoned timber. The combination of a lifetime of serious gospel study and countless hours spent in councils of the Church over the previous twenty-six years uniquely qualified him for the work.

REPROVING BETIMES WITH SHARPNESS

In the fall of 1972, Elder McConkie, at the request of a stake president in Bountiful, Utah, counseled with a couple in his stake who were teaching that salvation centers in obtaining a special relationship with Jesus, a relationship that could only be achieved by praying to Christ instead of the Father. The man involved was a marriage counselor and popular speaker. His wife accompanied him and sang at meetings they held. They claimed these teachings had aided them in saving many marriages. After a long discussion, the man seemed to mellow somewhat, but his wife remained adamant in her views, and her spirit was quite bitter. Not satisfied with the principles Elder McConkie had attempted to teach them, they insisted on meeting with President Harold B. Lee.

Having thoroughly reviewed the situation and the doctrinal explanations Elder McConkie had given the couple, President Lee declined to meet with them. He advised them by letter that if they did not find it in their hearts to follow the counsel that had been given them, the spirit of the adversary would have power over them. Of that experience Elder McConkie observed, "This is a perfect illustration of how doctrinal misjudgment can lead people away from the truth and eventually out of the Church. People begin to believe something that is not taught by the Church, then they refuse to accept the counsel of those whose right it is to interpret the doctrines, then they feel the Church is out of line and they are right, and finally they begin to criticize the Brethren. The spirit of the devil takes over in their lives, and unless they repent they go out of the Church to destruction."

This was not the last time Elder McConkie was called on to confront this doctrinal aberration. In October 1981, while presiding over a multistake conference at BYU, Elder McConkie encountered a similar circumstance. In the Saturday priesthood leadership meeting, he reviewed a "laundry list" of potential problems (discussed in chapter 16), only to discover that he had walked into a hornets' nest when he touched on the danger of students being encouraged to gain a "special relationship with Jesus."

By assignment from the Quorum of the Twelve, Elder McConkie returned to BYU a few months later to speak to the entire student body on the matter. In that address, entitled "Our Relationship with the Lord," given at a devotional March 2, 1982, he announced that he would "expound the doctrine of the Church relative to what our relationship should be to all members of the Godhead and do so in plainness and simplicity so that none need misunderstand or be led astray by other voices." In doing so, he said, "I am on my own ground and am at home with my subject." He invited "erring teachers and beguiled students to repent and believe the accepted gospel verities as I shall set them forth." Then, true to his promise, he established from scripture seventeen basic points illustrating the impropriety of singling Christ out of the Godhead for some kind of special relationship.

He began by quoting from a founding document of our dispensation, which declares that we are to love and worship God the Father and "serve him, the only living and true God, and that he should be the only being whom [we] should worship" (D&C 20:19). Christ, Elder McConkie reminded his listeners, came into the world to do the will of the Father, to implement his plan for the salvation of his children, to work out his own salvation, and through his atoning sacrifice to reconcile us with the Father. To worship as Christ worshipped is to worship the Father. To center our worship on anyone or anything other than the Father throws the entire plan of salvation out of balance. "If there were some need—which there is not!—to single out one member of the Godhead for a special relationship, the Father, not the Son, would be the one to choose."

He noted further that another peril for those so involved was that they often began to pray directly to Christ because of some

The Nature of His Ministry, 1946 to 1985

special friendship they felt had been developed. "In this connection," he pointed out, "a current and unwise book, which advocates gaining a special relationship with Jesus, contains this sentence: 'Because the Savior is our mediator, our prayers go through Christ to the Father, and the Father answers our prayers through his Son.'

"This is plain sectarian nonsense. Our prayers are addressed to the Father, and to him only. They do not go through Christ, or the Blessed Virgin, or St. Genevieve, or along the beads of a rosary. We are entitled to 'come boldly unto the throne of grace, that we may obtain mercy, and find grace to help in time of need' (Hebrews 4:16)."

Elder McConkie was quite aware that this address would give offense to some. To speak against the idea of a special relationship with Jesus, he said, was like "speaking out against mother love, or Americanism, or the little red schoolhouse." Nevertheless, he maintained, "the very moment anyone singles out one member of the Godhead as the almost sole recipient of his devotion, to the exclusion of the others, that is the moment when spiritual instability begins to replace sense and reason." Among those claiming this special relationship with Christ, he observed, one commonly found "an unwholesome holier-than-thou attitude" that made them condescending towards those they regarded as their spiritual inferiors.

Elder McConkie also warned against the notion popular among "intellectuals without strong testimonies" who advocate the idea that God is forever "progressing in truth and knowledge." "These," he declared, "unless they repent, will live and die weak in the faith and will fall short of inheriting what might have been theirs in eternity."[1]

His address caused quite a stir, and in the course of the next few weeks, his office responded to about three thousand requests for copies. Many of these in turn became master copies for further distribution. The address was reported in the *Church News* for

March 20, 1982. The following are typical of the hundreds of letters Elder McConkie received in response to his address. One reader wrote: "I almost wanted to shout hurrah! when I read it. It has been a subject which has troubled me for some time, and which I have felt *needed* to be addressed by someone in authority for the members of the Church." Another reader, the mother of seven children, wrote to Elder McConkie: "I have just finished reading the *Church News* (March 20). I am grateful for your article about our relationship to members of the Godhead. There has been much talk here about the 'personal relationship with Christ.' I have been troubled by it—and didn't even know why. Your talk was so clear and beautiful. I have wondered 'What is wrong with me?' The personal relationship with Christ theme made me feel uneasy and I desperately need your counsel. We have 7 children, with 2 of them in Seminary—where this theme has been pushed. I especially need your help as a mother. I teach Mother Education in our ward and have had other mothers ask me about this very thing. I shall be so happy to have your words to help. Thank you, thank you for helping us to stay on the path we should follow. It is a blessing to know that our priesthood leaders care enough to speak out boldly when it is called for—and put things back in perspective."

THE POWER OF FAITH

While on a stake conference assignment in 1961, Elder McConkie was invited to the home of the Pratts for something to eat between sessions. Their eighteen-year-old son, who had been afflicted since birth with an incurable skin disease, got out of his bed to meet Elder McConkie. He asked what was wrong with the boy. His response to the explanation was to inquire, "Have the elders administered to him?" He was told that they had, many times. Doctors could only offer the young man relief for his pain, recommending that he be kept comfortable until he died.

The Nature of His Ministry, 1946 to 1985

Sister Pratt recalled: "After the dinner the authorities left and went back to church to prepare for the second session of conference. I was trying to clean up the dishes so I could get back to church when I heard the door open and the booming voice of Bruce R. McConkie, saying, 'Sister Pratt, I want to give that young man a blessing before I leave here today. Have him at the church at the close of the meeting.'

"I got Ray ready and took him to the church. When they laid their hands on Ray's head, Elder McConkie was silent. I panicked, thinking there was no blessing for him. I was shedding tears when Elder McConkie started to speak. In his very distinct and articulate voice he said, 'Brother Ray Grant Pratt, the Lord has given you this affliction to prepare you for the work that lies ahead. I promise you in the name of the Lord Jesus Christ that your health will never stand in the way of your serving the Lord.'" The disease was rebuked, and the blessing of healing was soon realized.

Another remarkable instance of the power of faith is that of a woman, a mother of two, who had contracted a rare blood disease. Though not fatal, it prohibited her from having more children. In an administration at the hands of her husband, she received the promise that her body would heal itself. Yet all medical efforts proved painful, frustrating, and ineffectual. At a stake conference attended by a member of the Twelve, she experienced the impression that if her faith were great enough, she could be healed. She labored to increase her faith. Six months later another apostle, Elder Bruce R. McConkie, was sent to the stake in which they lived. Her children were ill that Sunday, and though she usually would have been the one to stay with them, she and her husband decided that she should attend the conference. "I took a seat in the middle of the auditorium," she wrote to Elder McConkie later, "and watched as you shook hands with many before the meeting. I was delighted as I watched the smiles of many I recognized enjoying your touch and smile.

"Throughout the meeting I found it difficult to concentrate, and as it came to a close, I could hardly remain seated. As the closing prayer was said, I felt very calm. Then," she continued, "the Spirit whispered to me, 'You could go up on that stage and be healed by Brother McConkie.' I replied, 'I don't want to bother him—look at all those people who want to talk to him. I'm just thrilled to be able to have heard him.' Then the Spirit reminded me—'just touch the edge of his jacket'—as I recalled the story of the woman who had touched the hem of the Savior's garment. I'm sure I literally shook my head and said, 'No. I can't possibly do that!'" She and the Spirit continued their debate. Finally she went.

"As I made my way through the crowd," she wrote, "I felt very anxious and wanted to turn around, but I edged forward until finally I was right behind you and you were engaged in conversation. I fixed my eyes upon your jacket edge and held my breath—you were so tall—I reached out and quickly touched with my index finger the hem of your jacket. Suddenly, you spun around and extended your hand to me. I shook it and tearfully uttered, 'Thank you.' You simply nodded and returned to your conversation, and I went to my car practically dancing!"

When she entered her home, she announced to her husband that she was healed. They knelt together in a prayer of thanksgiving. The doctor was baffled. At the time of her writing she had become the mother of three more children. Her faith had made her whole.

Stake Reorganizations

In his twenty-six years as a member of the First Council of the Seventy, Elder McConkie had never been responsible to call a new stake president or a new stake patriarch, the authority to do so not having been extended to his Quorum. This changed quickly with his call to the apostleship. The growth of the Church was such that by the time he had been an apostle four years, he had called more stake presidents than his father-in-law, Joseph Fielding Smith, had called in more than sixty years in that same office. The responsibility of identifying the man the Lord had chosen to lead a particular stake or to be its patriarch was one he greatly enjoyed. His experiences of being directed by the Spirit in this responsibility were innumerable. He never felt bound to follow a particular procedure; rather, he sought, as he did in speaking, to follow the lead of the Spirit.

Early in his experience, he was called on to reorganize two stakes into three. While interviewing Maxwell Richards Cannon, he felt impressed to call him to be a patriarch. No one had mentioned his name in the interviews. Brother Cannon evidenced no surprise at the call. He said, "My wife told me a week ago I was to be the new stake patriarch." Bruce replied, "That is interesting. The last time I called a patriarch, he told me his wife had told him the week before that he was to be called." Bruce recorded that "in ordaining Brother Cannon I felt impressed to tell him that his progenitors were interested in his call and pleased that he was being ordained to this high and holy office." He was a grandson of George Q. Cannon on his father's side and George F. Richards on his mother's side.

In another instance Elder McConkie interviewed thirty-two men, all but one of whom made the same recommendation. The one not making a recommendation was a former Congressman who, though repeatedly pressed, could not bring himself to make a recommendation. Elder McConkie said, "I thought to myself, Here is a real politician."

While sitting on the stand in a stake conference some years later, Elder McConkie said, "After the morning session had commenced, I decided by pure inspiration to call George I. Cannon to serve as a patriarch. I went down off the stand, got him out of the congregation, took him to a back room and interviewed him, and then returned in time to present the new stake presidency and the new patriarch for a sustaining vote."

In another instance, Elder McConkie recalled, "The new patriarch of the Caracas Stake is named Reuben Pacheco. He has 14 children, four of whom have been sealed to him in the Washington Temple. When he was preparing to go to the temple, he went to the bank to get the money. The bank placed the money in a sealed envelope and handed it to him. He did not open the envelope for several days, and when he did open it, he found that it contained 3,000 more bolivars than it should. This is about $750. He took the envelope back to the bank and returned to them the extra 3,000 bolivars. They told him they were missing that amount but had no idea where it had gone. He then went to the airport to take his family to Washington. When the price of the tickets was figured out, he was 300 bolivars short (about $75). As he stood in the ticket line discussing the matter with the ticket agent, someone tapped him on the shoulder and said, 'Do you have a problem?' He said, 'Yes, I am short 300 bolivars to pay for my tickets.' The man said, 'Perhaps I can be of assistance to you' and handed him the 300 bolivars. He turned and gave the money to the ticket agent and then turned back to thank the man for his help. The man had disappeared and was nowhere to be seen."

Garth L. Lee, a regional representative of the Twelve for the Bear Lake Idaho Region, recalled that on October 30 and 31, 1978, he aided Elder McConkie in dividing the Afton Wyoming Stake. After meeting with the stake president, they commenced interviewing each member of the high council and each of the bishops in order according to which stake they would be in following the division. "Brother McConkie chose to have me interview each person initially, asking the necessary questions: how he felt toward the Church, the strength of his testimony, the quality of support at home, his commitment to serve wherever called, etc., and asking him to name three brethren whom he felt would make a good stake president in order of preference." Elder McConkie asked whatever additional questions he felt to and then stood and extended "his great hand to him, gave a few words of encouragement," and excused him.

"After we had interviewed all the high council and bishops of the first stake, Elder McConkie looked at me and said, 'Who is it?' Startled that he should ask me, I said, 'Don't ask me. You are the apostle.' He replied, 'Yes, but you know who it is, don't you?' I replied, 'Yes,' and gave the name. It was very clear to me. Elder McConkie went to the office door and asked the stake president to bring in the candidate." He was then called and instructed to choose his counselors.

"We then interviewed high councilors and bishops who lived in the confines of the other stake, following the same pattern. After the last man had been interviewed, Elder McConkie again asked, 'You don't know who it is, do you?' I had to confess that I didn't. He then said, 'There are two of them, aren't there?' I agreed that there were two candidates in my mind. We discussed both men for a few minutes, pointing out the fine characteristics of both as revealed in their interview. Then Elder McConkie said, 'We're not getting anywhere.' He slipped to his knees; I did to mine. And I listened while he presented the case in prayer. He spoke of the great qualities of each man and told the Lord that they were both great men but that we needed to know which He had chosen.

"When we arose from our knees, he looked at me and said, 'What do you think, Brother Lee?' I replied, 'The thought came to me that you might speak to the stake president.' He replied, 'That's what I am thinking.' The stake president was invited in, was asked four or five questions, and was then excused. Again Elder McConkie turned to Brother Lee and said, 'You know who it is, don't you?' I did, as clearly as one can know." The call was then issued to that man.

In yet another stake reorganization, Elder McConkie and his companions (a member of the Seventy and the regional representative) had interviewed the outgoing stake presidency, the high council, and the bishops. While they were alone in the high council room, seated about ten feet from each other, Elder McConkie asked his companions to write down the names of the three men they thought should be in the new presidency, listing the president first and then the counselors in order. Elder McConkie read the list written by the regional representative, then that of the Seventy, and finally his own. Each of the three read the same names in the same order.

Elder McConkie told of making a mistake in a stake conference and being sent back by President Spencer W. Kimball to correct it. The stake president had moved out of the stake but, not wanting to be released, had kept the move a secret. It was only when he and Elder McConkie were seated and the seven o'clock priesthood leadership meeting was about to begin that the stake president casually mentioned the matter. Faced with the decision of canceling the other meetings that had been scheduled so he would have time to attend to the matter of interviews and calling a new stake president or going ahead as scheduled, Elder McConkie chose to go ahead as scheduled. That was, of course, the stake president's plan. The matter was corrected a couple of weeks later.

Teaching

In August 1973 Elder McConkie spoke at an eight-stake missionary meeting with some fifteen hundred investigators present. The meeting had been arranged by his brother Oscar, who was the president of the Arizona Tempe Mission. The subject was "Was Joseph Smith Called of God?" Oscar had called President Marion G. Romney to request a speaker. In doing so, he explained that what was needed was a speaker with good Redd blood. President Romney said, "Ask Bruce."

TROUBLESHOOTING

From mid-October to mid-December 1965, Elder McConkie presided over a mission in the British Isles because its president had gone home for medical treatment. Leaving Salt Lake City with less than twenty-four hours' notice, Elder McConkie found this a very unhappy experience because of "the endless problems" to which he could not give an enduring solution because he would be there for only a short time. "The mission itself was in a very poor condition, probably the worst of any mission I have ever had contact with," he noted. When he interviewed the missionaries and asked what their goals were, he was consistently told that their goal was not to baptize anyone unless they could be absolutely certain that the one they were baptizing would remain in the Church, because if the one baptized were to fall away, they would be held responsible at the bar of judgment. Because of this mission president's indoctrination, a negative spirit ruled the mission and the work of the Lord was at a standstill. When the mission president returned, Elder McConkie outlined what he had done in his absence, adding that he had not transferred any missionaries or made any organizational changes except those that were emergency in nature. The mission president's reply captured the spirit of the mission: "Well, it is a good thing you haven't changed anything, because anything you changed I would have changed back to exactly the way I had it."

On Thursday, March 29, 1973, in the monthly temple session attended by all the general authorities, President Harold B. Lee announced unexpectedly that disciplinary action had been taken against a former mission president for doctrinal matters and that Bruce McConkie would be sent to that mission to address and correct the situation. After April conference was over, Elder McConkie left to attend to the matter. He spent a full day in council with the new mission president and his wife. The next day was spent in a mission conference, in which he addressed the various doctrines involved for seven hours. The next day he attended a zone conference with about forty missionaries, going over various phases of the proselyting program and interviewing each of them. On Sunday, a district conference was held in which announcements were made relative to the teachings of the former mission president. The next Monday and Tuesday were filled with more zone conferences and interviews. From these interviews it became clear that more instruction was needed. Another mission conference was held. Elder McConkie addressed the missionaries for nine hours in this conference. "I started," he said, "on one row and went right down the row, back to the next and gave each missionary the opportunity to ask any questions." Of the doctrines involved, he said, they were "the most bizarre, unusual, speculative, and false notions that I have ever heard in all my experience."

Upon his return, Elder McConkie made a written report of his activities to the First Presidency. He also met individually with each of them, reporting his experience at length. Other councils were held, so that the former mission president might be properly dealt with.

One of the problems in this mission involved what is known as the Adam-God doctrine. "In the second mission-wide conference," Elder McConkie noted, "I was talking with some power and fluency about this doctrine, explaining that these interpretations were false and defining how and where the Church stood on Adam and on the members of the Godhead. In the midst of this discussion, under circumstances where I was far more fluent and expressive than my normal capacity allows, it suddenly seemed to me as though a pillar of light extended up from me endlessly and the clear, unmistakable impression came from the Spirit of the Lord that what I was teaching was true; that the interpretations made by various people of Brigham Young's quotations was totally false and that if I felt so inclined I was perfectly at liberty to speak in the Lord's name as to the truths I was then declaring. I did not so speak, reasoning that under the circumstances there had been so much sensational and unusual matter presented to these particular missionaries that I did not want to say something outside the usual bounds. As I look back, it seems to me that this experience was given primarily for my benefit and enlightenment."

Reorganizing the First Presidency

President Harold B. Lee passed away suddenly on the evening following Christmas in 1973. The remaining members of the First Presidency and the Quorum of the Twelve Apostles met in the temple the following Sunday to reorganize the First Presidency. On the Thursday before that meeting, Elder Marvin J. Ashton taught Elder McConkie, the junior member of the Quorum, on the procedure that would be followed in that meeting. He explained that each of the Brethren would be called on to express himself freely and frankly about what he thought ought to be done, starting with the junior member of that Quorum and proceeding with each man in turn to the senior member. He added that any motion should be made by one of the senior apostles. That Sunday, as the members of the Twelve walked from the Church Office Building through the parking lot and underground tunnel to the temple, Elder Thomas S. Monson repeated that same counsel to Elder McConkie.

When the men who had been set apart as members of the Council of the Twelve Apostles assembled in the upper room of the temple, they seated themselves according to seniority. Presidents N. Eldon

Tanner and Marion G. Romney, who had been counselors to President Lee, took their places in order of seniority in the Council of the Twelve. President Kimball, the senior apostle and the man who had been set apart as the president of that Quorum, conducted the meeting. At the point in the meeting when each man was to be called on to express himself, President Kimball, rather than starting with the most junior apostle, turned to Elder Benson, the next senior apostle, and asked him to speak first. Each of the apostles stood and voiced the feeling that it was appropriate for the First Presidency to be reorganized and that Spencer W. Kimball should stand at the head of the Church. When Elder Romney spoke, he said that he had attended Sunday School that morning in his home ward. In that meeting he was asked, "Does the President of the Council of the Twelve have to become the President of the Church?" and "Does the Council of the Twelve choose the President of the Church?" He said that his answer to each of these questions was yes and that as he understood the doctrine, the Lord arranged to have as president of the Twelve the man he wanted to be president of the Church and that then the Council of the Twelve chose him and installed him as such. He also indicated that the only way that order could be changed was for the revelation to do so to be given to the president of the Quorum.

Another of the Twelve observed that in his view the Prophet Joseph Smith chooses the president of the Church and that in this instance he had been influenced by President Heber C. Kimball. Elder McConkie said that he agreed with what had been said about Joseph Smith choosing the president of the Church, and he wanted to add that our ancestors have some influence on what positions we hold in the Church today. "I said I had been made aware that my father had been involved in my call to the Council of the Twelve and then said that in my judgment Bishop Marvin O. Ashton had a great personal interest in the assignments and labors of his son,

Marvin J. Ashton; that old Bishop Nathan Tanner had no greater concerns and interests than to know what his son, N. Eldon Tanner, was doing in the Council of the Twelve and in the First Presidency; that President George Romney had a similar concern and interest where his son, President Marion G. Romney, was concerned; and that surely President George F. Richards and others of the progenitors of LeGrand Richards exhibited the same interest where their descendant was concerned." Similarly, he said, this would be true of the interest that Ezra T. Benson had in his grandson Ezra Taft Benson.

Following the motion of Ezra Taft Benson, it was unanimously agreed that Spencer W. Kimball should preside over the Church. All of the Brethren stood in the circle as President Benson ordained and set apart President Spencer W. Kimball as the prophet, seer, and revelator to the Church.

THE DISCERNING OF SPIRITS

On March 22 and 23, 1974, Elder McConkie reorganized a stake in Columbus, Ohio, and held a stake conference with the Columbus Ohio East Stake. Saturday night a two-stake leadership meeting was held. Elder McConkie was the concluding speaker and spoke for about forty-five minutes on the eternal nature of the family. After the meeting, people crowded around to shake his hand and make brief expressions as is customary.

A man approached him and said, "I am a member of the Church of Christ." Spontaneously, Elder McConkie replied, "Well, you can repent just like anyone else." The man said a couple of things that Elder McConkie did not hear. Then the man said, "Are you an apostle?"

Elder McConkie replied, "'I am.' He said, 'Do you know the signs of an apostle?' I said, 'I do.' He began to quote a passage from Paul defining what they are. I said, 'I know what they are.' At this point he took off his glasses, held them out at arm's length, opened his eyes wide, and thrust his face up toward mine and said, 'I have weak eyes. I want you to heal me.' I said, 'Healings come by faith. There is no possible way for you to be healed because you do not have faith. You have an evil spirit.' He said, 'But Paul said in Corinthians that the signs of an apostle are—' and he began again to recite them. And he demanded again that I heal him. I said, 'I am doing exactly the same thing toward you that Peter or Paul would do, and that they did do, when people with evil spirits came to them.' He demanded yet again that I heal him. I said, 'You have an evil spirit, and there is something I want you to know. I am going to tell it to you and I want you to write it in your journal, and if you do not keep a journal, to write it on a piece of paper and your wife who is here listening will be a witness that I told it to you. I want you to know that unless you repent, you will go to hell. I have never told anyone else this before, but I am telling you.'"

At this point Elder McConkie turned and began talking to other people.

Elder McConkie shared that experience with Elder Marvin J. Ashton. During the temple meeting when they reported on their assignments, Elder Ashton asked him to share that experience with all present. He did so, to the great interest of President Kimball.

The Mark Hofmann Affair

During the late 1970s and the early 1980s, Mark Hofmann, one of the premier forgers of the century, was preying with marked success on a Latter-day Saint constituency. He forged a number of documents dealing with the early years of Church history. These documents consistently cast a shadow on doctrines and events important to our faith. One such document was purported to be a blessing given to Joseph Smith III by his father, the Prophet. In this blessing Joseph III was presumptively ordained to be his father's successor as the head of the Church. While supposed authorities were declaring the document authentic, Elder McConkie, in a memo to Elder Gordon B. Hinckley (who was handling the matter for the Church) suggested otherwise. There was still enough lawyer in him to question how a manuscript "carefully and painstakingly written in longhand" could represent a blessing as it was being given. This in turn, he felt, led to doubts about its provenance. "We have no knowledge of the source from which it was copied" or "whether it is an accurate transcription of an earlier record, or for that matter whether any prior record did or does exist," he wrote.

Nonetheless, his conviction that it simply could not represent the voice of Joseph Smith rested on theological grounds. As Dad reviewed his memo with me, he made particular note of the lack of any language indicating the conferral of keys. How could the man to whom all of the keys of the kingdom had been restored forget to bequeath them to his successor? He also noted a number of other doctrinal matters not consistent with his understanding of Joseph Smith. In a conversation with my brother Mark, Dad commented that he did not know anything about Mark Hofmann but he did know Joseph Smith, and what he saw in those documents was not Joseph Smith.

In his general conference talk given a few days later in April 1981, he found himself with a few moments of time at the end of his prepared text. He took the occasion to testify that this document did not accord with the witness of the Spirit. "May I add," he said, "speaking as an Apostle of the Lord, Jesus Christ, . . .—and I speak for myself and for my Brethren of the Twelve—that we know that God has in these last days restored again the fulness of his everlasting gospel for the salvation of all men on earth who will believe and obey; and that he has called Joseph Smith, Jr., to be his latter-day prophet, to be the first and chief Apostle in the dispensation of the fullness of times, and has given him every key and priesthood and power that Peter and the Apostles and the ancient prophets held in the days of their ministry; and that these keys and this holy Apostleship have descended in this manner: [he then listed each president of the Church in order]; and that this holy Apostleship and these keys will continue to descend from one Apostle to another until the Lord Jesus Christ comes in the clouds of heaven to reign personally upon the earth. And this I say not of myself, but in the name of the Lord, standing as his representative and saying what he would say if he personally were here."[2]

Of that experience he said in a talk to personnel of the Church Educational System: "I had in mind the document that had recently come to light purporting to be an account of a prophetic utterance or a blessing given by the Prophet Joseph to one of his sons. And so I felt impressed, after my formal remarks were concluded, to bear a witness of what was involved in succession in the presidency."[3] Having built on a sure foundation, Elder Bruce R. McConkie in this and a host of like instances had no difficulty in discerning between truth and error.

21

GREAT EVENTS

We live in a day of great events relating to the scriptures.
—Boyd K. Packer

Between 1975 and 1981, during the administration of President Spencer W. Kimball, three of the most significant events in the history of the restored Church in the twentieth century took place: the receipt of the revelation on priesthood, which announced that those of all races were invited to receive the fulness of priesthood blessings; the release of the Assistants to the Quorum of the Twelve and the ordering of the Seventy in accord with the scriptural pattern; and the publication of corrected editions of the standard works, including the first Latter-day Saint edition of the Bible. Bruce R. McConkie was privileged to participate in each of these events.

EXTENDING THE PRIESTHOOD TO ALL RACES

The revelation extending the full blessings of the priesthood to all races ranks among the great events of this dispensation. It is one of the singular events necessary for the fulfillment of prophecies that the fulness of the gospel would be taken to every nation, kindred, tongue, and people before the return of Christ.

The events that attended the receipt of this revelation constitute a classic illustration of how revelation is received. The time was right, and accordingly the Spirit of the Lord began to work on President Kimball. For months he labored with the issue, spending many hours in the most holy of places in the temple, importuning the heavens for direction. Preparatory to the receipt of this revelation, he was required—according to the pattern established in Doctrine and Covenants 9—to study, search, and counsel with those charged to direct the affairs of the Church. By his own acknowledgment, it was also necessary for him to rid his own heart and soul of any possible sense of racial superiority, particularly as such feelings were common to the community in which he had been raised.

President Kimball did not act alone on the matter. He sought the feelings of his counselors and the members of the Quorum of the Twelve Apostles. In March 1978 he invited any of the Twelve who desired to do so to make expressions to him in writing so that he could carefully consider them. Three members of that Quorum responded to this invitation: Elders Monson, Packer, and McConkie. Elder McConkie's memo centered on the doctrinal basis for conferring the Melchizedek Priesthood on the blacks. After the revelation was received, he freely shared with his family the scriptural chain of thought he had suggested to President Kimball. The power of it was in its simplicity. He simply saw things in scripture that the rest of us had conditioned ourselves not to see. He saw them in a new light and had no hesitation in moving forward.

He reasoned that inherent in any passage of scripture that promised that the gospel would go to all mankind was the promise that it—with all its blessings—must go to the blacks. The Third Article of Faith states, "We believe that through the Atonement of Christ, all mankind may be saved, by obedience to the laws and ordinances of the Gospel." The word *saved* as used in this text, he said, meant to be exalted or obtain all the blessings of the celestial kingdom. To illustrate the point, he quoted Doctrine and Covenants 6:13: "If thou wilt do good, yea, and hold out faithful to the end, thou shalt be *saved* in the kingdom of God, which is the greatest of all the gifts of God; for there is no gift greater than the gift of salvation," and Joseph Smith's statement that "salvation consists in the glory, authority, majesty, power and dominion which Jehovah possesses and in nothing else."[1]

He pointed out that all those who accept the gospel become the seed of the family of Abraham and are entitled to all of the blessings of the gospel. Jehovah told Abraham that his seed would take the gospel and the "Priesthood unto all nations" and that "as many as receive this Gospel shall be called after thy name, and shall be accounted thy seed, and shall rise up and bless thee, as their father" (Abraham 2:9–10). Jehovah also promised Abraham that when his literal seed took the message of salvation to "*all nations*," then "*shall all the families of the earth be blessed, even with the blessings of the Gospel, which are the blessings of salvation, even of life eternal*" (Abraham 2:9, 11; emphasis added). This, of course, is the doctrine of adoption into the house of Israel.

In his address at Elder McConkie's funeral, Elder Boyd K. Packer observed that "President Kimball has spoken in public of his gratitude to Elder McConkie for some special support he received in the days leading up to the revelation on the Priesthood."[2] It would be hard to suppose that this special help did not include the assurance of Elder McConkie's gospel understanding.

It is well within the mark to say that no member of the Church was more excited or pleased than Bruce McConkie about the revelation given to President Kimball on this matter. One evidence of his excitement about this momentous event is the freedom with which he spoke and wrote about the events that led up to the receipt of the revelation.

As the First Presidency and the Twelve discussed the matter the week before the revelation, Elder LeGrand Richards identified the presence of President Wilford Woodruff in their temple meeting. Perhaps it was given to Elder Richards to know this because he was the only one of their number old enough to have actually seen Wilford Woodruff, which he had done as a young boy. As to why President Woodruff was there, Elder McConkie reasoned that since he had presided over the Church when the revelation to reverse its course on the matter of plural marriage was given, it was natural that he would be called on to help direct the Brethren when a revelation was needed that represented a reversal of direction.

Elder Richards asked that the Twelve and the First Presidency keep his having seen President Woodruff a confidential matter because he did not want people thinking him some kind of a great man to have had that experience. Elder Packer felt it proper to make this knowledge public at Elder Richards's funeral.

The revelation was received on Thursday, June 1, 1978, about twelve noon in the upper room of the Salt Lake Temple. The normal order of the day was for the Twelve to meet and attend to their business and then be joined by the First Presidency. When the two quorums meet, they unite in prayer, according to the pattern of the temple. They then conduct their business, which normally ends about the middle of the afternoon. The Brethren then retire to a dining room for lunch, after which they leave the temple.

On Thursday, June 1, 1978, the Twelve met as usual. They were joined by the First Presidency, the Seventy, and the Presiding Bishopric at 9 A.M., and the normal meeting was held. It included partaking of the sacrament and the bearing of testimony. The Spirit of the Lord was present in great abundance. After the prayer closing that meeting, President Kimball took the unusual step of inviting the members of the First Presidency and the Twelve to remain in the room and excused the other Brethren. All had come to the meeting fasting. President Kimball told the Twelve that he would like them to continue during the rest of that day to fast with the First Presidency and that the normal luncheon at the end of the business meeting had been cancelled. He reminded the members of the Presidency and the Twelve that in recent months he had been giving extended serious, prayerful consideration to the matter of conferring the priesthood upon the blacks and that he felt the need for divine guidance. He had spent many hours alone in the upper room in the temple pleading with the Lord for counsel and direction. He said he hoped the Lord would give a revelation one way or another and resolve the matter. He indicated that if it was the mind and will of the Lord that the Church continue in the present course, denying the priesthood to the descendants of Cain, that he was willing to sustain and support that decision and defend it with all its implications to the death. He said, however, that if the Lord was willing to have the priesthood go to them, he hoped for a clear affirmation of this so there would be no question in anyone's mind.

A long discussion followed in which each member of the Quorum of the Twelve expressed himself. Elder McConkie recorded: "A strong, compelling spirit of unity was in the meeting. It seemed as though all of the Brethren were in effect joining in the prayers which President Kimball had recently been making on this tremendously important matter."

President Kimball suggested that they go forward with the prayer. He said that if it was agreeable with the Brethren, he would be voice. He importuned the Lord with great fervor and faith. He asked that a revelation be given manifesting the Lord's mind and will on this matter so that the issue could be resolved. "It was one of those occasions," Elder McConkie wrote in his journal, "when the one who was mouth in the prayer prayed by the power of the Spirit and was given expression and guided in the words that were used and the sentences that were said. The prayer he gave was dictated by the Holy Ghost."

While President Kimball prayed, the revelation came. When he ended the prayer, there was a great Pentecostal outpouring of the Spirit such as none of those present had ever before experienced. There are no words to describe what happened. It was something that could only be felt in the hearts of the recipients and which can only be understood by the power of the Spirit. Afterward, President Kimball, his counselors, and President Benson, representing the feelings of all who were present, expressed themselves to the effect that never in their experience in the Church had they felt or experienced anything in any way comparable to what occurred on this occasion.

The manner in which the revelation was given could not have been more perfect. It came through the prophet of the Lord, President Spencer W. Kimball, and at the same time was received by way of confirmation by twelve others. Thus, the prophet received the revelation with twelve men (two members of the First Presidency and ten members of the Quorum of the Twelve) all of whom had been set apart as apostles of the Lord and all of them receiving the same revelation at the same time to attest to the verity of the event.

Those absent were Elders Mark E. Petersen and Delbert L. Stapley. Elder Petersen was on assignment in South America, and Elder Stapley was ill in LDS Hospital in Salt Lake City. It was felt that they should be given opportunity to learn what had transpired and to be asked if they were in accord. A call was placed to South America for Elder Petersen, who was in complete accord with the feelings of his Quorum. Later that day, the First Presidency called upon Elder Delbert L. Stapley in the hospital. He, too, wholeheartedly sustained the revelation.

It was decided to present the matter to the rest of the general authorities the next Thursday, June 8, 1978. They were invited to attend the meeting fasting. The meeting enjoyed a marvelous outpouring of the Spirit that served both as a witness to all present that the time had come to give the priesthood to all races and also as a confirmation of the events of the previous week.

Reflecting on the timing of these events, Elder McConkie observed, "I think the Lord waited to give this new direction to his earthly kingdom until his Church was big enough and strong enough to absorb those of all races and cultures, without being overwhelmed by the world, as the primitive saints were when the Church in their day gained general acceptance in the Roman Empire."

While these events were taking place in Salt Lake City, Bruce's brother Brit was serving as a patriarch in the Philippines, where he was working as a legal counselor for the Church. In one of the blessings he gave, he told a woman with black ancestry that she would be married in the temple. She quizzed him about it, so he checked his recorded utterances, thinking that there might be a mistake. Upon finding it correct, he said, "That is what I was impressed to say." In another blessing, this one given to a young black man, Brit told him that he would hold the priesthood. Apparently the fellow was telling this to his friends, so Brit checked the recording of this blessing, and again, it confirmed that that was what he had said. When the young man asked him what he should do about it, he said, "Just wait." After the revelation had been received but before the public announcement was made, Brit called Bruce and asked what he should do about the promises he had given. Bruce said, "Just wait."

Organizing the Seventy in Accordance with Scripture

At the October conference in 1975, President Spencer W. Kimball called four new members of the First Quorum of the Seventy, expanding that quorum beyond its seven presidents for the first time in the twentieth century. One of those called was William R. Bradford, whose call had been made known to Elder McConkie and Elder James E. Faust three weeks before in Santiago in individual revelations. In the October 1976 conference, all the Assistants to the Twelve were released as such and called as members of the First Quorum of the Seventy. In addition, four others were called to that quorum, and its presidency was reorganized.

President Kimball explained: "In 1941, five high priests were called to assist the Twelve Apostles in their heavy workload, and to fill a role similar to that envisioned by the revelations for the First Quorum of the Seventy. The scope and demands of the work at that time did not justify the reconstitution of the First Quorum of the Seventy. In the intervening years, additional Assistants to the Twelve have been added and today we have twenty-one."[3]

It should be noted that any differences in the nature of the work being done by the Seventy and the Assistants to the Twelve had greatly narrowed in 1961 when President David O. McKay ordained the seven presidents of the Seventy to the office of high priest. It could also be noted that there is no scriptural provision for the office of Assistant to the Twelve. "With this move," President Kimball continued, "the three governing quorums of the Church defined by the revelations—the First Presidency, the Quorum of the Twelve, and the First Quorum of the Seventy—have been set in their places as revealed by the Lord. This will make it possible to handle efficiently the present heavy workload and to prepare for the increasing expansion and acceleration of the work, anticipating the day when the Lord will return to take direct charge of His church and kingdom."[4]

In October 1986, the calling of men to the office of seventy on the stake level was discontinued. The moving force behind these changes may be found in the following extract from Lucile C. Tate's biography of President Boyd K. Packer: "Laboring in faith and diligence, Brother Packer continued the quest, to know the Lord's will. He studied and pondered the passages in Doctrine and Covenants 107 that pertain specifically to the Seventy. As he read and reread, verse 10 suddenly stood out as if it had been newly placed there: 'High priests after the order of the Melchizedek Priesthood have a right to officiate in their own standing, under the direction of the presidency, in administering spiritual things, and also in the office of an elder, priest, . . . teacher, deacon, and member' (D&C 107:10)." What had previously not been seen was the obvious absence of reference to "seventy." It occurred to Elder Packer that it was not intended that the seventy labor on the stake and ward level. The office of seventy as intended by the revelation appeared to be one that functioned at the general level of Church government only. "I took [D&C 107:10] to Bruce McConkie first," Elder Packer noted, "and read it to him in that context. It was the first time that he had ever seen it in that light. Because it very declaratively said that a high priest could not officiate in the office of a Seventy."[5] It was not long afterwards that seventies quorums on a stake level were discontinued. The Church continues to grow in understanding—line upon line, precept upon precept—just as its members do.

New Editions of LDS Scriptures

The publication in 1979 of the LDS edition of the King James Bible was of immeasurable importance. It was followed in 1981 by a new edition of the Book of Mormon, the Doctrine and Covenants, and the Pearl of Great Price. Each of these books was linked to the others by a common system of footnotes and cross-references and a six-hundred-page topical guide and a dictionary included with the Bible. A decade of tedious work preceded these publications.

This labor had its beginnings under the direction of Harold B. Lee while he served as a counselor to President Joseph Fielding Smith. Elders Thomas S. Monson and Boyd K. Packer were assigned to direct this work. Later Elder McConkie was called to join them. It would be difficult to overstate the importance of this labor or the seriousness with which these men approached this task.

In this labor Elder McConkie supervised all text and reference matters and wrote the chapter headings and summaries for each of the standard works. Robert J. Matthews observed that these headings and summaries constitute a very helpful commentary on the scriptures. Of the entire scriptures project, Elder McConkie said, "I do not have any language to indicate how strongly I feel or how much I am assured that the work that has been done will benefit and bless the members of the Church and hosts of people who yet will hear the message of the Restoration."

Of those who labored under the direction of the Twelve on this committee, Elder McConkie said in a general authorities' training meeting October 2, 1981: "These brethren—Robert J. Matthews, Ellis T. Rasmussen, Robert C. Patch, and William James Mortimer—have literally been raised up by the Lord at this time and season to do the particular, difficult, and technical work that has been required. The Lord's hand has been in it." To that he added, "There is no question that major decisions were made by the spirit of inspiration and that the conclusions reached accord with the mind and will of the Lord."

The biography of President Packer recounts: "Early in the project, James Mortimer and Ellis T. Rasmussen had called at the

Cambridge University Press in Cambridge, England, which had been publishing the King James Bible since the first edition in 1611.

"'They met with Mr. Roger Coleman, director of religious publishing, to discuss the publication of a most unusual edition of the King James Bible. The printers were quite as skeptical about this proposal as Mr. Grandin had been nearly 150 years before. . . .

"'The text was to remain exactly as it was, no changes, not one. But all footnoting, cross-references, chapter introductions, indexes, and so on, were to be replaced. Only the chapter and verse numbering for the sixty-six books would be retained.

"'And that was just the beginning. This edition of the Bible would be cross-referenced with three other books of scripture: the Book of Mormon, the Doctrine and Covenants, and the Pearl of Great Price. The printers had barely heard of them.'

"The technical problems seemed insurmountable to these men. Clearly, 'it could not be done,' Elder Packer related. 'But in that meeting also was Mr. Derek Bowen, editor, a most remarkable man. . . . He was, perhaps, the one man in the world who could direct such a printing project.' [*Ensign,* Nov. 1982, 53.]"[6]

Because of his position on the Scriptures Publication Committee and his love of the revelations of the Restoration, Elder McConkie was in a position to recommend that Joseph Smith's vision of the celestial kingdom and Joseph F. Smith's vision of the redemption of the dead be added to the canon of scripture. In the April 1976 conference, President N. Eldon Tanner proposed that these two documents be added to the Pearl of Great Price at the general conference of the Church for a sustaining vote. They were later placed in the 1981 edition of the Doctrine and Covenants as sections 137 and 138.

Describing the experience of working on the Scriptures Publication Committee, Robert J. Matthews said to me: "For nearly a decade several of us worked with Elders Thomas S. Monson, Boyd K. Packer, and Bruce R. McConkie in the preparation of the new editions of the standard works. We saw them work with divine inspiration in the day-to-day activities of that Committee, and often marveled at their clarity of vision and quickness of perception in deciding the course to follow. Each of the Brethren had his respective areas of responsibility, all of which were important to the success of the undertaking.

"One of Elder McConkie's contributions was the chapter headings. In reality these headings constitute a doctrinal commentary of the particular chapter. I was fully conversant with these headings before publication, yet as I find them again in study, I am often re-impressed with the clarity and insight wherein he made so few words say so much.

"One time two of us discussed with Elder McConkie a number of headings which he had written for use in Isaiah, Jeremiah, and Ezekiel dealing with prophecies of a 'latter-day David.' We felt the wording might be misleading. I never saw him more open and congenial. We talked at length about the meaning of the particular scriptural passages and the wording of the headings. He carefully explained his views and then gave us permission to alter his wording if we cared to do so. The course of the conversation was mild in atmosphere and spirit. The convincing power of true doctrine slowly but surely changed our hearts, and we willingly agreed that his original wording was correct. There was no force, no intimidation, no threatening situation. It was neither by intellect nor by argument, but the Spirit bore testimony to us that what he had written was correct. It was an unforgettable experience.

"When discussing the relative importance of the JST as compared with other footnotes, he once expressed himself strongly that the Prophet Joseph Smith should not have to compete for room with the words of any Bible scholar's interpretation. At a later date he reconfirmed that by saying to me, with a twinkle in his eye, 'Let's have a little more JST and a little less Dictionary.'"

Great Events

Much that Elder McConkie had done before his service on the Scriptures Publication Committee bore a rich harvest at that time. This obviously included his years of study of the Joseph Smith Translation, which had its beginning in the scripture study he and Amelia did together in the first years of their marriage. When it came time for him to write the brief headnotes to each chapter in the scriptures, he was greatly aided by the headings he had written for his *Doctrinal New Testament Commentary*.

Elder McConkie observed: "There have been a couple of things happen in our lifetimes that have had more influence and will yet have a greater impact upon the Church than anything else of which I am aware, and both of them have come to pass as a result of the inspiration of heaven to President Kimball. One is the great organizational step that was taken when he had the wisdom and insight to fill up the First Quorum of the Seventy and begin to use its members in harmony with the provisions found in the revelations. Organizationally, this is what perfects the arrangement in the Church so that no matter how big the kingdom grows or how wide and varied its interests are, the framework is there for proper divine government.

"The other thing of such tremendous moment was the receipt of the revelation on priesthood—the revelation in which the Lord directed that the holy priesthood, the Melchizedek order, the highest and holiest order that God gives to men, should now go to those of all races and cultures, without reference to nationality or color of skin or any previous impediments, and that it should go solely and wholly on the basis of personal worthiness and righteousness."

Elder McConkie concluded, "I think that, organizationally, the First Quorum of the Seventy is the greatest thing that has happened in our lifetimes, and that, doctrinally, the taking of the priesthood to all people of every race and culture is the most significant thing that has happened."[7]

22

Special Contributions

If ever there was a man raised up unto a very purpose, if ever a man was prepared against a certain need—it was Bruce R. McConkie.
—Boyd K. Packer

The consuming passion of Bruce McConkie's life was teaching the gospel. When he stood to speak in a church meeting, he would go directly to his task. He felt no need to coddle his audience or to warm them up with wit or humor. One of his associates told him that if he would tell a few jokes, he would convert people by the thousands. Another told him that if he wanted people to listen to him, he would have to tell stories. He listened politely but had no intention of following their counsel. Years ago he said to me, "Doctrinal teachers will be quoted a hundred years after their death while the popular speakers who people find so entertaining will be long forgotten." Still another would-be mentor told him that if he wanted to be read, he should not write above a fourteen-year-old reading level. His private response was, "I will not do it. If I cannot raise the level of understanding in the Church, I will not write." When I inquired about a manuscript I noticed on his desk, he responded, "Oh, I have been asked to read that and see if I can

Special Contributions

think of any reason that it shouldn't be published." He then added, "I wish I had been asked if I could think of any reason why it should be."

The substitution of "goose pimples and fluff" for saving principles wearied his soul. He thought such things an insult to the gospel. By contrast, teaching from the scriptures always seemed to energize him. He greatly enjoyed the classes he taught at the Institute at the University of Utah and the classes he taught to the religion faculty at Brigham Young University. He typically had more energy at the end of those classes than he did when he began. He found them a refreshing change from his responsibilities at the Church Offices.

His Published Works

Between 1954 and 1956, the three-volume work entitled *Doctrines of Salvation* was first published. This work, which Bruce McConkie edited, consisted of doctrinal teachings of his father-in-law, Joseph Fielding Smith. Having then served for more than forty years as an apostle, President Smith had spent countless hours in front of his trusty old Underwood typewriter using the amazingly effective hunt-and-peck method to answer the endless flow of gospel questions that came to him. The mutual respect existing between him and his son-in-law gave rise to the idea that Bruce edit a three-volume work drawing on the many letters Joseph Fielding Smith had written over the years. It also created a wonderful opportunity for President Smith to mentor the young Seventy. Many interesting gospel discussions between the two men grew out of this work. In 2001, nearly fifty years after they were first published, the three volumes were combined into one and given as a Christmas gift to Church employees and CES personnel.

The first edition of *Mormon Doctrine* was published in 1958.

More than four decades have passed since it was first published, and yet it retains its place of respect among Latter-day Saints.

Elder McConkie wrote a three-volume *Doctrinal New Testament Commentary*, which was published between 1965 and 1973. It contains the text of the New Testament as found in the King James Bible and the text of the Inspired Version (or as it is called now, the Joseph Smith Translation). The word changes or additions in the Joseph Smith Translation are rendered in bold type. This expression of confidence in Joseph Smith's inspired translation of the Bible did much to acquaint the Church with it and to convert them to its importance. The rising generation has become so familiar with the Joseph Smith Translation footnotes in their Bibles that they are surprised to learn that in their parents' day this work was generally unknown to the membership of the Church. This situation reflected a distrust of what was known at that time as the Reorganized Church of Jesus Christ of Latter Day Saints (now called Community of Christ), who have possession of the original manuscripts from which this work comes and thus its copyright. The groundbreaking work of Robert J. Matthews to gain the confidence of RLDS Church officials and obtain permission to compare the original manuscript with the Bernhisel Manuscript (in the possession of the LDS Church) affirmed that the RLDS publications were true to the manuscripts. Any thoughts that the manuscript had been tampered with were thereby laid to rest.

The Joseph Smith Translation is not a translation in the literal sense, meaning to return the Bible to a more perfect form of the Hebrew and Greek in which it was originally written. Nor is it a translation in the traditional sense that it changes the text from one language to another. Rather, it is a doctrinal restoration, a restoration of the purity and intent of the original writers. Some in scholarly circles in the Church have viewed it with skepticism because it is not always in harmony with ancient manuscripts. The Prophet

Special Contributions

did not use ancient manuscripts in making his translation. He simply used the King James Version of the Bible and the gift and power of God. His was a translation by the Spirit of revelation. It thus forces the scholar to choose between the spirit of revelation as professed by Joseph Smith and loyalty to various ancient manuscripts, all of which are in some degree at variance with each other. For Bruce McConkie, that was not a difficult choice. One of the distinguishing characteristics of the Joseph Smith Translation is that it presents the reader with a greater Christ than any other translation of the Bible.

For instance, when Christ was in the temple at age twelve, we learn that he did not seek understanding from the learned men of his day, but rather they inquired of him (JST Luke 2:46). In Joseph Smith's translation of Matthew 3:25, we read that Jesus "served under his father, and he spake not as other men, neither could he be taught; for he needed not that any man should teach him." The Joseph Smith Translation also corrects the idea that in the temptations in the wilderness, the devil took Jesus from place to place. Satan has no power to lead Christ around; rather, we learn, it was the Spirit of the Lord that transported him from place to place (JST Matthew 4:5, 8).

After his call to the Twelve, Elder McConkie wrote his six-volume series on the Messiah. Standing between *The Promised Messiah*, with which the series begins, and *The Millennial Messiah*, with which it ends, is a four-volume treatment of the Savior's mortal ministry. This work, written sixty-four years after the publication of Elder James E. Talmage's classic work *Jesus the Christ*, drew upon revelation received since then—namely Joseph F. Smith's vision of the redemption of the dead (now D&C 138) and the flood of light available in the Joseph Smith Translation.

Elder McConkie also wrote a seven-hundred-page work entitled *A New Witness for the Articles of Faith*. He took an approach to the

Articles of Faith entirely different from Elder James E. Talmage's work eight decades earlier. Elder Talmage had sought to give credibility to Joseph Smith and to Mormonism by showing that its doctrines were based on the Bible. Elder McConkie, on the other hand, sought to explain them in the light of modern revelation. He felt that the best evidence that God has spoken in our day is found in what God has said today.

On August 23, 1984, about eight months before he passed away and before his work on the Articles of Faith was published, Elder McConkie wrote: "Incident to my recent illness, and the realization that all of us will soon meet our Maker and be called upon to give an account of our stewardship, I had some spiritual experiences that caused me to know that my life was being spared to preach the gospel and write about the doctrines of salvation. It is the spiritual impressions I then received that caused me to have such deep concern over the matter of declaring doctrine and writing doctrinal books."

This work, which was warmly received, elicited the following note of appreciation to Amelia from one of her husband's colleagues: "I read choice books a few pages at a time, so I can savor them and think about their implications. Proceeding in that manner, I have just finished reading *A New Witness for the Articles of Faith*. This is undoubtedly the most profound and inspirational doctrinal book I have ever read. It has and will have a great influence on my thinking and my ministry."

Defender of the Faith

Like his father, whom a patriarch had declared to be a pure Israelite, Bruce McConkie did not have so much as a single drop of doubting blood in his veins. The measure of a man, he held, was found in his loyalty to those principles revealed by the Prophet Joseph Smith. Nothing would please him more than to be measured by that standard for every talk he gave, and every word he wrote measures well by it. "This is the Lord's Church, and he runs it," he declared. The great thing about the gospel message, he constantly said, "is that it is true!" Jesus Christ was the literal son of God, and Joseph Smith was the great revelator of Christ for this dispensation. Such is the testimony that echoes from all that Bruce McConkie did. It was upon the altar of these principles that he placed his life. These principles directed his choice of subjects when he spoke, they determined the books he wrote, and they placed him—by choice— in the front ranks of the defenders of the faith and, as such, a rightful heir to the wrath of those who opposed such principles.

The body of manuscripts that Bruce McConkie regarded as scripture included measurably more than the standard works and the Joseph Smith Translation. His own list of scripture included the Wentworth letter, in which Joseph Smith briefly told the story of the First Vision and the coming of Moroni and to which he appended the Articles of Faith; the *Lectures on Faith*, which were published with the Doctrine and Covenants until 1921; the official Exposition of the First Presidency on the Origin of Man, issued in 1912; the Doctrinal Exposition of the First Presidency on the Father and the Son, issued in 1916; the King Follett Discourse given by Joseph Smith at a conference of the Church on April 7, 1844, and the similar discourse given in the Grove at Nauvoo in June of the same year. To him these documents could very properly have been added to our present canon.

The great love he had for the revelations of the Restoration did not diminish his love for the Bible. As he himself noted, he probably wrote more by way of explanation and testimony of the Bible than any other man in our dispensation. Our understanding and appreciation of this marvelous compilation of revelation was, in his judgment, hindered by two seals that men had placed on the book. The first was the seal of ignorance; the second, the seal of intellectuality. In his view, Joseph Smith and the revelations of the Restoration removed those seals.

Elder McConkie also spoke out with great vigor in defense of the *Lectures on Faith*, which draw the darts and arrows of those whose sight is impaired by their own egos. He said, speaking particularly of the Fifth Lecture, "In my judgment, it is the most comprehensive, intelligent, inspired utterance that now exists in the English language—that exists in one place defining, interpreting, expounding, announcing, and testifying what kind of being God is. It was written by the power of the Holy Ghost, by the spirit of inspiration. It is, in effect, eternal scripture; it is true."

Missionary Work

Bruce McConkie's philosophy of missionary work evolved naturally out of his studying and writing about the gospel. One of my colleagues asked what my impressions were after I read my father's missionary journal. He thought me outrageously arrogant when I replied that my father was a fine missionary but if he had served under my direction when I was a mission president, he would have been much more effective. My confidence in saying this centered on the principles I had learned from my father. They were, however, principles he had not fully understood as a young missionary. The more he advanced in gospel understanding, the greater his loyalty became to those truths restored by Joseph Smith and the more he realized that it is in the revelations of the Restoration that the great power of conversion is found. Recalling his experience as a young missionary in the Eastern States Mission, he said, "When I was a missionary, we distributed thousands of copies of an old tract entitled, 'Why I Believe the Book of Mormon to Be the Word of God,' by William A. Morgan. I thought it was a fine tract, but I didn't know any better in that day. Now, really, it isn't very valid; it supposedly proves that the Book of Mormon is true by quoting Biblical

Special Contributions

passages. It quotes Isaiah 29, Ezekiel 37, Psalm 85, and the statement in John about 'other sheep' and so on, and then proclaims, 'Here's the prophecy that is fulfilled in the Book of Mormon!' That's marvelous, nobody can contend with that except that it isn't the Lord's way of teaching the gospel. The fact is not that the Bible proves the Book of Mormon is true, but that the Book of Mormon proves the Bible is true. That's the Lord's approach to presenting the message of salvation." The principle he taught his sons was that it is easier to convert someone to the Book of Mormon than it is to convince them of the true meaning of the Bible. My own missionaries received a great testimony of this principle.

"I don't think there is anyone in the world who believes more of what's in the Bible, or who has attempted to study it more and figure out what is involved in numerous passages, than I have," stated Elder McConkie. "I have unbounded appreciation and respect for the Biblical word, as far as what I have had occasion to write about is concerned. I've written more about the Bible, a hundred times over, than I have about the Book of Mormon. However, I have used the Book of Mormon for the purpose of interpreting what's in the Bible. I have a three-volume doctrinal New Testament commentary. I have four volumes on the life of Christ, and another book on the Messianic prophecies, which is primarily Biblical. My point is, the Bible is what it is, and is a marvelous reservoir of scriptural truth. Don't let anyone be confused about that. Yet, in no single passage does the Bible give all the facts about what it's talking about. It just doesn't do it. We sometimes have the idea that things get translated and that the translation is what the Lord originally revealed. That isn't quite right. There is more than one translation for some passages, and both translations are correct. The classical illustration of this is the Malachi passage about the coming of Elijah. When Moroni comes, he changes what's involved in the

Malachi prophecy about the coming of Elijah. He talks about restoring the priesthood, and so on, by the hand of Elijah the prophet.

"The Prophet Joseph Smith, with full knowledge that this was the correct meaning of that passage, proceeded to translate the Book of Mormon and copy the King James language; then he proceeded to quote the King James version in a Doctrine and Covenants passage. This shows that it is possible to have a passage of scripture translated in two ways—one having a lesser meaning and one having a much higher meaning. Certainly we have a much greater meaning, a better meaning, in this Elijah passage when we take it the way Moroni quoted it. . . .

"The things in the fore part of the book of Genesis are true. But the fore part of Genesis is virtually rewritten in the book of Moses and there is a tremendous added flood of light and knowledge because of what the Prophet added by the spirit of inspiration. I don't know whether he added all of it because it was in the original record or whether some of it is inspired interpolation by him, but that doesn't matter. The point is that when he gives us the book of Moses, he's giving us a book that contains the sense and meaning of the early chapters in Genesis. So there are two translations, as it were, of the same thing, and both of them are true.

"I say that these are illustrations of the fact that there can be two translations of the same thing, and both of them can be true. One translation is designed to present the gospel to people who have a limited understanding, and the other is a translation for people who have grown in the things of the Spirit and are prepared and capable of receiving more. I say that about the Bible; it isn't complete in any instance.

"If Mormon could have just had the ancient records of Israel and done to them what he did to the records of the Nephites and given us an account of Israel's history by inspiration, and then if we could receive it in translation the way he gave it, the Old Testament would read just exactly the way the Book of Mormon reads. It would talk about atonement, faith and repentance, gifts of the Spirit, the fall of Adam, and so on, the same way that the Book of Mormon does.

"We began trying to figure out how we could get the concept through our missionary work that we believe in Christ. We came up with a system and revised our first discussion. We revised it so that the emphasis was put on the Lord Jesus in the first discussion. That on the surface sounds like a marvelous thing to do, but, unfortunately, it was the wrong thing to do. From the overall perspective I will tell you why. We had been selling, year in and year out, through the missionary program, more than a million copies of the Book of Mormon. So we changed the first discussion in our proselyting program, and immediately, the very first year, our sales of the Book of Mormon dropped 500,000, and we've gone on like that since. We're placing half the number of copies of the Book of Mormon that we used to place. We hope that we're going to get that corrected. As a matter of fact, we're in the process of revising the whole system of missionary discussions to get the Book of Mormon back in the position where it should be.

"Contrary to what a lot of well-meaning people may think, people don't get converted to the Church when you show them the uniformity which we have with them. If you show them that they're Christians and we're Christians, we'll never convert anybody. It just does not happen. When we give the first discussion now and they hear we believe in Christ, the way we present it, they say, 'That's lovely, we're glad you think like we do, and you're nice young men, but we're not interested in any more discussion.' Conversion comes from the differences and not the similarities. The reason people join the Church is that you show them the differences between us and the world; the personal God against the spirit essence, gifts of the Spirit, and revelation against the sealed heaven, and so on. It's the distinctive things about Mormonism that convert, and it's the distinctive things, the differences between us and the world, that get the fire of testimony burning in the lives of members of the Church. Well, we stumbled around a little, we the Brethren. I'm not condemning anyone else; I'm taking the responsibility for this. I was in on all the decisions. But we stumble around, and we make some mistakes, and the Lord lets us do it, and we hopefully learn from our mistakes and get back in the channel before we go off the deep end. . . .

"Now let me tell you, there isn't anybody on earth, not the Pope in Rome, not Martin Luther, not any of the reformers, not Bishop Jeremy Taylor, not the Archbishop of Canterbury, not anybody, no matter how much they know, who can ever discover the meaning of Romans until they've read the Book of Mormon. The Book of Mormon and latter-day revelation interpret the New Testament. They give the understanding and the background so that you know what Paul is talking about when he talks about justification and sanctification and the like."

Doctrinal Contributions

Elder McConkie will long be remembered as one of the great doctrinal teachers of the twentieth century. The great doctrinal labor of the last hundred years has been to grow up into the revelations received by the Prophet Joseph Smith. This is not to suggest that the heavens have been sealed during this period but rather that they have opened most readily to those who have faithfully built the house of their gospel understanding on the foundation that the Prophet laid. That is precisely what Bruce McConkie did. The key to obtaining a meaningful understanding of either the Old or the New Testament, Elder McConkie would tell us, is in the revelations of the Restoration. It is, for instance, to read the Old Testament as if Mormon or Moroni had translated it. That is how he read it.

It is the light of the Restoration that allows us to see what otherwise is obscured by the dark clouds of tradition and the difficulties associated with matters of translation and transmission. No gospel teacher of the twentieth century has surpassed the clarity with which Bruce McConkie taught the doctrine of the divine Sonship of Christ, the Abrahamic covenant, or the doctrine of the gathering of Israel. As an illustration, he took the lead in teaching the doctrine of the gathering in the Mexico and Central America area conference in August 1972. There he explained that we are now in a new era of Church growth and development. In the early days of this dispensation, it was necessary for the Saints to gather together in order to survive. Those accepting the gospel in foreign lands emigrated to America to join with the Saints there and to help establish a modern Zion. Had they not done so, the Church would not have survived nor could we have built our first temples. Now we are past that stage in our history. Congregations of the Saints are springing up in all parts of the earth. In fulfillment of prophecy we are becoming a worldwide church, a church which those of every nation, kindred, and tongue can attend. In our day the gathering consists of joining the Church, of coming to a knowledge of its saving truths, and of worshiping with the Saints in the place where we reside.

"The place of gathering for the Mexican Saints is in Mexico; the place of gathering for the Guatemalan Saints is in Guatemala; the place of gathering for the Brazilian Saints is in Brazil; so it goes throughout the length and breadth of the whole earth. Japan is for the Japanese; Korea is for the Koreans; Australia is for the Australians; every nation is the gathering place for its own people."[1] Church president Harold B. Lee subsequently quoted Elder McConkie on the same matter in the April 1973 general conference, placing, as it were the seal of his office on the explanation Elder McConkie had given. President Spencer W. Kimball took a similar action in an area conference in Lima, Peru. By assignment, Elder McConkie wrote an article on this subject for the *Ensign*.[2]

He Blessed Us by Teaching Us

Elder McConkie was a gospel teacher, not a cheerleader. He blessed us by teaching us. There is a great lesson in this. A letter of appreciation sent to him noted: "The Church membership and the world, in general, have benefited greatly from your research of the Scriptures, your written analysis and commentary on them and the articulate manner in which you have taught the gospel of Jesus Christ over the years. Your talks are forcefully delivered in a very persuasive manner. Your listeners always go away feeling inspired to live better lives.

"In every generation there are a few leaders who stand out above the rest in character, talent and example. You are one of the preeminent forces for good in our generation. Your perception and creativity mark you as a choice spirit who was foreordained to teach the Gospel with lasting impact.

"You will long be remembered by those whose lives you have touched and by your posterity as one of the greatest theologians and patriarchs in your family lineage and in the Church. Your name is imprinted in the Lamb's Book of Life for having served so faithfully and well during your mortal probation."

23

HIS FINAL TESTIMONY

Bristled hair . . . and guileless tongue . . .
Tear-filled voice, emotion wrung . . .
Manner strong and features kind . . .
Speech incisive . . . steel-trap mind.
—William Kent Wadsworth

About a year before Dad started to have trouble with his health, he felt impressed to move himself and Mother out of the family home on Dorchester Drive and into a condominium near the Church Offices. Toward the end of 1983 he started to experience some pain and discomfort in his stomach. There was no thought that the matter was particularly serious, though he seemed more tired on occasion than he ought to be and had a rather listless appetite. The doctors ran about a dozen tests on him for ulcers, cancer, and so forth. All the tests came back negative. A spot was noticed on his liver, so the doctors recommended surgery, just in case something was wrong. Elders James E. Faust and Neal A. Maxwell gave him a blessing, and the surgery took place on January 20, 1984. To our surprise and overwhelming disappointment, the doctors found cancer in Dad's system to such an extent that there was simply nothing they could do for him.

The doctors sewed him up so that he could go home and die in peace. They told the family that he had only "months" to live, meaning, we were later to learn, that they really thought he had "two weeks to two months" to live. Tears were shed, expressions of faith were made, and both the Smith and the McConkie families—including uncles, aunts, and cousins—united in fasting and prayer. Together their resolve was to walk in all "the ordinances of the Lord blameless" and to call down the blessings of heaven (Luke 1:6).

In typical Bruce McConkie fashion, he made every effort to keep the matter out of the public eye. Yet all efforts to that effect were unsuccessful. Rumors spread with speed rivaling that of light itself. In the hope of stemming the tide of rumor, Oscar announced the matter to the press. Don LeFevre, as spokesman for the Church, confirmed the report without adding to it. The seriousness of the situation was downplayed for the press, but no one who had any knowledge of this kind of cancer was fooled.

President Gordon B. Hinckley visited Dad and, at Dad's request, gave him a blessing. Elder Boyd K. Packer called Mother and asked if he could visit and give Dad a blessing. Of course she responded affirmatively. He came, saying that he had struggled with the matter for two days and that he was fighting mad: "Bruce was not to be taken." He gave Dad a blessing and told him that they were laboring on both sides of the veil to keep him here. Brit was also called to administer to him. He repeated Elder Packer's words and gave the same promises, though he was unaware that the earlier blessing had been given. Thousands of faithful Saints throughout the Church added their prayers with much effect. Dad was scheduled to go home from the hospital two weeks after the operation. He went home after a week. The doctors called it "a little miracle."

While he was still in the hospital, Sister Hulda Parker Young, who was the Relief Society president for the hospital, told Dad of a patient there who had been paralyzed for years. She was a young mother who had almost surrendered to despair. She had asked Sister

His Final Testimony

Young, "Couldn't I have one of the general authorities that come in to bless Elder McConkie come down and administer to me?" Dad said he would see to it. He got up out of his bed and said, "Come on, Mother." Together they went down to the room of this woman, and he gave her a blessing. She now walks.

He left the hospital on January 27 and began chemotherapy about two weeks later. In a letter to the family written February 20, Mother noted that "Dad has passed the first phase of the chemotherapy with relative ease—slight nausea and exhaustion, but no violent reactions." Notwithstanding his tolerance for the chemotherapy, his battle to live was attended by "pain beyond description."

While in the hospital he observed to Elder Packer that the early apostles had suffered much and perhaps this was the equivalent suffering for the Twelve of this day. "Suffering sanctifies," Dad said. He believed his affliction was a test, and he was determined to pass it well. In a talk written for, but not delivered in, the April 1979 general conference he said, "Life never was intended to be easy. We are here on probation. We need the experiences of mortality, experiences which could be gained in no other way." He then suggested that we must each face our own Gethsemane. We will all "be tried and tested to the full extent of our power to withstand," he wrote.

In the course of some months, another scan was made of his liver, which showed that there were no new cancer spots and the old ones were shrinking. His doctor told him that this was medically impossible. A couple of days later his doctor, not a member of the Church, visited his office to explain, "I don't think you understand. What has happened is not medically possible." Dr. Russell M. Nelson confirmed that. "No one recovers when the cancer has spread like it had in his liver."

Dad stood in April conference to say: "I am quite overwhelmed by deep feelings of thanksgiving and rejoicing for the goodness of the Lord to me.

"He has permitted me to suffer pain, feel anxiety, and taste his healing power. I am profoundly grateful for the faith and prayers of many people, for heartfelt petitions that have ascended to the throne of grace on my behalf.

"It is pleasing to that God whose we are when we fast and pray and seek his blessings; when we plead with all the energy of our souls for those things we so much desire; when, as Paul says, we 'come boldly unto the throne of grace, that we may obtain mercy, and find grace to help in time of need' (Heb. 4:16)."[1]

For a time Dad continued to improve. By the end of August he could jog five miles, but early in September he began again to lose his strength and the original symptoms returned. He was completely spent by the time he returned from the office in the evening. Tests showed that the cancer had returned with a vengeance. At about this time he asked the members of the Missionary Executive Committee—Elders Packer, Faust, and Dallin H. Oaks—to give him a blessing. Elder Packer was voice, and he gave a powerful and positive blessing. He indicated that people on both sides of the veil were laboring for his recovery, particularly President Joseph Fielding Smith. A second miracle occurred, and again his life was extended.

During this period of reprieve he was able to accomplish a number of things of particular importance to him, including three talks now regarded as classics by Latter-day Saint religious educators. The first of these, given June 3, 1984, dealt with missionary work, conversion, and the place of the Book of Mormon. It was given to teachers at Brigham Young University who were being trained to aid Religion faculty members in teaching Book of Mormon classes. In these remarks he showed how in our missionary efforts we have hindered the work by attempting to find common ground with people of other faiths. The attempt to show that we share a faith in

His Final Testimony

common—that we are Christians just like them—left those we were teaching without reason to hear the message of the Restoration. We exist as a faith because of our differences with historical Christianity, and only in those differences is reason found for conversion and the kind of faith it takes to be a Latter-day Saint, he said.

In August of that year he spoke by assignment to Church Educational System personnel. The title of his address was "The Bible, a Sealed Book," which identified the two seals that lock the meaning of this sacred record to the understanding of men. The first he identified as "the seal of ignorance" and the second as "the seal of intellectuality." He showed how the true meaning of the book could only be unlocked by the spirit of revelation.[2]

On Saturday, November 3, 1984, he gave another landmark talk entitled "The Doctrinal Restoration" at a symposium sponsored by the Religious Studies Center at Brigham Young University. In the keynote address he charged all who have been commissioned to teach the gospel to be true to the revelations of the Restoration. As to the Joseph Smith Translation, he said, "May I be pardoned if I say that negative attitudes and feelings about the Joseph Smith Translation are simply part of the devil's program to keep the word of truth from the children of men.

"Of course the revealed changes made by Joseph Smith are true—as much so as anything in the Book of Mormon or the Doctrine and Covenants.

"Of course we have adequate and authentic original sources showing the changes—as much so as are the sources for the Book of Mormon or the revelations.

"Of course we should use the Joseph Smith Translation in our study and teaching. Since when do any of us have the right to place bounds on the Almighty and say we will believe these revelations but not those?"[3]

I participated in this symposium and was scheduled to speak

immediately after Dad, perhaps so that he would be able to stay and hear my presentation. I had looked forward to this event because it would be one of the few times we shared the same platform. Immediately after his talk, however, he indicated to me that he did not have the strength to stay. Like everyone else present, I had no idea how difficult that presentation had been for him.

Another goal he was able to accomplish during his second reprieve from the ravages of cancer was planning a family trip. On August 28, 1984, Dad wrote to each of his children and their spouses to invite them to join him and Mother on a visit to the Holy Land. Because Brenda and I had had experience in leading such tours, he asked us to make the preparations. Among other things, a schedule of family study classes was drawn up. All who could attend were expected to take their turn instructing the group at our family nights. When it was Dad's turn, as something of a measure of his interest, he came with typed outlines twenty to thirty pages long.

Fighting the Good Fight

In the meantime, Dad's fight with cancer intensified. Elder John K. Carmack recounted events attending a weekend assignment during this period, when Elder McConkie and Elder David B. Haight were assigned to a twelve-stake conference in Santa Barbara, California. "We met to plan the conference in Elder Haight's office. I was the junior member of the team. Elder McConkie's only request was that we do what would be most convenient to the people of the twelve stakes. So we planned two four-hour leadership meetings on Saturday, one in Chatsworth and one in Santa Barbara, one hundred miles away. Sunday would find us doing two-hour meetings on the University of California, Santa Barbara, campus. We would return the one hundred miles to Los Angeles and arrive home about

His Final TESTIMONY

midnight. Elder Haight, ever solicitous of Elder McConkie, protested, but deferred to the senior apostle.

"I saw him that week in the General Authority dining room. 'John, let's go preach the gospel,' he said with obvious enthusiasm. He anticipated the chance to once more teach and exhort the Saints.

"On the Friday night before the conference, Shirley and I met Bruce and Amelia McConkie and David Haight at the Burbank Airport. Elder McConkie was completely exhausted. He had just had his chemotherapy shot. (Incidentally, Sister McConkie says that his doctor, who was not a member of the Church, did not quite know how to take Bruce. She said he would walk in on Friday for his shot, roll up his sleeve, and say, 'Seven more days of life, Doc!')

"After we met at the airport that night, Elder McConkie went straight to bed without dinner. Over dinner, Amelia shared with us his cooperative disdain for the illness which was obviously consuming him."

As to the conference meetings, Elder Carmack recalled: "Many felt he was never more powerful than he was at that conference, nor was there a finer regional conference than that on Saturday and Sunday in Chatsworth and Santa Barbara. He was back where his father, Oscar McConkie, had presided in such power. . . .

"Experiencing some difficulty with the sound on Sunday, he grasped the microphone on the podium and pulled it close to his mouth. 'I didn't come all this way not to be heard,' he announced. Everyone heard and everyone understood his message of salvation.

"We drove back to Los Angeles and awaited the late arrival of our flight to Salt Lake City. In the airport many recognized him and Elder Haight and spoke to them. He could travel to no location in the world without being recognized. He and all of the rest of us were tired as we arrived in Salt Lake City at midnight.

"On Tuesday following that exhausting weekend, I saw him at

the office. 'How are you feeling?' I asked. He jumped instantly into the air, clicked his heels, and exclaimed, 'Great!'" It was the importance of what he was doing that gave him strength, Elder Carmack concluded. "Soon he would join his Savior, but he must endure to the end. This he did with courage and power beyond anything I have witnessed."[4]

During this period he also filled conference assignments and reorganized a number of stakes. In at least one instance his pain was such that he called a stake president while lying on the floor of the stake office.

Among the notes written on pieces of scratch paper in my father's desk, I found part of an envelope printed by an airline containing a flight ticket. It was dated January 27, 1985. On it Dad had written the following little verse, obviously written as he returned from what was a very difficult conference assignment:

> We are late, late, late;
> And getting later.
> It is dark, dark, dark;
> And getting darker.
> I am tired, tired, tired;
> And getting tireder.
> Oh Hell!

A Family Blessing and Promise

In mid-February 1985, the family was informed that Dad's situation was again getting worse. His chemotherapy treatments no longer seemed to be working, so they were stopped.

On Sunday, February 27, the family gathered at the home of my sister Sara and her husband, Jerry Fenn, to seal our fast and importune the heavens in Dad's behalf. Mother had invited us to do this without Dad's knowledge for fear he would not want us to make a fuss over him. The spirit of the meeting was positive. Mother indicated that

His Final Testimony

Dad had asked the boys to come down to their apartment and give him a blessing. When we were seated in the apartment, she turned to me and asked me to take charge. I briefly recounted for Dad what had taken place and then told him he was surrounded by men of faith who would be pleased to give him a blessing if he desired it. He said, "I would like that," in a manner that indicated he meant it. He asked me to be voice in giving the blessing. As we gathered around him, I asked if he would like us to anoint him also. He responded in the affirmative and asked Stanford to perform that ordinance. In the blessing we told Dad that he was encircled in the love of his family and that each of us who laid our hands on his head had received the priesthood or its saving ordinances at his hand and now deemed it an honor to place our hands on his head to bless him as he had blessed us. We rebuked the disease in his body, telling him that as the Lord had told Joseph Smith the bounds of his enemies were set, so the bounds of this affliction were set. We commanded the disease to recede to those bounds. We also told him that like Joseph Smith, his days were known and would not be numbered less. We told him that he would be required to rest and recuperate but that the Lord would return that time to him. We assured him that he would "yet bear every testimony, teach every doctrine and write every word that he had been foreordained in the councils of heaven to accomplish." We sealed upon him the blessing given by our Grandfather McConkie to that effect—and, I suppose, if not in word, then surely by implication—the blessing given in the councils of heaven. We then asked for a blessing beyond mortal ability for the doctors who would attend him.

One week later, before he went into the hospital, the Quorum of the Twelve Apostles and President Hinckley also blessed Dad. He called to tell me about the blessing, saying that President Hinckley "sealed upon him the blessing given by his family."

Dad then went into the hospital for what was supposed to be a two-week stay in which they would shoot chemotherapy directly into his liver. He was told that this procedure had a 40 percent chance of working. The therapy worked, and Dad was sent home from the hospital after about the ninth day. All that could have been hoped for was accomplished. Still, he was very weak and had a serious case of jaundice. The treatment also robbed him of his appetite.

His doctors came to the apartment to check on him. Describing these events to the family, Mother wrote as follows: "This morning the chemo doctor came in while I was here. He did his usual thorough and expert checking on Daddy, and after all the thumping and feeling and listening he said that his liver was smaller than it had been and he could not detect any indication of fluid in the area." These were both positive signs, suggesting that the treatment was having the desired effect. Dad was also doing well at maintaining his weight.

To her report Mother added, "Dr. Maurice Taylor, an old friend and devoted follower of Daddy's came in. He is a fine old Gentleman and Stake Patriarch. After a little visit he was about to leave and then turned and asked Daddy if he would like to have him give Dad a blessing." Dad indicated that he would. A beautiful blessing followed, which Dad felt was the most positive he had received.

"It was interesting," Mother continued, "to hear a blessing with a physician talking to the 'Great Physican' and using medical expressions like, 'As you know the cells are producing _____, which is causing _____, and he needs to have "this or that" take place in order to throw off this disease, etc.' He rebuked the cells that were rebellious and refusing to act as they should normally do and blessed Daddy that the terrible itching and other problems he's had would cease. He also said that Daddy was well loved in the Church and his work was not finished and he would remain until he had done all he should."

His Final Testimony

Perhaps the last photograph taken of Mother and Dad together, March 1985

Dad had a very pronounced case of jaundice, which we understood to be a good sign because it meant the treatment was working. His bilirubin count was up, and the doctors attributed the itch to that. Pills could relieve the itching but with the side effect of drowsiness. He would take them only at night.

About this time I received a call to serve as the president of a Brigham Young University student stake. It was one of the young married stakes and had in it fourteen hundred returned missionaries. When I told Dad about my call and described the stake, I said, "What do you think Joseph Smith would have done if he had had fourteen hundred returned missionaries with whom to begin the labors of this dispensation?" He answered, "I don't know, but in a few weeks I will ask him."

On March 10, 1985, Dad went down to the Motion Picture Studio in Provo to film his part of a short film introducing the new editions of the scriptures. The experience took most of the day and left him so exhausted that when it was finished, he got into the car and fell asleep as Mother drove him home.

Conference Week

Sometime before April conference, probably the last Saturday in March, Mother recounted, "Dad came into the kitchen and said, 'Would you like to hear what I have prepared for General Conference?' I was making him a pie, because his appetite had begun to go downhill, and I thought, maybe he'd like an apple pie. I had the apples all ready to put in it, and I was rolling up the dough, the oven was on, everything was ready, and he came in and sat down and started to read me his talk and the tears streamed down his face, and he didn't get more than a couple of sentences out and I thought to myself, 'You don't make apple pies when somebody is saying these things to you.' So I sat down, dropped everything, and listened to him. I asked him, 'How are you going to be able to get up and read this?' Because there he was, having a hard time saying what he was saying because he was so touched. And he said, 'I don't know, but I'm going to do it.'"

On Monday, April 1, Brit gave Dad a blessing. He said he still had work to do, that the devil had been rebuked, and he blessed him to have the strength to get through conference. Elder Packer came on Tuesday and blessed him and again affirmed that he had more to do.

On Tuesday evening, April 2, Mother called our home. I answered the phone and could tell immediately from the tone of her voice that something was seriously wrong. She said, "I called to wish you a happy birthday tomorrow." She then explained that Dad's blood tests had come back, and they were very bad. "The doctors can do nothing for him," she said. They had told her "to take him home and make him as comfortable as possible" for what they said would be the last few days or weeks of his life. She told us that Dad

His Final Testimony

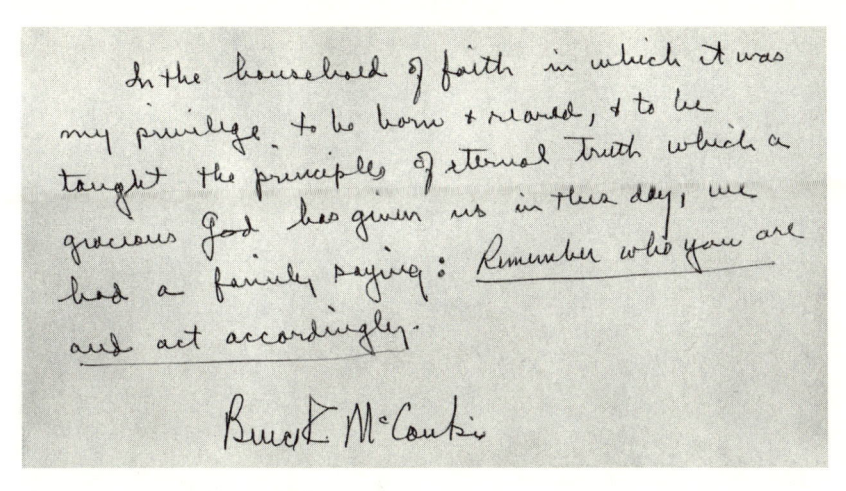

> In the household of faith in which it was my privilege to be born & reared, & to be taught the principles of eternal truth which a gracious God has given us in this day, we had a family saying: <u>Remember who you are and act accordingly.</u>
>
> Bruce R. McConkie

A note written on a scrap of paper

had instructed her that the family was to accept the will of the Lord and that they were not to fast and pray for the extension of his life.

As to conference, she reported that the doctors said that he would be too weak to speak and that should he try, he would likely pass out in front of a national television audience and embarrass the whole Church. "Nevertheless," she said, "your father wants to give that talk. It means more to him than anything he has done in this life," but he could not even finish reading it to her. Each time he attempted to do so, he broke down in tears.

After Mother's call, with Vivian's help we contacted each of our brothers and sisters to relay Mother's message and to unite the family in a fast—not contrary to his wishes in pleading for the extension of his life but rather that he might be granted both the strength and the emotional control he needed to give the talk he had written.

During the day, Dad would rest on his bed with his clothes on, refusing to make the concession of remaining in bed. He also refused to eat in the bedroom. Regardless of how bad he felt, he would go to the kitchen to attempt to eat.

Wednesday evening, Brenda and I went up to visit Mother and

Dad being greeted by President Ezra Taft Benson before the Saturday morning session of conference, April 1985

Dad. He had just returned from his meetings and was exhausted. While he took a nap, Mother insisted on cooking some hamburgers for us. Dad came in and sat at the table. This was especially gracious of him because he had no appetite, and the smell of food nauseated him. He too ate, which greatly pleased Mother. Brenda gave him a supply of a diet supplement in the form of an odorless pill, something like an energy bar but smaller. He could eat them because they were odorless. They may have been his primary food supply for the next few days. I remember seeing him put one in his mouth just before he got up to speak at conference.

By Saturday the family had gathered. Mark and Mary Ann had come from Colorado, Mike and Becky from Iowa, and Stephen and Shauna from California. The rest of us—Brenda and I, Vivian and Carlos, Stanford and Kathy, Mary and Ben, Sara and Jerry, all lived within an hour's drive of Salt Lake City. Sara and Jerry, who had

His Final Testimony

Elder McConkie delivering his final testimony

bought the family home on Dorchester Drive, generously made it our headquarters.

In the Saturday morning session on April 6, 1985, Dad gave his final talk in a general conference of the Church. As he rose to speak, his face was drawn and thin, his skin so yellow that many must have been tempted to adjust the color on their television sets, his steps those of a man many years his senior; nevertheless, he stood tall and spoke as he always had, with confidence and power. The family prayer that he might have both the strength and emotional control to give the talk was answered. The Spirit took over as Dad had prayed it would, and one of the most powerful talks ever given in the Tabernacle was delivered.

With a trembling voice, he concluded: "I am one of his witnesses, and in a coming day I shall feel the nail marks in his hands and in his feet and shall wet his feet with my tears.

"But I shall not know any better then than I know now that he is God's Almighty Son, that he is our Savior and Redeemer, and that salvation comes in and through his atoning blood and in no other way."[5]

On Sunday, April 14, Elder Packer visited and blessed Dad for the final time. He said the promises given in the previous blessings were fulfilled in his conference address and that it was a miracle we had had him this year. In effect, Elder Packer indicated in the blessing that Dad's life's ministry was completed. Afterward, Dad turned to Mother and said, "Do you know what he said?" Mother told him she would try to live to be an honor and a credit to him. He cried.

Elder Packer visited with Mother and left. His instructions to the family were to yield to the will of the Lord. When Mother and Elder Packer left the room, Dad got up and with what little strength he had remaining, he undressed, pulled the covers back, and got into bed, thus signaling that the battle was over. Thereafter he declined food but would sometimes take a little water.

Brenda and I went up to see them. Mother was tired, and even though she had invited us up, she probably would have preferred that we not come. There had been a constant parade of people in that day. We visited with Mother for a few minutes in the living room and then she said, "Joseph, you can go in and sit by your dad if you would like to." I entered the bedroom very quietly. I thought he was asleep. He was lying on the far side of the bed with his back to me. I didn't want to wake him; it was enough just to be present. He said, "Hello, Joseph." I responded, "Hello, Dad." I then walked around the bed to be closer to him. He turned his back to me. I started back to the other side so that I could face him. He asked me if I would scratch his back. I rubbed his back for about ten minutes. It seemed a special honor. My thoughts were of those privileged to anoint the broken body of the Savior. When I thought him awake, I said to him, "Dad, I wanted to come up to tell you that I love you." He was unable to respond. After I had rubbed his back for that short time, he rolled over onto his back, and we talked. I said, "You remember Farrell Smith, who I served with in Vietnam?" He responded in the affirmative.

I told him Farrell was a stake president in Arizona and that he was holding a stake priesthood meeting that night in which they were showing the video of his talk and building their meeting around it. I told him again that I thought more people had been affected by his talk than any talk ever given in a general conference. He said, as he had before, "I wanted to give that talk if it was the last thing I ever did!" I told him that my children wanted to come up and tell him that they loved him, but we were afraid it would wear him out. I said that they were good children, that I had taken Joseph Jr. home teaching with me that day, that he had given the lesson, that he was getting tall and handsome, and that he would be a great missionary. Dad said he knew they were good children and that he was proud of them. He said, "Joseph, I love you."

Mother came into the room, and when she saw that we were talking, she asked me to get Brenda. I did so. Brenda came in. A moment or two after she came into the room, Dad opened his eyes and saw her. He said, "Hello, Brenda," with a special kindness and love in his voice like that with which he had greeted me. She said, "Dad, our children wanted us to tell you how much they love you. Shanna felt bad she hadn't told you that when she was here last week." Dad said, "I know they do. I love them and am proud of them. You have a good family, Brenda." Then she said, "We want to thank you for all that you have done for us." He responded, "It was a privilege."

At this point Mother sat down and began rubbing Dad's back again. She made some comments about his having a son and a brother and a father who were waiting to see him. We said we would leave and said good night. Mother excused herself from Dad and walked us to the door. I thanked her for letting us come, and she said we were welcome any time we wanted to come and we did not need to call. We hugged and left.

The next few days family members and close friends came to bid Dad farewell. Each experience contained its own tenderness. The tone of the visit with his mother, Vivian Redd McConkie, was somewhat different, however. She visited Dad to give him instruction. "When you see Daddy," she said, referring to his father and her companion, from whom she had now been separated for twenty years, "you tell him my suitcase is packed and I am waiting at the curb." Grandmother, who had hardly been sick a day in her life, was now in her ninety-fifth year—no great thing, particularly, considering that her mother, Lucinda Pace Redd, had lived to be 104. Yet Grandmother McConkie was ready to meet Granddaddy and fully expected Dad to see that the matter was attended to. Three weeks and one day after Dad's death, she herself died.

Early Friday morning, April 19, Elder Russell M. Nelson came by to check Dad. He took Mother into the living room and told her that Dad would pass away that day. He was leaving for a multiregional conference in Boston, to which Dad had been assigned. He was going with President Ezra Taft Benson, who lived across the hall.

Calls were made, and the family assembled. It was sometime after noon before everyone who was able to be there had arrived. We took chairs into Dad's room for everyone. Mother suggested that we kneel and have prayer. She asked me to be voice. Stanford's wife, Kathy, who is a registered nurse, had just taken Dad's heartbeat, observing that it was strong and regular and would be the last thing to go. Mother, Kathy, and Dad's nurse had bathed Dad, changed his clothing, and prepared everything needful prior to this gathering.

Vivian described what followed: "We all knelt around the bed. Joseph prayed. He thanked the Lord for Dad's life and asked him to have regard for Dad's condition and his obedience and if it was us. We spent some sacred moments together on the Mount of Beatitudes according to our appointment. At the Garden Tomb outside the walls of the Old City in Jerusalem, we found a quiet place and sat in a circle to listen to a recording of Dad's last talk. As we listened, a dove flew down into the center of our group, where it remained until Dad's final amen.

McConkie family trip to Israel, 1985

possible, to release his spirit and call him home. Immediately upon the phrase 'call him home,' Dad's spirit left his body, and he was gone. The others were aware he had quit breathing. Joseph asked the Lord to allow Dad to be with us in Israel on the Mount of Beatitudes where the first Twelve were ordained, if it were appropriate."

Within ten minutes Dr. J. Poulson Hunter came by. No one had called him. He just appeared. He phoned the mortuary and took care of a few other things. Elder Packer called at about the same time. He had just returned from commencement exercises at Brigham Young University. It seemed uncanny how these things were happening. Dr. Hunter called President Hinckley. At about 2:30 P.M. someone looked out the window and saw that the flag at the Church Offices was at half mast.

That spring, according to Dad's wish, the family made the trip to the Holy Land that we had been planning. Brit and his wife, Beth, as well as Dad's secretary of many years, Velma Harvey, joined

24

REFLECTIONS OF A SON

The Lord placed him as an Apostle for a purpose. He has taken him for a reason.

—President Gordon B. Hinckley

The life of Bruce McConkie ended, as it had begun, with a miracle. All that took place in between clearly evidenced the hand of the Lord. At age nineteen he was told that the time would come when all who knew him would look to him "for counsel and for the witness of the truth" and that he would become "a chosen vessel," "exalted among [his] brethren in the holy order of the priesthood of our God." By divine design, as a young missionary he was sent to the Eastern States Mission, where he spent thirteen months of his mission laboring in the immediate proximity of the Sacred Grove and the Hill Cumorah. There the spirit of the Restoration and the testimony of Joseph Smith sank deeply into his soul.

From the time he was ordained a missionary, he hungered to preach the gospel with power. At the end of his mission, an inspired mission president asked him to extend his mission for six weeks and go on a speaking tour of the mission.

Bruce McConkie had as mentors two lions of the Lord. The first was his father, Oscar W. McConkie, a man who could move mountains with his faith, preach with the voice of thunder, raise the dead, and heal the sick. He was a man who dreamed dreams and saw visions. The second was his father-in-law, Joseph Fielding Smith, destined to stand at the head of the Church as its prophet, as his own father had done before him, and destined to defend the teachings of the Prophet Joseph Smith, according to the words of a patriarch, in its highest councils. President Heber J. Grant called him the "best posted" man in the Church on the scriptures. Such was President Smith's integrity that my uncle Oscar, a law partner in the firm that handled many legal matters for the Church, told me once, "Joseph Fielding Smith is so honest that if the Church wasn't true, he would call a press conference and announce it." Both men, one in high position, the other not, loved the Church, the gospel, and the Savior more than life itself. Both would rather have talked scripture than eat. Both were guileless, and as preachers neither knew any gospel other than the gospel of plainness nor cared a fig for public favor. In Bruce McConkie one could plainly see the likeness of his mentors.

Called to the First Council of the Seventy at age thirty-one, Bruce never had the opportunity to serve as a bishop, high councilor, or member of a stake presidency. He had not held any position of leadership outside his mission experience and his service as a seventy. As a general authority, he was sent out to train men, many of whom had served in leadership positions longer than he had been alive. Knowing he could not teach what he did not know, he taught what he did know: the gospel. He taught principles, he quoted scripture, and in the process honed the ability to rely on the Spirit and teach as holy men had taught in days long past. The more he did it, the more confident he became that there was power in the message and that only in the message could one find "the power of God unto salvation." "Principles are eternal," he said. "Procedures are man-made."

Some seek safety in ambiguity and refuge in uncertainty, but Bruce McConkie was not one of them. When he tromped through the intellectual thicket inhabited by critics attempting to hide their lack of devotion, those critics consistently sought to confuse what Paul called "much assurance" with arrogance, and the "undeviating course" with narrow-mindedness. So it is that men like Joseph Fielding Smith, Bruce R. McConkie, and Boyd K. Packer become as lightning rods for the discontented, the unconverted, and the avowed enemies of truth. Anyone who speaks as one having authority is to them a threat; anyone who marks a sure path offends their predilection to wander. "The measure of a man," taught Bruce McConkie, "is not in who profess to be his friends but in who his enemies are."

Of Bruce McConkie, President Gordon B. Hinckley said: "He was a Disciple of the Lord Jesus Christ, an Apostle with an understanding of what that meant."[1] As such, when his answer to a question or the authority by which he answered questions was challenged, he had no hesitation in saying, "You can just quote me on that." It did not trouble him when others made mistakes, and he claimed the right to do so himself. Yet, he was never slow to accept correction or embrace new light and truth as it was manifest. People have often quoted his statement correcting what he wrote in *Mormon Doctrine* about when the priesthood would be granted to the seed of Cain: "I was wrong! It is a new day and we have new light. Disregard all that I or anyone else said previously."[2]

Like his mentor Joseph Fielding Smith, Bruce McConkie was consistently called on to defend the teachings of the Prophet Joseph Smith, even among those from whom such a defense should not have been necessary. He played a leading role in the conversion of the twentieth-century Church to the use of Joseph Smith's inspired translation of the Bible, first in his *Doctrinal New Testament Commentary* and later in his membership on the Scriptures Publication Committee. The seeds planted in the early years of his marriage, when he and his bride read and carefully compared again and again the King James Version and the Joseph Smith Translation of the Bible, grew to produce a bountiful harvest. He brought the spirit of Joseph Smith into the great labor that produced the first Latter-day Saint edition of the King James Bible. Today we have a generation of gospel students who would be surprised to learn that the Joseph Smith Translation was virtually unknown to their parents.

His Written Testimony

As to the power of his pen and the books he wrote, it must be noted that that for which he was most criticized in life, he was most praised in death. Said Elder Boyd K. Packer: "Elder McConkie came to know two things as few mortals know them: the law and the prophets. . . .

"If you know ecclesiastical history at all, if you know the dealings of the Lord with men and of men with men, you should not be surprised that the one characteristic which the Lord pressed upon him was the very thing that many, even some closely, misunderstood. As is often true, the great ones are not fully understood or appreciated while they live. Perhaps one day we will see how great a man has walked among us. He was not less than Elder Talmage or the others that we revere from the past. His sermons and writings will live on. In these he will live longer than any of us. The scriptures have something to say about testimonies being in fuller force after the death of the testator (Hebrews 9:15–18)."[3]

As an author, Bruce McConkie is perhaps best known for the book *Mormon Doctrine*. Perhaps no single book, scripture excepted, has equaled its influence in identifying and defining the faith of the Latter-day Saint people. Much that was criticized when the book was first published now finds expression in the dictionary in the LDS edition of the Bible. The number of copies—376,000—sold during the lifetime of the author is quite remarkable when it is remembered that at its release, the Church numbered only a million and a half members.

No one in the history of the Church has written more by way of testimony of Christ than did Bruce R. McConkie. The ten volumes he wrote, which average more than seven hundred pages each, all center on doctrinal and scriptural commentary. They have made him one of the Church's leading theologians. No one is quoted more often on doctrinal matters.

In a devotional talk given at the Institute at the University of Utah a few months after his death, his wife, Amelia, observed that when she went through his effects, she found enough notes and papers to fill a number of boxes. These were handwritten outlines for talks or lessons, even a long list of titles for books he would like to have written. "I realized that this was what was important to him. He had not accumulated things that pertained to this world. He was not interested in them. He accumulated things that had something to do with the gospel until I had boxes full of them.

"I quote from one such scrap of paper: 'People are everlastingly asking me: "When do you find time to write? On your schedule how can you possibly write all the things you do?" Amelia (my beloved wife) has an answer. She says, "He does it on my time." This answer, true as it may seem to her, is wrong. Or at best it contains only a few grains of truth. Oh yes, because most of my days are programmed and full, [I] spend evenings and holidays and the occasional free hour at my typewriter. There is no such thing as maintaining continuity of thought or hope of project completion unless one maintains a rugged wearisome routine. There are many 12-hour days with an occasional 14-hour stretch thrown in for variety.'"

This note suggests something of his sense of devotion and the discipline that was his. There was, however, one more line on this scrap of paper: "But all this is not my writing schedule, far from it." The expression that completed that thought was not found. The intimation is, and this is always the case, that there was a great deal more involved in accomplishing what he did than twelve- and fourteen-hour days.

Of his work, Eleanor Knowles, then executive editor and publishing director for Deseret Book, said, "His writing is very poetic in style, very biblical in the phrasing of sentences. His manuscripts were wonderful to work on. Elder Bruce R. McConkie was one of the finest writers in the Church. We did less editing on his work than on any other. He was very accurate and used excellent grammar. His were the most carefully thought-out manuscripts I have ever seen."

His Last Testimony

"None who heard his last sermon on the Atonement of Jesus Christ will ever forget his witness," said President Ezra Taft Benson. "His testimony bears repeating because his was a sure witness as an Apostle of the Lord Jesus Christ and as a special witness of His name."[4]

Of that testimony President Gordon B. Hinckley observed: "None who were in the tabernacle that recent Saturday morning of General Conference, or who saw it or heard it over the air, will forget his final testimony when he declared in a voice shaking with emotion: 'I am one of His witnesses, and in a coming day I shall feel the nail marks in His hands and in His feet and shall wet His feet with my tears.

"'But I shall not know any better then than I know now that He is God's almighty Son; that He is our Savior and Redeemer; and that salvation comes in and through His atoning blood and in no other way.'

" .... That testimony touched the hearts of tens of thousands across the Church, and will continue to do so in the years to come."[5]

The *Salt Lake Tribune* said in an editorial tribute: "Few testimonies of a personal belief in divine redemption can rival for power and conviction Elder McConkie's words during the Church's spring conference in Salt Lake City earlier this month. A cancer victim, acutely aware of his earthly mortality, the emotional, yet intellectually unbowed speaker attested to a mercy and blessedness, for those practicing scriptural constancy, so sublime and certain as to permanently affect all who heard him describe it." The editorial went on to say that he was more "than theologian and instructor, although as both he excelled beyond measure. He was striding taller than most, counseling more fervently than many, still one with his companion worshippers, profoundly interested in their struggles, concerned for their eternal salvation. As a diligent servant of his church, as inspiration for its congregation, he will be missed. But with the acknowledgment that death awaits every man, humble or great, Bruce R. McConkie deserves to live now in those exalting recollections forever graced by reverence, affection, and gratitude."

At the time of this writing, nearly eighteen years have passed since that testimony was given, and yet people constantly share with members of the family their feelings at the time it was given. Those expressions have included people not of our faith, conversion stories, and other memories and impressions that have been indelibly impressed on their hearts and minds. We have received calls and letters from mission presidents, stake presidents, and others from the ends of the earth requesting copies of it. Typical is this note addressed to Elder McConkie before his death: "Yesterday, as I listened to your testimony I wept with you as you testified of Christ. The Holy Ghost bore witness to me again of the truth and reality of the Savior's redeeming sacrifice. I thank you for it and the many other times that I have been blessed and inspired by your life and sermons."

Yet another note records: "I distinctly remember as if it was yesterday sitting downstairs at my parents' watching conference that year, having recently returned from my mission and listening to Elder Bruce R. McConkie bear his final testimony to the world. It was the most powerful testimony I have ever heard and I felt the Spirit so strongly I remember losing all control of my emotions and running up to my room afterwards and bawling for some time. The Spirit bore witness to me so strongly on that occasion of the divinity of the Savior and his Atonement, I would have to say more strongly than any testimony I have received in my lifetime."

In 1989, shortly after I arrived in Scotland to preside over the mission there, a couple requested that I baptize them. In response to my asking why they wanted me to perform their baptism, they said because their conversion had come while they were listening to a tape of Dad's last conference talk.

Reflections of a Son

Objectivity, like humility, is least to be expected among those who make the greatest pretense to it. I can but see through the eyes that were given me. Were the reader to ask me if I thought my father perfect, the answer would be, "Yes, in some things." His assurance that Amelia Smith was the girl he was destined to marry was perfect. On that matter he never experienced a moment's doubt. He surprised the student body at the Brigham Young University when he told them he had never prayed about the girl he should marry. That to him was as obvious as life itself. He may have prayed about how to ask her to be his wife but not about whether he wanted her as such. In like manner, his testimony of gospel principles was perfect. He never doubted that God lives, that Jesus of Nazareth is His Only Begotten Son, that Joseph Smith is the great prophet of the Restoration. Nor did he pray to know the truthfulness of these or any other eternal verity. He prayed and labored constantly to grow

Reflections of a Son

in knowledge and understanding of these principles, but the principles themselves he never doubted. His knowledge of them was perfect. On all other matters he, like Elijah, was a man of "like passions as we are" (James 5:7). He differed from others only in the energy and zeal with which he sought to perfect himself. He constantly challenged himself to reach higher, to be better. "I shall pray," he wrote in 1967, "with the faith of Alma, repent with the determination of Paul. Write with the pen of Peter. Labor with the zeal of Moroni. Speak with the tongue of Aaron. Walk in the way of Jesus. Testify as did Joseph Smith. Submit to the divine will as did Job. Walk with God as did Enoch. Heal the sick as did my father. Preach as did Nephi."

When I was set apart as a mission president, Elder Neal A. Maxwell welcomed my family warmly into his office and observed that it had once been my father's office. The rolltop desk in the corner was his, noted Elder Maxwell. "I tend to go and just sit there sometimes and soak up the inspiration."

In the Eyes of Those with Whom He Labored

"To me," stated Elder Boyd K. Packer at the funeral service for Elder McConkie, "there was one great crowning contribution and achievement in Brother McConkie's ministry. Some may not agree because he accomplished and contributed so many things. But I am sure, quite sure of this, if ever there was a man who was raised up unto a very purpose, if ever a man was prepared against a certain need—it was Bruce R. McConkie. It had to do with the scriptures. All members of the Presidency and the Quorum of the Twelve had important work to do in the publication of the new editions of the scriptures with all of the aids, the footnotes, the corrections, the topical guide, the dictionaries, the indexes, the re-versification, the new chapter headings, the additional revelations and more.

"This work, while hardly appreciated yet, will one day emerge as a signal inspired event in our generation. Because of it we shall raise up generations of Latter-day Saints who will know the gospel and who will know the Lord.

"Brother Monson and I served for years on the Scriptures Publication Committee with Brother McConkie. I know full well that the work could have been accomplished without me. I venture to suggest as well that Brother Monson was not crucial to that work, but it could not have been done without Elder Bruce R. McConkie. Few will ever know the extent of the service he rendered. Few can appraise the lifetime of preparation for this quiet, crowning contribution to the on-rolling of the restored gospel in the dispensation of the fullness of times."[6]

In that same service President Hinckley said, "I agree with Elder Packer concerning [Elder McConkie's] scholarship and the preparation of his earlier years to assist in the project of bringing out the LDS edition of the King James Version of the Bible, as well as the new editions of the Book of Mormon, the Doctrine and Covenants, and the Pearl of Great Price." President Hinckley continued: "The Lord put Elder McConkie where he was. The Lord has now taken him. The Lord placed him as an Apostle for a purpose. He has taken him for a reason."[7]

As to Bruce McConkie the preacher, Elder Packer observed: "His manner of delivery was unique, something of an Old Testament scriptural quality about it. It was not granted to Brother McConkie to judge beforehand how his discourses would be received and then alter them accordingly. He could not measure what he ought to say and how he ought to say it by, 'What will people think?' Would his sermons leave any uncomfortable? Would his bold declarations irritate some in the Church? Would they inspire the critics to rush to their anvils and hammer out more 'fiery darts,' as the scriptures call them? Would his manner of delivery offend? Would his forthright declarations in content or in manner

Reflections of a Son

of presentation drive some learned investigators away? Would he be described as insensitive or overbearing? Would his warnings and condemnations of evil undo the careful work of others whose main intent was to have the world 'think well of the Church'? Perhaps it was given to other men to so measure their words in that way, but it was not given to him. We have talked of this and when he was tempted to change, the Spirit would withdraw a distance and there would come that deep loneliness known only to those who have enjoyed close association with the Spirit, only to find on occasion that it moves away. He could stand what the critics might say and what the enemies might do, but he could not stand that. He would be driven to his knees to beg forgiveness and plead for the renewal of that companionship of the Spirit which the scriptures promise can be constant. Then he would learn, once again, that what was true of the Holy Men of God who spake in ancient times applied to him as well. He was to speak as he was moved upon by the Holy Spirit. What matter if it sounded like Bruce R. McConkie so long as the Lord approved. I knew him well enough to know all of that."[8]

Similarly, President Hinckley said: "He had his own unique style. With measured words, firm and unequivocal and with order and logic, he wove the patterns of his discourses. His language was clear, its meaning unmistakable. There was a cadence to it. There was a peculiar strength and beauty in its pattern. He spoke from a cultivated mind, but also from a sincere heart."[9]

Elder Russell M. Nelson observed: "Elder Bruce R. McConkie was a great friend. His door was always open to me, and I frequently imposed upon his graciousness, asking him questions that possibly only he could answer." Considering that Elder McConkie had been diagnosed with terminal cancer eighteen months before his death, Elder Nelson said, "I look upon the extra year of life that he was granted as a period for the training of Elder Dallin H. Oaks and me. We are greatly in his debt and miss him very much."[10]

Bruce McConkie understood the sacred nature of the office he held and extended himself in every way he could to honor it. He knew he could not change the way he preached without offending the powers of heaven upon which he was wholly dependent. In an effort to convey his love and concern for those to whom he preached, it became his practice wherever possible to go through the audience row by row before the meeting started and shake hands with everyone present. Many have mentioned to members of the McConkie family how they appreciated his doing so. The following extract from a letter to his Amelia illustrates:

"About 15 minutes before the meeting started, I noticed Elder McConkie come into the chapel. He went up to the stand, which was already full of choir members and other important people, and began to shake their hands and greet them. I was impressed with that gesture of kindness on his part, to think that he would take the time to greet all the people on the stand. However, he didn't stop there! He came down to the first row of the chapel, which was starting to become full, and shook all their hands, too, and continued moving row by row through the chapel. Without hurrying, he kindly greeted everyone personally in the chapel and was very soon shaking my hand. I said simply, 'Good morning, Sir,' and he passed to the next person. I was in awe. I assumed that he was going to greet everyone in the chapel and then return to the stand. I was wrong. By this time the gym was full, and he met and shook hands with each and every one of them. I watched as he shook hands with everyone on the stage, and then he walked back to the stand. The meeting started precisely on time, and Elder McConkie had already personally met everyone in the congregation. I will never forget the only time I met Elder McConkie in person and face to face."

There is a deep sense of reverence that the membership of the Church holds for the office of apostle. Such feelings did not differ from his own. Bruce McConkie shared with all of the household of faith a profound respect for the office with which he had been entrusted. When my brother Mark asked Dad if he liked being an apostle, he responded, "Yes. Now people listen to what I say." He also indicated that there was a much greater outpouring of the Spirit among those with whom he labored and in the temple meetings of the Twelve than he had imagined would be the case.

Reaching back some fifty years to the experiences they had shared in the mission field, Sister Carol Read Flake, after listening to his last conference address, wrote to him:

"You were President McConkie when I first met you. How quickly I learned to admire and love my District president. . . .

"I recall your introducing me to that 'cowboy from Arizona,' on October 23rd, 1935.

"I can't describe the feelings I had, listening to your powerful, sweet and humble address on the atonement of our Savior. . . . Your own tearful testimony reduced me to shed tears with you, and then to listen to that magnificent poetry of yours in song by the Choir—*I Believe in Christ! He Is My King!* Bless you, dear Bruce, the Spirit of the Lord was so strongly apparent, and I know now that it was he who bore you up and gave you strength to deliver the greatest testimony of your life of testimony bearing, and being His Special Witness as an Apostle of the Lord Jesus Christ. Thank you for making that great sacrifice for all the Church!"

OUR COVENANT

In the October 1984 general conference, Elder McConkie spoke as follows: "The Church is like a great caravan—organized, prepared, following an appointed course, with its captains of tens and captains of hundreds all in place.

"What does it matter if a few barking dogs snap at the heels of the weary travelers? Or that predators claim those few who fall by the way? The caravan moves on.

"Is there a ravine to cross, a miry mud hole to pull through, a steep grade to climb? So be it. The oxen are strong and the teamsters wise. The caravan moves on.

"Are there storms that rage along the way, floods that wash away the bridges, deserts to cross, and rivers to ford? Such is life in this fallen sphere. The caravan moves on.

"Ahead is the celestial city, the eternal Zion of our God, where all who maintain their position in the caravan shall find food and drink and rest. Thank God that the caravan moves on!"[11]

In one of the last conversations between my parents, when Mother asked Dad what she would do without him, he responded, "Carry on." As for himself, he said, "It makes not a particle of difference whether I preach the gospel here or in the next world. I will preach the gospel."

For his family and those who are committed to the same cause, his counsel remains as it was given in his inaugural speech as an apostle: "Whatever the past has been—let this then be our covenant, that we will walk in all the ordinances of the Lord blameless. Let this be our covenant, that we will keep the commandments of God and be living witnesses of the truth and divinity of this glorious work, which is destined to sweep the earth as with a flood and which shall cover the earth as the waters cover the sea.

"O God, grant that I and my family and all the faithful members of the house of Israel may walk in truth and light, and having enjoyed the fellowship and kinship and association that is found nowhere else on earth outside the Church, let us enjoy that same spirit, that same fellowship in its eternal fulness, in the mansions and realms which are ahead."[12]

His parting words to Amelia, the love of his life, were "Carry on."

Notes

Introduction
  1. *Ensign*, May 1985, 16.

Chapter 1: "Let This Then Be Our Covenant"
  Ensign, January 1973, 37.
  1. *Ensign*, January 1973, 36.
  2. *Ensign*, January 1973, 37.
  3. *Improvement Era*, January 1952, 926; emphasis added.
  4. *Ensign*, January 1973, 36–37.

Chapter 6: Service as a Missionary, 1934 to 1936
  1. See, for example, Conference Report, October 1918, 23–24; October 1934, 123; April 1941, 4–5; October 1942, 25–26.

Chapter 7: Marriage to Amelia and the Death of Bruce Jr., 1937 to 1941
  1. See, for example, Bruce R. McConkie, *Mormon Doctrine* (Salt Lake City: Bookcraft, 1966), s.v. "Celestial Marriage."
  2. Joseph Fielding Smith, *Life of Joseph F. Smith* (Salt Lake City: Deseret News Press, 1938), 456.

Notes

CHAPTER 8: THE WAR YEARS, 1942 TO 1946
1. Conference Report, April 1942, 60.
2. Conference Report, October 1942, 58.

CHAPTER 9: CALLED AS A SEVENTY, 1946 AND 1947
1. Conference Report, October 1946, 146.
2. Francis M. Gibbons, *George Albert Smith: Kind and Caring Christian, Prophet of God* (Salt Lake City: Deseret Book, 1990), 321.
3. Conference Report, April 1947, 39.
4. Conference Report, April 1947, 41.

CHAPTER 10: THINGS GREAT AND SMALL, 1948 TO 1961
1. *Church News*, June 17, 1961, 3.
2. Joseph Smith, *History of The Church of Jesus Christ of Latter-day Saints*, edited by B. H. Roberts, 2d ed. rev., 7 vols. (Salt Lake City: The Church of Jesus Christ of Latter-day Saints, 1932–51), 2:476.
3. Conference Report, October 1961, 81.
4. *Deseret News*, June 1877, 274.
5. *Deseret News*, June 1877, 274.
6. Conference Report, October 1961, 90.

CHAPTER 11: THE MORMON DOCTRINE SAGA, 1958 AND 1966
1. Philip E. Johnson, *Reason in the Balance: The Case against Naturalism in Science, Law, and Education* (Downers Grove, Ill.: InterVarsity Press, 1995), 198–99.
2. Bruce R. McConkie, *The Mortal Messiah*, 3 vols. (Salt Lake City: Deseret Book, 1979–81), 1:xviii.

CHAPTER 12: THE AUSTRALIA YEARS, 1961 TO 1964
1. Bruce C. Hafen, *A Disciple's Life: The Biography of Neal A. Maxwell* (Salt Lake City: Deseret Book, 2002), 433.

CHAPTER 15: THE NATURE OF THE MAN
1. *Hymns* (Salt Lake City: The Church of Jesus Christ of Latter-day Saints, 1985), no. 21.
2. Bruce R. McConkie, Mexico City Area Conference Report, August 1972, 41–46.
3. Harold B. Lee, Conference Report, April 1973, 6–7.
4. Spencer W. Kimball, Lima Area Conference Report, February 1977, 34.

Notes

5. John K. Carmack, *Speeches* (Provo, Utah: Brigham Young University, 1985), 110.

CHAPTER 16: AS HE SAW IT

1. Joseph Fielding Smith, *Ensign*, December 1971, 10.
2. Bruce R. McConkie, "All Are Alike unto God," address delivered to personnel of the Church Educational System, Salt Lake City, Utah, August 18, 1978, in *Charge to Religious Educators*, 2d ed. (Salt Lake City: The Church of Jesus Christ of Latter-day Saints, 1982), 152–55.
3. Bruce R. McConkie, *The Promised Messiah* (Salt Lake City: Deseret Book, 1978), 515.

CHAPTER 17: A TIME TO LAUGH

1. *Church News*, April 28, 1985, 13.
2. Edward L. Kimball and Andrew E. Kimball Jr., *Spencer W. Kimball* (Salt Lake City: Bookcraft, 1977), 281–82.
3. Bruce R. McConkie, *Mormon Doctrine*, 2d ed. (Salt Lake City: Bookcraft, 1966), 283–84.

CHAPTER 18: CALL TO THE APOSTLESHIP

1. Bruce R. McConkie, *Ensign*, July 1972, 109.
2. *Hymns* (Salt Lake City: The Church of Jesus Christ of Latter-day Saints, 1985), no. 134; *Ensign*, July 1972, 109.
3. Bruce R. McConkie, Mexico City Area Conference Report, August 1972, 41–46; Harold B. Lee, Conference Report, April 1973, 6–7.
4. L. Brent Goates, *Harold B. Lee: Prophet and Seer* (Salt Lake City: Bookcraft, 1985), 494–95.
5. Edward L. Kimball and Andrew E. Kimball Jr., *Spencer W. Kimball, Twelfth President of The Church of Jesus Christ of Latter-day Saints* (Salt Lake City: Bookcraft, 1977), 194.
6. *Church News*, July 8, 1972, 13–14.
7. J. Reuben Clark Jr., *Improvement Era*, June 1951, 412.
8. Bruce R. McConkie, *Ensign*, May 1977, 14.

CHAPTER 19: AMONG THE NATIONS, 1968 TO 1982

1. Rulon P. Madsen, "Reunion with a Son," *Improvement Era*, April 1969, 43.
2. James E. Faust, address at funeral of Bruce R. McConkie, April 22, 1985, Special Collections, Harold B. Lee Library, Brigham Young University, Provo, Utah, typescript, 5–6.

Notes

CHAPTER 20: THE NATURE OF HIS MINISTRY, 1946 TO 1985

1. Bruce R. McConkie, "Our Relationship with the Lord," in *Speeches* (Provo, Utah: Brigham Young University, 1982), 97–103.
2. Bruce R. McConkie, *Ensign*, May 1981, 77.
3. Bruce R. McConkie, *The Foolishness of Teaching* [address delivered to Church Educational System personnel, September 18, 1981] (Salt Lake City: The Church of Jesus Christ of Latter-day Saints, 1981), 3.

CHAPTER 21: GREAT EVENTS

Boyd K. Packer, "Teach the Scriptures," address delivered to Church Educational System personnel, October 14, 1977, in *Charge to Religious Educators*, 2d ed. (Salt Lake City: The Church of Jesus Christ of Latter-day Saints, 1982), 21.

1. *Lectures on Faith*, compiled by N. B. Lundwall (Salt Lake City: Deseret Book, 1985), 7:9.
2. Boyd K. Packer, address at funeral of Bruce R. McConkie, April 22, 1985, Special Collections, Harold B. Lee Library, Brigham Young University, Provo, Utah, typescript, 11.
3. Spencer W. Kimball, *Ensign*, November 1976, 9.
4. Kimball, *Ensign*, November 1976, 9.
5. Lucile C. Tate, *Boyd K. Packer: A Watchman on the Tower* (Salt Lake City: Bookcraft, 1995), 236.
6. Tate, *Boyd K. Packer*, 219.
7. Bruce R. McConkie, *The Foolishness of Teaching* [address delivered to Church Educational System personnel, September 18, 1981] (Salt Lake City: The Church of Jesus Christ of Latter-day Saints, 1981), 1.

CHAPTER 22: SPECIAL CONTRIBUTIONS

Boyd K. Packer, address at funeral of Bruce R. McConkie, April 22, 1985, Special Collections, Harold B. Lee Library, Brigham Young University, Provo, Utah, typescript, 9.

1. Bruce R. McConkie, Mexico City Area Conference Report, August 1972, 45.
2. See Harold B. Lee, Conference Report, April 1973, 6–7; Spencer W. Kimball, Lima Area Conference Report, February 1977, 34; Bruce R. McConkie, *Ensign*, May 1977, 115–18.

CHAPTER 23: HIS FINAL TESTIMONY

1. Bruce R. McConkie, *Ensign*, May 1984, 32.
2. Bruce R. McConkie, "The Bible, a Sealed Book," in *Supplement to a*

Notes

Symposium on the New Testament, 1984 (Salt Lake City: The Church of Jesus Christ of Latter-day Saints, 1984), 3.

3. Bruce R. McConkie, "The Doctrinal Restoration," in Monte S. Nyman and Charles D. Tate Jr., eds., *Joseph Smith Translation: The Restoration of Plain and Precious Things* (Provo, Utah: BYU Religious Studies Center, 1985), 14.
4. John K. Carmack, "The Testament of Bruce R. McConkie," in *Speeches* (Provo, Utah: Brigham Young University, 1985), 109–10.
5. Bruce R. McConkie, *Ensign*, May 1985, 11.

CHAPTER 24: REFLECTIONS OF A SON

Gordon B. Hinckley, address at funeral of Bruce R. McConkie, April 22, 1985, Special Collections, Harold B. Lee Library, Brigham Young University, Provo, Utah, typescript, 14.

1. Hinckley, address at funeral, 14.
2. See Bruce R. McConkie, "All Are Alike unto God," address delivered to personnel of the Church Educational System, Salt Lake City, Utah, August 18, 1978, in *Charge to Religious Educators*, 2d ed. (Salt Lake City: The Church of Jesus Christ of Latter-day Saints, 1982), 153.
3. Boyd K. Packer, address at funeral of Bruce R. McConkie, April 22, 1985, Special Collections, Harold B. Lee Library, Brigham Young University, Provo, Utah, typescript, 10.
4. Ezra Taft Benson, address at funeral of Bruce R. McConkie, April 22, 1985, Special Collections, Harold B. Lee Library, Brigham Young University, Provo, Utah, typescript, 2.
5. Hinckley, address at funeral, 15.
6. Packer, address at funeral, 9.
7. Hinckley, address at funeral, 14.
8. Packer, address at funeral, 11.
9. Hinckley, address at funeral, 15.
10. Russell M. Nelson, in Spencer J. Condie, *Russell M. Nelson: Father, Surgeon, Apostle* (Salt Lake City: Deseret Book, 2003), 194.
11. Bruce R. McConkie, *Ensign*, November 1984, 85.
12. Bruce R. McConkie, *Ensign*, January 1973, 37.

Index

Pages on which photographs appear are designated in italic type.

Aaronic Priesthood, 35, 66–67
Aborigine, 229
Abraham, 375
Adams, Carlos, 412, *417*
Adams, Vivian McConkie, 14, 125, *131*, 416, *417*
Administrator, 296
Agency, 248, 257
Allen, Rhea B., 332
Ancestors, 14–29, 368–69
Ann Arbor, Michigan, 43, 71–72
Apocrypha, 274–75
Apostasy, 343
Apostle, 369–70, 430–31
Articles of Faith, 4, 389–90
Asay, Carlos E., 267
Ashton, Marvin J., 367, 370
Ashton, Marvin O., 148
Asia, 334–42
Assistants to the Twelve, 380
At Random, 203–5
Australia, 199–201

Australians, 206, 211
Authority, 258

Babies, death of, 124
Balance, 261, 277, 290–93, 321
Ballard, Melvin J., 93, 328
Bancroft, Louis, 208–10
Baptism, 205–10, 294
Beelzebub, 96–97
Benson, Ezra Taft: defends BRM, 220; BRM on aging of, 266; sends BRM to Vietnam, 336–37; dedicates Indonesia, 340–41; with BRM, *412*; on testimony of BRM, 424
Bible: BRM and Amelia read, 117–18; Book of Mormon key to understanding, 256, 393–96; LDS edition of, 381–85; BRM's love for, 391; as sealed book, 403. *See also* Joseph Smith Translation
Bible Dictionary, 384

439

Index

Bickerstaff, George, 186–87
Bishops, 206, 283–84, 319
Blanding, Utah, 60, 62
Blessings: father's, 82–84, 196, 238–39; of healing, 168–69, 337–38, 358–60, 369–70, 400–401, 407; special, 293. *See also* Patriarchal blessing
Blue Mountain Irrigation Company, 60, 76
Blue Mountains, 59, 66
Bluff, Utah, 60
Book of Mormon: and Emma Somerville McConkie, 34; BRM defends, on television, 204; as key to understanding Bible, 256, 393–95; as key to missionary work, 302, 395–96, 402–3; results of missionary survey about, 305; new edition of, 381
Books, 235, 237, 254, 274–75
Bookcraft, 186–87, 191
Boulder, 70
Bowen, Albert E., 129–30, 145
Bradford, William R., 346, 380
Broadbent, David A., 231
Buddhists, 343
Brockbank, Bernard P., 174
Burgoyne, Ed, 197
Butler, Caroline Skeen, 17–19, 22–23
Butler, John Lowe, 17–19, 29
Butler, Keziah Jane. *See* Redd, Keziah Butler
Butler, Margot, 316–17

Cabins, 32–33
Calhoun, Margaret. *See* Pace, Margaret Calhoun
California Mission, 46–52
Calling and election made sure, 294
Calling(s), 255–56, 330–31, 368–69
Canberra, 197–98
Cancer, 399, 401, 404
Cannon, George I., 362

Cannon, George J., 81, 85
Cannon, Maxwell Richards, 361
Cannons, 19
Caravan, Church as, 431–32
Carmack, John K., 404
Carter, Dominicus, 16
Catholic priest, 203–5
Cave, story about, 296–97
Celestial kingdom, 295
Change, 300–301
Chemotherapy, 401, 408
Childbirth, 27, 56–57
Chile, 352–53
China, 351
Christensen, Leatha Hair, 103
Christmas, 242–44
Church of Jesus Christ of Latter-day Saints, The, 298, 333, 397, 431; headquarters of, 296
Clark, J. Reuben, Jr.: reads First Presidency statement, 129; advises BRM, 150, 151–52; quotes BRM, 157; converses with Marion G. Romney, 252; on serving, 330
Clawson, Rudger, 93
Cochapas, 50–51
Colonia Dublán, 26, 155
Colonia Juárez, 26, 155
Colonia Pacheco, 26, 33, 155
Colton, Don B., 80, 87, 99, 104
"Come, Listen to a Prophet's Voice," 273
Commandments, 45
Commentary, scriptural, 3–5
Condie, Spencer J., 324–25
Confidence, 9
Constitution, 38–39, 138–40
Conversion, 395–96
Converts, 333
Coon Chicken Inn, 78
Council Bluffs, 21
Covenants, 11, 12, 54–55, 432
Cowley, Matthew, 147
Cremation, 51

440

Index

Criticism, 185, 189, 265–66, 286–87, 300
Critics, 421, 428–29
Culture, 297–98
Cumorah District, 87–88

Dalton, Emma, 61
Dating, 258–59, 293
Daynes, Bob, 326
Death, 125, 228
Decision, 293
Dedication: of Hill Cumorah Monument, 91–95; of Indonesia, 340–41; of Santiago Chile Temple, 352–53; of Mount Timpanogos Temple, 353
Deseret News, 140, 144
Dialogue at Golgotha, A, 32
Directness, 327
Discipline, 184
Disease, 358–60
Doctrinal expositions of First Presidency, 391
Doctrinal New Testament Commentary, 3, 301, 314–15, 388, 422
Doctrine and Covenants, 10, 306, 381
Doctrine(s): BRM focuses on, 5, 396–98, 421, 423; fruits of, 261–62; changing, 299–301; will all be known in next life, 331; false, 366–67
Doctrines of Salvation, 3, 301, 387
Donoho, Ben, 412, *417*
Donoho, Mary Ethel McConkie, 14, *162*, *200*, 412, *417*
Dover, Ed, 49–50
Dreams: of Lemuel Hardison Redd, 25; of Emma Somerville McConkie, 27–28; Oscar W. McConkie and BRM have gift of, 31, 36–37, 39–40, 51, 54–55
Dunn, Loren C., *158*
Dunn, Paul H., *158*

Dunyon, Eileen, 220–22
Dyering, Morgan, 317

Eastern States Mission, 81
Eastley, Jay R., 201–2
Edmunds-Tucker Act, 25
Elijah, 394
Enemies, 265, 421
Europe, 297–98
Evans, Jessie Ella. *See* Smith, Jessie Ella Evans
Evans, Oakley, 332
Evans, Richard L., 147, *149*
Evolution, 188–89, 298–99
Example, 55
Expositions of the First Presidency, 391
Extremism, 292

Faith: BRM on, 5–6; of BRM and Oscar W. McConkie, 31; inheritance of, 46; personal responsibility for, 255; healing experience as lesson in, 337–38; power of, 358–60
Family: BRM on, 246, 256, 329, 330–31; eternal nature of, 343
Family home evening, 257
Fanaticism, 277, 291, 294
Farr, Louise, 84
Fathers, 246–48
Faust, James E., 307, 345, 399
Fenn, Jerry, 406, 412, *417*
Fenn, Sara Jill McConkie, 14, *162*, *200*, 406, 412, *417*
Fife, Bill, 198
Fife, Lois, 198
First Presidency, 7, 8, 10, 259, 367–69, 391
Flake, Carol Read, 98–100, 102–3, 105–6, 431
Flake, Dennis, 97–100
Foreordination, 295
Forgeries, 370–72
Fort Douglas, 129

Index

Friends, 265, 421
Fruits, 261–62

Gadianton robbers, 37
Gallatin, Missouri, 18
Garden, 260–61
Garden Grove, 19
Gathering, 325, 397
Genealogical Society, 124
General authorities, 319–21
General conference: BRM sustained as member of Quorum of the Twelve in, 8–9, 10–11; Oscar W. McConkie speaks in, 52–54; during WWII, 129; BRM called to Council of the Seventy during, 144; BRM gives first talk in, 156–57; and family tradition, 259; BRM gives bold statement in, 265; and "I Believe in Christ," 322, 332; BRM's final testimony in, 413–14, 424–26, 431
Genesis, 394
Gentile, 27
Germany, 350
Gethsemane, 401
Gibbons, Francis, 154
Glade, Earl J., 93, 141
God the Father, 356
Godhead, 292–93, 355–58
Gospel, understanding of, 31, 240–41
Grant, Heber J.: dedicates Hill Cumorah Monument, 91, 94–95; and BRM's wedding day, 116; performs marriage of Joseph Fielding Smith and Jessie Smith, 120; and Melvin J. Ballard, 328; on Joseph Fielding Smith, 420
Grasshoppers, 22
Great Basin, 24
Greatness, 256
Greece, 350
Gundersen, LaMont, 153

Haight, David B., 404
Hair, Leatha. *See* Christensen, Leatha Hair
Hales, Sam, 202
Hammond, Francis A., 58–59
Hanks, Marion D., 229
Harding, Brother, 339
Hardy, Elaine, 337, 339
Hardy, W. Brent, 335, 337, 339
Harvester, The, 215
Harvey, Velma, 417
Hay, 65
Headings, chapter, 384
Healing, blessings of, 168–69, 337–38, 358–60, 369–70, 400–401, 407
Heart, 329
Heaven, 296
Heresies, 186
High priests, 178–81
Hill Cumorah Monument, 91–95
Hill Cumorah Pageant, 105
Hinckley, Gordon B.: in Australia, 221–24, *222*; at temple dedication in Chile, 352; gives blessing to BRM, 400; notified of BRM's death, 417; on BRM, 421, 428; on BRM's final testimony, 424
History of the Church, 178
Hofmann, Mark, 370–72
Holy Ghost: Emma Somerville McConkie feels, 34; as source of testimony, 156–57; BRM on tuning our souls to, 226; teaching with, 241, 265–66; all can be prompted by, 252; BRM on leadership being guided by, 302; BRM on presence of, during priesthood revelation, 378. *See also* Spirit
Holy Ghost, The, 32
Horses, 65
Humor, 307

442

Index

Hunter, Milton R., 147, *149*, *158*, 167
Hunter, J. Poulson, 417
Hyde, Lyle, 66
Hymns, 270–73, 322–23, 343

"I Believe in Christ," 273, 322–24, 332
Ice delivery truck, 111
Idaho Falls Temple, 137
Indians, 22, 24, 50–51, 62
Indonesia, 339–41
Inspired Version. *See* Joseph Smith Translation
Isaacson, Thorpe B., 158
Israel: gathering of, 278–81; McConkie family trip to, 404, *417*, 417–18
Ivins, Antoine R., 147, 148–49, *149*

Japan, 334, 343
Jehovah's Witness, 203–5
Jesus Christ: BRM's testimony of, 9, 322–24, 390–9, 413–14; second coming of, 292; personal relationship with, 292–93, 355–58; people offended by, 304, 322–24, 332; as child in temple, 389
Jesus the Christ, 389
Jerusalem, 341–42
Johnson, Philip E., 189
Joseph Smith Translation: introduced in *Doctrinal New Testament Commentary*, 3; BRM and Amelia study, 117–18, 422; BRM gives priority to, 384–85; as restoration, 388–89; BRM on, 403, 422

Kangaroo skins, 202
Kimball, Spencer W.: set apart as president of Quorum of the Twelve, 8; BRM on, 153; and *Mormon Doctrine*, 183, 187, 191; BRM obeys, 260; BRM on aging of, 266; on talk given by BRM, 278; trades coats with BRM, 318, *319*; on ancestors, 329; set apart as prophet, 368–69; and revelation on priesthood, 374–79; organizes Seventy, 380–81, 385
King Follett Discourse, 391
Kirkham, Oscar A., 147, *149*
Kirton, Wilford W., 339
Knowles, Eleanor, 424

Lamanites, 51. *See also* Indians
Leadership, 331
Learning, 300
Lectures on Faith, 391, 392
Lee, Garth L., 362–64
Lee, Harold B.: becomes prophet, 8–9; tours Oscar W. McConkie's mission, 46, 50; on loving everyone, 152; on organizational changes, 178; quotes BRM, 278; on BRM's conference talk, 324; in Mexico City, 325; on choice of BRM as apostle, 327–28; declines to meet with couple, 355; death of, 367
Lee, John D., 16
LeFevre, Don, 400
L. H. Redd Company, 63–64
Liberty, 38–39
Lifestyles, 297
London, 349
Love, 45, 336
Lucifer, 54, 205
Lutheran minister, 343–44

Madsen, Rulon P., 336
Malachi, 393–94
Man's Search for Happiness, 342
Manual, Sunday School, 131–36
Marriage, 45–46, 115, 153, 258–59, 293
Matthews, Robert J., 382, 383–84, 388

Index

Maxwell, Neal A., 219, 399, 427
McConkie, Amelia Smith, 14; on death of father, 7; hears voice of Oscar W. McConkie, 12, 328; BRM courts, 76–80; on BRM leaving for mission, 86; receives letter from father, 107; becomes engaged to BRM, 110; at graduation, *112*; visits Chicago, 112; as child, *113*; marriage of, 114–17, *115*; patriarchal blessing of, 115, 346; reads scriptures with BRM, 117–18; gives birth to Bruce Jr., 121; goes to Yellowstone, 137; travels to Monticello, 159–60; moves family to Lambourne Avenue, 162; as Relief Society president, 163, 277; relaxes with BRM, *165, 168, 316*; teaches son to save for mission, 171; learns of BRM's call as mission president, 195–96; moves to Australia, 197–99, *199, 200, 224, 226*; receives blessing from BRM, 212; letter to, from BRM, 212–13; on visit of Belle S. Spafford, 221–22; picks up Gordon B. Hinckley from airport, 223–24; speaks in stake conference, 224; on Joseph Fielding Smith's visit, 224–25; on missionaries' deaths, 227–28; on visiting Kalgoorlie, 228–29; cooking skills of, 235; on BRM's lack of musical talent, 272–73; gives BRM a black eye, 308; drawing of, *309*; BRM's poems about, 313; on leaving dinner for BRM, 317–18; on first trip to Asia, 334–35; visits son Joseph in Vietnam, *338*; visits Indonesia, 340–41; visits Jerusalem, 341–42; in Tahiti, *347*; at the Vatican, *348*; visits Saudi Arabia, 348–50;
visits China, 351; in Peru, *353*; speaks at temple dedications, 353; moves to condominium, 399; on BRM's health, 408, 410; last photo of, with BRM, *409*; on BRM preparing last conference talk, 410; in Israel, *417*; on BRM's accumulated notes, 423; letter to, about BRM, 430; BRM's last words to, 432

McConkie, Beth, 417
McConkie, Brenda, 253, 411–12, 415, *417*
McConkie, Briton, 14, 68, *109, 128*; birth of, 61; pays tithing as child, 65–66; in runaway wagon, 70; fights in Europe in WWII, 127, 130; as patriarch in Philippines, 379; gives blessing to BRM, 400; goes to Israel with BRM's family, 417
McConkie, Bruce, Jr., 14, 121–25
McConkie, Bruce Redd

Character traits
spiritual gifts, 9, 10, 263, 287–88, 360–64; testimony, 9, 160–61, 322–24, 371–72, 390–92, 413–14; gospel understanding, 31; sense of humor, 98, 268, 307–321; works to become better, 100–103, 158–59, 276–77, 427; lack of musical talent, 103, 270–73, 316–17; work ethic, 156; shoe size, *163*, 345; delegation, 177, 283–86; obedience, 184, 260; teaching style, 251, 267–68, 306, 386, 396–98, 420; loyalty to Joseph Smith, 256, 390–92, 421; family home evening, 257; study habits, 273–75; speaking style, 276–77, 327, 428–29; confidence and boldness, 281–83; respect for priesthood

444

Index

offices, 283–86, 429–31; false stories about, 288–89; love of teaching, 296, 299, 386; changes own views, 299–301, 421; drawings, *309, 310*; on being mistaken for other general authorities, 312; becomes ill during talk, 315–16; trades coats with Spencer W. Kimball, 318, *319*; sense of duty, 329; concern for others, 345; experience with shoeshine boy, 345; buys sheepskin coat, 346; discerning of spirits, 369–70; love of Bible, 391; love of revelations, 391; greets individuals, 430

Childhood and young adult experiences
birth, 43, 56–57; as child, *57, 58*, 68; builds path, 60; prays for father, 61; ailments, 61–62; on herding turkeys, 62; on Indian war, 62; on childhood winters, 62–63; on Monticello Co-op, 63–64; baptism, 66; ordained deacon, 66; fistfights, 66, 67; early schooling, 67; saved by father from runaway horse, 69; on runaway wagon, 70; on summer school, 71; completes high school early, 73; on debate team, 74; plays saxophone, 74; plays football, 74, 75; auditions for play, 74–75; in ROTC, 75; uses broom to stand straight, 320

Church service
called to Quorum of the Twelve, 8; conference addresses, 9, 156–57, 322–24, 332, 371–72, 413–14; speaks at funeral of Joseph Fielding Smith, 12, 262; speaks with Joseph Fielding Smith, 119; letter to superintendent of Sunday School, 132–36; called to First Council of Seventy, 146, *149*, 150–51, *158, 159*; on Spencer W. Kimball, 153; visits Colonia Juárez, 155–56; stake conference in Monticello, 159–60; ordained high priest, 177; speaks on gathering, 278–81, 325–26; receives hate mail, 286–87; in Vietnam, *337, 338*; with Ronald Reagan, *344*; at the Vatican, *348*; in China, *352*; in Peru, *353*; with Ezra Taft Benson, *412*; goes to Mexico City, 324–25; called to the Twelve, 324–29; travels, 334; supervises missions in Asia, 334–42; gives blessings in evacuation hospitals, 337–38; at dedication of Indonesia, 340–41; visits Jerusalem, 341–42; serves in South America, 345–47; serves on Scriptures Publication Committee, 347, 381–85, 422, 427; visits Polynesia, 347; visits Saudi Arabia, 348–50; visits China, 351; goes to temple dedication in Chile, 352–53; gives controversial talk at BYU, 356–58; gives blessing to boy with skin disease, 358–59; woman with blood disease, 359–60; stake reorganizations, 360–64; fills in as mission president, 365; sent to mission to correct false doctrine, 366; comments on Hofmann forgeries, 370–72; revelation on priesthood, 373–79, 385; organization of Seventy, 380–81, 385

Family and friends
related to Marion G. Romney, 11; father, 13; mother, 13; ancestors, 14–29; respect for parents, 30;

445

similarities with Oscar W. McConkie, 30–32; on Grandfather Redd, 68; on Grandmother McConkie, 69; courts Amelia, 76–80; arrives home from mission, 108–9; proposes to Amelia, 110; drives ice delivery truck, 111; attends ROTC summer camp, 111–12; graduation, *112*; marriage, 114–17, *115*; reads scriptures with Amelia, 117–18, 422; has pneumonia, 120–21; with family, *128*; as young father, *131*; goes to Yellowstone, 137; moves family to Lambourne Avenue, 162; relaxes with Amelia, *165, 168, 316*; as neighborhood organizer, 165–66; climbs mountain, 167; Glen Rudd on, 175–76; letter to Amelia, 212–13; gives haircuts to children, 232–33; with son, grandson, and son-in-law, *233*; encourages children, 236; letters from, 237; answers gospel questions, 238; teaches children to work, 238; gives father's blessings, 238–39; parenting style, 246–48; encourages son to write, 249–50; teaches children to find own answers, 250–51; counsels son about marriage, 253; teaches children to back up beliefs, 253–55; plants garden, 260–61; love for Amelia, 309–10; friendship with S. Dilworth Young, 311–13; visits son Joseph in Vietnam, 336–38; last photo with Amelia, *409*

Final days
cancer diagnosis, 399; receives blessings of healing, 400; gives blessing to woman while in hospital, 401; receives chemotherapy, 401; on suffering, 401; medical miracle, 401–2; receives blessings from Elder Packer, 402, 410, 414; plans family trip to Israel, 404; weekend assignment in California, 404–5; reorganizes stakes during sickness, 406; family fasts for, 406–7, 411; receives blessing from Twelve, 407; sons give blessing to, 407; receives blessing from Maurice Taylor, 408; prepares last conference talk, 410; receives blessing from Brit, 410; final conference talk, *413*, 413–14, 424–26, 431; in final days of life, 414–17; death of, 417; last words to Amelia, 432

Interests and work experiences
works for newspaper, 31; studies law, 118; tries first criminal case, 126; serves at Fort Douglas, 130; writes for *Deseret News*, 138, 140, 149; hiker, *234*, 234–35; physical fitness, 242, 315; disregard for fashion, 266; birdwatcher, 268–70; mountain-climbing experience, 269–70; on Australian plumbing, 311; interest in rocks, 313–14; writes light-hearted poetry, 313–15; unable to use microwave, 317–18

Missionary experiences
receives mission call, 80–82; ordained an elder, 82; receives father's blessing, 82–84; has jaundice, 84; receives patriarchal blessing, 84, 86; farewell, 84–85, *85*; says goodbye to Amelia, 86; assigned to Cumorah District, 87–88; holds street meeting, 89; photos, *90, 109*; writes about Amelia, 90; performs baptisms,

Index

91; attends dedication of Hill Cumorah Monument, 91–95; meets members of the Twelve, 93; twentieth birthday, 95–96; purchases car, 96; seriousness of, 96; Seneca District president, 97–100; is teased about Amelia, 104; Palmyra District, *104*; journal entries, 104–5; travels with Joseph Fielding Smith, 106–7, 119; extends mission six weeks, 108; called as mission president, 195; receives father's blessing before becoming mission president, 196; in Australia, *199, 200, 222, 224, 226*; Jay R. Eastley on, as mission president, 201–2; appears on Australian television, 203–5; implements "Testify and Challenge" program, 205; at district conference in Perth, 206–10; and Australian youth, 211–12; responds to Protestant radio ministry, 213–14; writes "Missionaries' Commission" and "My Mission," 215–16; purchases adding machines, 219–20; receives visit from Elder Gordon B. Hinckley, 221–24; holds meeting on Mount Wellington, 225; television analogy, 225–27; learns of missionaries' deaths, 227–28; photographs Aborigine, 229; on being a mission president, 229–30; on missionary work, 259–60, 392–96, 402–3; views of missionary work, 302–6, 392–96

Teachings
writings, 4–5, 275–76, 387–90, 422–24; *Mormon Doctrine*, 182–93; on errors, 190; on sermons, 192; on teaching with scriptures, 241, 387; on success, 260; on family, 246; on teaching by the Spirit, 265–66; on fanaticism, 277; one-liners, 278; on gathering, 278–81, 325–26; encourages balance, 290–93; on practical gospel, 293–97; on decentralizing, 296–97; on evolution, 298–99; on scriptures, 301–2; views of missionary work, 302–6, 392–96; experience at World's Fair, 303–4; "I Believe in Christ," 322–23; on callings, 330; on Jesus Christ, 332; counters false doctrine, 355–58, 366; *Doctrines of Salvation*, 387; *Doctrinal New Testament Commentary*, 388; *Messiah* series, 389; *A New Witness for the Articles of Faith*, 389–90; and documents regarded as scripture, 391; on Bible and Book of Mormon, 393–96; on Restoration, 403–4; on Church as caravan, 431–32

McConkie, Elizabeth Slade, 26–27, 32

McConkie, Emma Eliza (daughter of George and Emma Somerville McConkie), 14, *33*

McConkie, Emma Somerville, 14, *27*, 58; as chief architect of Oscar W. McConkie's character, 15, 33–34; birth of, 20–21; marriage and family of, 26–28; shares cabin with Elizabeth Slade, 32; relocates, 33, 35; Book of Mormon, 34; has spirit of discernment, 37; faith of, 46; covenant of, 54–55

McConkie forebears, 14; hear gospel, 15–16, 26; promise given to, 54–55

McConkie, George Wilson, 14, 26–27, 32, 33

Index

McConkie, George Wilson, Jr., 14, 32, *33*, 35–36

McConkie, James, 14, *109*, *128*; birth of, 61; fights in Europe in WWII, 127, 130; gives blessing to son, 168–69; death of, 169–71

McConkie, James, Jr., 168–69

McConkie, Joseph Fielding, 14; birth of, 125; as young child, *131*; on trip to Monticello, 160; with BRM in Wyoming, 167; attends BYU, 171; mission of, 171–75; with Joseph Fielding Smith, *174*, *241*; with BRM, brother-in-law, and son, *233*; learns about agency, 248; writing of, 249–50; marriage of, 253; as chaplain in Vietnam, 335–38, *338*; called as BYU stake president, 409; hears BRM's final conference talk, 412; visits father in final days of BRM's life, 414–15; in Israel, *417*

McConkie, Kathy, 412, 416, *417*

McConkie, Margaret. *See* Pope, Margaret McConkie

McConkie, Margaret Vivian Redd, 14; union of, with Oscar W. McConkie, 13–15; BRM on, 30; with children and grandchildren, *39*; attends University of Utah, 41; Oscar W. McConkie courts, 41–43; with basketball teammates, *42*; marriage of, 43; at time of marriage, *43*; in Michigan, *44*; letters about, by Oscar, 44–45, 45–46; in middle years, *45*; patriarchal blessing of, 45; faith of, 46; missionary farewell program, 47; gives birth to BRM, 56–57, *57*; home of, in Monticello, 60; gives birth to children in Moab, 61; buys turkeys, 62; makes butter and cheese, 64; moves to Ann Arbor, 71; moves to Salt Lake City, 71–72; with family in 1938, *109*; with family, *128*; visits BRM before his death, 416; death of, 416

McConkie, Mark Lewis, 14, 162, *200*, 326–27, 412, *417*

McConkie, Mary Ann, 412, *417*

McConkie, Mary Elizabeth, 32

McConkie, Mary Ethel. *See* Donoho, Mary Ethel McConkie

McConkie, Oscar, Jr., 14, *109*, *128*; hears in conference that his father will speak, 52–53; birth of, 61; recalls stake conference preparations, 65; set apart as missionary by BRM, 152; on directness of McConkies, 327; on Joseph Fielding Smith, 420

McConkie, Oscar Walter, 14, *53*; similarities between, and BRM, 30–32; gospel understanding of, 31; law practice of, 31; watches Kentucky Derby, 31; gift of, to dream dreams, 31, 36–37, 38–39, 51; as author, 32; faith of, 32; with siblings, *33*; in Mona, Utah, 33–34; mother of, 33–34; story of, about goats and cheese, 34; called as president of deacons quorum, 35; on cutting and hauling wood, 35; fasts for brother George, 35–36; patriarchal blessing of, 36; and politics, 37–39; letter of, to posterity, 38–39; with children and grandchildren, *39*; has typhoid fever, 40–41; and Word of Wisdom, 40–41, 49; attends University of Utah, 41; presides over California Mission, 41, 46–52; courts Margaret Vivian Redd, 41–43; as editor of *San Juan Journal*, 41–44, 59; marriage of, 43; at time of marriage, *43*; in

Index

Ann Arbor, Michigan, *44;* letters of, about Vivian, 44–45, *45–46;* missionary farewell program of, 47; heals eyesight of elder, 48; and Mark Johnson Vest, 50–51; gives blessing to George Albert Smith, 52; speaks in general conference, 52–54; sees vision of Satan, 54; sees vision of his mother's posterity, 54–55; gives wife blessing at birth of BRM, 56; with BRM, *57;* home of, in Monticello, 60; five-year-old BRM prays for, 61; passes bar exam, 61; camps with sons, 66; discourages fighting, 67; obeys prompting and saves BRM, 69; holds church in home in Ann Arbor, 71; returns to law school in Ann Arbor, Michigan, 71; moves family to Salt Lake City, 71–72; gives BRM father's blessings, 82–84, 196; with family, *109, 128;* at son's graduation, *112;* on death of Bruce Jr., 124–25; as mission president, 140; boards plane to be with son and grandson, 169; obeys God's will, 169–70; and *Mormon Doctrine,* 192; speaks to grandchildren before his death, 243; honored by BRM's call to Twelve, 328; as mentor for BRM, 419–20

McConkie, Rebecca. *See* Pinegar, Rebecca McConkie

McConkie, Russell, 14, 32, *33*

McConkie, Sara Jill. *See* Fenn, Sara Jill McConkie

McConkie, Shauna, 412, *417*

McConkie, Stanford, 14, 162, *200, 407,* 412, *417*

McConkie, Stephen, 14, 162, *200,* 412, *417*

McConkie, Susan Smith, 26–27, 32

McConkie, Vivian. *See* Adams, Vivian McConkie

McConkie, William, 14, 68, 76, *109, 128*

McDonald, Alexander F., 26

McKay, David O.: speaks at dedication of Hill Cumorah Monument, 94; calls BRM to First Council of Seventy, 145–46; speaks at James McConkie's funeral, 170; and reorganization of Seventy, 178–80; on high priests, 181; and *Mormon Doctrine,* 183; BRM on aging of, 266

Melbourne, Australia, 199–200, 223–24

Melchizedek Priesthood, 40

Merrill, Joseph F., 147, 152

Mesa Verde National Park, 66

Messiah series, 4, 252, 254, 389

Methodist minister, 203–5

Mexican colonies, 25–26, 27, 155–56

Mexico City, 325–26

Millennial Messiah, The, 4, 254, 292, 389

Millennium, 295–96, 331

Mission call, 80–82, 236

Mission president, former, 366

Missionaries, 152, 259, 282, 304–5, 333

"Missionaries' Commission," 215

Missionary Training Center, 304–5

Missionary work: miracle of, 100; and baptism, 205–6; in Europe, 298; BRM's views on, 302–4, 392–96, 402–3

Mississippi River, 20

Missourians, 18

Moab, Utah, 32, 35

Mob, 17, 19–20

Mona, Utah, 24, 33–34

Money, 31

Monson, Thomas S., 220, 367

Index

Monticello Co-op. *See* L. H. Redd Company
Monticello, Utah, 41, 57–61, 75–76, 159–61
Monticello Utah Temple, 60
"Mormon Airlines," 338–39
Mormon Battalion, 21
Mormon Doctrine: influence of, 3, 387–88, 422–23; dedication in, 32; controversy surrounding, 182–93; quote in, about general authorities, 319
Mormon Pavilion, 342–45
Mormon Tabernacle Choir, 119, 332
Mormons, hostility against, 17, 18
Moroni, statue of, 93, 97
Mortal Messiah, The, 190
Mortality, 294
Mortimer, William James, 382
Moses, 394
Motherhood, 44–45
Mount Olympus, 234–35
Mount Pisgah, 19, 21
Mount Timpanogos Utah Temple, 353
Mount Wellington, 225
Moyle, Henry D., 170, 172, 177, 185
Music, 235, 270–73, 316–17
"My Mission," 215–16

Nauvoo, 15–20
Nauvoo Legion, 19
Nauvoo Temple, 19, 20
Negativity, 365
Nelson, Russell M., 401, 416, 429
Neslen, Clarence, 80, 81
New Testament, 3–4, 117, 388
New Witness for the Articles of Faith, A, 4, 389
North British Mission, 174

Oaks, Dallin H., 4, 351, 429
Oaks, June, 351
Offense, 265, 304
Oil, 350

Okazaki, Chieko N., 342
Okazaki, Edward Y., 342
Ordain, 151
Organ, 342
Ottley, Jerold, 332

Pace, James, 15, 16, 19, 21–24
Pace, Lucinda Alvira. *See* Redd, Lucinda Alvira Pace
Pace, Lucinda Strickland, 16, 19
Pace, Margaret Calhoun, 14, 15, 23
Pace, William, 14, 16, 19, 21–22
Pacheco, Reuben, 362
Packer, Boyd K.: at Santiago Chile Temple dedication, 352; speaks at BRM's funeral, 375; studies about the Seventy, 381; gives BRM blessings, 400, 414; calls McConkie family, 417; on BRM, 422, 427–29
Palmyra, 91–92, 103
Palmyra District, *104*
Parents, 245–46
Parker, Hulda, 216–18
Patch, Robert C., 382
Path, straight and narrow, 293–95, 317
Patience, 31, 247
Patriarchal blessing: promises in, 28–29; of Oscar W. McConkie, 36; of Margaret Vivian Redd McConkie, 45; of BRM, 86; of Amelia Smith McConkie, 115, 346
Patriarchal order, 331
Patrick, Edith, 262
Paulsen, Finn, 165, 167, 196, 269–70, 346
Payson, Utah, 22
Peace Mission, 24
Pearl of Great Price, 382
Perfection, 294
Perry, J. Wesley, 88, 101, 102
Peterson, Mark E., 148, 152, 378
Philippines, 335

Index

Pigeons, 308
Pinegar, Mike, 412, *417*
Pinegar, Rebecca McConkie, 14, 162, *200*, 412, *417*
Pioneers, 15
Politics, 30, 37–39
Polygamists, 25, 26, 33
Pope, Margaret McConkie, 14, 61, 65, *109*, *128*
Posterity, 28–29, 54–55
Pratt family, 358–59
Pratt, Orson, 15
Pratt, Parley P., 254
Pratt, Ray, 358–59
Prayer, 293, 356–57, 402
Prejudice, 92
Premortal life, 294–95
Preparation, 250–51, 257
Priesthood: healings by, 19, 56, 169; promise of, given in blessings, 29; respect for, 54–55, 184, 238; and order of heaven, 180; misuse of, 257; BRM and, 287–88, 338; revelation on, 299, 373–79, 385. *See also* Aaronic Priesthood; Melchizedek Priesthood
Principles, 421
Promise, 54
Promised Messiah, The, 254, 389
Propaganda, 303
Prophets, 265, 306, 331
Protestant ministers, 213–14

Quecie Club, 76
Quorum of the Twelve Apostles, 7–8, 376–79
Quorums, 178–81

Rabbits, 64
Rasmussen, Ellis T., 382
Read, Carol. *See* Flake, Carol Read
Reagan, Ronald, *344*
Rector, Harman, Jr., *158*
Redd, Eliza Ann Westover, 24
Redd, James Monroe, 23, 59, 68, 70

Redd, James Monroe ("Roe"), Jr., 60, 64
Redd, Jay, 63, 66
Redd, Jim, 68
Redd, John Hardison, 16–17, 21, 23–24
Redd, Keziah Butler, 15, 17, 22, 23
Redd, Lemuel Hardison: Marion G. Romney on, 11; marries Keziah Butler, 17, 22; contracts cholera, 21; has dreams about water and San Juan River, 24–25; settles in San Juan River valley, 24–25; goes to Mexico, 25–26; death of, 26
Redd, Lemuel, Jr., 24
Redd, Lucinda Alvira Pace, 23–24, 41, 59, 68–69, 416
Redd, Lula, 24
Redd, Margaret Vivian. *See* McConkie, Margaret Vivian Redd
Redd, Ray, 70
Regional Representative, 283–86
Reorganized Church of Jesus Christ of Latter Day Saints, 388
Repentance, 294
Resolutions, 95–96
Responsibility, 253–55
Restoration, 15, 139, 302, 396–98, 403–4
Resurrection, 124
Revelation(s): of Restoration, 2–3, 256, 391, 396; modern, 9, 299–300; on priesthood, 299, 373–79, 385
Reynolds, Harold G., 81
Rich, Abel S., 93
Richards, George F., 153, 331
Richards, LeGrand, 376
Richards, Wayne, 106, 108
Righteousness, 5–6, 53
Roberts, B. H., 149
Roman Catholicism, 182–83

451

Romney, George S., 93
Romney, Marion G.: set apart as president of Quorum of the Twelve, 8; related to BRM, 11; on scholars of the world, 252; as BRM's stake president, 291–92; receives impression about BRM, 324; in First Presidency, 325; on BRM, 365; on choosing the next prophet, 368
Romney, Miles P., 26
Rudd, Glen: BRM's friendship with, 163; on BRM as neighborhood ringleader, 164; on personality of BRM, 166–67, 175–76; on Joseph Fielding McConkie's mission call, 172; visits BRM in Australia, 219–20; letter to, from BRM, 315
Rudd, Marva, 163

Sabbath, 256
Saigon, 338
Salt Lake Tribune, 425
Salvation, 293, 329, 355
San Juan Journal, 43
Santiago Chile Temple, 352–53
Satan. *See* Lucifer
Saudi Arabia, 348–50
Sawyer, S. Nelson, 91
Saxophone, 271
Scandinavia, 297
Scholars, 252
Schomas, A. J., 309–10
School, 67
Schwendiman, Fred, 198
Schwendiman, Lillian, 198
Scriptures: BRM's study of, 31, 273–75, 329; BRM and Amelia read, as newlyweds, 117–18; BRM on, 254; BRM on interpreting, by Spirit, 257, 291, 301–2
Scriptures Publication Committee, 347, 381–85, 427–28
Second Coming, 280
Seneca District, 95, 96

Seventies, 178–81, 380–81, 385
"Share the Gospel Nights," 203
Sill, Sterling W., 218–19
Singapore, 335
Skeen, Caroline. *See* Butler, Caroline Skeen
Slade, Elizabeth. *See* McConkie, Elizabeth Slade
Slaves, 17, 18
Smith, Amelia. *See* McConkie, Amelia Smith
Smith, Carlos, 339, 340
Smith, Douglas, 112, 114
Smith, Eliza. *See* Somerville, Eliza Smith
Smith, Ethel Reynolds, 76–77, *112*, 113
Smith, Farrell, 336, 415
Smith, George Albert, 52, 141–42, 147, 150–51, 153–54
Smith, Jessie Ella Evans, 119–20, 224, *224*
Smith, Joseph: BRM's testimony of, 9, 256, 390–92, 421; James Pace as bodyguard of, 16; John Butler as bodyguard of, 18; Palmyra mayor comments on, 91–92; Heber J. Grant has vision of, 94–95; reorganizes quorums, 178–81; McConkie children give talks about, 240; loyalty to, 256, 264, 390–92; and conflicting interpretations, 301; as key to missionary work, 302–5, 392–96; forgeries about, 370–72; celestial kingdom vision of, 383; laid foundation for gospel understanding, 396. *See also* Joseph Smith Translation
Smith, Joseph F., 12, 122, 147, 383
Smith, Joseph Fielding: BRM consults, 3; death of, 7, 262, 324; funeral of, 12, 262, 324–25; speaks at farewell of BRM, 84;

Index

visits Palmyra, 105–7; writes to daughter Amelia, 107; at daughter's graduation, *112*; takes trip to Chicago, 112–13; takes BRM to conference assignment, 119; remarries, 119–20; gives Bruce Jr. name and blessing, 123; learns of son's death, 128–29; with grandson, *174, 241*; Glen Rudd on, 175; and *Mormon Doctrine*, 190–91; visits Melbourne, Australia, *224*, 224–25; and Sabbath, 256; birth and naming of, 262; study habits of, 273–74; gives BRM olive, 308; and *Doctrines of Salvation*, 387; as mentor for BRM, 420
Smith, Lavon, 339
Smith, Lewis, 112, 114, 127, 128
Smith, Mary Fielding, 18
Smith, Mercy Josephine, 121
Smith, Milton, 112, 114
Smith, Nicholas G., 84
Smith, Reynolds, 112, 114
Smith, Richard L., 103
Smith, Silas, 122
Smith, Susan. *See* McConkie, Susan Smith
Smith, Winslow Farr, 80–81, 85
Snow, Eliza R., 94
Snow, Erastus, 23
Solemn assembly, 8
Somerville, Andrew, 36–37
Somerville, Annie, 35
Somerville, Eliza Smith, 14, 20, 24
Somerville, Emma. *See* McConkie, Emma Somerville
Somerville, Ray, 35
Somerville, William, 14, 15, 19–21, 24, 35
South America, 345–47
Spafford, Belle S., 220–21
Spanish Fork, Utah, 21
Spirit: BRM learns by, 31; Oscar W. McConkie prompted by, 36–37; BRM becomes dependent on, 101; BRM teaches by, 257, 263, 265–66, 324, 367; companionship of, 258, 429; leading by, 361; and revelation on priesthood, 378; BRM testifies by, 413. *See also* Holy Ghost
Spirit, evil, 370
Spirit world, 51, 331
Spiritual gifts, 9, 31, 100, 263
Spiritual maturity, 238, 256
Stake conferences, 333–34
Stake president, 284–86, 287
Stake reorganizations, 360–64
Stapley, Delbert L., 378–79
Success, 260
Suffering, 401
Sunday, 292
Sunday School, 240
Superintendent of Sunday School, 131–36

Talmage, James E., 252, 389
Tanner, N. Eldon, 8, 325, 367, 383
Tanner, Sara, *347*
Taylor, John, 188
Taylor, John H., 143
Taylor, Maurice, 408
Teacher, BRM as, 251, 267–68, 296, 299, 306, 386–98, 420,
Teaching, 241, 251, 257, 265–66, 306, 387
Teasdale, George, 95
Television, 225–27, 233
Temple. *See* Idaho Falls Temple; Monticello Utah Temple; Mount Timpanogos Utah Temple; Nauvoo Temple; Santiago Chile Temple
"Testify and Challenge," 205, 217
Testimony: of BRM, 9, 156–57, 322–24, 371–72, 390–92; of John Butler, 29; about Joseph Smith, 161, 390–92; in meetings in Saudi

453

Arabia, 350; BRM's final, 413–14, 424–26, 431
Threshing, 64
Thurber, Albert D., 26
Tithing, 294
Tithing office, 66
Traditions, 242–44, 297
Translation, 394, 397
Traveling, 112–13, 156, 334
Truth, 289, 302
Tuttle, A. Theodore, 158
Typhoid, 40–41

Unity, 377
University of Utah, 41

Vacation, 160
Vatican, 348
Vest, Mark Johnson, 50–51
Vietnam, 239, 253, 335–38
Vision: of the celestial kingdom, 383; of the redemption of the dead, 383, 389. *See also* Dreams

Wallin, Marvin, 191
Warren, Earl, 130
Weeks, Ernest, 349
Wentworth letter, 391

Westover, Eliza Ann. *See* Redd, Eliza Ann Westover
Wirthlin, Joseph L., 158
Witnesses, of BRM's call to the Twelve, 324–27
Woodruff, Wilford, 30, 208, 376
Word of Wisdom, 40–41, 49
Work, 238
World War II, 127, 130
World's Fair, 342–45

Yellowstone National Park, 137, 167
Young Ambassadors, 351
Young, Brigham, 16, 19, 179–81
Young, Hulda Parker, 400–401
Young, Levi Edgar, 147, *149*
Young, Ray, 339
Young, Seymour Dilworth, *149, 158*; in First Council of the Seventy, 147; BRM travels with, 152; Joseph Fielding McConkie meets with, 172; friendship of, with BRM, 311–13; discovers BRM's heavy conference schedule, 334

Zion, 280